T5-CQB-732

REFORM AND RENEWAL
IN THE MIDDLE AGES AND
THE RENAISSANCE

STUDIES IN THE HISTORY OF CHRISTIAN THOUGHT

EDITED BY
HEIKO A. OBERMAN, Tucson, Arizona

VOLUME XCVI

THOMAS M. IZBICKI AND CHRISTOPHER M. BELLITTO

REFORM AND RENEWAL IN THE MIDDLE AGES AND THE RENAISSANCE

Louis B. Pascoe, S. J.

REFORM AND RENEWAL IN THE MIDDLE AGES AND THE RENAISSANCE

STUDIES IN HONOR OF LOUIS PASCOE, S. J.

EDITED BY

THOMAS M. IZBICKI

AND

CHRISTOPHER M. BELLITTO

BRILL
LEIDEN · BOSTON · KÖLN
2000

This book is printed on acid-free paper.

Library of Congress Cataloging-in-Publication Data

The Library of Congress Cataloging-in-Publication Data is also available.

Die Deutsche Bibliothek - CIP-Einheitsaufnahme

Reform and renewal in the Middle Ages and the Renaissance : studies in honor of Louis Pascoe, S. J. / ed. by Thomas M. Izbicki and Christopher M. Bellitto. – Leiden ; Boston ; Köln : Brill, 2000
(Studies in the history of Christian thought ; Vol. 96)
ISBN 90-04-11399-1

ISSN 0081-8607
ISBN 90 04 11399 1

PRINTED IN THE NETHERLANDS

CONTENTS

INTRODUCTION

The idea for this *festschrift* emerged at a conference where members of the American Cusanus Society remarked that Louis B. Pascoe, S. J., was one of those scholars and teachers whose impact extended far beyond his publications. Others had published more than he, but Fr. Pascoe's particular influence cannot be measured by the list of books and articles on a *curriculum vitae*. His is the impact of a kind colleague who will read a chapter or draft sent to him with the close attention he would lavish on his own work or on the papers of his students. Indeed, historians and theologians have had to wait nearly two decades for Fr. Pascoe's promised study, *Apocalypticism and Church Reform: Bishops, Theologians and Canon Lawyers in the Thought of Pierre d'Ailly*, because he always put a student or fellow scholar's work ahead of his own. These efforts stemmed from what Fr. Pascoe once identified as the three joys of his life: his priesthood, his teaching, and his Jesuit vocation. It is this generosity of spirit that has given Fr. Pascoe his well-deserved reputation as a gentleman and a scholar.

Fr. Pascoe grew up in eastern Pennsylvania and planned a career as a teacher. He received a BA in History at the University of Scranton where he found that God and the Jesuits had other plans for him, at least immediately. Fr. Pascoe received his philosophy degree from Woodstock College, an MA in History at Fordham where he first met Gerhart Ladner and produced a thesis on Bernard of Clairvaux, a license in theology from Woodstock, and a Ph.D. in History at UCLA where he worked on Jean Gerson under Dr. Ladner. During his Jesuit training, Fr. Pascoe taught at Georgetown, then began his post-doctoral teaching at Woodstock in 1971 where he was also involved in the circle of medievalists at Columbia University. He moved to Fordham in 1973 and reached the rank of full professor there in 1981. He held fellowships at Georgetown, Woodstock, and Fordham, a research grant from Fordham, and travel grants from the American Council of Learned Societies and the Centro Italiano di Studi, Spoleto. At Fordham, Fr. Pascoe served as chair of the history department (1987-1990) and Acting Dean of Fordham College (1992).

Fr. Pascoe's publications are marked by the careful scholarship drilled into him by Dr. Ladner. The studies in this *festschrift* have been designed to reflect the path of Fr. Pascoe's own interests in education, reform, humanism, apocalypticism, and theology. His first article, published while still a graduate student, took him slightly beyond the late medieval period where he spent most of his career: "The Council of Trent and Bible Study: Humanism and Scripture," *Catholic Historical Review* 42 (1966): 18-36. He converted his dissertation into a monograph, *Jean Gerson: Principles of Church Reform* (Leiden: E. J. Brill, 1973) and followed with a series of articles on Gerson for *Traditio*, *Viator*, *Annuarium Historiae Conciliorum*, *Dictionary of the Middle Ages*, et al. In the late 1970s, though he continued to publish on Gerson, Fr. Pascoe moved onto Pierre d'Ailly with a tightly-argued article on his conception of the papal plenitude of power for *Annuarium Historiae Conciliorum* and "Pierre d'Ailly:

Histoire, Schisme et Antéchrist," in *Genèse et débuts du Grand Schisme d'Occident* (Paris: CNRS, 1980), pp. 615-622. His reputation grew internationally as he gave papers in France, Germany, England, and Finland, and reviewed nearly three dozen books in French, German, and Italian. From 1993 to 1996, he served on the executive council of the American Catholic Historical Association, which held a panel for him at its convention in New York City, January 1997. The response to that panel was so enthusiastic (indeed, more than one scholar noted that if anyone deserved to be honored for his quiet achievements, it is Fr. Pascoe) that this *festschrift* quickly took shape.

We are grateful for the encouragement and financial support of the following, all of which were eager to honor one of their own: the New York Province of the Society of Jesus, the Association of Jesuit Colleges and Universities, and Fordham University, especially Dean Robert Himmelberg, Graduate School of Arts & Sciences. Professor Heiko Oberman, who published Fr. Pascoe's book on Gerson in his Brill series Studies in Medieval and Reformation Thought, happily supported this project for inclusion in Studies in the History of Christian Thought. The editors at E. J. Brill provided their accustomed support. Kim Breighner provided the necessary computer expertise for the production of a seamless whole from diskettes in a variety of formats.

T. M. I.
C. M. B.

FOR LOUIS B. PASCOE, S. J.

Joseph F. O'Callaghan

On a winter's day one is apt to encounter Reverend Louis B. Pascoe, S. J., Professor of Medieval History at Fordham University, as he makes his way with measured gait from his office in Dealy Hall, past Edward's Parade to his classroom in Keating Hall, where a group of eager young scholars awaits him. One will notice that he wears a black Russian fur hat which is almost as tall as he is. His kindly demeanor is apparent to all who pass him by. Indeed, his journey is often interrupted as he stops to talk to students, colleagues, secretaries, maintenance men, and children.

I first met Lou Pascoe more than twenty-five years ago when he joined the Fordham History Department in 1973. His arrival was quite timely because our Department, of which I was then chairman, would soon have to face an evaluation of our doctoral program by the State Board of Regents. The addition of Lou to our staff of medievalists gained our program in medieval history high praise from the state visitors who declared in 1974 that it was without a superior in New York State.

Lou brought to our program an important dimension in medieval religious and intellectual history. His undergraduate courses on the Medieval Mendicants and Medieval Universities were consistently well attended. Graduate students quickly found themselves introduced to the great themes of reform and renewal which Lou's mentor at UCLA, Gerhart Ladner, had done so much to develop. Students whose Latin was a bit rusty also learned in his seminars to handle the language with proficiency. He always took the business of teaching with the utmost seriousness. He regularly set aside hours for preparation of both undergraduate and graduate classes and would only depart from that schedule in case of dire emergency. His preparation was reflected in the high quality of his lectures and his direction of seminar discussion. That careful preparation has also been apparent in the many doctoral comprehensive examinations in which he has participated. Students have come to expect a clear and logical inquiry into the matter at hand; though he might be disappointed with a student's performance, he was always kind and eminently fair in his judgments.

Although my own interest was primarily in institutional and Spanish history, I greatly appreciated his emphasis on medieval religious history. I was pleased that he continued to offer graduate classes in Medieval Monasticism which my own mentor Jeremiah F. O'Sullivan had introduced many years before. As I had also studied with Gerhart Ladner at Fordham before he went to UCLA I was familiar with Ladner's work on the idea of reform. Lou's dissertation on *Jean Gerson: Principles of Church Reform,* published at Leiden by E. J. Brill in 1973, is an outstanding contribution to the history of the intellectual and theological milieu of the late medieval church. His work on another major figure of the conciliar epoch, Pierre d'Ailly, tentatively entitled, *Apocalypticism and Church Reform: Bishops, Theologians and Canon Lawyers in the Thought of Pierre d'Ailly,* has been delayed by his acceptance of many responsibilities aside from his daily teaching routine. Recognizing his talents, his Jesuit superiors called on him to serve as Acting Dean of Fordham College and his Jesuit confrères entrusted him with many tasks as their representative. One hopes that with greater leisure he will soon bring his study of Pierre d'Ailly to happy completion.

Long recognized as a distinguished scholar by the medieval community, Lou has been a consistent participant in the Columbia University seminars and at the meetings of the Medieval Academy of America and the American Historical Association. He has been an esteemed member of the Executive Council of the American Catholic Historical Association.

His colleagues in the Department of History also know him as someone whose opinions are highly valued. Whether as chairman of the Department or simply as a member, he has always been thoughtful and deliberate when considering the issues at hand. Indeed at times his slowness in reaching a decision has exasperated some, but the time he takes to weigh all aspects of a problem ultimately has proven to be wise. When confronted with ideas or suggestions that he thought lacked merit or neglected to take into account the general good of the Department, he clearly expressed his disagreement. If the discussion became heated (as sometimes happened!), he nevertheless was always courteous, though firm in defending his own position.

Lou has always been an entertaining companion and a good story teller who is not afraid to laugh at himself. His description of his walks on the beach during his early days in California is truly hilarious. There he was, wearing black shorts, black socks, and black shoes, with a white shirt (though not a Roman collar!). To all the world he seemed like an alien amidst the bronzed bodies lolling on the sand.

How many times did he invite me to lunch before doctoral comprehensive examinations or on other occasions? I recall those lunches - which sometimes stretched for two hours or so - with great pleasure, as we had long discussions about the Department, the University, our students, the state of the Catholic church, the tensions between Irish pastors and Italian congregants, my family and his, and especially his love and care for his aged mother.

In every bone of his body he exemplifies the Ignatian ideal of the *cura personalis*. I have been struck by how often those words constantly and naturally fall from his lips. As a good Jesuit, faithful to the ideals of St. Ignatius Loyola, he always tries to give personal care or, if you will, the personal touch, not only to students, colleagues, and friends but to everyone with whom he has contact. People of all ages and conditions of life have sought his counsel not just on academic matters, but also on those of a spiritual or more personal nature.

His most significant contribution as a member of the Department of History is his constant concern to uphold the Jesuit and Catholic tradition of the University, a task that has become more and more difficult in recent years as the importance of that tradition has come under question.

For me personally it has been a distinct honor and pleasure to count him as a colleague and a friend for so many, many years. As he reaches retirement, I salute him as one who has in his own person embodied the Jesuit motto, *ad majorem Dei gloriam!*

Lou, *ad multos annos!*

THE INFLUENCE OF GERHART LADNER'S *THE IDEA OF REFORM**

Phillip H. Stump

Gerhart Ladner's *The Idea of Reform*[1] after forty years remains the definitive study of reform ideas. Quite simply, it defined a new sub-discipline of history. Ladner delineated the boundaries, established the methodology, and posed the fundamental questions of this new discipline. Then he demonstrated its practice by tracing the first six hundred years of its history in magisterial fashion—so magisterial that he left little new to say about patristic reform ideas, and it is striking that Ladner's *Idea of Reform* has had its greatest single impact on researchers exploring the idea of reform in the high and late Middle Ages. In this paper, after a few general remarks about Ladner's influence, I would like to examine the impact of *The Idea of Reform* on five different, but not mutually exclusive, audiences: 1) patristic scholars and historians of the late Roman and early medieval periods; 2) historians of renascences and of "*The* Renaissance"; 3) historians of the medieval and Reformation church; 4) contemporary ecumenical thinkers and post-Vatican II reformers; and 5) historians interested in historical ideas of change. Then I will return to the question of the book's importance for those studying late medieval reform.

The standard dictionaries and other works which deal with renewal ideas usually cite Ladner's works in their first paragraph or footnote as the definitive starting point.[2] Fortunately, this is usually more than an obligatory nod to a time-worn classic, for Ladner's work is still eminently readable and still invites the full engagement of the reader—engagement not only with *The Idea of Reform* itself, but also with Ladner's many other works on reform and renewal and with his art historical studies which converge with his studies of reform, especially when they address Christian representations of humanity created in the

* An earlier version of this paper was delivered at a panel entitled "Gerhart Ladner's *The Idea of Reform*: Forty Years After," at the joint meeting of the American Catholic Historical Association and the American Society of Church History in Washington, D.C., January 9, 1999. The other panelists included Fr. Pascoe and Christopher Bellitto. Gerhart Ladner was the beloved mentor of both Fr. Pascoe and myself. I would like to express my admiration and deep gratitude to Fr. Pascoe for his perceptive advice and special friendship over the years.

1 Gerhart B. Ladner, *The Idea of Reform: Its Impact on Christian Thought and Action in the Age of the Fathers* (Cambridge, Massachussetts, 1959; rev. ed. New York, 1967).

2 Eike Wolgast, "Reform, Reformation," in *Geschichtliche Grundbegriffe* (Stuttgart, 1984), 5.313-360; Richard Kieckhefer, "Reform, Idea of," in *Dictionary of the Middle Ages* 10.281-288; Konrad Repgen, "'Reform' als Leitgedanke kirchlicher Vergangenheit und Gegenwart," *Römische Quartalschrift* 84 (1989): 5-30; J. Gribomont, "Riforme," in *Dizionario degli istituti di perfezione*, 7.1748-1751; Gerald Strauss, "Ideas of *Reformatio* and *Renovatio* from the Middle Ages to the Reformation," in *Handbook of European History, 1400-1600*, ed. Thomas Brady et al. (Leiden, 1995), 2.1-30; and Johannes Helmrath, "Reform als Thema der Konzilien des Spätmittelalters," in *Christian Unity: The Council of Ferrara-Florence 1438-39-1989,* ed. Giuseppe Alberigo (Louvain, 1991), pp. 75-152.

divine image.[3] We now have two indispensable guides for viewing these diverse writings within the entire context of Ladner's intellectual development: 1) a rich article by John Van Engen, one of Ladner's students, which traces this development; and 2) Ladner's own recently published memoirs, entitled simply *Erinnerungen*.[4] These make clear how much the influence of *The Idea of Reform* is inseparable not only from Ladner's other writings, but also from the influence he exerted through his personal friendships with the foremost scholars in many diverse fields of scholarship.

I

Ladner's impact on two of the leading scholars of the transition between the late antique and early medieval periods, Herwig Wolfram and Walter Pohl, is evidenced by the fact that they were the editors of the Austrian edition of Ladner's *Erinnerungen*. The profound admiration which *The Idea of Reform* evoked among leading patristic and early medieval scholars is revealed in the reviews published by Henri Marrou, Herbert Musurillo, Robert Grant, Christine Mohrmann, Heinrich Fichtenau, Friedrich Kempf, and Klaus Thraede.[5] Patristic scholars admired it for its fresh exploration of an idea found in nearly all the Church fathers, but never before investigated systematically in their writings, probably because the fathers themselves did not think in categories of reform which are familiar to the modern ear. As Musurillo puts it, for Ladner "many great theological controversies, such as Pelagianism, the patristic discussion of the divine image in man, the meaning of the City of God, may all be fruitfully examined in the light of reform theology."[6] Patristic scholars appreciated the depth of Ladner's erudition in both Greek and Latin sources and the breadth of his vision that enabled him, not only to present this fresh new perspective, but also, as Marrou suggests, to demonstrate parallels between specific reform themes in Greek and Latin authors and to offer many new insights and syntheses on

[3] Almost all of Ladner's separately published articles were collected by him (with addenda for many articles) in *Images and Ideas in the Middle Ages: Selected Studies in History and Art* [hereafter *Selected Studies*], 2 vols. (Rome, 1983).

[4] John Van Engen, "Images and Ideas: The Achievements of Gerhart Burian Ladner, with a Bibliography of His Published Works," *Viator* 20 (1989): 85-115; Gerhart B. Ladner, *Erinnerungen*, ed. Herwig Wolfram and Walter Pohl (Sitzungsberichte der Österreichischen Akademie der Wissenschaften, Phil.-Hist. Kl. 617; Vienna, 1994).

[5] Henri Marrou in *Revue d'histoire ecclésiastique* 55 (1960): 139-141; Herbert Musurillo in *Theological Studies* 21(1960): 472-474; Robert Grant in *Speculum* 36 (1961): 140-142; Christine Mohrmann in *Vigiliae christianae* 16 (1962): 235-237; Friedrich Kempf in *Historisches Jarhbuch* 81 (1962): 328-331; Heinrich Fichtenau in *Mitteilungen des Instituts für Österreichische Geschichtsforschung* 69 (1961): 116-118; and Klaus Thraede in *Jahrbuch für Antike und Christentum* 4 (1961): 168-170.

[6] Musurillo, p. 472.

individual questions, each of which would have been worthy of a separately published note or article.[7]

Patristic scholars recognized that the principal achievement of *The Idea of Reform* was to demonstrate convincingly the existence of an idea of reform among the Church fathers which was above all an idea of personal renewal grounded in the theology of the Pauline epistles and to trace the subtle, but significant divergences of that idea in the East and West. Without denying that there was much overlap between Greek and Latin patristic reform ideas, Ladner claimed that the main emphasis in the East lay on reform as restoration of the pristine image of God in the soul, a return to the paradisiac state of Adam before the fall, whereas the fathers in the West, beginning with Tertullian and culminating in Augustine, envisaged a *reformatio in melius*, a movement forward to a state better than that of Adam in paradise. Placing primary emphasis on the Incarnation, Greek fathers conceived of reform as a process of purification of the divine image in man, purgation with the goal of returning to paradise (recapitulation); in its most sublime statement in Gregory of Nyssa, this essentially mystical idea of reform was one of assimilation to God, which in turn was seen as equivalent to attaining the vision of God. The Latin fathers, placing their primary stress on the passion of Christ, conceived of reform in more practical ways; and Augustine, in particular, in the wake of the Pelagian controversy stressed the role of divine grace in the reform of the individual.

The fact that the major theme of patristic reform in both East and West thus emerged as the personal reform of the individual Christian might not at first seem too promising for connections with later reform ideas which are so predominantly supra-individual in scope. Yet, Ladner also clearly demonstrated that the divergences between these reform conceptions had profound implications for ideas of the right ordering of Christian society in the East and West.[8] In the East, the leadership fell in different ways to the emperor and the monks, with their different visions of the deification of man through Christomimesis. In the West, under the powerful influence of Augustine, Christian society was seen as a city of pilgrims in need of continual renewal rather than as a perfect kingdom; and the leadership fell to the priesthood, but a priesthood that was urged by this same Augustine to live as cenobitical monks. This "monasticization of the clergy" was grounded partly in the supra-personal reform motif of imitation of the primitive church in Jerusalem.[9] Because of its fusion of active and

[7] Marrou, p. 139.

[8] The best analyses of Ladner's arguments in *The Idea of Reform* and their implications for the larger cultural history of the Byzantine Empire and the Western Middle Ages are to be found in the reviews by Friedrich Kempf and Heinrich Fichtenau; see above, n. 5.

[9] Pier Cesare Bori, *Chiesa Primitiva: L'immagine della comunità delle origini - Atti 2,42-47; 4,32-37 - nella storia della chiesa antica* (Brescia, 1974), pp. 111-112. Bori cites the section from Ladner's *Idea*, pp. 129-132, which speaks of St. John Chrysostom's effort to "reform the 'Polis' within the 'Basileia,'" which had failed because the tension between the two "cities" which pervaded the thought of Augustine was lacking in Chrysostom's thought.

contemplative life, of mystical and apostolic spirituality, it was of highest importance for later development of supra-personal reform in the West.

The differing Greek and Latin ideas of reform, as elucidated by Ladner, in turn, shed important light on what has been called the "political theology" of the late antique world. Lester Field, one of the last UCLA students to have studied under Ladner, acknowledges his own and many other scholars' indebtedness to Ladner's insights in this area.[10] Field believes that Ladner and his close friend Ernst Kantorowicz both led the way toward a new appreciation of the continuity between the late antique and the early medieval and Byzantine worlds.

Marrou, Kempf, and Fichtenau all eagerly called attention to Ladner's promise in *The Idea of Reform* that he would explore the implications of the patristic ideas fully for later periods in the future volumes of his work. Indeed, Ladner's previous studies had already laid the groundwork for such connections, in particular his studies of the Gregorian reform and his investigation of the relationship between the late medieval reform idea and ideas of "renaissance."

II

The impact of *The Idea of Reform* on historians studying the medieval renascences and "*The* Renaissance" has been threefold. First, the book clearly defines the generic relationship, but also the specific differences, between ideas of renascence and ideas of reform, two species of renewal ideas.[11] For Ladner, reform ideas are ideas of conscious, intentional change, whereas ideas of renaissance are ideas of vitalistic renewal which involve spontaneous change. Secondly, Ladner's approach in *The Idea of Reform*, supplemented by his other writings about various renascences, contributed to a widespread interest among medievalists in renascences before the Renaissance, such as a Theodosian or a Carolingian Renaissance (although Ladner was skeptical about the former and

[10] Lester Field, *Liberty, Dominion, and the Two Swords: On the Origins of Western Political Theology (180-398)* (Notre Dame, 1998), p. xi. In a personal letter dated December 14, 1998, Field referred to a second book manuscript he is readying for publication which will "analyze the twentieth-century historiography and hermeneutics that had decisively shaped current perceptions of the 'political' in theologies of Late Antiquity, including those that, by older conventions, seem early-Byzantine or early-medieval." He notes that Ladner's work will be a chief focus of this study.

[11] Ladner, *Idea*, pp. 16-26, esp. p. 26: "Contrary to all vitalistic renewal ideas, the idea of reform implies the conscious pursuit of ends. Whether reform be predominantly contemplative or active, its starting point is the element of intention rather than spontaneity, urge, or response." Ladner gently faults earlier studies—including those of Konrad Burdach and Friedrich Heer—which had treated these ideas together but sometimes did not sufficiently distinguish them. In his discussion on these pages of *The Idea of Reform*, Ladner looks specifically at the so-called "Theodosian Renaissance" of the fourth century C. E., asking to what extent the vitalistic terminology is present.

treated the latter more as a reform movement than a Renaissance)[12]—but above all the "twelfth-century Renaissance." Ladner's close personal friendships with Erwin Panofsky and Giles Constable insured a mutual influence here.[13] In 1977 Ladner participated in a symposium organized by Constable to commemorate the fiftieth anniversary of the publication of Charles Homer Haskins' work which had coined the phrase "Renaissance of the twelfth century."[14] Ladner's contribution was close to Haskins' own in its emphasis on the secular aspects of this Renaissance foreshadowing the Italian Renaissance, whereas even in 1977 Constable was stressing the Christian, and especially monastic, reform elements in ways that culminated in his recent rich monograph, *The Reformation of the Twelfth Century*.[15] Thirdly, Ladner's analysis of Greek patristic concepts of the dignity of human nature paralleled and reinforced the conclusions of Renaissance historians who realized the impact of these patristic ideas on Italian humanists.[16]

12 Cf. Ladner, *Idea*, p. 303: "in the great reform periods, for instance, in the so-called Carolingian Renaissance."

13 On these friendships, see *Erinnerungen*, pp. 69, 71.

14 The volume of proceedings is *Renaissance and Renewal in the Twelfth Century*, ed. Robert Benson, Giles Constable, and Carol Lanham (Cambridge, Massachusetts, 1982). Ladner's contribution was entitled "Terms and Ideas of Renewal in the Twelfth Century," pp. 1-33.

15 Giles Constable, *The Reformation of the Twelfth Century* (Cambridge, Massachusetts, 1996).

16 Here one thinks immediately of the monumental study of Charles Trinkaus, *In Our Image and Likeness*, 2 vols. (Chicago, 1970); but Ladner's book had a particularly great impact on Fr. John O'Malley's investigation of ideas of human dignity in the rhetoric of Renaissance preachers at the papal court in Rome. See John O'Malley, *Praise and Blame in Renaissance Rome: Rhetoric, Doctrine, and Reform in the Sacred Orators of the Papal Court, c. 1450-1521* (Durham, North Carolina, 1979). In patristic reform thought, the divine image was located almost invariably in the soul or spirit rather than the body. Ladner's wonderful little book, *Ad imaginem Dei*, suggests the impact of this spiritualization on the Christian art of the early Middle Ages, but also shows how high medieval artists began reintroducing classical motifs which harmonized with Christian ideas of the dignity of humanity guaranteed by Christ's incarnation in a human body. There was a concomitant new emphasis of the artists on the humanity of Christ and the dignity of the human body made visible in the Incarnation; see Gerhart B. Ladner, *Ad imaginem Dei: The Image of Man in Medieval Art* (Latrobe, Pennsylvania, 1965), pp. 58, 64-65. The Renaissance humanists and artists shared the tendency of Greek patristic reform thought to stress the Incarnation as the central mystery of the faith. The Renaissance artists went further in portraying the Incarnation visually, even to the point of explicitly portraying Jesus's sexuality, a neglected fact which Leo Steinberg has explored in his book entitled *The Sexuality of Christ in Renaissance Art and Modern Oblivion* (New York, 1983). Because of his understanding of the background in patristic reform thought for this Renaissance artistic practice, Fr. O'Malley was invited to make remarks concerning Steinberg's findings at a public lecture given by Steinberg, who then asked to have O'Malley's remarks published as a postscript to his book. Fr. O'Malley's postscript appears on pp. 199-203. O'Malley had discovered the same kind of themes and explicitness about Jesus's sexuality in sermons preached at the Renaissance papal court for the Feast of the Circumcision.

III

For all its impact on historians of the Renaissance, *The Idea of Reform* has had surprisingly little influence on historians of the Reformation (I mean the Protestant Reformation here), even among historians looking for some continuity between late medieval reform and the Reformation. Steven Ozment, in his book, *The Age of Reform, 1250-1550,* cites it only once, for a minor point.[17] Yet, as Fr. Pascoe notes, Ozment was one of few historians of late medieval reform who in fact pursued Ladner's approach of examining the principles and ideologies of reform that underlay specific reform proposals.[18] Interestingly, Ladner's *Idea of Reform* did have an indirect impact on Ozment through his reading of Fr. Pascoe's own study of Gerson's reform ideas. Ozment's mentor, Heiko Oberman, is one of the few Protestant historians of the Reformation who have given extensive attention to Ladner's work, and he has also been very interested in the work of Ladner's students, including Fr. Pascoe. This I would see as a reflection of his commitment to study both late Middle Ages and Reformation together. The lack of attention given by most Reformation historians to Ladner's book is, I would conjecture, a measure of how fully the Protestant reformers themselves rejected the medieval concept of reform (and with it, surprisingly, the patristic concept as well, in spite of their interest in returning to the purity of the early Church). Ladner himself notes in *The Idea of Reform* that "primitive Protestantism had on the whole not much use for a religiously founded idea of repeated reforms," since early Protestant reformers regarded their changes as final and complete.[19] But the medieval idea of reform itself, with its stress on the dignity of human nature and on voluntary self-reform of the individual, was highly problematic for Luther, because of his anxieties about human perfectibility, and for Calvin, because of his convictions about the total depravity of human nature after the fall.[20] Consequently,

[17] Steven Ozment, *The Age of Reform, 1250-1550: An Intellectual and Religious History of Late Medieval and Reformation Europe* (New Haven, 1980), p. 85 and n. 37 (for a statement of Augustine praising the monastic life). However, Ladner did influence Ozment indirectly through the work of Fr. Pascoe on Gerson; see p. 75 and n. 5. One excellent survey of late medieval and Reformation reform thought is that of Gerald Strauss cited in n. 2 above.

[18] Louis Pascoe, *Jean Gerson: Principles of Church Reform* (Leiden, 1973), p. 2, where he praises Ozment's "The University and the Church: Patterns of Reform in Jean Gerson," *Mediaevalia et Humanistica,* n. s. 1 (1970): 111-126.

[19] Ladner, *Idea*, p. 33-34. Ladner hastened to add that "later Protestant reformers saw that it could become necessary to proceed 'even to the reforming of the Reformation itself' (here citing Milton's *Areopagitica*). Konrad Repgen (see above, n. 4), p. 22, has also called attention to the later Calvinists' concept of an *ecclesia semper reformanda*, the first occurrence of which he finds among mid-seventeenth century Dutch Calvinists; Repgen argues that such an idea would be foreign to Calvin's thought.

[20] See Karl Morrison, *The Mimetic Tradition of Reform in the West* (Princeton, 1982), pp. 230-240. Morrison, concerned with reform as *mimesis*, says

Protestant historians of the Reformation have too often tended to dismiss the medieval reform concepts as irrelevant. Ladner's work makes it very clear that they do so at the peril of retaining a very truncated view of the Christian heritage of reform ideas.

Ironically, while rejecting much of this heritage themselves, Protestant reformers, by causing the very word "reform" to be suspect for Catholics, had also caused Catholics to neglect this heritage.[21] For Catholic historians, Ladner's book has, I believe, played a major role in rehabilitating reform as a positive part of the Catholic heritage. Ladner's scrupulous and erudite investigation has made accessible a rich realm of patristic and medieval ideas of reform and shown them to be in full harmony with the traditional teaching of the church.

IV

For this reason the book has also had an important, though indirect, impact on the renewal of the church associated with Vatican II and the ecumenical movement. Ladner did not write it as a work of advocacy, but rather as a work of appreciation for an idea which he believed had profoundly influenced

that Luther rejected the idea of the "mimetic mediation" of Christ because "for him, Christ as mediator performed a single act: propitiation." Luther did entertain other ideas of reform, especially a whole range of conciliar reform ideas together with ideas of the German *Gravamina* movement, which he set forth in his *Letter to the German Nobility*. But he seems to have dropped these after 1520. Congar has suggested that for Luther, reform became focused almost solely on theological reform. It may well be that, ironically, his theological reform stance caused him to reject medieval and humanist reform concepts. Many sincere reformers of Luther's time in turn rejected Luther's reformation. Paula Datsko Barker described this phenomenon in a bold thesis concerning Caritas Pirckheimer in a paper she delivered at the Kalamazoo Medieval Congress in 1996: This great German humanist abbess rejected the Reformation because it stood in direct contradiction to her understanding of reform. See Barker's article "Caritas Pirckheimer: A Female Humanist Confronts the Reformation," *Sixteenth Century Journal* 26 (1995): 259-272. In my discussion with Barker, she mentioned the importance of Ladner's *Idea* for her understanding of medieval reform ideas.

[21] J. Gribomont, "Riforme," col. 1748: "Nel Cinquecento la Riforme protestante andò ben al di là del concetto tradizionale di riforme, e nel suo sforzo di ritornare alle origini cadde nella rottura. Il termine di riforme, cosí compromesso, si trovò quasi proibito ai cattolici..." See esp. Guiseppe Alberigo, "'Réforme' en tant que critère de l'Histoire de l'Église," *Revue d'histoire ecclésiastique* 76 (1981): 72-81 at p. 74: "Dans ce cadre, la thématisation de la réforme de l'Église avait automatiquement aux yeux des catholiques une coloration protestante ou moderniste, c'est-à-dire qu'elle n'était proposable. La culture catholique acceptait à une très large majorité une confiscation protestante de l'idée de réforme de l'Église, au point que s'était couramment créée une identification ou au moins une connexion entre réforme de l'Église et réforme protestante (aggravée par l'existence d'un seul substantif dans les langues latines)." See also p. 80, where Alberigo hails Ladner's historical work as running parallel to the theological work of Congar and others and acting in synergy with the work of Jedin on the "Catholic Reformation" and the reforms of the Council of Trent. All these efforts have helped reclaim the heritage of reform thought within the Catholic church.

people's thought and action. The scholarly detachment with which Ladner posed his questions has insured that his book, when used in debates about contemporary issues, will serve to provide historical depth and accuracy of understanding about those issues. This was evident in his contribution to an ecumenical dialogue organized at Harvard University in 1964 by Giles Constable.[22]

Well before Vatican II, Fr. Yves Congar had raised some of the issues of reform in his book *True and False Reform in the Church*.[23] The second edition of Congar's book reveals careful reading of Ladner's *Idea of Reform*. Congar acknowledged the book's important contribution to the early history of reform ideas, noting that Ladner showed the central focus of these ideas to be a theme of Christian anthropology—the reform of the image of God in the individual Christian.[24] In a later article Congar mentioned Ladner's book in this context again with admiration, but also with a caveat to those who would reduce ecclesiastical reform to individual reform while neglecting structural reform.[25] Congar cited four examples of reform movements in the church which were *both* spiritual and structural at the same time. The first two of these—the Gregorian reform and the mendicant reforms—were, in fact, the two which Ladner also singled out to address when he participated in the Harvard dialogue.[26] At that dialogue the discussion of forward- and backward-looking reform ideas clearly reflected the influence of Ladner's analysis in *The Idea of Reform* of reform as restoration vs. *reformatio in melius* in the Greek and Latin Church Fathers.[27] Ladner's other writings on reform, especially those on the Gregorian reform,

[22] Gerhart B. Ladner, "*Reformatio,*" in *Ecumenical Dialogue at Harvard: The Roman Catholic-Protestant Colloquium* (Cambridge, Massachusetts, 1964), pp. 172-190.

[23] Yves Congar, *Vraie et fausse réforme dans l'Église,* 2d. ed. (Paris, 1968).

[24] Ibid., p. 156 and n. 46b, where Congar cites a passage from Jerome using one of Ladner's footnotes as his mediate source. Congar (p. 322) accepts as definitive Ladner's study of the early uses of the word reform in the writings of the Church fathers and the liturgy; Ladner's study makes clear that the context of these uses was Christian anthropology: "C'est l'oeuvre de l'Incarnation rédemptrice."

[25] Yves Congar, "Renouvellement de l'Esprit et réforme de l'Institution," in *Écrits réformateurs* (Paris, 1995), pp. 197-206 at pp. 198-199, where he notes that to take seriously the reform of oneself according to the norms of the Gospel can lead very far, but is not sufficient. Too often this theme has been developed by defenders of authority, of the status quo, who say, if you just reform yourself, everything will be fine. Congar points to very spiritual movements of self-reform like the Friends of God and the *devotio moderna* which did not have an effect on the institutions of the church. Then he points to four reform movements which were both spiritual and structural at the same time: Gregorian reform, mendicants' reform, Tridentine reform, and the reforms of Vatican II.

[26] Ladner, "*Reformatio,*" p. 190. Ladner speaks of Pope Gregory VII and St. Francis as two complementary reform figures.

[27] Giles Constable, "Seminar III: Reformatio," in *Ecumenical Dialogue at Harvard,* pp. 330-343 at pp. 332-333.

shed light on the ideas of institutional reform of the church which enriched the discussions of reform surrounding Vatican II.

Vatican II was convened in 1963; we know that two years earlier Angelo Roncalli, Pope John XXIII, had read Ladner's book; he sent word to Ladner in 1961 that the book had brought him much consolation and stimulation.[28] However, John XXIII's concept of change which became the *leitmotif* of the Council—*aggiornamento*—referred to the updating of the church's practices, and some have questioned whether it was, strictly speaking, an idea of reform.[29] In fact, O'Malley argues that the word reform itself was used very infrequently in the Vatican II documents, but he does call attention to the notable exception in the Decree on Ecumenism (*Unitatis reintegratio*), which calls for a "continual reformation (*perrenis reformatio*)."[30] O'Malley believes that the recent church has been sorely lacking in deep theological reflection about the meaning of reform and needs especially a thoroughgoing history of reform which would carry Ladner's pioneering effort up to the present.[31]

V

The lack of use of the word "reform" in the documents of Vatican II does not mean that reform was slighted at the council. Even the casual observer would conclude that the council brought an enormous renewal of the church. There is an interesting parallel to the Gregorian reform here. Gerd Tellenbach has pointed to the infrequency with which Gregory VII used the word reform.[32] Ladner's study of Gregory's terminology revealed, however, that, although he used the word *reformare* infrequently, he often used related reform terms, such as *renovare, emendare,* or *corrigere.* Tellenbach was arguing that the Gregorian reform was less a reform than a revolution, and here, while deeply influenced by Ladner, he also took issue with him. This example brings us to the last and

[28] Ladner, *Erinnerungen*, p. 67, where he tells of receiving a letter from the pope, signed by the papal secretary thanking Ladner for the gift and among other things saying that it had brought the pope "viel Trost und Erquickung." Yves Congar also reports that the pope had read and annotated his *Vraie et fausse Réforme dans l'Église;* see Congar, *Réforme*, p. 8 and n. 2.

[29] John O'Malley, *Tradition and Transition: Historical Perspectives on Vatican II* (Wilmington, Delaware, 1989), pp. 44-49. O'Malley suggests that the idea of *aggiornamento* was, in fact, a revolution in reform thinking, because earlier reforms had always stressed that "men must be changed by religion, rather than religion by men."

[30] Ibid., p. 64. O'Malley speculates that the avoidance of the word "reform" was because it had been tainted by Protestants, but more likely because its use would imply that the church had made errors which needed correcting, and this was something Vatican II was reluctant to do.

[31] Ibid., p. 44-45 and n. 2.

[32] Gerd Tellenbach, *The Church in Western Europe from the Tenth to the Early Twentieth Century* (Cambridge, 1993) p. 348 and n. 5.

potentially largest audience influenced by Ladner's work: historians and other scholars interested in past concepts of change.

The appeal of Ladner's *Idea of Reform* to this audience is suggested by an article by Gerhart Niemeyer in *Review of Politics,* which reviewed Ladner's work jointly with a book of collected essays by the political philosopher Leo Strauss.[33] Niemeyer contends that Ladner's theoretical constructions are highly significant for political scientists, above all because of the way in which they set off the concept of reform

> against the idea of cosmological rebirth (cyclical renewal), the idea of renaissance (vitalistic new growth), and the idea of the millennium (total perfection). Reform is neither "merely response nor sterile return to a dead past." It implies the "conscious pursuit of ends." It is "characterized by the belief both in ineradicable terrestrial imperfection and in a *relative perfectibility* the extent of which is unforeseeable."

Thus, in Niemeyer's appreciation of Ladner's formulation, "the concept of reform differs significantly from the perennial human tendency to 'make a new beginning'." One might add that, ironically, ideas of change which most stress "newness" are thus often quite conservative, because the newness they envision is a return to the beginnings, whereas ideas of "reform" often anticipate change to something truly new, in the sense that it has not existed before. Such concepts of reform owe much to Augustine's central emphasis on a *reformatio in melius*, in turn reminding us that a large part of the impact of *The Idea of Reform* stems from its central focus on, and consummate analysis of the Augustinian ideas which, in turn, have been central to the entire history of the idea of reform in the West.

However, ideas of "new beginnings" can also envisage revolutionary change, especially if the past era to be recapitulated is very distant and imperfectly understood. Part of the appeal of the "idea of reform" as defined by Ladner has undoubtedly been its vision of change within continuity, the possibility it suggests of change without the violent rupture of revolution. Yet here, as Tellenbach's criticism suggests, the boundary between reform and revolution may not always be so distinct as Ladner makes it out.

While acknowledging his indebtedness to *The Idea of Reform* for an understanding of the monastic reform ideas which played such a fundamental role in eleventh century reform, Tellenbach differed sharply from Ladner's assessment of the Gregorian reform itself, which Ladner had set forth in his *Habilitationsschrift* concerning the political and theological background of the investiture contest.[34] Ladner did call attention to Gregory's use of Tertullian's

[33] Gerhart Niemeyer, "What Is Political Knowledge?" *Review of Politics* 23 (1961): 104-107. (The internal citations are from Ladner's *Idea of Reform.*)

[34] Gerhart B. Ladner, *Theologie und Politik vor dem Investiturstreit: Abendmahlstreit, Kirchenreform, Cluni und Heinrich III.* (Baden, 1936; reprint

statement, "Our Lord Christ has called Himself truth, not custom," which many have taken to express the radical, and even revolutionary nature of Gregory's program.[35] But Ladner believed that Gregory distinguished between bad new customs and good old customs, and that the main thrust of his idea of change was a restoration of the good Roman canons from the past which had fallen into disuse. Ladner's characterization of Gregory's movement as reform rather than revolution was based above all on his criteria stated in *The Idea of Reform* for distinguishing reform ideas from ideas of revolution. This distinction, though endorsed in the revised edition of Karl Griewank's standard work on the modern concept of revolution,[36] has probably been the one aspect of *The Idea of Reform* which has undergone most questioning.

As Karl Morrison puts it, "other authors have perceived that reform and revolution are not mutually exclusive and that, in fact, many reforms may cumulatively produce—and may be planned to produce—a radical change of social order."[37] In his far-ranging study, Morrison considers reform as *mimesis*, a strategy of change for the better, specifically a strategy of mediating the asymmetries between what is and what should or might be. For Morrison even the revolutionary thought of Marx falls within this tradition of mimetic reform. Morrison acknowledges the major impact of Ladner's *Idea* on his own work and is in fundamental agreement with Ladner on the central role of Pauline and patristic thought in establishing the main patterns of mimetic reform thought.[38] But he argues for a much heavier input of pre-Christian Greek ideas into the early Christian ones than Ladner would see.

Whereas Morrison sees *mimesis* as one species of reform strategies, Ladner sees the idea of reform as one species of renewal ideas. Although Ladner may have underestimated the overlap between ideas of reform and revolution, he gave much attention to the combination of reform ideas with other ideas of renewal. Ladner's categorization of ideas of renewal in *The Idea of Reform* has opened many vistas for scholars of change in all epochs, for renewal ideas are

Darmstadt, 1968). Tellenbach, *Europe*, p. 348 and n. 5. Ladner had disagreed with Tellenbach in his article "Aspects of Mediaeval Thought on Church and State," *Review of Politics* 9 (1947) 403-422 [*Selected Studies*, pp. 435-456, 1028-1029, and 1045 at p. 449 and n. 45.] Tellenbach said that Ladner's objections "only confirm me in my opinion." However, elsewhere Tellenbach spoke highly of Ladner's *Idea of Reform* and its analysis of monastic reform thought: p. 377 and n. 16.

35 Gerhart B. Ladner, "Two Gregorian Letters on the Sources and Nature of Gregory VII's Reform Ideology," *Studi Gregoriani* 5 (1956): 221-242 [*Selected Studies*, pp. 675-682].

36 Karl Griewank, *Die neuzeitliche Revolutionsbegriff*, ed. J. Horn-Staiger, 2d ed. (Frankfurt, 1969).

37 Morrison, *Mimetic Tradition*, p. 421.

38 Ibid., pp. 419-421, for the influence of both *The Idea of Reform* and *Ad imaginem Dei*.

ideas of change which encompass both forward-looking and backward-looking elements.[39] Ladner developed this taxonomy of renewal ideas further for the ancient world in his article "Erneuerung" in the *Reallexikon für Antike und Christentum* and for the later medieval and Renaissance periods in a series of articles.[40] His work has had a great influence on his students and other scholars. The volume *Renaissance and Renewal in the Twelfth Century*, cited above, is a prime example of such influence.[41] One of Ladner's students, Michael Phelps, wrote his doctoral dissertation on three kinds of renewal ideas associated with the Franciscan movement.[42] Phelps distinguishes the ideas of reform of Francis and his immediate followers from two other kinds of renewal ideas associated with his life and work: vitalistic renewal ideas of Pope Gregory IX and others who saw Francis as bringing a renewal of the whole church, and apocalyptic ideas of renewal among Spiritual Franciscans who saw Francis and Dominic as ushering in a new age of the Spirit. In my own studies of late medieval conciliar reform ideas, I have repeatedly observed that very concrete and limited reform proposals are described by their advocates in very grandiose renewal imagery.[43]

Ladner's investigation of the imagery of renewal, which is so compatible with his art historical training and research, offers rich insights into mentalities of reform. I believe it is thus compatible in many ways with the work of French historians Georges Duby and Jacques Le Goff which explores the medieval "imaginary."[44] In *The Idea of Reform* Ladner paid special attention to

39 Ladner himself tells us of one of the most interesting influences of *The Idea of Reform* in his *Erinnerungen*, p. 67. Ivan Illich, Mexican pedagogue and critic of technology, was fascinated by *The Idea of Reform*, and invited Ladner to his institute in Cuernavaca in 1971 to conduct a one-month seminar on renewal ideas.

40 "Erneuerung," in "*Reallexikon für Antike und Christentum,* vol. 6 (Stuttgart, 1964), pp. 240-275; "Die mittelalterliche Reform-Idee und ihr Verhältnis zur Idee der Renaissance," *Mitteilungen des österreichischen Instituts für Geschichtsforschung,* 60 (1952): 31-59 [*Selected Studies*, pp. 559-593, 1030]; "Vegetation Symbolism and the Concept of Renaissance," in *De artibus opusula XL: Essays in Honor of Erwin Panofsky* (New York, 1961), 1.303-322 [*Selected Studies*, pp. 727-763, 1033-1035, 1044, 1066].

41 See above, n. 14.

42 John Michael Phelps, "A Study of Renewal Ideas in the Writings of the Early Franciscans, 1210-1256," Ph.D. diss., University of California at Los Angeles, 1972.

43 For an example, see Phillip H. Stump, *The Reforms of the Council of Constance (1414-1418)* (Leiden, 1994), p. 209 and n. 9.

44 Georges Duby, *Les Trois Ordres ou l'Imaginaire de féodalisme* (Paris, 1978); Jacques Le Goff, *L'Imaginaire médiéval: Essais* (Paris, 1985) trans. Arthur Goldhammer: *The Medieval Imagination* (Chicago, 1988), pp. 6-7: "To study the imagination (*imaginaire*) of a society is to go to the heart of its consciousness and historical evolution. . . . All the great 'images' of the Middle Ages—man as microcosm, the 'mirror,' the Church as mystical body, society as organism, danse

the imagery used by patristic authors to describe the effacement and the restoration of the divine image-likeness in humanity.[45] In other articles he noted the imagery which describes the renewal of the church in agricultural terms of weeding, hoeing, and pruning.[46] In my doctoral dissertation and subsequent book concerning conciliar reform at the Council of Constance, I investigated a number of such patterns of imagery associated with reform of the Church.[47] Alongside the agricultural images I found images of reform as purgation, the refinement of precious metals, but also, and above all, reform as healing of the church as the body of Christ.

VI

At first glance the profusion and the diffuseness of renewal terms and images in the late Middle Ages might seem to defy any meaningful analysis, but it is especially here that the application of Ladner's methodology does yield significant results, not only because Ladner's taxonomy enables us to sort out the overlap among different types of renewal ideas, but also in three other ways.

First, Ladner's method challenges us to look for reform ideas and principles which inform the myriad specific and concrete reform demands. Frs. Pascoe and O'Malley did so magisterially in their studies of the reforming principles of Jean Gerson and Giles of Viterbo, respectively.[48] Second, it has taught us to look at reform terms and images in their textual and historical contexts before arriving at conclusions about the reform ideas and principles. It is now possible to do a much more complete and accurate search for terms in context using new textual databases and computer search facilities. Ladner was actually on the forefront of such computer-aided research back in 1973, when he did a study of the reform ideas in Gregory's *Moralia* using a database prepared by classicist David Packard in the era before scanners.[49] Michael Phelps also used it to analyze the Franciscan reform ideas. It was Phelps, possibly using a

macabre, symbols of social rank from clothing and furs to coats of arms, symbols of power such as flags and oriflammes, royal investitures and entries—this entire corpus of images simply reproduces in outwardly visible signs the profound mental images of medieval men and women, more or less sophisticated according to their social status and level of culture." See also Stump, *Reforms*, p. 19.

45 Ladner, *Idea*, pp. 92-93.

46 Ibid., pp. 16-26; see also Ladner, "Mittelalterliche Reform-idee," pp. 31-59; and Ladner, "Vegetation," p. 304 and n. 4.

47 See Stump, *Reforms*, pp. 218-226.

48 John O'Malley, *Giles of Viterbo on Church and Reform: A Study in Renaissance Thought* (Leiden, 1968). See, for example, p. 52 n.3.

49 Gerhart B. Ladner, "Gregory the Great and Gregory VII: A Comparison of Their Concepts of Renewal," *Viator* 4 (1973): 1-27 [*Selected Studies*, pp. 629-664].

computer database of Gregory IX's letters, who first made me aware that the watchword of late medieval reform, "reform in head and members," was in fact first used in the papal chancery, at least from the time of Innocent III. (The context was the reform of ecclesiastical corporations, such as monasteries and cathedral chapters.) In the meantime one of Harald Zimmermann's students, Karl Augustin Frech, has traced the whole history of this usage in an admirable study which shows how deeply Frech has drunk at Ladner's well.[50]

This brings me to the third and final way in which *The Idea of Reform* has had an impact on students of late medieval reform: Again and again, seemingly new patterns of reform ideology in fact have long histories, histories which often lead us back more or less directly to the patristic reform ideas Ladner investigated so definitively in *The Idea of Reform*.[51] Fr. Pascoe has traced many such lineages in the reform thought of Gerson and d'Ailly—for example, Gerson's evocation of Augustine's idea of the trinitarian divine image in the soul (which may have helped give a trinitarian cast to Gerson's entire reform ideology); also the Pseudo-Dionysian ideas of hierarchical reform, and ideas of reform relating to the pre-Constantinian *ecclesia primitiva*. One of Fr. Pascoe's students, Christopher Bellitto, in his recent fascinating study of Nicholas de Clamanges' reform thought, traces the major emphasis of it back to patristic ideas of personal renewal and argues that this major emphasis may account for much of Clamanges' ambivalence to the institutional reform ideas of the conciliar movement.[52] Bellitto's study also reminds us that the connection between humanism and reform in France may be traced back into the late fourteenth century, and here, once again, ideas of reform intersect with ideas of renascence, a convergence which for later periods has been investigated so admirably in the work of Fr. John O'Malley and Nelson Minnich on Giles of Viterbo and the Fifth Lateran Council.

[50] Karl Augustin Frech, *Reform an Haupt und Gliedern: Untersuchungen zur Entwicklung und Verwendung der Formulierung im Hoch- und Spätmittelalter* (Frankfurt, 1992); see especially pp. 91-108.

[51] Helmrath, "Reform as Thema," p. 150. Helmrath has shown how reform ideas have long lives in medieval conciliar and monastic sources and sometimes, after repeated enunciation, finally find implementation years, and indeed centuries, later. One group of reform documents which found a particularly long life was the ninth-century Pseudo-Isidorian Decretals. Constantin Fasolt has brilliantly demonstrated the role these decretals played in the seminal conciliar reform ideas of William Durant the Younger; see Constantin Fasolt, *Council and Hierarchy: The Political Thought of William Durant the Younger* (Cambridge, 1990). The decretals in turn transmitted to the later Middle Ages much earlier conciliar sources, many of which were from the patristic era; this example also reminds us again of the importance of canon law sources for reform, which Ladner underscored in a chapter of *The Idea of Reform;* see Ladner, *Idea*, pp. 298-315.

[52] Christopher M. Bellitto, "Nicolas de Clamanges: Personal and Pastoral Reform in the Late Medieval Church," Ph.D. diss., Fordham University, 1996.

The rich diversity of the late medieval reform ideas and their convergence with ideas of Renaissance are, I believe, two principal reasons why Ladner's *Idea of Reform* has had its most concentrated impact among scholars working in the area of late medieval reform. A third reason is that so much work remains to be done in sorting out the complex late medieval ideas. Ladner's students, and his students' students, as well as many other scholars in diverse fields are now engaged in the task. As we investigate the rich harvest of late medieval reform ideas, their connection with ideas of rebirth, and their continuity or discontinuity with the Reformation, we will often return, humanist fashion, *ad fontes*; and we will find the sources, more often than not, already awaiting us again in Gerhart Ladner's venerable, but ever new, *Idea of Reform*.

POPE URBAN II, A PSEUDO-COUNCIL OF CHARTRES, AND *CONGREGATO* (C.16, Q.7, C.2 "PALEA")

Robert Somerville

Pope Urban II's journey to France in 1095-1096 has been studied in detail, by historians of the First Crusade especially but also by those who are interested in the pontiff's activities in the general context of the reform of the eleventh-century church.[1] Urban's activities in France were conducted in familiar circumstances, for he was born at Châtillon-sur-Marne, and made a career at Reims and Cluny before going to Rome in 1079/1080 to serve Gregory VII as cardinal-bishop of Ostia.[2] Why he came north in the summer of 1095 is a complicated question. Perhaps a plan to seek military aid for the Byzantine Empire against the Turks, and even to conquer Jerusalem, was already well formed when he left Italy in mid-summer of 1095, but whether or not that was so, surely he hoped to disseminate his version of the program for ecclesiastical reform inherited from his predecessors. Councils provided an excellent opportunity for both tasks, through promulgating general legislation (commonly called "decrees" or "canons"), and providing a captive audience to hear the Crusade appeal.[3] Urban II convened synods at Clermont (November 1095), Tours (March 1096), and Nîmes (July 1096). Once it was thought that Limoges should be added to that list (Christmastime 1095), but this is now known not to be the case.[4] Yet the phantom "Council of Limoges" illustrates that documentation

1 The work of Alfons Becker, *Papst Urban II.*, 2 vols. (Monumenta Germaniae Historica, Schriften 19; Stuttgart, 1964ff) [hereafter Becker, *Urban*], is now the starting point for treating Urban's itinerary - see 1.214ff., and 2.435ff., with a map on p. 458. See also idem, "Le voyage d'Urbain II en France," in *Le concile de Clermont de 1095 et l'appel à la croisade* (Collection de l'École française de Rome 236; Roma, 1997), pp. 127-140 (map on p. 128; see in n. 12 below). The works of René Crozet remain useful: "Le voyage d'Urbain II et ses arrangements avec le clergé de France (1095-1096)," *Revue historique* 179 (1937): 271-310 [hereafter Crozet, "Voyage"], and "Le voyage d'Urbain II en France (1095-1096) et son importance au point de vue archéologique," *Annales du Midi* 49 (1937): 46-69.

2 Becker, *Urban,* 1.24-62; and Robert Somerville, "Urban II, Pope," in *Dictionary of the Middle Ages,* vol. 12 (1988): 302-304.

3 For Urban's motives in coming to France see now Robert Somerville, "Clermont 1095: Crusade and Canons," in *La primera cruzada novecientos años después: El concilio de Clermont y los orígenes del movimento cruzado,* ed. Luis García-Guijarro Ramos (Madrid, 1997), p. 69 [hereafter Somerville, "Crusade and Canons"]; and for the "general councils" of the eleventh/twelfth-century papal reform see idem, "Councils, Western (869-1179)," in *Dictionary of the Middle Ages,* vol. 3 (1983): 632-639. Jonathan Riley-Smith, *The First Crusaders, 1095-1131* (Cambridge, 1997), p. 75, makes the intriguing observation that "a high proportion of the first crusaders known to me came from localities within a day or two's ride of [the path of Urban's journey]."

4 Robert Somerville, "The French Councils of Pope Urban II: Some Basic Considerations," *Annuarium Historiae Conciliorum* 2 (1970): 56-65 (reprint in idem, *Papacy, Councils and Canon Law in the 11th-12th Centuries* [Variorum Collected

about late eleventh-century assemblies can be both scarce and unclear, and attested synods for which very little is known include Gregory VII's at Salerno in 1084 and Urban's at the Lateran in 1097.[5] Is there reason to think that Urban II, during his stay in France, held a council or councils other than the well-known gatherings at Clermont, Tours, and Nîmes?

Despite the pope's own statement implying that Nîmes was the third synod which he celebrated in France, this question requires some thought in light of a text added to what probably is an early thirteenth-century copy of Gratian's *Decretum* found in MS 2009 of the Biblioteca del Cabildo at Seo de Urgel.[6] The *Decretum* is accompanied on fol. 2v-193v (through C.36, q.2, dpc.11), by the first recension of the apparatus *Ius naturale* of Alanus Anglicus, without the preface, and beginning *Tractatutus de iure canonico Gratianus incipiens.* Among a group of texts added to Gratian's work at the end of C.12 is one which is inscribed *Urbanus secundus,* and begins, "In a synod of many bishops assembled in the city of Chartres a question was brought before us by certain people...."[7] The text continues, describing the issue and its resolution:[8]

Studies CS312; Aldershot, 1990], and see the "Additions & Corrections" at the end of the volume) [hereafter Somerville, "French Councils"]. See also Becker, *Urban,* 2.442-443.

5 Robert Somerville, "The Councils of Gregory VII," *Studi Gregoriani* 12 (1989): 36; and Francis J. Gossman, *Pope Urban II and Canon Law* (The Catholic University of America, Canon Law Studies 403; Washington, 1960) [hereafter Gossman, *Urban*], p. 11.

6 For Nîmes as the *tertia synodus* see Somerville, "French Councils" p. 60. MS 2009 from Seo de Urgel and the text therein to be discussed here were kindly pointed out to the author by the late Gérard Fransen, who in 1957 published a note about the anonymous commentary to the *De consecratione* in MS 2009, "Un commentaire au 'De consecratione'," *Traditio* 13 (1957): 508-509. Prof. Antonio García y García generously provided a copy of the relevant pages from the typescript of a forthcoming *Catálogo de los manuscritos jurídicos de la Biblioteca del Cabildo de Seo de Urgel,* in preparation by Professor García y García et al., where a fuller bibliography will be given. See in the meantime, Antonio García y García, "Los manuscritos del Decreto de Graciano en las bibliotecas y archivos de España," *Studia Gratiana* 8 (1962): 168-169; Richard M. Fraher, "Alanus Anglicus and the Summa 'Induent sancti'," *Bulletin of Medieval Canon Law,* n. s. 6 (1976): 47-54, especially pp. 47-50; and Gérard Fransen, "Les gloses de Melendus et l'apparat d'Alain l'Anglais sur le Décret de Gratien," *Cahiers de Fanjeaux* 29 (1994): 32-33.

7 Fol. 105vb: "Congregato [MS: Congregacio] apud Carnotensem urbem multorum episcoporum sinodali conventu, opposita est nobis a quibusdam questio...." The word quibusdam probably refers back to episcopo*rum,* although it need not.

8 Ibid.: "...opposita est...questio de ecclesiis vel ecclesiasticis possessionibus a clericis vel monachis usque in presenciarum inconsultis episcopis. Nos autem usi [MS: nisi] saniori consilio eorundem episcoporum, condescendentes pro tempore providentesque ecclesiastice paci vel quia aliter absque inevitabili scandali periculo huiusmodi questio non poterat procedere, apostolica auctoritate decrevimus ut ea, que a clericis vel monachis a quibuscumque personis, prout potuerunt

> ...a question...about churches and ecclesiastical possessions acquired by clerics and monks up to the present time behind the backs of bishops. Drawing, however, on wiser counsel of the same bishops, acquiescing for the time being and providing for ecclesiastical peace—and because otherwise a question of this sort was unable to proceed without the inevitable danger of scandal—we decreed by apostolic authority that those things which up to today were acquired by clerics and monks, just as they were able, from anyone at all, should be held as forever stable and inviolable, nevertheless, with this understanding, that in the future they should not presume to do such things behind the backs of bishops.

Did Urban II preside at a synod in Chartres for which no evidence until now has come to light, where this question about church property was raised and settled? Bishop Ivo of Chartres and the pope were on cordial terms, for Urban supported Ivo's claims to his see in the face of opposition, and had consecrated him at Capua in 1090.[9] Yet this text is nearly identical to a canon which appears in thirteenth-century manuscripts of Gratian's *Decretum,* as a "palea" at C.16, q.7, c.2, and in which the location of the dispute is not a synod at Chartres, but the Council of Clermont.[10] Legislation from Urban's French councils was repeated from one to the other, so repetition does not per se argue against a synod at Chartres.[11] What virtually precludes such an event, however, is an examination of the papal itinerary.

Based on what is at present known, Urban seems to have come no closer to Chartres than Le Mans and Vendôme.[12] He is found in Le Mans, where he

[MS: potuerñt], usque hodie fuerunt [MS: fuerñt] acquisita, rata perenniter et inconvulsa permaneantur, hoc tamen tenore, ne inposterum inconsultis episcopis talia presumant."

9 For Ivo see now Jean Werckmeister, *Yves de Chartres, Prologue* (Sources canoniques 1; Paris, 1997), pp. 13ff.

10 See Robert Somerville, *The Councils of Urban II, I: Decreta Claromontensia* (Annuarium Historiae Conciliorum, Supplementum 1; Amsterdam, 1972), p. 133 [hereafter Somerville, *Decreta*], with reference to Jacqueline Rambaud-Buhot, "Les paleae dans le Décret de Gratien," in *Proceedings of the Second International Congress of Medieval Canon Law,* ed. Stephan Kuttner & J. Joseph Ryan (Monumenta iuris canonici, Subsidia 1; Cittàdel Vatican, 1965), pp. 23-44. *Congregato* can be found in printings of the late sixteenth-century "Roman Edition" of Gratian - e.g., this author has seen it in the printings from Venice 1584 and 1595 - and in the edition by Emil Friedberg, *Corpus Iuris canonici,* pars prior: *Decretum Magistri Gratiani* (Lipsiae, 1879) [hereafter Friedberg, *Decretum*]. For the "Roman Edition" see Augustine Thompson, James Gordley, and Katherine Christensen, *Gratian, The Treatise on Laws* (Studies in Medieval and Early Modern Canon Law 2; Washington, 1993), p. xix.

11 For this repetiton see Somerville, "French Councils" pp. 62-63.

12 The emergence of new information cannot be discounted: for a recent discovery which adds Saumur to Urban's itinerary see George T. Beech, "Urban II, the Abbey of Saint-Florent of Saumur, and the First Crusade," in *Autour de la Première*

arrived from Sablé and Angers, on February 15/16-18, 1096, and on February 26 his presence is recorded at the abbey of La Trinité in Vendôme. He then appeared in Tours on March 3, and opened his synod there nearly two weeks later, on the 16th. Writing in the middle of the second decade of the twelfth century, Abbot Geoffrey remembered that the pope and his entourage stayed at La Trinité for eleven days.[13] Even if Geoffrey's memory is faulty or if he exaggerated, there is no reason to doubt that Urban spent several days at this important monastery. It is possible that at some point he might have made the relatively brief journey from Vendôme to Chartres before turning southward toward Tours, but if so he could not have remained very long, and most likely would not have held a council there in view of the upcoming synod at Tours, for which preparations surely were underway in late February. Crozet also pointed out the obvious political considerations associated with a papal journey very far north of the Loire. Urban's relations with King Philip I were rocky, and "la crainte d'un coup de force de Philippe Ier" surely was in the mind of the pope and his advisers.[14] To a very high degree of probability, therefore, the canon added to C.12 of Gratian in MS 2009 is wrong in speaking of a council of Urban II at Chartres, and its *Carnotensem urbem* must be a corruption of *Claromontensem urbem,* as found in the "palea" of C.16, q.7, c.2. This text seems generally to have been ignored by those dealing with monks, canons, and lay and episcopal rights at the end of the eleventh century, although from time to time it has been noticed in discussions of Pope Urban's conciliar legislation.[15] In that context the point was made as long ago as the sixteenth century that the provisional character of the

Croisade, ed. Michel Balard (Byzantina Sobornensia 14; Paris, 1996), pp. 57-70, with a map on p. 70; see also the map in Michael Matzke, "De origine Hospitalariorum Hierosolymitanorum: Vom klösterlichen Pilgerhospital zur internationalen Organisation," *Journal of Medieval History* 22 (1996): 12 (for other maps see n. 1 above). For the discussion which follows see Becker, *Urban,* 2.435ff.

13 Geneviève Giordanengo, *Geoffrey de Vendôme, Oeuvres* (s, l. 1996), p. 292, no. 139. Becker, *Urban,* 2.446, writes, somewhat ambiguously, that the eleven-day interval was "vielleicht Febr. 19/20-März 2/3."

14 Crozet, "Voyage," p. 308.

15 Cinzio Violante is an exception, and has dealt with *Congregato* in two studies; see "Monachesimo Cluniacense di fronte al mondo politico ed ecclesiastico (secoli x e xi)," in idem, *Studi sulla Christianità medioevale,* ed. Piero Zerbi, 2nd ed. (Cultura e storia 8; Milano, 1975), pp. 38ff (originally published in *Spiritualità cluniacense* [Todi, 1960]); and in "Pievi e parrocchie nell'Italia centrosettentrionale durante i secoli XI e XII," in *Le istituzioni ecclesiastiche della "Societas Christiana" dei secoli XI-XII: Diocesi, pievi e parrocchie* (Miscellanea del Centro di Studi medioevali 8; Milano, 1977), pp. 691ff. See the general discussion in Gossman, *Urban,* p. 130, and Somerville, *Decreta,* pp. 131-135.

text suggests that it does not derive from the canonical legislation enacted at Clermont, and it is, in fact, absent from all such lists (such as they are).[16]

Aside from the versions in Seo de Urgell MS 2009, and the "palea" at C.16, q.7, c.2, a third occurrence of *Congregato* in a manuscript of Gratian's *Decretum* has long been known. First reported by Mansi, the text appears in a copy of the *Decretum* which still is to be found in that city.[17] MS 20 [6] of the Archivio Archivescovile, dating from the late twelfth or early thirteenth century, contains *Congregato* at fol. 124ra, seemingly as a marginal gloss not to C.16, q.7, c.2, but to C.16, q.6, c.6 [7] (*Episcopo*), and bearing the enigmatic inscription *Item Albinus.*[18]

Beyond these occurrences in Gratian, *Congregato* also is transmitted in three late twelfth-century collections of papal decretal letters.

1. The systematic collection of decretals known as the *Collectio Francofurtana,* which remains to be throughly analyzed and edited, survives in four manuscripts which differ significantly among themselves. The earliest form of the collection, represented by MS T below, probably was assembled during the pontificate of Pope Lucius III (1181-1185), and probably in Sens.[19] The following manuscripts are known, with *Congregato* found in title 16 ("How distribution of ecclesiastical benefices ought to be done."), c.7.[20]

16 Ibid., with reference on p. 133 to this view of Antonio Agustín (+1586), and passim, for the chaotic state of the transmission of the canons.

17 Ibid., pp. 132-134.

18 The author is grateful to John F. Kenney who, during a visit to Lucca in 1968, saw this manuscript and made some notes from it. Mansi incorrectly read the inscription as Item *Albino*. See now Rudolf Weigand, *Die Glossen zum Dekret Gratians,* 2 vols. (Studia Gratiana 25-26; Roma, 1991), 2.818-820, especially p. 818 for the dating, and for *Albinus*.

19 A study of this important collection is to be prepared by Peter Landau: see idem, "Die Entstehung der systematischen Dekretalensammlungen und die europäische Kanonistik des 12. Jahrhunderts," *Zeitschrift der Savigny-Stiftung für Rechtsgeschichte,* Kan. Abt. 67 (1979): 137-143 (reprint with "Retractationes" in idem, *Kanones und Dekretalen* [Bibliotheca eruditorum 2; Goldbach bei Aschaffenburg, 1997]) [hereafter, Landau, "Entstehung"; Landau *Kanones*]. André Gouron, "Une école ou des écoles? Sur les canonistes français (vers 1150-vers 1210)," in *Proceedings of the Sixth International Congress of Medieval Canon Law,* ed. Stephan Kuttner and Kenneth Pennington (Monumenta iuris canonici, Subsidia 7; Città del Vaticano, 1985), p. 237, suggests Auxerre as the home of the *Francofurtana.*

20 *Qualiter ecclesiasticorum beneficiorum debeat fieri distributio.* For the manuscripts, and bibliography, see the list in *Decretales ineditae saeculi XII,* from the papers of the late Walther Holtzmann, edited and revised by Stanley Chodorow and Charles Duggan (Monumenta iuris canonici, Corpus Collectionum 4; Città del Vaticano, 1982), p. xxvi. The "sigla" used here are taken from there. The author is grateful to Peter Landau for access to materials from the papers and photostats of Walther Holtzmann which are housed at the Stephan Kuttner Institute of Medieval Canon Law in Munich, and to Jörg Müller and Otto Vervaart for kindly providing

i) Frankfurt, Stadt- und Universitätsbibl., Barth. 60, fol. 2-85 (=F), *Congregato* at fol. 27v.

ii) London, Brit. Lib., Egerton 2901, fol. 1r-97v (=M), from St. Maximin, Trier (once Phillipps MSS 7369, and 7790), *Congregato* at fol. 26r.[21]

iii) Paris, BNF, lat. 3922A, fol. 173r-209r (=R), from Rouen, *Congregato* at fol. 182v.

iv) Troyes, Bibl. de la Ville 961, fol. 1r-96v (=T), from Clairvaux, *Congregato* at fol. 34r-v.

2. The *Liber extravagantium* of Bernard of Pavia—often called the *Compilatio prima* as the earliest of the five basic compilations which Raymond of Peñafort used in the 1230s in preparing the *Decretales* of Pope Gregory IX —is an extensive work existing in different versions which date between 1190 and 1198.[22] There is no modern edition. The compilation was edited in the sixteenth century by Antonio Agustín, and in 1882 Friedberg published what amounted to a register of its contents, printing the canons which neither were in Gratian nor in the *Decretales* of Gregory. *Congregato* is found as c.1 in the third book, title 32 "Concerning churches of monks and other religious."[23] *Comp. I* then added another text of Urban II, in some versions appended to the end of *Congregato* without a break—a canon dealing with the old issue of monks performing parish work, beginning *In ecclesiis,* and preserved in the legislative tradition of the Council of Clermont.[24]

3. The *Collectio Sangermanensis,* which employed *Comp. I* as one of its sources, was assembled in Normandy around the year 1198. It survives in one manuscript, Paris, BNF, lat. 12459, fol. 1-106v (=P - the immediate provenance of this manuscript was the Abbey of St.-Germain-des-Prés in Paris). *Congregato* is found in book 7, canon 137, at fol. 83v, and as in *Comp. I* is followed by *In ecclesiis,* here without a separate attribution but as a separate

copies of such items, and answering various inquiries.

21 For this copy see Peter Landau, "Studien zur Appendix und den Glossen in frühen systematischen Dekretalensammlungen," *Bulletin of Medieval Canon Law,* New Series 9 (1979): 5ff (reprint in Landau, *Kanones*).

22 See Robert Somerville and Bruce C. Brasington, *Prefaces to Canon Law Books in Latin Christianity* (New Haven, 1998), pp. 216ff.

23 *De capellis monachorum, et aliorum religiosorum* in Antonio Agustín, *Antiquae collectiones decretalium* (Ilerdae, 1576), reprinted in Agustín's *Opera omnia* (Luca, 1769), 4.202-203 [hereafter Agustín, *Opera*]; Emil Friedberg, *Quinque compilationes antiquae* (Lipsiae, 1882), p. 40 [hereafter Friedberg, QCA]. For these works see Stephan Kuttner, "Antonio Agustín's Edition of the Compilationes antiquae," *Bulletin of Medieval Canon Law,* n. s. 7 (1977): 1-14; see p. 11, on the high quality and ease of use of the Luchese reprint of Agustín's *Antiquae collectiones.*

24 Somerville, *Decreta,* p. 133.

text.[25] Given its variegated transmission, it is impossible at this point to provide a critical edition of *Congregato,* which in several cases is embedded in works which themselves have a complicated textual history which remains to be delineated. Yet in order to assess in more detail the nature of this text, and to attempt to see what Urban II and the bishops at Clermont are said to have done, it is important to present its various forms as far as they are now known. For this purpose what appears to be the earliest appearance of the text, in MS T of the *Collectio Francofurtana,* will be transcribed (with editorial capitalization and punctuation), with variants from the other versions noted (other than spelling differences, which are indicated only in the case of forms for "Clermont"). Because T seems to be the earliest manuscript where *Congregato* occurs, however, does not mean that its text presents the earliest version, and the relationship among the manuscripts of the *Coll. Francofurtana* needs to be clarified.[26] The *Francofurtana,* furthermore, seems not to have influenced *Comp. I,* and Bernard of Pavia admitted that he used canonical collections from before the time of Gratian in putting together his *Liber extravagantium.*[27] Finally, where MSS L and S derived their text, and what underlies the thirteenth-century tradition of the "palea" which appeared at C.16, q.7, are open questions.

The following "sigla" are used below in the critical apparatus; variants, for ease of reference, will be given following the alphabetical order of the "sigla", although anything noted from MS T will be listed first, and those from the *Coll. Francofurtana* will be given together, after "F."

B = Bernard of Pavia, *Comp. I,* 3.32.1, as printed in Agustín, *Opera,* 4.202-203. *Collectio Francofurtana:* for MSS F, M, R, and T, see above.

G = C.16, q.7, c.2, "palea" in Gratian's *Decretum,* as printed in Friedberg, *Decretum,* cols. 800-801.

L = Lucca, Archivio Archivescovile 20 [6], fol. 123ra.

P = Paris, BNF, lat. 12459, fol. 83v, *Collectio Sangermanensis.*

S = Seo de Urgel, Biblioteca del Cabildo 2009, fol. 105vb.

25 Heinrich Singer, *Neue Beiträge über de Dekretalensammlungen vor und nach Bernhard von Pavia* (Sitzungsberichte der Kais. Akademie der Wissenschaften in Wien Phil.-Hist. Klasse 171.1; Wien, 1913), p. 309; and Landau, "Entstehung," pp. 144-146. Singer's detailed analysis of the collection does not indicate any titles under which the texts in bk. 7 are arrayed.

26 See Landau, "Entstehung," p. 125, and also p. 142, n. 92, indicating that a layer of glosses occurring in T "im wesentlichen" also appears in M and R.

27 Ibid., pp. 125, 135-137, and 142-143, for *Coll. Francof.* and *Comp. I.* See Somerville and Brasington, *Prefaces,* pp. 219-220 for Bernard, and also Friedberg, QCA, p. xi. Ibid., p. xvii, Friedberg listed no source for *Congregato* in *Comp. I,* only noting its appearance as a "palea" in Gratian.

Item Urbanus II.
Congregato apud Claremontensem urbem multorum coepiscoporum
sinodali conventu, proposita est nobis a quibusdam eorum questio
de ecclesiis vel ecclesiasticis possessionibus, a clericis vel monachis
5 usque in presentiarum inconsultis episcopis acquisitis. Nos autem
usi saniori consilio eorum episcoporum, condescendentes questioni
providentesque ecclesiastice paci, vel quia aliter absque inevitabilis
scandali periculo huiusmodi questio non poterat procedere, apostolica
auctoritate decrevimus, ut ea, que a clericis vel a monachis a
10 quibuscumque personis, prout potuerunt, usque hodie fuerint
acquisita, rata perhenniter et inconcussa permaneant, hoc tamen
tenore, <ne> inposterum inconsultis episcopis talia presuma<n>t.

1 Item-II.] Urbanus II. In concilio Claromontensi. B; Unde Urbanus II. G; Item Albinus. L; Urbanus II in concilio Daromontensi. P; Urbanus secundus. S 1-2 Item-multorum *om.* M

2 Congregatio *corr. ad* Congregato T; Congreto *corr. ad* Congregato R; Congregacio S Claromontensem G B; Clarenontensem L; Claromontem P; Cleremontensem R; Carnotensem S episcoporum B F M G S episcoporum multorum P

3 opposita S nobis est G eorum *om.* L S

4 de ecclesiis vel *om.* P vel] de *add.* B G, a *add.* P

5 antem P

6 usi] nisi S saniorum R

6 eorum

6 condescendentes questioni] condescendentes pro tempore B G L P S; ruine condescendentes F M questioni] pro tempore *corr. ad.* questioni R providentes quia T; providentes P

7 ecclesiastice paci] non *potest legi* L, vel *om.* P R inevitabilis] inevitabili B P S; *non potest legi* L

8 scandali *repetit et cancell.* R huiuscemodi F; huius M R P

9 decernimus B P ut ea *repetit et cancell.* R vel] et F

9 a(1) *om.* B G L R S [monachis] vel *add.* B G quibusdam B a(2)] vel F potuerint G; potuert L S

10 fuerunt B F R; fuert L S inconcussa inconvulsa S

11 permaneant] et *add.* T; permaneantur S inconcussa episcopis inconsultis L ne B F M R G L P S

12 presumant B F M R G L P S *In fine add.* B: In ecclesiis, ubi monachi habitant, populus per monachum non regatur, sed capellanus, qui populum regat, ab Episcopo per consilium monachorum instituatur, ita tamen, ut ex solius Episcopi arbitrio, tam ordinatio, quam depositio, & totius vitae pendeat conversatio.

From an examination of this text and the accompanying variants the following set of four issues can be raised.

1. Other than the strange *Item Albinus.* in L, *Congregato* has not been found inscribed to anyone other than Urban II. A twelfth-century figure named *Albinus,* who could be either the author of a work in which *Congregato* appears, or who, as Mansi assumed by changing *Albinus* to *Albino* (see at n. 18 above), could be the recipient of the text, has not been found. It once was suggested that this excerpt might be found in the *Gesta pauperis scholaris Albini,* assembled late in the twelfth century by the Cardinal Bishop of Albano, but that guess turned out to be incorrect.[28] The best solution to the puzzle might be to conclude that the curious inscription is a corruption of *Item Urbanus.* - not the easiest transformation to imagine but within the realm of possibility.

2. The reference to the Council of Clermont in the inscription in B, and, distorted, in P, cannot mean that the compilers of those collections thought that the text as such originated at Clermont. Reading through *Congregato* makes clear that it was composed after the synod, and is describing something that occurred therein. The excerpt is written in the first person plural, the normal papal mode of expression, and thus is presented as a segment of a papal letter from Urban II which refers back to an episode from Clermont involving circumstances and persons which must remain unknown unless the full letter comes to light. It can be surmised that such a letter would have been sent to someone in the French church, for in their correspondence with this region popes of the time, including Urban himself, recounted decisions from Clermont.[29] A French destination for the letter also fits with the emergence of *Congregato* in the French *Collectio Francofurtana* in the 1180s, although its presence in the Lucchese Gratian, and in *Comp. I,* serve as reminders that the paths by which texts appear in the canonical tradition are complex.

3. There are two places where the collated versions of *Congregato* present substantively different readings, lines 5-7, and lines 9-10.

a) Line 6: aside from *eorundem* versus the *eorum* attested in T, L, and before correction in R, and the question in line 7 of *inevitabilis* versus *inevitabili,* what is to be made of the variants in line 6? The sense is clear: in the face of opposition, but with the approval of some bishops at the synod and with a view toward a peaceful solution, Urban handed down his ruling. The words *condescendentes questioni* in line 6 can be translated "paying careful attention to the question", with or without the sense of "condescension".[30] The variant readings, however, offer both *condescendentes pro tempore,* and *ruine condescendentes,* i.e., "paying careful attention to circumstances" or "to the

[28] Somerville, *Decreta,* p. 134.

[29] Ibid., pp. 139-141 (Appendix II).

[30] See *Mittellateinsiches Wörtbuch* (München, 1995), 8/2.1241.

devastation". No form of the word *condescendentes* has been found with any of these three terms elsewhere in Urban's extant correspondence, and the verb itself has been located only once, in a different context (and in an obviously corrupt text).[31] The word *ruina* also has not turned up in Urban's known texts, but *pro tempo* appears, especially in his turbulent early years.[32] None of this, of course, sheds great light on the origin of *Congregato,* but one suggestion can be offered.

Perhaps the original reading was *condescedentes pro tempore,* a feasible assumption on grounds of similarity to other texts of Urban II, and from the fact that it occurs in all versions transmitted independent of the *Collectio Francofurtana.* The provisional aspect of the papal judgment might have troubled the compiler of the *Francofurtana,* who, nonetheless, having his own reasons for including the text conceivably altered the wording at this point.[33] A study of the *Collectio Francofurtana* with specific attention to conditional rulings might shed light on this suggestion.

b) The word *vel* was inserted before the words *a quibuscumque personis* (see line 10) in the "palea" found in Gratian, and by Bernard of Pavia, and with the preposition *a* missing before *quibuscumque* in MS F of the *Francofurtana.* The word *persona* then carries the meaning "priest" (i.e, "parson"), and the prepositional phrases *vel a monachis vel a quibuscumque personis,* as correlatives, qualify *a clericis* of line 9, specifying those who can keep the questionably acquired property. Without *vel,* the words *a quibuscumque personis* designate the source of what the clerics and monks have acquired (see the translation above).[34] In substantive terms the choice between a reading with and

31 JL 5405 = Urban II, *Collectio Britannica,* no. 43, in Robert Somerville *Pope Urban II, the Collectio Britannica, and the Council of Melfi (1089),* (Oxford, 1996), pp. 163-164 [hereafter, Somerville, *Britannica*]. JL = papal letters cited according to Philipp Jaffé et al., *Regesta pontificum Romanorum,* 2nd ed., vol. 1 (Lipsiae, 1885), section revised by Samuel Loewenfeld.

32 These results concerning *condescendere* and *ruina,* of course, are not exhaustive, and something could have been overlooked, although it is fair to say that neither was a frequently used term in Pope Urban's texts. The author is grateful to Robert Scott and Iain Kennedy of Columbia University's Electronic Text Service for their cordial assistance in using online resources for pursuing this question. For *pro tempore* see, e.g., JL 5353 = Urban II *Coll. Britannica* 4; JL 5363 = Urb. CB 16; JL 5380 = Urb. CB 25; JL 5383 = Urb. CB 30; Council of Melfi (1089), c. 9 - Somerville, *Britannica,* pp. 48, 68, 94, 105, and 255. The list could be expanded, especially with expressions which convey similar meaning. For the turmoil and concomitant legislative maneuvering in the early years of Urban's pontificate especially see ibid., passim, but particularly pp. 31ff. The authenticity of texts from the *Collectio Britannica* is a complicated matter, although it cannot be proven that any of the excerpts therein is a forgery; see ibid., pp. 27ff.

33 A point already made in the sixteenth century by Antonio Agustín: see Somerville, *Decreta,* p. 135 n. 67.

34 For *persona* see Franz Kerff, "'Altar' und 'Person'," in *Dialektik und Rhetorik im früheren und hohen Mittelalter,* ed. Johannes Fried (Schriften des

a reading without *vel* in line 9 is not obvious. In a letter written at an undetermined time after the Council of Melfi (September 1089) by Pope Urban's chancellor John of Gaëta to the abbot of Molesme, and which deals with issues similar to those in *Congregato,* John spoke of "churches given by princes to monasteries" (*ecclesiae a principibus datae monasterii*).[35] The canons of Urban II's Council of Melfi do not survive in an official version but c. 6 of the "textus receptus" decreed that an abbot or a provost should not receive "from the laity" (*a laicis*) things which pertain to ecclesiastical jurisdiction.[36]

It can be wondered why the author of *Congregato* would not have found less ambiguous phrasing at this point if he wished to designate from whom donations were received - John of Gaëta, for example, spoke not only of churches given *a principibus,* but also of things *per principes data monasteriis* - but even so, the choice, perhaps incorrect but with an eye on *a clericis vel monachis* of line 4, was to follow MS T (and the majority of the manuscript testimony) and not insert *vel* before *a quibusque personis.*

4. Does the canon *In ecclesiis,* found in some manuscripts of *Compilatio prima* at the end of *Congregato,* form part of the longer text, or did it become attached because of similar subject matter, and/or because of its association with the Council of Clermont? *In ecclesiis* stipulates that in monastic churches chaplains should be appointed by the local bishop, albeit in consultation with the monks, and that the bishop has control over both the appointment and the conduct of the appointee. Nothing is said about accepting property. *In ecclesiis* appears in a series of canons from Clermont associated with the church at Thérouanne, and the author of *Congregato,* whether it originated in Pope Urban's chancery or elsewhere, could have found and incorporated this text. Given the presence of the combination only in versions of *Comp. I,* however, it seems more reasonable to assume that the marriage was performed at the end of the twelfth and not at the end of the eleventh century.

Considering these four points, the view that *Congregato* formed part of a letter from Urban II written to an unidentified recipient sometime after November 1095, that is, after the Council of Clermont, is possible but unproven. The excerpt's form is the form of papal correspondence, but as 3a shows, the verdict about its language as characteristic of Urban II is mixed. That the text survives only in canon law books composed decades after Urban's day is not an argument against its authenticity, given the survival of texts from other pontiffs of the

Historisches Kollegs, Kolloquien 27; München, 1997), pp. 269-296. The author is grateful to Dr. Kerff for supplying a copy of this article.

35 This letter will be treated in some detail below. The text can be found in Philippe Labbe and Gabrel Cossart, *Sacrosancta concilia ad regiam editionem exact.* (Lutetiae Parisiorum, 1671), 10.497 (also available in Johannes D. Mansi, *Sacrorum conciliorum nova et amplissima collectio* [Venetiis, 1775], 20.726) [hereafter Mansi, *Collectio*]. See the discussion in Somerville, *Britannica,* pp. 199-202.

36 Ibid, p. 254.

Reform Age only in decretal collections.[37] A tentative vote can be cast for *Congregato's* authenticity, if only because it is hard to imagine why anybody in the late twelfth century would invent such a text, with a conditional ruling, and place its origin in the Council of Clermont.

Cinzio Violante, assuming that *Congregato* derives from Urban II, situates it within a discussion about ecclesiastical property and church structure during the papal reform, and also cites the afore-noted letter from Urban's chancellor John of Gaëta.[38] John noted that canonical decrees place all ecclesiastical possessions under episcopal control, nonetheless in earlier times secular princes were allowed to give churches to monasteries.

This permission was interpreted loosely, and princes even sold churches to monks. Gregory VII forbade that practice, John continued, but due to this prohibition bishops began to despoil monasteries (presumably snatching away donations of all sorts).

Whence Gregory decided, in a council in his antepenultimate year, that the possessions and churches given to monasteries by princes before that council should be retained. But with the struggle raging against the Henricians, Gregory's ruling was not followed, hence Urban II at the Council of Melfi commanded that whatever had been given by princes to monasteries up to that point should remain their property. John concluded by indicating a degree of

37 See Uta-Renate Blumenthal, "Decrees and decretals of Pope Paschal II in twelfth-century canonical collections," *Bulletin of Medieval Canon Law,* n. s. 10 (1980): 15-30 (repr. eadem, *Papal Reform and Canon Law in the 11th and 12th Centuries* [Variorum Collected Studies Series CS618; Aldershot, 1998]), for texts which survive only in collections from the mid-twelfth century onward; cf. Walther Holtzmann, "Kanonistische Ergänzungen zur Italia pontificia," *Quellen und Forschungen* 37 (1957): 55-102; 38 (1958): 67-175; and separately, under the same title, (Tübingen, 1959), especially nos. 42, 55, and 179 (Popes Paschal II and Honorius II).

38 See n. 15 above. John's letter is printed in Mansi, *Collectio,* 20.726: "Omnes ecclesiarum res in manu episcoporum canonica decreta constituunt. Sed praeteritis temporibus principibus saecularibus licuit etiam ecclesias monasteriis tradere. Hac vero licentia nimis laxe principes usi sunt, ut etiam ecclesias monachis venderent. Hoc papa Gregorius septimus acriter prohibuit. Propter quam prohibitionem episcopi monasteria acrius spoliare coeperunt. Unde idem moderatione hac uti volunt in concilio antepenultimi anni sui, ut quaecumque res vel ecclesie ante ipsum concilium a principibus datae monasteriis fuerant, in eorum possessione persisterent. Post haec secundo pontificatus sui anno dominus noster Urbanus papa concilium apud Melfiam urbem Apuliae celebravit. Sane quia Gregorii papae praeceptio Heinricianae persecutionis urgente periculo minus celebrata fuerat, ipse quoque dominus Urbanus papa praecepit in eodem concilio Melfitano, ut quae usque ad illud concilium per principes data monasteriis fuerant, firma & integra permaneant. De caetero abbates ab adquisitione hujusmodi abstinerent. Hoc sane concilium Melfitanum celebratum est anno dominicae incarnat. 1089. Porro per hujusmodi temperamentum & abbates ab ecclesiarum invasionibus cessaverunt, & episcopi non omnino spoliare monasteria voluerunt. Plures enim inter eos querelae sic postea in nostra Romana ecclesia definitae sunt."

success as a result of Urban's provision: abbots ceased to usurp churches, bishops did not wish to ruin monasteries, and many disputes between them were subsequently settled in the Roman church.

This is not the place for a new discussion either of this letter composed by the future Pope Gelasius II or of the very complex issue of the disposition of church property during the papal reform.[39] A search among the known decrees from Urban's synod at Melfi for texts which convey the decisions which Chancellor John was recalling does not yield as clear a result as might be hoped. Some version of what are edited as cc. 5-6 must have been in his mind - those canons stating that laity should not make donations of churches to monasteries or houses of canons without episcopal (or papal) approval, nor should any abbot or head of a house of canons accept them.[40] Nothing is said in those decrees about amnesty for such donations made before the time of the council, although such an adjustment might not find a place in the formal synodal legislation. But what can be said specifically about John of Gaëta's letter in comparison with *Congregato*?

The episode in *Congregato* arose from a specific question raised by bishops, it is noted near the beginning of the excerpt, perhaps even a dispute of the sort which John had in mind when he spoke at the end of his letter to Molesme of episcopal-abbatial conflicts being settled in the Roman church (which can be extended to include papal synods even when they convened far from Rome). The chancellor's letter is silent about the abuse at issue in *Congregato,* i.e., monks and canons gaining ecclesiastical possessions without their bishops' knowledge, yet it opens with a reminder of the general policy of the reform papacy to reiterate episcopal authority over all goods of the church, i.e., "Canonical decrees state that all the possessions of churches are in the hand of bishops."[41]

This declaration establishes a link with *Congregato,* at the end of which Pope Urban is said to warn that his compromise was made with the proviso that in the future monks and clerics "should not presume to do such things behind the backs of bishops." But this canonical, pro-episcopal stance is not the only link between John's letter and *Congregato.* Both also reveal papal decisions made on

39 For some of the issues raised by this text see Somerville, *Britannica,* pp. 199-202.

40 Ibid., p. 254, and see also pp. 278-279. On papal approval see Giles Constable, "Monastic Possession of Churches and 'Spiritualia' in the Age of Reform," in *Il monachismo e la riforma ecclesiastica (1049-1122)* (Miscellanea del Centro di Studi Medioevali 10; Milano, 1971), p. 320 (reprint in idem, *Religious Life and Thought (11th-12th centuries)* [Variorum Reprint CS89; London, 1979]).

41 Mansi, *Collectio,* 20.726: "Omnes ecclesiarum res in manu episcoporum canonica decreta constituunt;" cf. Melfi, c. <1b>, = Somerville, *Britannica,* p. 252: "Episcopus omnia sui episcopatus membra . . . sine venalitate disponat."

a *pro tempore* basis. John pointed out that in the face of bishops despoiling monasteries a council of Gregory VII - "who was by no means an unbending doctrinaire," as Stephan Kuttner reminded us in another context[42]—employed moderation and permitted monks to keep goods and churches given by princes before that synod. Urban II did the same, first at Melfi, and as it seems from *Congregato* again six years later at Clermont, *quia aliter absque inevitabilis scandali periculo huiusmodi questio non poterat procedere.*

In both councils, therefore, Urban was, as *Congregato* put it, *condescendentes questioni, providentes ecclesiastice paci;* but neither does the "condescension" find any echo in the synods' canonical legislation.

Clermont reiterated the decrees of Urban II's earlier councils, thus re-enacting Melfi's canons, noted above, absolutely forbidding lay donations to religious houses without episcopal consent.[43]

If that reenactment was, so to speak, "in the air" at Clermont, it is understandable that bishops on hand for the case described in *Congregato* balked at Urban's permission that such gifts received before that time could be retained.[44] Violante rightly points out that in adjudicating that case the pope may well have lacked the support of a majority of bishops, given *Congregato's* allusion to chapter 64 of the *Rule of St. Benedict,* i.e., *Nos autem usi saniori consilio eorum episcoporum.*[45] Perhaps the dissenters also recalled a canon from the council held at Poitiers in 1078 by the papal legate Hugh of Die, where it was decreed (c.6):[46]

> That abbots, monks [and] canons should not buy churches which they never possessed, nor claim them for themselves in any way without

[42] Stephan Kuttner, "Urban II and the Doctrine of Interpretation: A Turning Point?," in *Post Scripta: Essays on Medieval Law and the Emergence of the European State in Honor of Gaines Post,* ed. Joseph R. Strayer and Donald E. Queller (*Studia Gratiana* 15; Roma, 1972), p. 66 (reprint with "Retractationes" in idem, *The History of Ideas and Doctrines of Canon Law in the Middle Ages* [Variorum Reprint CS113; London, 1980, 2nd ed. with "New Retractationes", 1992]).

[43] See Somerville, *Britannica,* p. 202.

[44] Somerville, "Crusade and Canons," pp. 70ff indicates how little is known about the legislative procedures at Clermont, and it is not a simple process to say what bishops on hand at any given moment of the proceedings would know about canons being promulgated or reenacted.

[45] Violante, "Pievi," p. 693-694. Chapter 64 of the *Rule* is the famous discussion of the election of an abbot.

[46] Mansi, *Collectio,* 20.498: "Ut abbates, monachi, canonici ecclesias, quas nunquam habuerunt, non emant, nec alio modo sibi vendicent, nisi consentiente episcopo, in cujus fuerint diocesi. In illis vero, quas hactenus absque calumnia habuerunt, redditus beneficiaque obtineant." See Violante, "Monachismo," p. 38, n. 69, and "Pievi," p. 691. Useful in general is the discussion by Gerd Tellenbach, *The Church in Western Europe from the Tenth to the Early Twelfth Century,* trans. Timothy Reuter (Cambridge, 1993), pp. 286ff.

consent of the bishop in whose diocese they [presumably the churches] were. But in those which they held up to now without calumny they should obtain the revenues and benefices.

The case in *Congregato,* annoyed bishops could have argued, was one distinguished by disception, with property held by monks and *clerics inconsultis episcopis acquisitis.*

A discussion of *Congregato* in the framework of Urban II's pontificate and of Clermont must be speculative, and the same is true about the text's interpretation in the world of post-Gratian canon law. A few words can be offered, nonetheless, in conclusion, on the position and interpretation of *Congregato* in the decretal collections. Its place in the *Francofurtana* and the *Sangermanensis* can only be assessed when these works are analyzed in detail, but one example of how late twelfth-century canonists used the excerpt is seen in *Compilatio prima.* Bk. 3, tit. 32 of *Comp. I.* Ideals with churches under the control of monks and others in the religious life, and contains three canons. The title opens with *Congregato,* amalgamated now with *In ecclesiis* about monks performing parish duties. The second canon is a long segment of c. 9 from the Lateran Council of 1179 (Lateran III).[47] This decree is concerned with regulating matters between local bishops and the Templars and the Hospitallers, and criticizes the military orders on several fronts for exceeding the privileges granted to them, including their practice of receiving churches from the laity. These orders and all other religious are forbidden to obtain churches and tithes in this way, and even those recently thus gained are to be relinquished.[48] After a statement about the need to avoid those who have been excommunicated or interdicted by bishops the text continues and stipulates that in churches where these orders lack full jurisdiction (*quae ad eos pleno iure non pertinent*), priests who are to be installed should be presented to the bishops, to whom they are responsible in matters of pastoral care, while an account is to be given to the religious for the temporalities (although priests who already have been installed without episcopal approval are not to be removed). Canon 3, finally, is JL 13829 (cited in Friedberg according to Jaffé's first edition as J 8894).[49] This excerpt from a letter of Pope Alexander III to the monks in the province of Canterbury commands that when a vacancy occurs in churches where they have the right to present clerical candidates, the monks should present to the diocesan

47 Friedberg, QCA, p. 40. See also *Conciliorum oecumenicorum decreta,* ed. Giuseppe Alberigo et al., 3rd ed. (Bologna, 1972), pp. 215-216.

48 This seems an odd statement, i.e., "even" those acquired recently should be given up: ". . . dimissis etiam quas contra tenorem istum moderno tempore receperunt." Perhaps it has something to do with specific privileges which the military orders recently received, and are misapplying.

49 Jaffé, *Regesta.*

bishop appropriate clergy who should report to him on religious matters and to them on temporal issues.

Taking these canons together, the second repeats in a papal conciliar text provisions of *Congregato,* with special emphasis on two of the new military orders, and with some other issues added. But there is a significant difference. *Congregato* allowed the possessions obtained from laity up to the time of the Council of Clermont to be retained; the text from Lateran III ordered that even those recently acquired be returned. The third canon of the title addresses the issue of monastic patronage, which also had been dealt with in the decree from the Lateran III, and repeats the same traditional division found in the Lateran text of religious and temporal obligations. This issue was, in fact, also treated at the Council of Clermont by Urban II, but it is not the question dealt with either in *Congregato* or in the appended canon *In ecclesiis.*[50]

Why *Congregato* was felt to be appropriate in this title is unclear. Perhaps its differences from c. 9 of Lateran III recommended it to Bernard of Pavia. His purpose, as related in the preface to *Comp. I,* was to present students of canon law with "a richer supply of allegations and judgments" (*uberior allegationum uel iudiciorum copia*).[51]

Three overlapping papal texts under the title *De capellis monachorum et aliorum religiosorum,* each addressed to different situations, might have seemed to Bernard to offer a stimulating array of opinions to be pondered by those studying the canons. When more is known of his sources, and if it ever becomes clear where he found these texts, perhaps that information will explain their presence in *Comp. I.*

When Raymond of Peñafort assembled the great collection of *Decretales* which were promulgated by Pope Gregory IX in 1234, he chose to omit *Congregato* but to include *In ecclesiis.*[52]

Furthermore, Raymond attributed that text, found at 3.37.1 in his work, to "Urban III". Raymond knew and used *Compilatio prima,* perhaps a version in which *Congregato* and *In ecclesiis* appeared as two separate canons (see above, in the discussion of *Comp. I* before the edition of *Congregato*).[53] The mistake in papal attribution is easily explained. But Raymond had great editorial discretion in handling his sources, and, whether attached to *In ecclesiis* or occurring as a separate canon, perhaps he found *Congregato* unsuited to his purposes and omitted it. On the other hand, perhaps he did not include it because by the

50 See Somerville, *Decreta,* p. 148, no. 43.

51 Friedberg, QCA, p. 1. See also the translation of the full text, and the commentary, in Somerville and Brasington, *Prefaces,* pp. 218-219, 230-231.

52 Emil Friedberg, *Corpus Iuris canonici,* pars secunda: *Decretalium collectiones* (Lipsiae, 1881), col. 607.

53 See Somerville and Brasington, *Prefaces,* pp. 216-217.

1230s the text was well established in C.16, q.7 of Gratian as a "palea."[54] Either way, *Congregato's* transmission appears to stop with Bernard of Pavia, and thus this probable witness to the Council of Clermont, and to a little noticed episode in which Pope Urban II's actions *pro tempore* again are visible, did not enter the Roman church's official corpus of canon law.

[54] Somerville, *Decreta,* p. 133.

REFORMATION OF THE INTELLECT IN THE THOUGHT OF AELRED OF RIEVAULX

Daniel Marcel La Corte

In his article entitled "Terms and Ideas of Renewal," Gerhart Ladner identifies the issue central to the spirituality of twelfth-century monastic writers: the reforming of the *imago Dei* in the human soul.[1] Writers such as John Scotus Erigenus, Hugh of Saint Victor, and many Cistercian authors each produced their own works on the reformation of the *imago Dei*.[2] In their teaching on the soul's imaging of God, these authors trace the harmful effects of sin on the image of God found in the soul's created condition, the need for restoration due to original sin, and its future glory when reformed. Ladner states that this reformation is a "progressive assimilation" of the soul, which comes about through continual contact with God's grace.[3] And elsewhere, in *The Idea of Reform*, Ladner points out that Saint Augustine's doctrine on the *imago Dei* and the process of its reformation had considerable influence on the twelfth-century writers.[4] Saint Augustine's doctrine states that the rational soul is composed of the *memoria, intelligentia,* and *voluntas*.[5] Unfortunately, because of original sin, the *imago Dei* "has become deformed and discolored, and man only recovers it when he is reformed and renewed."[6] Saint Augustine teaches that each of the soul's faculties may, through continual contact with God's grace, be reformed to their original condition.[7] Thus, the twelfth-century writers each reflect, to varying degrees, Saint Augustine's doctrine of the process of the *imago Dei's* reformation through grace.

[1] Gerhart B. Ladner, "Terms and Ideas of Renewal," in *Renaissance and Renewal in the Twelfth Century,* ed. Robert Benson, Giles Constable, and Carol Lanham (reprint, Toronto, 1991), pp.14-15.

[2] Marie-Dominique Chenu, *Nature, Man, and Society in the Twelfth Century,* ed. and trans. Jerome Taylor and Lester K. Little (Chicago, 1968), pp. 30-37, 46-55. See also Charles H. Talbot, "Introduction," to Aelred of Rievaulx's *Dialogue on the Soul* (Cistercian Fathers series 22 [hereafter CF]; Kalamazoo, 1981), pp. 17-27; David N. Bell, "The Tripartite Soul and the Image of God in the Latin Tradition," *Recherches de théologie ancienne et médiévale* 47 (1980): 16-52.

[3] Ladner, "Terms and Ideas of Renewal," p. 15.

[4] Ladner, *The Idea of Reform: Its Impact of Christian Thought and Actions in the Age of the Fathers,* rev. ed. (New York, 1967), pp. 167-202. See also Ladner, "St. Augustine's Conception of the Reformation of Man to the Image of God," in *Augustinus Magister: Congrès international augustinien, Paris 21-24 1954* (Paris, 1954), 2.867-878.

[5] Augustine's *De Trinitate* 10.11, PL 42.983.

[6] ". . . imago deformis et decolor facta est; hanc recipit cum reformatur et renovatur. . . .," *De Trinitate,* 14.16, PL 42.1053.

[7] See *De Trinitate*, 14-19, PL 42.1053-1056.

The Cistercian fathers, William of Saint Thierry and Saint Bernard of Clairvaux, each produced treatises indebted to Augustine's doctrine.[8] In their teaching on the soul's imaging of God, these authors traced the harmful effects of sin on the soul's faculties: the intellect, will, and memory. Then they detailed the need for the soul's restoration due to original sin and its future glory when reformed, in terms of a process of reformation. While much work has been done on the reformation of the triune soul in the thought of Bernard of Clairvaux and William of Saint Thierry's,[9] little systematic study has been devoted to the contribution on this question of Bernard's fellow Cistercian, Aelred of Rievaulx, whose leadership greatly influenced Cistercian monasticism in Britain.[10]

Aelred also wrote a treatise on the soul, entitled simply, *De anima*.[11] Throughout his treatise he follows more closely than Bernard the traditional model of the soul found in Augustine's *De Trinitate*.[12] Aelred's teaching on the soul's restoration also focuses on the triple condition of the soul's existence: created, fallen, and glorified.[13] Still following Augustine, he explains that the distinctive human faculties of the soul are "memory, reason, and the will."[14]

8 Bernard of Clairvaux, *Sermo super Cantica canticorum* 11, 5, in *Sancti Bernardi Opera,* Jean Leclerq et al., 8 vols. in 9 (Roma, 1957-1977) [hereafter SBOp], 1.57; William of St. Thierry's *Aenigma Fidei,* PL 180.429.

9 For a recent analysis of Bernard of Clairvaux on this issue and a fine bibliography, see John R. Sommerfeldt, *The Spiritual Teachings of Bernard of Clairvaux* (Cistercian Studies series [herafter CS] 125; Kalamazoo, 1991); for William of Saint Thierry, see David N. Bell, *The Image and Likeness: The Augustinian Spirituality of William of Saint Thierry* (CS 78; Kalamazoo, 1984).

10 While not exhaustive, the following studies are foundational for Aelred's thought: Ailred Squire, *Aelred of Rievaulx: A Study* (London, 1969); and Amédée Hallier, *The Monastic Theology of Aelred of Rievaulx: An Experiential Theology*, trans. Columban Heaney (CS 2; Kalamazoo, 1969).

11 *De Anima,* (Corpus Christianorum Continuatio Mediaevalis 1 [hereafter CCCM]; Turnholti, 1989) 1.685-754; an English translation can be found in CF 22 Kalamazoo, 1981.

12 See *De Trinitate* 10.11, PL 42.983. See too, Ladner, *Idea,* pp. 153-283; see also Elizabeth Connor, "Saint Bernard's Three Steps of Truth and Saint Aelred of Rievaulx's Three Loves," in *Bernardus Magister: Papers Presented at the Nonacentenary of the Birth of Saint Bernard of Clairvaux, Kalamazoo, Michigan, Sponsored by the Institute of Cistercian Studies, Western Michigan University, 10-13 May 1990* (CS 135; Kalamazoo, 1992), pp. 355-362.

13 "Et potestis notare triplicem statum humanae carnis: secundum creationem, secundum damnationem, secundum glorificationem," *Sermo ad abbates,* 31.5, CCCM 2a.251. See also, Charles H. Talbot, "Introduction," to Aelred's *Dialogue on the Soul*, CF 22.17-27; and Hallier, *Monastic Theology,* pp. 5-9.

14 "Igitur haec tria, memoria, ratio, uoluntas, aut ipsa anima sunt, aut certe in anima," *De anima* 1.32; CCCM 1.694; CF 22.50. The tripartite model of the soul is found througout the *De anima* as well as in *Speculum caritatis* 1.3.9; CCCM 1.116; CF 17.92: "Tria haec memoriam dico, scientiam, amorem siue uoluntatem." See also *Sermo in die pentecosten*, in *Sermones inediti B. Aelredi Abbatis Rievallensis*, ed. Charles H. Talbot (Rome, 1952) [hereafter SI], p. 107; and *Sermo beate Virginis*, SI,

This description of a triune soul, Aelred teaches, establishes the means by which the human creature achieves its happiness. In the primordial state, the human soul shared in the image of God:

> Indeed, in this image, which we have distinguished for our part, God impressed his likeness, a celestial vision in the memory, a divine understanding in the intellect, and true love in the will. Hence man untiringly embraced God through his memory, understood without error through his reason, and tasted through true love without self-seeking desire for anything else.[15]

The fulfillment of human happiness is God. Before the effects of sin, the soul existed in a state of happiness with each of its faculties fulfilled by adhering to God. Man's happiness or despair depends on his use of the soul's faculties: "Through reason the soul searches out or finds or considers God; through the will it chooses or neglects him, loves or despises him; through the memory it recalls, holds, and embraces Him."[16] However, it is through the intellect that the reformation process might begin. Therefore, according to Aelred, restoration of the intellect is central to process of the soul's reformation.

The human intellectual faculty has a leadership role in the triune soul in that its function is to acquire knowledge. Indeed, this ability to acquire knowledge distinguishes the human creature from other creatures.[17] In Aelred's thought it is also the human intellect which discerns right from wrong.[18] Aelred maintains that the intellect is responsible for distinguishing "between truth and falsehood, justice and injustice, and, since the intellect has the capacity for wisdom, it is through reason that knowledge of God is attained."[19] Thus, central to the importance of reason is its ability to apprehend knowledge. Aelred knows

p. 137. For Augustine's tripartite image in humans, see *De Trinitate* 10.17, PL 42.983. For Bernard's use of this model, see *De gratia et libero arbitrio* 7.21-22; SBOp 3.182, CF 19.79.

15 "Huic namque imagini, quam pro modulo nostro distinximus, suam similitudinem impressit deus, memorie celestem visionem, rationi divinam cognitionem, voluntati caritatem. Ita, homo deum suum per memoriam amplectabatur sine fatigatione, per rationem cognoscebat sine errore, per caritatem gustabat sine alterius rei cupiditate," *Sermo de emissione Filii et Spiritus Sancti,* SI, p. 108.

16 ". . . Anima proinde deum ratione vel investigat vel invenit vel considerat, voluntate eligit vel negligit, diligit vel contempnit, memoria recordatur, tenet, amplectitur," *Sermo beate Virginis,* SI, pp. 137-138.

17 "Est autem tanta uis rationis, ut per eam a caeteris animalibus discernamur," *De Anima* 2.14; CCCM 1.711; CF 22.78.

18 "Dicitur et secundum iudicium, quo et reprobanda reprobat, et approbat approbanda," *De Anima* 2.22; CCCM 1.714; CF 22.83.

19 "Ratione distinguimus inter uerum et falsum, inter iustum et iniustum, quae cum capax sit sapientiae, per ipsam ad Dei notitiam peruenitur," *De Anima* 2.18; CCCM 1.713; CF 22.80.

that no "approach to it [truth] is possible without [the aid of] the intellect."[20] Created in God's image, humans experienced a perfect harmony among the powers of the soul, each enjoying clarity of function and fulfillment of its respective end. The condition of the human creature, while in its primordial and happy condition, was afforded special qualities and dignity, "He was able to choose the good without false interpretation, to desire the good without false pleasure, to make use of the good without violence and contradiction."[21] Moreover, as originally created, the soul was free from distractions from the body so that "not even the desires of the flesh contravened the spirit."[22]

Aelred knows that there exists a deformity in the present condition of humanity and identifies the sin of humankind's first parents as its source. Aelred teaches that free choice had permitted humanity to "delight forever in the memory and knowledge of God and could have existed in perpetual happiness."[23] However, the choice of our first parents to "divert their love to something less"[24] changed all this. Humanity's fall brought with it an ignorance, which Aelred assigns to the action of pride as loving self rather than loving God.[25] Indeed, according to Aelred, the central cause for that disordered choice is particular to the sin of pride, which begins in a defective intellect:

> I will be, he [Adam] says, like a god! O intolerable pride! Shortly after being formed of earth and clay, do you insolently strive to become a god? . . . Thus, pride paves the way for disobedience. These two sins, pride and disobedience, are the wretched condition and cause of all our sins.[26]

Pride, for Aelred, is the root of all sin; its effects are destructive for the soul and provide a host of other disorders: "There remains the ultimate war against pride, which is divided into five vices, which are like five kings. We see

[20] " . . . Sed ad eam sine ratione nullus esse potest accessus," *De Anima* 2.18; CCCM 1.712; CF 22.79.

[21] "Bonum potuit eligere sine mali interpellatione, bonum appetere sine mali delectatione, bono uti sine molestia et contradictione," *Sermo in adventu Domini,* SI, p. 38.

[22] "Non enim caro concupiscebat adversus spiritum [Gal 5:17]," *Sermo in adventu Domini,* SI, p. 38.

[23] ". . . Parens noster libero muneratus arbitrio poterat . . . ipsum Deum perpetuo amando in eius memoria notitiaque perpetuo delectari perpetuoque beatus existere," *Speculum caritas* 1.4.11, CCCM 1.17; CF 17.92.

[24] "Potuit et ipsum amorem suum ad aliquid minus reflectere. . . ," *Speculum caritas* 1.4.11, CCCM 1.17; CF 17.92.

[25] *Speculum caritas* 1.4.12, CCCM 1.17-18; CF 17.93.

[26] "Ero, inquis, sicut deus [Gn 3.5]. O intolerabilis superbia. Paulo ante de limo formatus et luto, dei similitudinem insolenter affectas? . . . Ita superbia perperit inobedientiam. Hec duo peccata, superbia et inobedientia, omnium sunt peccatorum nostrorum miseria et causa," *Sermo in nativitate Domini,* SI, p. 38. See also *Speculum caritas* 1.4.11, CCCM 1.17; CF 17.92.

pride under the forms of vanity, ambition, boasting, contempt of God, and love of self."[27] He argues further that ". . . self-love occurs when we spurn the judgment of others and delight in our own supposed virtues and not in those of God."[28] When pride exists in the soul, all knowledge is oriented towards the self, and thus the will is blinded in its choices.

The results of the prideful fall have devastating effects to that original created, happy condition of the soul. Further, the sin of pride affects the original likeness of God in the soul by cloaking it in sin and the soul is unable to retain its blessed and dignified condition. Because of the fall, Aelred writes, by the sin of pride "God's likeness is rightly garbed in the likeness of beasts."[29] Aelred teaches that the splendor, dignity, and beauty bestowed on our first parents, the likeness of God, vanished because humans clothed themselves with the concerns of the brute animals.[30] The soul thus lost its likeness to God and cast itself into a land of unlikeness, the *regio dissimilitudinis*.[31] Life in the land of unlikeness is the present condition of humanity; and the effects of this unlikeness, due to pride, continue the rift not only between God and man, but also "between angelic and human nature, between celestial and terrestrial creation."[32]

The result of the fall and the introduction of sin into the world had profound consequences for the human soul and for the intellect in particular. Aelred insists that the effect of the fall on the intellectual faculty is confusion in the function of the *ratio* itself. After the fall, sin affected human knowledge by "clouding it over with error"[33] and thus disorienting the intellectual faculty of the soul. The resultant deficiency in knowledge Aelred makes specific by an example given in a sermon *On the Annunciation*. There, Aelred identifies the intellect as an eye and the specific disorder inherited by the fall as a sort of

[27] "Restat ultimum bellum adversus superbiam, que in quinque vitiis, quasi in quinque regibus, dividitur. Ad superbiam quippe spectat vanitas, ambitio, iactantia, contemptus dei, amor sui," *Sermo in festo sancti Benedicti*, SI, p. 69.

[28] ". . . Amore sui, quando homo, spreto aliorum iudicio, in suis, ut putat, virtutibus non in domino delectatur," *Sermo in festo sancti Benedicti*, SI, p. 69. See also *Sermo de oneribus* 13, PL 195.410.

[29] "Dei usurpat similitudinem, merito iumentorum induit dissimilitudinem," *Speculum caritas* 1.4.11, CCCM 1.17; CF 17.93.

[30] "Homo in honore positus non intellexit, comparatus est iumentis insipientibus et similis factus est illis, et, amissa dei similitudine, similis factus est illis. . . ," *Sermo in die pentecosten*, SI, pp. 108-109.

[31] For further study of the term *regio dissimilitudinis*, see Hallier, *Monastic Theology*, pp. 12-16; A. E. Taylor, "*Regio dissimilitudinis*," *Archives d'histoire doctrinale et litteraire du moyen age* 9 (1934): 305-306; and Etienne Gilson, "*Regio dissimilitudinis* de Platon à Saint Bernard de Clairvaux," *Mediaeval Studies* 9 (1947): 108-130.

[32] ". . . Inter angelicam et humanam naturam, inter caelestem et terrestrem creaturam," *Sermo in nativitate Ioannis baptistae* 14.12, CCCM 2A.116-17.

[33] ". . . Scientiam quoque sed subditam errori. . . ," *Speculum caritatis* 1.4.12, CCCM 1.17; CF 17.92.

blindness in which condition humans cannot properly perceive God: "Without a doubt the human mind has been completely covered and thus blinded by darkness, so that the interior eye can in no way be directed toward the divine light."[34] To properly respond to God, the human person must have a properly functioning intellect to assess sense data so that it can offer the will the proper object to love. As a result of pride, the intellect, because of its defective analysis of the world and itself, is often incapable of recognizing the good; consequently, it misinforms the will which in turn attaches itself to inferior goods. The proper object of the intellect, the truth, is obscured from its sight.

However, Aelred is optimistic in his teaching and posits a sense of hope in this land of unlikeness because, while the human likeness to God has been destroyed, the image of God remains.[35] With confidence Aelred reminds his listeners once again that this condition need not be permanent:

> From the corruption of our nature stems the urge to pride, from which we patiently suffer. From it comes the urge to inordinate pleasure, the urge to anger, the motivation for pride, the urge for ambition. But, if we do not consent, God will not impute this to us. . . .[36]

The *imago Dei* remains because humans retain the faculties of the soul, however disoriented in their fallen condition.[37] Aelred is confident that, following the fall, the reformation of mankind is indeed possible because human beings "did not cease to be and to live, and they were still able to return to their pristine form, reformed by Him who had formed them. But, this reformation is in wisdom; truly, the road along which we are brought back is education."[38] The curriculum for this education in wisdom is God Himself. Since the human person is guided by a disordered soul, beclouded in its intellect, "we know in what we must believe, in what we must hope, and what we must love."[39] True knowledge of oneself and God, the object of the intellect, begins humanity's re-education and consequent restoration. But Aelred is no Pelagian or Semipelagian. While humans were created for a share in divinity and are always eager to return

[34] "Sine dubio enim mens hominum ita erat in tenebris peccatorum obuoluta et excaecata, ut nequaquam posset interiorem oculum in illam diuinam lucem intendere," *sermo in annuntiatione Domini* 9.7, CCCM 2A.72.

[35] ". . . Etsi non imagine, diuina tamen similitudine. . . ," *Speculum caritas* 1.2.6, CCCM 1.15; CF 17.90.

[36] "Ex corruptione naturae nostrae sunt motus concupiscentiae quos inuiti patimur. Inde motus libidinis, motus irae, motus superbiae, motus ambitionis. Sed, si non consentimus, non imputat nobis Deus ista. . . ," *Sermo in die pasce* 12.10, CCCM 2A.100.

[37] *Sermo in die pentecosten*, SI, pp. 108-109.

[38] ". . . Nec tamen desiit esse et vivere: qui posset ad pristinam formam, eo qui formaverat reformante, redire. Ipsa autem forma, sapientia est; via vero, per quam ad ipsam formam redeatur, eruditio," *Sermo de oneribus* 2, PL 195.363.

[39] ". . .Ut sciamus quid credendum, quid sperandum, quid sit amandum. . . ," *Sermo de oneribus* 2, PL 195.363.

to this condition, "by themselves, they are quite incapable of this happiness."[40] The happiness which the rational creature desires cannot come about through human means; Aelred teaches that reformation and perfection are accomplished in them through God's grace.[41] The intellect, thus, requires teaching by Wisdom Himself, because the deformed creature can be reformed by none other than the Holy Spirit.[42] For the soul, therefore, to be restored and receive the wisdom necessary for its re-education, it needs to be reformed by an encounter with the Christ Himself. Aelred defines this encounter as an experience of Love itself.[43] Aelred maintains that an encounter with divine love has the power to re-educate in and of itself: "Divine love will raise us far up from the contemplation of inferior things in which the Creator is discovered in his creatures; it will elevate us to that height and purity, free from all veils, in which we shall behold and love with our whole heart and soul and strength."[44] The veils which Aelred describes are those sorts of self-centered, self-imposed vices resultant of pride. The benefits to the intellect of this upward gazing is the beginning of its re-education in humility.[45]

Humility, the proper evaluation of the human condition and the recognition of one's limitations, is central to the restoration of the intellect. Aelred teaches that the beginning of the restorative process begins in "reflection on our weakness, and extends to the dawn of our restoration. Just as pride is the beginning of all sin [Sir 10:15], all justice begins in humility. . . . Now the soul, which knows herself in humility, begins to know God in gratitude."[46] As a result of the intellect's growth in humility, it can properly evaluate the worth of things and provide this accurate information to the will. The soul can now begin to know God and love Him; assisted by grace it can seek out love. This pursuit is required by Christ's own commandment to love and Aelred stresses

[40] "Rationalis quippe creatura sicut beatitudinis capax condita est, ita ipsius beatitudinis auida semper est; sed ad beatitudinem nequaquam ipsa sibi sufficiens est," *Speculum caritas* 3.8.22; CCCM 1.115, CF 17.235.

[41] *Speculum caritas* 3.8.22, CCCM 1.115; CF 17.235-236.

[42] *Sermo in adventu Domini,* SI, p. 34.

[43] See *Sermo in adventu Domini*, SI, p. 34.

[44] ". . . Caritas divina sustulerit, quatinus ab illa inferiori contemplatione, qua creator in sua cernitur creatura, ad illud summum et purum, remoto omni velamine, transeat intuendum, et diligendum ex toto corde et tota anima et ex tota virtute," *Sermo in adventu Domini*, SI, p. 35.

[45] ". . . Quia sicut non pedum passu, sed mentis affectu a summo bono recedens, et in semetipsa ueterascens humana superbia, Dei in se corrupit imaginem, ita mentis affectu ad Deum accedens humana humilitas, renouatur in imaginem eius, qui creauit eum," *Speculum caritatis* 1.8.24, CCCM 1.22; CF 17.100.

[46] ". . . Id est ex consideratione nostrae infirmitatis, et tendit in mane nouae nostrae reparationis. Et sicut initium omnis peccati superbia, ita ab humilitate incipit omnis iustitia et est primus ad regnum caelorum ascensus," *Sermo in festivitate omnium sanctorum* 27.12, CCCM 2A.224-225.

that the new commandment "contains the divesting of the old man, the renewal of his mind, and the reforming of the divine image."[47] This divestment results in the reorientation of an intellect now freed from pride, a condition which must continually be addressed and assisted by grace (divine love). This grace initiates the transformation of the human person by restoring sight to the blinded intellect and enabling one to begin to see and to seek out God. However, the acquisition of humility does not occur by simply identifying the need for this virtue; growth in wisdom of God and consequent reformation of self-knowledge is assisted and accomplished by divine love along its path of re-education.

Aelred clarifies his doctrine on the properties and benefits of God's graces which come from true love by stating, "True love flows in from above; by its warmth it melts one's sloth; it lifts one to higher levels, . . . [so that one can] fly to that pure and sublime Goodness to which it owes its birth."[48] Once the soul recognizes that self-centeredness is less gratifying than being filled with true love, it can take on a new life in Christ.[49] The recovery of humility—a properly balanced view of the world and one's place in it—can now come about by rejecting those actions, thoughts, and objects that enslave the person to self-centeredness (*cupiditas*) and pride. Humans desire freedom from the slavery of that *cupiditas* which Aelred does not limit to disordered desires of the flesh. He teaches that the will must freely reject "the concupiscence the apostle calls 'of the flesh,' [see Gal 5:17] not because every evil concupiscence is of the flesh . . . but because this comes not from God but from man."[50] True love cannot be motivated by such self-centered impulses; through the assistance of wisdom and contact with divine love, humility restores a properly functioning intellect to the soul and assists in the reformation of the image and likeness of God. Thus, when the intellect can discern reality with humility, the will can be freed from self-centered desires; it is allowed to seek God as its happiness and take on a new life in true love.

Aelred's teaching on the most beneficial approach to reformation of the soul, not surprisingly, can be found in his teaching on the monastic life, a life

[47] "Ideo saluberrime nobis indicitur istius unius praecepti compendium, in quo et ueteris hominis exspoliatio, et mentis renouatio, et diuinae imaginis consistit reformatio," *Speculum caritatis* 1.8.24, CCCM 1.22; CF 17.100.

[48] ". . . Caritate desuper influente, ac innatum torporem suo suo calore dissoluente, ad altiora se surrigit, sic quie exuens uetustatem, ac induens nouitatem, sortitur pennas columbae deargentatas, quibus ad illud sublime et purum bonum euolet, de quo et genus ducit. . . ," *Speculum caritatis* 1.8.25, CCCM 1.23; CF 17.100-101.

[49] ". . . O anima mea . . . esto quasi vas perditum, quatenus a temetipsa deficiens, et tota in Deum transiens, nescias tibi uiuere, nec tibi mori; sed ei qui protemortuus est, et resurrexit," *Speculum caritatis* 1.16.48, CCCM 1.32; CF 17.114.

[50] ". . . Concupiscentiam scilicet quam carnis esse dicit Apostolus, non quod omnis concupiscentia mala ex carne sit . . . sed quod non ex Deo, sed ex homine sit. . . ," *Speculum caritatis* 1.10.28, CCCM 1.22; CF 17.102.

which he describes as a journey.[51] The *Rule* of Saint Benedict establishes a disciplined way of life that provides continual assistance in the reformation, and thus the perfection, of the whole human being. The purpose of the monastic life according to Aelred, the end towards which every activity and practice is focused, should be the restoration of each of the soul's faculties, its re-education in wisdom and a life of habitual virtue. Knowing the central role love plays in the restoration of the human soul, it is not surprising that Aelred preaches that life lived according to the *Rule* is a sure way to arrive at true love.[52] Aelred's words on the monastic practices elucidate clearly the importance of the monastic exercises in the reformation of the intellect. His abbatial teachings emphasize the importance of living out the Cistercian life of daily physical and spiritual exercises described in the *Rule* which are central to reformation of the intellect and the other faculties of the soul: "Our profession and *Rule* consist of both virtue and observance, and it is necessary for us to practice them both."[53] Although Aelred divides the monastic observances into two groups, physical and spiritual, he often lists them together, describing them allegorically as cities:

> Moses constituted six cities of refuge for the sons of Israel [see Nm 35:11-14; Dt 19:2-10; Jos 20:2-6]. . . . It has been seen that these six can symbolize the six kinds of exercises which have been instituted for us. Three of them are physical, they are labor, vigils, and fasts. . . . There are also three spiritual [exercises], *lectio*, prayer, and meditation.[54]

Each group of activities promotes and maintains the reforming virtues necessary for the soul. However, the effects of both physical and spiritual exercises are not limited to a specific virtue but nourish the entire monk on his journey back to God.

With regard to the first of these three spiritual exercises, Aelred encourages his monks to spend some of their day in the meditative reading of Scripture. The monastic tradition called this spiritual activity *lectio divina*, but *lectio* is not purely an intellectual activity. Medieval monks read Scripture

[51] Aelred develops the theme of the monastic journey in *Sermo VI in natali sancti Benedicti*, where he compares Benedict's leadership in the monastic journey to Moses' role in the Exodus from Egypt. See also CCCM 2A.51-60.

[52] See *Sermo in natali sancti Benedicti* 8.12-14, CCCM 2A.67-68.

[53] ". . . Professionem nostram et Regulam in utrisque, uirtutibus scilicet obseruantiisque constare, ac proinde utraque a nobis necessario seruanda non neget," *Speculum cariatis* 3.35.94, CCCM 1.150; CF 17.286.

[54] "Constituit ille Moyses sex ciuitates confugii filiis Israel. . . . Videntur mihi sex [civitates] istae significare posse sex illa generalia exercitia quae nobis instituta sunt. Tria corporalia , id est labores, uigiliae, ieiunia. . . . Tria autem sunt spiritualia, scilicet lectio, oratio, meditatio," *Sermo in natali sancti Benedicti* 8.13-15, CCCM 2A.67-68. See also *Speculum caritatis* 2.6.15, CCCM 1.72 and *Sermo in assumptione sanctae Mariae* 21.44, CCCM 2A.174.

slowly in a low voice, "feeling" every word.[55] Pronouncing the words - usually aloud -imprints those words both physically and mentally on the monk. This divine reading requires the use of the intellect not only to understand what is being read but also to reflect on all the possible meanings of the Word. Aelred insists that the monk will experience the Lord's grace, so necessary to the reform of the intellect, in the exercise of *lectio divina* and asks, "'But who will roll back the stone door to the sepulcher for us [Mk 16:3]?' That is, who will remove that which covers Scripture, so that we can find what we seek? His angel, His grace, is present."[56] Contact with Scripture is one of the most certain means by which the monk encounters Christ. These encounters bring with them a variety of effects. Aelred tells his monks that knowledge of how to pray or what to do can be discerned in the light of Scripture,[57] and reading and hearing Scripture in the oratory reveals hidden meanings to the monk.[58] Furthermore, the monk begins to sense and experience the effects of love in his meditative readings. The experience of love in meditative reading draws the monk to perform these exercises with increasing joy. To explain this awareness of Christ's love, Aelred offers an analogy in which assiduous meditation on Scripture is likened to the flight of a bee over a field of flowers. Here, the will is the bee searching for the sweet nectar which it desires:

> There, in the sayings and examples of the saints, the bee collects certain spiritual flowers, from which a wonderful enjoyment and a great pleasure of celestial sweetness comes into its heart and thus it experiences that the Spirit of the Lord is sweeter than honey.[59]

If time spent reading the Word meditatively is the vital catalyst which readies the soul, and specifically the intellect, for the Creator - not in some distant future, but in the present time - then all the spiritual practices ought to be performed properly, patiently, and, when possible, joyfully. By reading Scripture meditatively, the intellect is perfected by wisdom, which is freely given by God.[60] Therefore, the purpose of *lectio divina* is to open the human heart and to interact with the Word of God. It initiates the human intellect to the Wisdom of God, a fundamental requirement for the reformation of the intellect.

[55] Jean Leclercq, *Love of Learning and the Desire for God* (New York, 1962; reprint, New York, 1988), p. 78.

[56] "Sed quis reuoluet nobis lapidem ab ostio monumenti, id est tegumentum huius Scripturae, ut possimus inuenire quod quaerimus? Angelus eius, gratia est," *Sermo in die pasce* 11.28, CCCM 2A.95.

[57] See *Sermo in nativitate sanctae Mariae* 22.9, CCCM 2A.178.

[58] See *Sermo in adventu Domini* 2.4, CCCM 2A.18.

[59] "Ibi ex dictis et exemplis sanctorum quosdam spiritales flores colligit, ex quibus fit in corde eius mira delectatio et magna supernae suauitatis dulcedo, et ita experitur quia Spiritus Domini super mel dulcis sit," *Sermo in nativitate sanctae Mariae* 22.24, CCCM 2A.182.

[60] See *Sermo in purificatione sanctae Mariae* 34.18, CCCM 2A.283; see also *Sermo in natali sanctorum apostolorum Petri et Pauli* 16.4, CCCM 2A.132-33.

Aelred advises his monks that "we ought to ponder [Scripture] with a diligent mind"[61] and thus teaches his monks the exercise of *lectio divina*:

> Let us, I say, who profess the cross of Christ, by taking up the key of God's word, unbar the barrier of our breast. By penetrating as far as the division between soul and spirit, between joints and marrow, let us discern the thoughts and intentions of our heart.[62]

Thus, the perfection of the intellect through constant contact with the Word is one of the main goals of the spiritual exercises within the monastic curriculum.

Aelred describes another spiritual practice particularly useful to the restoration process: meditation. This private practice requires the monk to "discern the thoughts and intentions of our heart [Heb 4:12]. Without any self-flattery, let us scrutinize what lies deeply hidden in the inner recesses of our soul and work mightily to dig out the diseased roots themselves."[63] Self-reflection and consideration can be one of the most useful objects of one's meditation. Aelred describes the effects of meditation:

> The highest of the intellectual virtues is to meditate continually and rigorously, so that the mind may obtain by its efforts what it desires, or that it might understand what ought to be desired. Thus, those may be believed to have advanced not a little who have learned, by an understanding of virtue, how far they are from virtue.[64]

Moreover Aelred knows that there are a variety of effects beyond self-knowledge associated with the practice of meditation. Meditation can lead to a truthful evaluation of one's place in relation to one's neighbors and God; this is the foundation of humility, the requisite virtue for the *ratio*'s reformation. The fruits of contact with the Word can be seen in the advice Aelred gives his monks on how and when they should pray:

> And He [Jesus] came, through the Spirit, into the Temple [Lk 2:27]. And so you, surely if you would seek [Him], in your quiet,

61 ". . . Sollicita mente pensemus. . . ," *Sermo in ascensione Domini* 13.38, CCCM 2A.113.

62 ". . . Nos, inquam, professores crucis Christi, assumpta claue uerbi Dei, reseremus claustra pectoris nostri, et penetrantes usque ad diuisionem animae ac spiritus, compagum quoque ac medullarum, discernamus cogitationes et intentiones cordis. . . ," *Speculum caritatis* 2.1.3, CCCM 1.67; CF 17.164.

63 ". . . Discernamus cogitationes et intentiones cordis et sine adulatoria palpatione quid in ipsis animae recessibus secretius latitet peruidentes, ipsas potius morborum radices eruere conemur," *Speculum caritatis* 2.1.3, CCCM 1.67; CF 17.164.

64 "Vnde uirtuosae mentis est sublimia sempre et ardua meditari, ut uel adipiscatur optata, uel lucidius intellegat et cognoscat optanda; cum non parum credendus sit profecisse, qui uirtutis cognitione didicit quam longe sit a virtute," *De Spirituali amicitia* 1.26, CCCM 1.293; CF 5.56.

> little bed, even in the city, must sometimes read meditatively, at others times must pray, at other times must meditate. . . .[65]

Aelred knows that prayer, *lectio divina*, and meditation are not separate and distinct activities. He acknowledges this by his frequent grouping of the three exercises, "reading, meditation, and prayer."[66] Chrysogonus Waddell reminds us that the early Cistercians had a dynamic understanding of the integral relationship of these three spiritual activities:

> Reading, meditation, prayer and contemplation interpenetrated with the others so powerfully in actual practice that it was more a matter of varying degrees of intensity of contact with the Word than a matter of four distinct though related spiritual activities.[67]

Prayer might lead the monk to meditation or in his meditative readings he might be moved to either prayer or meditation. The constant contact and presence with the Word imprints it on the heart, making it a part of the soul, thus acting as a motivation as well as an object for the monk. These effects foster the monk's continual reformation. The practice thus becomes an encounter with Christ and a personal experience of love. In an encounter with Christ through His Word, reflection leads to humility and may restore the intellect in love. Through all these encounters with Scripture in prayer, reading, and meditation, the intellect is recreated and love is consequently perfected.

The monastic life, properly lived, also employs physical exercises which assist in the reformation of the whole person and aid in the reformation of the intellect as well. Aelred often lists three physical exercises and their effects alongside the spiritual exercises: "Just as through labors, vigils, and fasts, the flesh is corrected, so too through reading, meditation, and prayer is the soul recreated."[68] Yet, the effects of labor, vigils, and fasting do not affect only the flesh; they have an impact also on the spirit, "Because without a doubt he who undertakes to enter this heavenly temple, . . . to ascend the mountain of God, to stand in his holy place, is required to fast and labor, . . . and thus he is able to be purified from iniquities of the spirit and the flesh."[69] The physical activities in the monastery therefore have a dual role: they assist in purifying both body and

[65] "Et venit in spiritu in templum. Et tu, igituer, si utique quesieris, videlicet in lectulo quietis tue, nuc legendo, nunc orando, nunc meditando. . . ," *Sermo in ypapanti Domini de diversis moribus*, SI, p. 51.

[66] See *Speculum caritatis* 2.6.15, CCCM 1.72; and *Sermo in purificatione sanctae Mariae* 32.27, CCCM 2A.273.

[67] Chrysogonus Waddell, "The Place and Meaning of the Work of God," *Cistercian Studies Quarterly* 23 (1988): 31.

[68] "Sicut enim per labores et uigilias et ieiunia caro castigatur, ita per lectionem, meditationem, orationem, animus recreatur," *Sermo in purificatione sanctae Mariae* 32.27, CCCM 2A.273.

[69] "Quia sine dubio qui cupit ingredi in illud caeleste templum . . . et ascendere ad montem Domini et stare in loco sancto eius, necesse habet ieiunare et laborare ferre temptationes et aerumnas huius uitae, ut sic possit purgari ab omni inquinamento carnis et spiritus. . . ," *Sermo in purificatione sanctae Mariae* 5.21, CCCM 2A.50.

soul. The path of *caritas* consists in "labor and toil, in vigils and fasts."[70] Aelred's attitude and insistence on labor is characteristically Cistercian. Part of the Cistercian's insistence on self-support and simplicity required them to do manual labor.[71] There is also a spiritual benefit in the economic realities which required the Cistercian monk to labor. Through the laborious practices which help reassert the monk's will over his bodily desires, "we put to death our members through abstinence, vigils, and labor."[72] The reordering of the body's desires requires that the monk "restrain the mind from wantonness by engaging in physical activities."[73] However, the intellect plays a part in initiating the physical exercises, as well; Aelred clearly suggests that the initiative for the restorative practices of labor is first taken by the *ratio*. The monk, growing in humility:

> . . . is to turn his attention to those passions by which he is attacked. Then he should examine which of these wearies him the most. Finally he should search diligently, with keen attention, for those tools which oppose these passions more effectively.[74]

After careful meditation, in which the monk identifies a particularly troublesome passion, he should then apply the appropriate tool or monastic practice. For example, Aelred suggests that "limiting the stomach easily curbs the passion of lust. The fatigue of vigils fortifies the wandering and unstable heart. Silence tempers anger, and the care expended on labor checks boredom."[75] Hard work also results in fatigue which limits the concerns of the mind. This labor, in turn, frees the soul from the superfluous demands of the body.

Fasting and abstinence also assist in the restoration of humility and the reordering of the body's demands on the will. The monastic diet denies meat except to those who are ill. In addition, there are periodic fasts according to the church calendar. The Cistercians returned to a more strict adherence of the *Rule*'s

70 ". . . Via caritatis per quam oportet nos incedere: in labore at aerumna, in uigiliis et ieiuniis," *Sermo in natali sanctorum apostolorum Petri et Pauli* 15.40, CCCM 2A.130-131.

71 See Charles Dumont, "Saint Aelred: The Balanced Life of the Monk," *Monastic Studies* 1 (1963): 25-38.

72 ". . . Mortificemus membra nostra in abstinentia, in uigiliis, in laboribus. . . ," *Sermo in natali sancti Benedicti* 37.10, CCCM 2A.302.

73 ". . . Mentis refrenare lasciviam. . . ," *Sermo beate Virginis*, SI, p. 143.

74 ". . . Ut passiones quibus impugnatur attendat, deinde quae sint quibus maxime fatigatur inspiciat; postremo quae instrumenta, quibus passionibus magis obuient sagaci circumspectione perquirat," *Speculum Caritatis* 3.33.79, CCCM 1.144; CF 17.276.

75 "Denique passionem libidinis facile comprimit uentris restrictio, uagum cor et instabile uigiliarum confirmat afflictio, iram silentium mitigat, taedium mentis operis sollicitudo castigat," *Speculum caritatis* 3.33.70, CCCM 1.144; CF 17.276-277.

requirements on diet,[76] and Aelred's community at Rievaulx followed these requirements carefully. Aelred knows fasting to be beneficial to the monk's spiritual growth and he teaches that fasting fosters prayer, devotion, and chastity, three necessary conditions for the restoration and perfection of the monk: "Fasting is an impenetrable shield against all trials, . . . an unfailing support for our prayers. . . . So fasting ought always be the guardian of our devotion; without it our chastity could not be maintained."[77] Like labor, fasting helps the monk free himself "from total concern for the body."[78] Aelred also suggests fasting for tempering the sin of envy, which is a condition of self-centeredness.[79]

Vigils similarly restore discipline and control over the flesh by crushing self-centeredness and restoring humility to the intellect. Monastic vigils or watches begin the monks' day; they are observed in the early hours of the morning, several hours before sunrise. At vigils, the monk listens to lessons drawn from Scripture and the works of the fathers, sings responsories or verses relating to the subject of the lessons, and prays the psalms. Aelred knows vigils are a form of bodily control.[80] He also maintains that the discipline required for rising in the early hours helps redirect the deformed soul: "The fatigue of vigils strengthens the wandering and unstable heart."[81] In this way, vigils help lessen the temptation to sloth. However, simply participating in the office and practices of vigils is not sufficient; the monk must attend these actions with due attention. Indeed, all the monk's external works must be performed with the proper interior intention to be reckoned good. Aelred advises his monks, in each and every exercise, ". . . to flee temptation, [and thus] in whatever exercise to have in himself a greater grace."[82] The activities of labor, vigils, and fasting here identified as penitential acts assist the monk to relinquish his proud and self-centered motivations. These activities of purgation also have a positive effect in assisting the monk's progress in the spiritual life, leading to greater virtue: "Those who are in any way wise, who are converted to the Lord, will walk from virtue to virtue, from self-knowledge to penitence, from penitence to humility,

[76] See Louis Lekai, *The Cistercians: Ideals and Reality* (Kent, Ohio, 1977), p. 26.

[77] "Est ergo ieiunium contra omnia tentamenta impenetrabile scutum, . . . orationibus nostris. . . . Licet autem religionis comes semper debeat esse ieiunium, sine quo castitas tuta esse non potest. . . ," *De institutione inclusarum* 1.11, CCCM 1.646-47; CF 2.57-58.

[78] ". . . Sunt liberos . . . a cura corporis absolute," *Sermo de tribus generibus et diversis causis ieiuniorum,* SI, p. 61.

[79] *Sermo de tribus generibus et diversis causis ieiuniorum*, SI, p. 60.

[80] "Carnis insolentia crebris uigiliis ac ieiuniis castiganda. . . ," *Speculum caritatis* 2.19.59, CCCM 1.204; CF 17.204.

[81] ". . . Uagum cor et instabile uigiliarum confirmat afflictio. . . ," *Speculum caritatis* 3.33.79, CCCM 1.144; CF 17.276.

[82] ". . . In temptatione confugere, in quo inuenerit se maiorem gratiam habere," *Sermo in natali sancti Benedicti* 8.17, CCCM 2A.69.

from humility to chastity."[83] The physical practices of monasticism can purge a sinful soul and assist a monk in growing in those virtues which protect the spiritual castle.

As a foundation for his monastic teaching, Aelred views the monastic life as a holistic method of reform which aids the healing of body and soul and transforms the intellect by properly ordering it toward God and others. Manual labor, vigils, and fasts each contribute necessary assistance to prioritize a monk's physical appetites and desires; this reappraisal and control lead to a truer understanding of oneself, the essence of humility. The spiritual exercises give the progressing soul the opportunity to express its desire for love itself, filling it with true knowledge, the object for which it was created. He insists that, through God's loving gift of grace, the monk will sense a movement in his soul, a sense of love itself being poured into his soul, which will give him the strength and courage to continue in his quest to live the life of love. Aelred insists that the more frequent the encounter with Christ, whether in the *opus Dei, lectio,* or meditation, the more the intellect is reformed in the likeness of God.

While Aelred's ideas on the benefits of the monastic life reflect a traditional understanding of the reformation process, his articulation of the monastic life does seem to be reflective of something new, something particular to the twelfth century. Aelred reflects his generation's theology of love. Furthermore, Aelred formed his monks according to his understanding of a loving God and reformation as a gift from a God who is "ever gentle, tender, loving and compassionate."[84] God's love is "the reason why He created what was to be created, guides what needs guidance, aids what needs assistance, moves what needs moving, advances what needs advancement, and perfects what needs perfecting."[85] Aelred's view of the world ultimately was formed by his understanding of this love. Therefore, the reformation of the human person, according to Aelred, comes about through love. As Aelred defines it, love is Christ Himself. Love is also a gift of the Holy Spirit which perfects the human soul in a variety of ways, in particular through the intellect. Due to this understanding of reformation, and particularly the Cistercian interpretation of the monastic process, Aelred communicated the life of love in England as successfully as his brethren did on the Continent.

83 ". . . Id est sapiens quisque, conversus ad Dominum, ambulat de virtute in virtutem, de sui cognitione ad poenitentiam, de poenitentia ad humilitatem, de humilitate ad castitatem," *Sermo de oneribus* 26, PL 195.469.

84 ". . . Dulcissimo, suauissimo, piissimo, compatientissimo. . . ," *Speculum caritatis* 2.5.10, CCCM 1.71; CF 17.170.

85 "Ipsa sola causa cur creauit creanda, regit regenda, administrat administranda, mouet mouenda, promouet promouenda, perfeicit perficienda," *Speculum caritatis* 1.19.56, CCCM 1.35; CF 17.119.

FRANCISCAN POVERTY AS A BASIS FOR THE REFORM OF THE CHURCH IN UBERTINO DA CASALE'S *ARBOR VITAE CRUCIFIXAE JESU*[1]

Gregory S. Beirich

Gerhart Ladner's seminal work *The Idea of Reform* has produced a host of studies devoted to exploring the nature and place of reform ideology in the history of the West. One area in desperate need of further examination involves the notion of reform which existed in the medieval Franciscan order. To date, only one study has addressed the role of reform ideology in the order, and that was limited to the first few decades of the order's existence.[2] Thus there is room for a further analysis of the reform dimensions found within the order. In particular, an elucidation of the reform ideas of the Franciscan Spiritual Ubertino da Casale (1259-c.1340) helps to illuminate how some in the order of the early fourteenth century viewed the possibility of reform. His position as a Spiritual Franciscan leader in the controversy over the poverty of the order provides a special opportunity to investigate his theory of reform because he ultimately links the possibility of reform to the proper practice of Franciscan poverty which he so ardently defended. He presents his ideas on reform in his most detailed work, the *Arbor vitae crucifixae Jesu* (1305).[3] While he does not advance here a specific program of reform for the church of his day, he does conclude that in the end times the church will in fact be reformed. This reform will be occasioned by the Spiritual Franciscans, whom Ubertino identifies with the elect discussed in Revelation. The basis for the reform of the church will be the practice of the poverty of Francis, itself modeled on the poverty of Christ and his apostles. He holds that this practice has been diluted and therefore destroyed in the years preceding the composition of the *Arbor*, a situation compounded by the approach of the apocalypse. Ubertino believes that a return to the true and faithful practice of Franciscan poverty as exemplified by Francis and his companions, and continued by the Spirituals, will result in both the final triumph of good over evil and a reformed church in the final age of history.

In venturing down the road which leads to the reform of Franciscan practice and, therefore, to the reform of the church, Ubertino must examine the roots of the order itself. For him, the starting point of the Franciscan order is

1 This article was first presented at the 32nd International Congress on Medieval Studies at Kalamazoo, Michigan, in May, 1997. I would like to thank Louis B. Pascoe, S. J. for introducing me to the world of medieval reform ideology and for his support in the completion of my dissertation concerning the reform elements of Ubertino's *Arbor*.

2 John Michael Phelps, "A Study of Renewal Ideas in the Writings of the Early Franciscans, 1210-1256," Ph.D. diss., University of California at Los Angeles, 1972.

3 The single best biography of Ubertino is found in Frédégand Callaey, *L'idéalisme franciscain spirituel au XIVe siècle: Étude sur Ubertin de Casale* (Louvain, 1914). A discussion of Ubertino's apocalyptic thought may be found in Gian Luca Potestà, *Storia ad escatologia in Ubertin da Casale* (Milano, 1980). The edition of *Arbor* used here is Ubertino da Casale, *Arbor vitae crucifixae Jesu*, ed. Charles T. Davis (Torino, 1961). This is the only complete printed edition of the *Arbor*.

found not in Francis and his *Rule,* but in the coming of Christ. He wants it understood that there would have been no Franciscan *Rule* or order without the example and practice of Christ and his first disciples as demonstrated in what he calls the evangelical life. Ubertino thinks that the primary component of the evangelical life, to be imitated by all who practice it, is poverty. More than anything else, it is the poverty of Christ and the apostles which provides the link between the evangelical life of Christ and that of the Franciscan *Rule.* It is therefore imperative for Ubertino to furnish a more detailed analysis of Christ's poverty.

Ubertino begins his exploration of Christ's poverty by addressing the foundation of Christ's life and the place of poverty in that foundation.[4] He says that Is 61:1 predicted that Christ would preach and observe poverty when it said "the spirit of the Lord is upon me, he anointed me, and he sent me."[5] He continues that the perfection of Christ arose from the poor of Israel who exulted, as Is 29:19 says.[6] Furthermore, Ubertino says that Christ made a conscious effort to emphasize his poverty, as Paul notes in 2 Cor 8:19 when he says that even though he was rich, Christ became poor "for us."[7] As a result, Ubertino argues that Christ wanted the poverty of his own person to be the foundation of the Christian religion.[8]

A major component of Christ's foundation was his renunciation of property, designed to combat evil. Ubertino notes that the evil of covetousness is in opposition to Christ's ideal of poverty since 1 Tm 6:10 says that it is the root of all evil, leading some astray from their faith.[9] The antidote to covetousness is the "highest perfection of poverty," which was instituted by Christ so that he might combat the works of the devil, as 1 Jn 3:8 says.[10] It is

[4] Much of Ubertino's defense of Franciscan poverty is drawn from Bonaventure's *Apologia pauperum.* For a discussion of the *Apologia pauperum* in the *Arbor,* see Potestà, *Storia ed escatologia,* pp. 193-206.

[5] Ubertino da Casale, *Arbor,* III, 3, 184b: "Circa primum scias quod christum paupertatem predicaturum et observaturum singulariter predixere prophite: Isaias lxi [: 1]: *super me: quod unxerit me: misit me*." All subsequent references to the *Arbor* will be cited according to book, chapter, page, and column numbers.

[6] *Arbor,* III, 3, 184b: "Et quod perfectio christi singulariter ad pauperes deberet transfundi quod Isaias xxix[:19] dicit: *Pauperes homines in sancto israel exultabunt.*"

[7] *Arbor,* III, 3, 184b: "Propter quod et apostolus dicit ii Cor. viii[:9]: *Sicut gratiam domini nostri iesu chrsti: quam cum dives esset propter nos egenus factus est.*"

[8] *Arbor,* III, 3, 184b: "Christus ergo fundamentum religionis christiane pauper in se esse voluit."

[9] *Arbor,* III, 3, 184b: "Cupiditas autem omnium malorum est radix: quam quidam appetentes erraverunt a fide: [1] Thy. vi[:10]."

[10] *Arbor,* III, 3, 184b: "Et ideo benedictus iesus qui in hoc apparuit *ut dissolvat opera diaboli* [1 Jn 3:8] oppositum cupiditatis paupertatem altissimam perfectionis instituit fundamentum."

through this spirit of poverty that "we" are configured to Christ; it is the root and foundation of evangelical perfection according to its analogy and connection to faith and charity, making for an almost identical relationship between those who practice evangelical poverty and Christ.[11] Furthermore, Christ himself related highest poverty to evangelical perfection when he said in Mt 19:21, "If you want to be perfect, go and sell all that you have and give to the poor, and you will have treasure in heaven; then come follow me." The fulfillment of this call results in evangelical perfection since, as Jerome said, "It is an act of apostolic perfection and of perfect virtue to sell all one has and give to the poor."[12]

While the ideal of evangelical perfection may be to relinquish one's property, the reality is that one still needs the necessities of life in order to survive. To address this situation, Ubertino turns to the two dimensions of temporal goods so critical to all Franciscan practice: their ownership and their use. He says that evangelical poverty consists in renouncing the ownership and property of earthly things. He further says that use may be retained, but that it should be limited, as 1 Tm 6:8 says: "Having food and sufficient clothing, with these let us be content."[13] Ownership itself has a twofold dimension: it may be either private or common, with the first type relating to a person and the second to a group. One may renounce the former while retaining the latter, as well as renounce both together.[14] As a result, there are two types of the profession of poverty. In the first, a person renounces all private and personal dominion over temporal goods and is sustained by things shared by a community. In the second, a person renounces all dominion and all rights over temporal goods, both on a personal and a communal level, and is sustained by things that belong to someone else, meaning that sustenance is piously provided by an outsider.[15]

[11] *Arbor*, III, 3, 184b: "Propter quod perfectionis evangelice per quam christo configuramur ipsa paupertas spiritus secundum quandam analogiam et coherentiam ad fidem et caritatem radix est fundamentum."

[12] *Arbor*, III, 3, 184b: "Dicens *Si vis perfectus esse. Vade et vende omnia que habens et da pauperibus: et habebis thesaurum in celo et veni sequere me*. Mat. xix [:21]. Quem locum tractans: hieronymus in epistola ad demetriadem ait. 'Apostolici fastigii est perfectemque virtutis omnia vendere.'" Cf. Jerome, *Epistolae*, 130 (alias 8):14.

[13] *Arbor*, III, 3, 184b-185a: "Cum autem circa temporalium possessionem duo contigat considerare dominium scilicet et usum: sit quam usus annexus necessario vite presenti usus dico facti non viris: evangelice perfectionis est possessiones terrenas quantum ad dominum proprietatem et ius utendi relinquere usum vero non omnio relinquere seu reiicere sed artare tantum. . .Iuxta illud Apostoli [1] Thy. vi[:8]: *habentes alimenta et quibus tegamur his contenti simus*."

[14] *Arbor*, III, 3, 185a: "Hoc autem dupliciter contingit. Cum enim sit duplex rerum dominium: privatum scilicet et commune: unum quidem spectans ad determinatam personam: alterum vero ad determinatum collegium. Et cum primum abdicari possit secundo remoto: possit etiam abdicari secundum cum primo."

[15] *Arbor*, III, 3, 185a: "Duplex est secundum hic professio paupertatis: una quidem qua quis omnium temporalium abdicato privato dominio sustentatur de non suo

The first is exemplified by the traditional form of the cenobitic life, while the second is reflected in the apostolic life.[16] This apostolic life, personified in Christ and passed on to the apostles, is one of "extreme and penurious poverty."[17] Those who are truly poor have no money or food; they wear simple clothes, and they walk without shoes.[18]

Once Ubertino has discussed the nature of Christ's poverty, he turns to the question of what form of poverty the apostles practiced. In the first place, Ubertino notes that Christ assumed extreme poverty as an example so as to display and demonstrate the perfection of this particular virtue.[19] His followers, the apostles, were to maintain, under this precept, the form of extreme poverty practiced by Christ, as Mt 10:9, Mk 6:8-9, and Lk 9:3 make clear.[20] Ubertino then enlists a variety of authorities to support the notion that the apostles imitated the poverty of Christ. For instance, he cites John Chrysostom, who says of Mt 10:9 that "He [Christ] was to send teachers throughout the world; for this reason, he changed them, so to speak, from men into angels, relieving them of all solicitude for this life."[21] Other authorities used by Ubertino include Rabanus Maurus, Bede, Ambrose, Augustine, Bernard, and Jerome. All of these sources, and Ubertino as well, conclude that voluntary and strict poverty--which consists in living without possessions, either personally or communally, but in the greatest need--was imposed on the apostles and practiced by them.[22]

id est non sibi proprio: nec suo collegio: tamen iure cum alliis [sic] de collegio suo possessio. Alia vero est qua quis omnium rerum abdicato dominio: et omni iure tam proprio quam communi sustentatur de non suo id est nec sibi proprio nec [sic] suo collegio in communi: sed alieno: pie tamen sibi ab alio pro sustentatione collato."

[16] *Arbor*, III, 3, 185a: "Hinc etiam fuit tradita forma ecclesiastice seu cenobice vite. . . . Secundum autem paupertatis exemplum processit in vita apostolorum."

[17] *Arbor*, III, 3, 185a: "In his igitur verbis [Mt 10:9ff] dominus apostolis et predicatoribus veritatis: extreme ac penuriose paupertatis formam observandam imponit quantum ad carentiam non solum possessionum: sed etiam pecuniarum et aliorum mobilium."

[18] *Arbor*, III, 3, 185a: "Ut tanquam veri pauperes in summa rerum constituti penuria: carerent pecuniis: alimenta non ferrent: simplici vestitu contenti essent et sine calciamentis incederent."

[19] *Arbor*, III, 3, 186a: "Quia vero magister paupertatis iesus hanc pro nobis sic penuriosam paupertatem assumpsit ut perfectionem huius virtutis in se ostenderet et nobis exemplo monstraret."

[20] *Arbor*, III, 3, 186a: "Ideo sanctis apostolis tanquam sue sanctitatis imitatoribus perfectis hanc extreme paupertatis formam servari precepit: sicut in evangelio legitur Mat. [10:9] Mar. [6:8f] et luce [9:3]."

[21] *Arbor*, III, 3, 186a: "'Et in orbem terrarum doctores erat missurus [sic]: propter hic angelos eos ex hominibus ut ita dicam constituit ab omnibus absolvens eos vite sollicitudine.'" Cf. Chrysostom, *Homiliae*, 32 (alias 33): 4.

[22] *Arbor*, III, 3, 186b: "Ex his omnibus aperte colligitur scriptam paupertatis formam: qua nihil possidetur: nec in proprio: nec in communi: et in summa rerum penuria vivitur apostolis fuisse preceptam: et ab eisdem servatam."

After he has established the centrality of evangelical poverty to both the life of Christ and the lives of the apostles, Ubertino next connects Francis and his *Rule* to Christ's foundation. He starts by speaking of the decay of the practice of Christ's evangelical life after the Savior's death. The evangelical rule, founded by Christ and passed on to the apostles, had over time declined and disappeared. The church, therefore, came to be in need of reform, to be accomplished via Francis.[23] This renewal of the church had its roots in Francis' conforming himself to the likeness of Christ: he was the most perfect imitator of Christ, especially in terms of his humility and his renunciation of the world.[24] Francis consciously tried to conform himself to the image of Christ as he understood it.[25] As far as Ubertino is concerned, Francis was similar to Christ because of the excellence of his way of life, and his likeness to Christ allowed for the renewal of the evangelical life in the church.[26]

Crucial to Ubertino's thesis of Francis' likeness to Christ is the degree to which Francis imitated Christ's poverty. In the first place, Francis embraced a practice of poverty modeled on that of Christ and observed with all his effort.[27] Francis became the most perfect advocate of highest poverty, a poverty which can truly be called evangelical.[28] Implicit in Francis' practice is his role in the renewal of evangelical poverty: just as the Magi came to Christ in the manger on the thirteenth day after his birth, so too did a renewal of the evangelical life of poverty occur in the thirteenth century in the person of Francis.[29] Francis not only follows Christ in the practice of his poverty, he renews it through his own practice.

Francis' embrace of the evangelical life would have had very little significance if he had been the only one who practiced it. But this situation

[23] *Arbor*, V, 5, 443b: "Hec [the evangelical rule] in ecclesia non fuit per apostolos transfusa ut dictum est supra: nec eam habebat ecclesia quando ipsam benedictus iesus in Franciscum renovare incepit."

[24] *Arbor*, V, 3, 423b: "In humilitate vero profunda et extirpatione totius mundane glorie sic perfectissime imitatus est christum."

[25] *Arbor*, V, 3, 430a: "Quoniam vero amicus sponsi iesu Franciscus in fervore charitatis et desiderio fraterne salutis ipsi iesu se studuerit conformare."

[26] *Arbor*, V, 3, 432b: "Sic ergo paret quoniam franciscus fuit similis benedicto iesu fastigio conversationis."

[27] *Arbor*, V, 3, 425b: "Franciscus emulator similitudinis iesu a sue conversationis primordio ad sanctam paupertatem querendam et omni studio secundum christi similitudinem observandam totum suum convertit conatum."

[28] *Arbor*, V, 3, 430a: "Perfectissimus zelator fuerit altissime paupertatis et illius que vere evangelica debet dici."

[29] *Arbor*, II, 7, 129b-130a: "Attende autem quod sicut decimotertio die facta fuit manifestatio iesu tribus magis in presepio. Sic in xiii centenario facta est multa manifestatio in ecclesia dei sapientie christiane multiplicatis multum divine sapientie radiis et religioni paupertatis maxime renovata evangelica vita in pauperum patriarcha francisco."

turned out not to be the case, particularly since Francis understood that his mission was to encourage the evangelical life in other devout souls. With this idea in mind, Ubertino describes the next step in the renewal of the evangelical life in the church: Francis' composition of a rule for his followers. The Franciscan *Rule* was to embody the proper practice of the apostolic and evangelical example. After several different incarnations, Francis recorded the final version of the *Rule* in the year 1223 while on retreat at Mt. Alverna.[30] Ubertino notes that it was here that Christ planted, founded, and confirmed the *Rule*.[31] He also establishes that the very structure of the *Rule* showed its apostolic character: it was divided into twelve chapters, reminiscent of the twelve apostles.[32] Even more important to Ubertino than the *Rule's* structure, however, was the role Christ played in producing it. He claims that while Francis was at Mt. Alverna, the spirit of the devil, who from the very beginning of the *Rule* sought to work against it, moved a group of brothers to seek out Elias, one of Francis' first adherents and a future Minister General of the order, and have him approach Francis concerning the *Rule's* contents. Elias related to Francis that the brothers of Italy knew he was writing a new *Rule* and that he might demand things of them that he demanded of himself. They wanted him to know that what he wrote was for him, but not for them.[33] Hearing Elias' words, Francis turned to Christ for guidance, asking him if he knew what the assembled brothers were saying.[34] Christ responded, in a voice heard throughout the valley, that it was he who had written the *Rule*, and that Francis added nothing new to it. Furthermore, the *Rule* was to be followed literally, without gloss.[35]

[30] The story goes that Francis wrote a *Primitive Rule* around 1209 for his first eleven followers. This *Rule* has not survived. Francis composed a subsequent *Rule*, called the *Regula non bullata*, sometime in the years 1220-1221. This *Rule* apparently fell short of the expectations of the order, so Francis wrote a third *Rule*, called the *Regula bullata* because it was confirmed by Pope Honorius III in 1223. This is the *Rule* of the order to this day.

[31] *Arbor*, V, 4, 441a: "His modis est allata tua sanctissima et seraphica regula: quam hic [Christ] plantasti: fundasti: et confirmasti in monte hereditatis tue [Mt. Alverna]."

[32] *Arbor*, V, 5, 445b: "Et in signum quod hec est apostolica regula: ipsam in xii distinxit capitula: quasi in xii fundamenta apostolica."

[33] *Arbor*, V, 5, 445a-445b: "Spiritus diaboli qui a principio contra hanc sacratissimam regulam offendicula excitavit: timore humano commovit multitudinem ministrorum et aliorum qui reputabantur discreti convenire reate: qui accedentes ad fratrem Heliam sibi dixerunt: quod ex parte ipsorum ascenderet ad virum sanctum: et diceret sibi verba que infra scribentur. . . . Cui ille helias ex omnium persona alta voce repsondit. Isti sunt ministri et discreti fratres italie: qui cognoscentes tui rigorem spiritus: et audientes quod novam conscribi facis regulam tibi denunciant pro se et pro aliis quod nolunt quod aliquid facias scribi quod eos obliget."

[34] *Arbor*, V, 5, 445b: "Audiens hec vir sanctus eiulatu magno vocem levavit ad celum dicens: fortissime domine audis quid isti iam dicunt?"

[35] *Arbor*, V, 5, 445b: "Ita quod per vallem et montem intellecta fuit et audita vox clara dicens: 'Franciscus, ego sum iesus qui tibi loquor de celo. Regula per me est

Francis added that clearly it came from Christ and not from him.[36] Thus Ubertino believes the author of the *Rule* to be Christ, not Francis.

Ubertino then goes on to address the poverty found in the *Rule.* He says that simplicity and poverty were the very beginning and foundation of the Franciscan order.[37] The brothers were transformed through highest poverty into the legitimate seraphic sons of Francis.[38] This poverty was recorded in the *Rule;* it was pure in its practice and involved full obedience in order to arrive at the foundation of complete evangelical perfection.[39] Since Franciscan poverty drew its definition from the gospels, the followers of Francis were to possess neither gold nor silver; they were to have neither money nor a purse to carry it in while on their travels; and they were to have only one tunic, no shoes, and no walking staff.[40] The brothers were to imitate Francis, and therefore the apostles, in their penurious use of things.[41] Ubertino thus holds that Francis' conception of the poverty of the order was clear in terms of its foundation, which included the gospels and the *Rule,* and its practice, as shown by the words and example of Francis himself.

Part of Francis' conception of the poverty of the order, in Ubertino's mind, was the idea that the *usus pauper* was included in the Franciscan vow. The notion of poor or restricted use can be found in Bonaventure's *Apologia pauperum* (1269); but the association of the *usus pauper* with the Franciscan vow originated with Peter John Olivi (d. 1298), the first of the great Spiritual leaders. He concluded, based on his reading of Franciscan sources, papal pronouncements, the words of the Gospels, and the evidence found in the *Rule,*

faciam: et tu nihil ibi posuisti de tuo. . . . Volo quod servetur ad litteram sine aliqua glosa.'"

[36] *Arbor,* V, 5, 445b: "Videtis aperte quod regula est domini nostri iesu christi: non mea: et quod ipse quicquid est ibi posuit."

[37] *Arbor,* V, 3, 429a: "Unde quasi pro nihil reputant viam simplicitatis et huius paupertatis: que fuerunt initium et fundamentum nostre religionis."

[38] *Arbor,* IV, 7, 304b: "Et idcirco sunt totaliter in christo passiones et dolores et penurias transformati per altissime paupertatis amorem: hi sunt viri seraphici legitimi filii francisci."

[39] *Arbor,* V, 5, 444b: "Ideo sapiens iesus et spiritus sanctus hec clarificans posuit mundissimam puritatem extremam paupertatem: obedientiam plenissimam et abnegationem sui perfectam: tamquam totius evangelice perfectionis fundamenta sub voto stabili et firmo omnia alia in quibus verbum precepti vel equipollens non exprimitur sub consiliis continentur: sive in regula: sive in evangeliis conscribantur."

[40] *Arbor,* V, 5, 444a: "Nam motivum fuit auditus evangelii dum missam audiret de apostolis cum lectum est evangelium in quo discipulis ad predicandum mittendis formam tribuit evangelicam in vivendo: ne videlicet possideant aurum vel argentum: nec in zonis peccuniam nec peram in via: nec duas tunicas habeant: nec deferant calciamenta: nec virgam."

[41] *Arbor,* III, 9, 206b: "Cum aperte clarescat quod christum iesu primum paupertatis magistrum et eius apostolos et primos patres ordinum fundatores et maxime pauperum patriarcham franciscum in rerum penuria satagant imitari."

that the *usus pauper* and the vow were intimately intertwined, a position he defended throughout his life despite repeated attacks.[42] Ubertino too accepts Olivi's reasoning, going so far as to defend his mentor and friend before a papal investigation.[43] In the *Arbor*, he presents the relationship between the *usus pauper* and the Franciscan vow in the context of discussing the Franciscan *Rule*.

Ubertino begins his examination of the *usus pauper*'s connection to the Franciscan vow by exploring the many charges made against this theory in his own day. He is amazed that there exists a monstrous idea, contrary to sacred doctrine, which holds that the *usus pauper* is included neither in the vow of evangelical perfection nor in the profession of highest poverty taught by Christ and imposed on the apostles, and that it was not promised by Francis in his *Rule*.[44] He continues that the above misconceptions about the *usus pauper* advance in his own times at the behest of those who live false and hypocritical lives. Not only is it insufficient for those who engage in this evil to live in a lax fashion, they conclude that the *usus pauper* is not part of the substance of evangelical poverty.[45] Ubertino believes such a conclusion to be ridiculous, one which would also seem so not only to those who are learned in the Sacred Scriptures, but also to every learned person.[46] He asks rhetorically who had heard that temporal things are relinquished by someone so that he may flee poor use and enjoy a life of opulence.[47] He who wants to use things abundantly and

[42] David Burr, *Olivi and Franciscan Poverty: The Origins of the Usus pauper Controversy* (Philadelphia, 1989), pp. 58-60.

[43] The principal works on Ubertino's defense of Olivi in the papal investigation of 1309-1312 are: the *Apologia* for Olivi, in *Achiv für Litterature und Kirchengeschichte*, ed. Franz Erhle and Heinrich Denifle [hereafter ALKG] 2 (1886): 374-416; *Sanctitas vestra*, ALKG 3 (1887): 48-49; the *Rotulus*, ALKG 3 (1887): 89-137; the *Declaratio*, ALKG 3 (1887): 160-195; and Ubertino's work on the *usus pauper*, the *Super tribus sceleribus*, ed. A Heysse, *Archivum Franciscanum Historicum* [hereafter AFH] 10 (1910): 123-174. For a bibliography of all the works known to have been produced for the Franciscan controversy, 1309-1312, see idem, *"Anonymi Spiritualis reponsio 'Beatus Vir' contra 'Abbreviaturum Communitatis,'"* AFH 42 (1949): 231-316. On Ubertino's role in the defense of Olivi, see Burr, *Olivi and Franciscan Poverty*, pp. 50-51, 107, 110, 146.

[44] *Arbor*, III, 3, 187a: "Miror ergo unde meis temporibus hic monstruosa: et contra dictam sanctorum doctrina: quod usus pauper non includitur in voto perfectionis evangelice: et in professione altissime paupertatis a christo docte: et apostolis imposite: et a beato francisco in regula promisse."

[45] *Arbor*, III, 3, 187a: "Sed video quod idem processus: idem et alia mala his temporibus in mundo venerunt a falsitate religionis et apperentie hypocritalis: que ad tantum malum pervenit: ut non sufficiat eis laxate vivere. . .dicitur quod pauperes uti rebus non est de substantia evangelice paupertatis."

[46] *Arbor*, III, 3, 187a: "Quod tamen ridiculosum videtur mihi: quod non solum sapientibus et doctoribus in sacra scriptura: sed etiam puto quod omnibus scolaribus appere debeat monstruosum."

[47] *Arbor*, III, 3, 187a: "Quis enim unquam audivit quod temporalia ab aliquo relinquantur: ut fugiat usum pauperem et habeat opulentum."

to abandon nothing, and still call himself one of the evangelical poor, in fact blasphemes both God and the apostles.[48] Those who argue that the *usus pauper* is too difficult a burden are wrong, too. Ubertino says that it was not the intention of the teachers and servers of poverty, nor of the holy apostles, nor of the renewer Francis, that the *usus pauper* be accepted in the vow of profession in an indivisible and unchangeable way, such that one always eats the same thing, or wears the same thing, or uses the same house. Instead, he argues that the *usus pauper* should be considered a middle virtue, a virtue not destroyed by one act, but one which arises out of evangelical perfection.[49]

It is this element of evangelical perfection which ultimately connects the *usus pauper* with the Franciscan vow. Ubertino claims that there is a great difference between poverty that results from necessity and poverty chosen through the charity of the holy gospel. In the first, the poor, when they enjoy an abundance of goods, gorge themselves. In the second, the poor always carry the love of poverty with them.[50] While both are poor, the evangelical poor are restrained, so that they do not go from house to house looking to fill their bellies, but instead make Christ their example; after all, Christ came to call the sinners to penance, not the just.[51] The evangelical poor also use goods in a temperate fashion.[52] When in others' houses, they stay away from superfluity and therefore maintain the strict observance of holy poverty.[53] When they are in the courts of the rich and powerful they preach poverty through the example of

[48] *Arbor*, III, 3, 187a: "Vele ergo abunde uti rebus: et nihil deficere: et cum hic se pauperem evangelicum dicere videat quantam blasphemiam christo et apostolis imponat."

[49] *Arbor*, III, 3, 187a-187b: "Ad clarificationem ergo huius sancti pauperis usus dicunt pauperes evangelici: quod non fuit intentio paupertatem docentis et servantis christi iesu: nec sanctorum apostolorum eius: nec sui renovatoris francisci: quod usus pauper accipiatur in voto profitentis in attomo indivisibili et incommutabili: ut semper eodem cibo: eodem indumento: eodem utantur habitaculo. . .sed usus pauper habet medium virtutis: quod medium semper destruitur uno actu qualicumque: sed isto modo usus pauper semper est de necessitate evangelice perfectionis."

[50] *Arbor*, III, 3, 187b: "Licet magna sit differentia iter pauperes quos facit necessitas: et quos sancti evangelii faciunt charitas. Primi sepe dum abundant se ingurgitant: secundi semper secum sue paupertatis amorem portant."

[51] *Arbor*, III, 3, 187b: "Et ideo ubique sunt pauperes et temperati: propter quod non sunt tales admodum glutonum qui libenter circuunt domos divitum: ut impleant ventrem suum: quinimmo si ad tales declinant hoc faciunt exemplo iesu christi: qui non venit vocare iustos sed peccatores ad penitentiam."

[52] *Arbor*, III, 3, 187b: "Et sic temperate illorum bonis utuntur."

[53] *Arbor*, III, 3, 187b: "Veri autem paupertatis amatores in alienis domibus quantum presentibus superfluitatem reprimunt: et in habitaculis eorum usibus a fidelibus concessis: sancte paupertatis strictum usum custodiunt."

their works.[54] They thus display themselves as true contemptors of the world.[55] By maintaining the *usus pauper*, they imitate Christ and observe their vow. It must be understood therefore that for Ubertino the *usus pauper* is always integral to the notion of evangelical perfection.[56]

The analysis by Ubertino of both Franciscan poverty and the *usus pauper* is required in order for him to repulse the actions of those who have continually sought to alter and therefore destroy Francis' foundation. As far as he is concerned, these actions were first launched by the hierarchy of the church, and particularly the papacy, which tried to modify Francis' wishes, beginning with the changes suggested at the time of the composition of the *Rule* of 1223. Notwithstanding Pope Innocent III's support of Francis' conception of his order in 1209 or 1210, the first Cardinal Protector of the order, Hugolino, wanted to alter its direction. Ubertino says that Hugolino came to Francis while the two were attending a meeting of the General Chapter at the Portiuncola and attempted to convince him that the Franciscans should gradually adapt their order to the ways of previously established orders, since these were sufficient guides for the whole world.[57] Francis responded, according to Ubertino, that Christ had selected him for his dedication to the life of Christ. It was a new perfect life, representing a new status. Francis continued that Hugolino should not tell him differently since Christ had manifested to the fullest the intent of His will to His unworthy servant.[58] The implication of Ubertino's tone is that to contradict Francis is to contradict Christ.

Even though Hugolino initially backed down from modifying Franciscan practice, he ultimately was convinced that changes to the order's practice should be made. After his election to the papacy as Gregory IX in 1227, he had greater authority to intervene in the affairs of the order; and, therefore, he proceeded through his bull *Quo elongati* (1230) to alter Francis' wishes by rescinding the ban on the acquisition of property by the order found in Francis' deathbed

[54] *Arbor*, III, 3, 187b: "De his vero qui morantur in curiis quibuscumque per obedientiam. . .sint paupertatis predicatores per exemplaritatem operum."

[55] *Arbor*, III, 3, 187b: "Et sic se ostendant veros mundi contemptores."

[56] *Arbor*, III, 3, 187a-187b: "Usus pauper semper est de necessitate evangelice perfectionis."

[57] *Arbor*, V, 7, 450a: "Idem pater et protector ordinis qui ex magna devotione ad sanctam mariam de portiuncula ad capitulum generale advenerat beatum franciscum vocavit ad patrem: et dixit. Frater franciscus bona tibi fecit altissimus et inter alia magnos tibi dedit prudentes et literatos: et qui noverunt dicta sanctorum et priorum ordinum instituta: qui et sunt sufficientes: et non solum ordinem: sed et mundum regere: opportet ergo te eorum consiliis regi: et paulatine prioribus ordinibus conformari."

[58] *Arbor*, V, 7, 450a-450b: "Cui illuminatus a deo franciscus humiliter et constanter respondit. . . Fratres mei hominem simplicem et sine aliqua sufficientia vas perditum sine scriptura sine aliquo bono me iesus christus elegit. . . et statum novum et vitam suam perfectam voluit mihi et vobis ex inestimabili misericordia dare indignis. . . . Non ergo allegetis mihi aliquid aliud: quia ipse voluntatem suam plenissime mihi indigno manifestat."

admonition, the *Testament.* The bull directly contradicted Francis, whom Ubertino says wanted no bulls or privileges for the order unless they state that his teaching on poverty cannot be weakened.[59] Francis himself was afraid of the weakening of his poverty, since Ubertino notes that he believed the greatest threat against his admonition would come from future dispensations.[60] *Quo elongati* seems to have confirmed Francis' fear. Ubertino asserts that it led to the conclusion by some that the brothers are obliged to follow the dictates of the pope, including his dispensations from the *Rule* and *Testament.* But Ubertino rejects this idea, saying that he refuses to be absolved from the paternal ties to Francis.[61] He does so because he thinks that if one lives by papal privilege, he lives against the dictates of the *Rule* and the wishes of Francis, thus creating for himself a new status and destroying the first one.[62]

Ubertino viewed *Quo elongati* as the first of many efforts made by the papacy to alter the proper practice of the Franciscan *Rule.* These efforts grew out of a general movement within the papacy, which extended down throughout the church and even to some in the order, to embrace temporal possessions. The devotion to temporal things began the descent into the abyss, where petitions fostered by the papacy resulted in the destruction of the *Testament.*[63] Ubertino holds that the relaxation which entered the order after the destruction of the *Testament* was due in part to the inclination of subsequent popes who acted in the mistaken belief that they imitated the piety, compassion, and sound providence of God.[64] He believes Nicholas III to be particularly important in the modification of the *Rule.* In fact, his bull *Exiit qui seminat*, issued in August of 1279, defined the evangelical nature of Christ's poverty and concluded that such poverty was the poverty of the Franciscans.[65] But Ubertino understood Nicholas' bull to be a detriment to the order; he calls it a millstone tied to the

[59] *Arbor*, V, 3, 426b: "Idcirco nullam voluit bullam: nullum privilegium: nisi hoc solum quod sua paupertas maculari non posset."

[60] *Arbor*, V, 5, 447a: "Respondeo quia hoc previdit futurorum inspector Franciscus scilicet hanc status sui dissipationem magis quia dispensationem futuram."

[61] *Arbor*, V, 5, 447a: "Sed dicis: si papa nos absoluit: tamen nos obligas. Dico quod nolo absolui ego a successione paterna."

[62] *Arbor*, V, 5, 447b: "Sic et vivere secundum privilegia papa iam contra id quod est in regula promissum: vel a sancto expressum: est facere unum alium novum statum: et destruere primum."

[63] *Arbor*, V, 5, 447b: "Ibi ergo devotio inchoavit que descendit in hac abyssum in qua nulla servatur declarario: ubi petitia est destructio sanctissimi testamenti."

[64] *Arbor*, V, 7, 453a: "Tam ab inclinatione pontificum qui credebant se in hoc dei pietatem et misericordiam et salubrem providentiam imitari."

[65] Malcolm D. Lambert, *Franciscan Poverty: The Doctrine of the Absolute Poverty of Christ and the Apostles in the Franciscan Order, 1210-1323* (London, 1961), pp. 141-148.

belly of the order.[66] In his mind, Nicholas had removed the practice of highest poverty.[67] Nicholas was just one example which illustrates that the popes falsely believed themselves to serve God, making acceptable in their minds the bending of the spiritual rigor of the *Rule*.[68] By Ubertino's time, this mistaken belief had developed into what he calls a "faulted pomposity" on the part of many within the church, including the popes, cardinals, and other prelates.[69]

The attempts made by the church to change the practice of the *Rule* were themselves encouraged by those within the order who wanted moderation. In Ubertino's mind, the ruin within the order began with the questioning of the Franciscan precept on poverty.[70] The brothers who wanted change became motivated not by a zeal to save souls but by a lust for wealth and temporal possessions.[71] He even charges that many Franciscans sought to emulate the Dominicans who had betrayed the foundation of Dominic, brothers who claimed a variety of offices and privileges as if they were kings, cardinals, princes, and potentates, and who acquired and multiplied their temporal possessions.[72] The modifying Franciscan brothers, like the Dominicans, make appeals to the pope for permission to change their practice.[73]

The brothers who have sought to alter Franciscan practice were first led by the aforementioned Elias. Ubertino thinks that no other single person is more responsible for the onset of the relaxation of the *Rule* than was he, and his position as Minister General allowed him wide latitude regarding the order's development. One example of Elias' role provided by Ubertino is his wish to

[66] *Arbor*, V, 3, 432a: "Nicolaus tertius ultimam declarationem fecti quantum potuit visa est regulam exponere. . .ac si lapsis molaris fuisset appensus ad ventrem ordinis."

[67] *Arbor*, V, 6, 448a: "Dominus ioannes de ursinis qui fuit postea nicholaus papa tertius qui sibi novam regulam ipse composuit cardinalis existens et ab altissima paupertate deiecit."

[68] *Arbor*, V, 7, 453a: "Et idocirco summi pontifices huius status prompti et liberales ad spiritualem rigorem regule inflectendum. . .in hoc crediderunt deo servire."

[69] *Arbor*, V, 6, 448b: "Quia falerata [sic] pompositas que nostris temporibus abundavit in tanta gratia summorum pontificum cardinalium prelatorum aliorum."

[70] *Arbor*, V, 7, 452a: "Et si bene notas principium omnis ruine fuit questionatio de precepto."

[71] *Arbor*, V, 3, 431b: "Quod luce clarius pater ex capitis vanitate procedere. . .non ergo est animarum zelus sed humane cupiditatis questus."

[72] *Arbor*, V, 7, 453b: "Et intellice quod secundum proportionem suam eodem modo in ruina processit ordo fratrem predicatorem a perfectione primaria qua beatus dominucus propagavit. . . . Nam emulant se invice in acquisitione libertatum et privilegiorum in familiaritatibus regum cardinalium: principum: et potentus: in acquisitione et multiplicatione rerum temporalium."

[73] *Arbor*, V, 3, 432a: "Et hanc concordiam voluerunt per auctoritatem summi pontificis obtinere."

change the way in which the Franciscan habit was styled. He wanted to take the one habit the brothers could possess and alter the length, width, and size of the hood, and have it made of better quality cloth.[74] As Ubertino sees it, this change would result in the brothers beginning to walk with raised heads and puffed chests, saying in an inflated and insipid voice, "Good people, the Lord gives you peace."[75] Elias himself was well aware of these dangers, since Ubertino claims that the Spirit spoke to him, telling him that the "bastards of the order" are beginning to creep in and that changes have been made to pious custom.[76] But Elias' negative role and input is even more profound than the above example suggests. Francis, by the authority of the Spirit, tells him that, because of his haughty pomposity and carnal knowledge, he is leading the order to its destruction and renders void the truth of the evangelical spirit.[77] Ubertino clearly holds Elias responsible for the beginnings of trouble within the order.

Ubertino further contends that operating hand-in-hand with Elias' efforts to alter the practice of Franciscan poverty was the acceptance of his efforts by some in the order. He says that the onset of the ruin of the order came from those who questioned what Francis said.[78] In order to make his point more clear, Ubertino employs as a metaphor the account of the serpent leading Eve astray, found in Gn 3:1-7, to explain what happened to the order. He understands that the verse which relates the serpent's questioning of Eve about her eating the fruit of the trees of the garden (Gn 3:1) refers to the damage done to the observance of God's command and the apparent usefulness of transgression.[79]

[74] *Arbor*, V, 7, 449b: "Nam cum frater helias qui semper videbatur sicut caro concupiscere contra spiritum sancti: licet sub specie discretionis et boni fecisset unum habitum: qui in longitudine et latitudine et magnitudine manicarum et caputii: et preciositate panni illam vilitatem multo deformem quam sanctus instituerat videbatur excedere: vocans illum coram multis fratribus dixit quod sibi prestaret habitum quem portabat: qui illum induens super suum."

[75] *Arbor*, V, 7, 449b: "Facta subcictura et gestibus in rugatione tunice et aptatione caputii in capite et in toto corpore: quos in spiritu previdebat fiendos a filiis cepit elevato capite: inflato pectore. . . et cum vocis boatu fratres in aspectu stupentes salutare inflata et insipida voce dicendo. Bone gentes dominus det vobis pacem."

[76] *Arbor*, V, 7, 449b: "Quo facto in fervore spiritus cum iracundie signo contumeliose extrahendo habitum: longe proiecit et dixit ad heliam audientibus aliis. Sic incedent bastardi ordinis: postea in suo habitu despecto brevim et stricto: in quo sicut ceteri primi fratres mundi crucifixo videbatur: mutata facie in mansuetudinem piam."

[77] *Arbor*, V, 7, 449b: "Sanctus pater spiritus auctoritate recepta super ipsum clamando respondit: helia helia tua fatuosa pompositas et carnis prudentia: et tui similium ordinem meum ducet ad nihilum: et totam veritatem evangelici spiritus vacuabant."

[78] *Arbor*, V, 7, 452a: "Si bene notas principium omnis ruine fuit questionatio de precepto."

[79] *Arbor*, V, 7, 452a: "*Cur*, inquit, *precepit vobis deus* etc. [Gen. 3:1]' Damnum in observantia et utilitatem in transgressione suggessit."

Once the serpent has raised the issue of disobeying God's command, he can then demonstrate the benefits that can be expected. The serpent told Eve that when she eats the fruit, her eyes will be opened and she will be like God. Ubertino understands that the serpent of course misled Eve, making her blind to the observance of God's command and wise in the ways of transgression. He believes that the same situation is true for those within the order who disobeyed Francis' command. They were themselves misled, so that they did not see the evil precept. For them, the blindness seemed to be bright, and they knew through transgression all the evil that comes over them.[80] As was the case for Eve, once their eyes were opened, they saw all the delights of the world. As a result, the power or strength of the holy *Rule* was obscured.[81]

The pursuit of the delights of the world is best demonstrated by the growth of learning within the order. The original impetus behind the rise of learning was based on good intentions: in order to preach more effectively, the friars should be well-versed in the scriptures. Ubertino holds, however, that the drive for learning caused them to become more and more immersed in learning for learning's sake. While Francis himself was aware of the need for the brothers to have some education, he wanted to make it clear where the brothers' priority should lie. He did not want the brothers to be lovers of wisdom and books. Instead, they should strive for a pure and holy simplicity, holy prayer, and Lady Poverty.[82] Francis repeatedly told the brothers that they could lose their vocation if they became involved in teaching others.[83] The danger was that by their teaching they might well believe themselves to be "afire" for the devotion and love of God because of their understanding of Scripture, but in reality they might remain cold and empty inside. They can thus not return to their "pristine" vocation, especially since they have lost time in living according to that vocation.[84] For those who argued that these risks were outweighed by the rewards associated with preaching, such as instructing the people and leading them to penance, Ubertino includes a response from Francis. It is the Lord, not

[80] *Arbor*, V, 7, 452a: "Dicitur *Scit deus quod aperientur oculi vestri. Inquacumque die comederitis eritis sicut dii* etc [Gn 3:5]: videtis quod cecitatem in observantia: scientiam in transgressione mentitur. Sed vere non videbant malum observantes preceptum et sic erat cecitas luminosa: sciverunt per transgressionem omne malum quod venit super eos."

[81] *Arbor*, V, 7, 452a: "*Eritis sicut dii* [Gn 3:5]: Nam sic eorum aperuit oculos: ut eis pulchra faceret omnia delectabilia mundi: que virtus sancte regule obscurabat."

[82] *Arbor*, V, 3, 428a-428b: "Similiter dicit frater leo: quod beatus franciscus nolebat quod fratres essent cupidi de scientia et de libris: sed volebat et fratribus predicabat: ut studerent habere puram et sanctam simplicitatem: orationem sanctam et dominam paupertatem."

[83] *Arbor*, V, 3, 428b: "Et etiam multotiens fratribus dixit: quod fratres multi sub occasione edificandi alios dimitterent vocationem suam."

[84] *Arbor*, V, 3, 428b: "Accidet illis quod unde crediderunt postea accendi ad devotionem et amorem dei propter intellectum scripture: inde occasionaliter remanebunt intus frigidi et quasi vacui: et sic ad pritinam vocationem reverti non poterunt: maxime quia amiserunt tempus vivendi secundum vocationem."

their words, who instructs and converts through holy prayers.[85] Ubertino's point is clear: even though Francis recognized the function of preaching in the Franciscan vocation, he wanted the brothers to remember that preaching was not an end in and of itself.

Ubertino no doubt believed that the order had in fact become lost in the ways of the world; after all, he himself was educated at the University of Paris, where the Friars Minor held great sway. But the real danger which arose from the alteration of Francis' wishes is only made completely clear when one considers Ubertino's apocalyptic understanding of history. He believes that church history dictates a reform of the Franciscan practice of poverty. Once Franciscan poverty has been reformed to bring it into line with Spiritual Franciscan practice, then history will be fulfilled and the church saved. The first step in examining Ubertino's conclusions is to dissect, in brief form, his understanding of church history.[86]

Ubertino divides church history into seven periods based on the seven visions expressed in Revelation.[87] He says that the first period deals with the primitive foundation and was constituted by the apostles. The second period involves an approving confirmation through the deeds of those martyred at the hands of the pagans throughout the world. He continues that the third period entails an illuminative doctrine related to clarifying faith and confounding heresies. The fourth period comprises the anchorite life lived in the most austere solitude. The fifth period, he says, is characterized by condescension, in that monks and clerics accepted temporal possessions. Ubertino holds that the sixth period is of critical importance because it witnesses the renovation of the evangelical life and the defeat of the sect of the Antichrist under voluntary poverty. He concludes by saying that the seventh period involves a quiet and miraculous participation in future glory as the New Jerusalem descends from the heavens.[88]

85 *Arbor*, V, 3, 428b: "Quam quos credunt suis verbis edificari vel ad penitentiam converti: dominus edificat et convertit orationibus sanctorum fratrem."

86 The greater amount of Ubertino's apocalyptic thought is borrowed verbatim from Olivi's *Lectura super apocalypsim* (1297 or 1298). On the content of the *Lectura* and its place in the Franciscan apocalyptic exegetical tradition, see David Burr, *Olivi's Peaceable Kingdom* (Philadelphia, 1993).

87 The seven visions are: the seven churches (Rv 2:1-3:22); the opening of the seven seals (Rv 4:1-8:1); the blowing of the seven trumpets, which Ubertino says begins at Rv 6, but which actually include Rv 8:2-11:18; the events involving the women pursued into the desert, the rise of the two beasts, and the angel who announces the fall of Babylon (Rv 12:1-14:20); the seven vials (Rv 15:1-16:20); the damnation of the whore of Babylon, which Ubertino says begins either at Rv 16:18 or at Rv 17; and the final damnation of the reprobates and the glorification of the elect, which begins either at Rv 20:11 or at 21:1.

88 *Arbor*, V, 1, 409b: "Quantum ergo ad primum sciendum quod primus status est fundationis primitive: et precipue in iudaismo ab apostolis facte. Secundus confirmationis probative per martyria facta a paganis in toto orbe. Tertius doctrine illuminative ad clarificandum [sic] fidem: et hereses confundendas. Quartus fuit anachoritice vite in solitudine viventis austerissime. Quintus fuit condescensive sub

Ubertino also connects the foundation of each period with concrete events in church history. He says that the first period began with the coming of Christ and the preaching of his mission.[89] The second period was initiated with the persecution under Nero, or the stoning of Stephen, or the passion of Christ, all clearly included in the acts of the martyrs. He believes that the third period dates from the time of the conversion of Constantine, or from the time of the blessed Silvester, or from the Council of Nicaea, the last especially exemplifying the clarification of doctrine. The fourth period commenced with such renowned anchorites as the hermit Anthony or the first hermit Paul, or, according to Joachim of Fiore, from the reign of the emperor Justinian. The reign of Charlemagne signaled the beginning of the fifth period, which also saw the church, according to Ubertino, grow in terms of temporal possessions. The coming of Francis marked the beginning of the sixth period. The seventh period will begin with the killing of the Antichrist and end with the arrival of the New Jerusalem.[90]

Included in Ubertino's discussion of the periodization of the church's history is an analysis of the activities or offices found in each period. In the first period the preeminence of prelacy and pastoral care is visible, while the second has the burden of suffering passion and the triumphal struggle. The third period includes the sound of preaching and the magisterial trumpet, the fourth involves sanctity and the singular life, and the fifth entails the righteous zeal and the judicial wrath, as well as the decline in the conventual life. He believes that the sixth period witnesses the model of Christ's life at work in the reform of the church, while the seventh period will see God in His glory receiving the church.[91] Ubertino continues that based on these offices, one can see the different people who embrace them. Thus the pastors of the Catholic church

monachis et clericis temporalia possidentibus. Sextus est renovationis evangelice vite: et expugnationis secte antichristiane sub pauperibus voluntariis nihil possidentibus in hac vita. Septimus prout spectat ad vitam istam est quedam quieta et mira participatio future glorie: ac si celestis hierusalem videatur ascendisse in terram."

89 *Arbor*, V, 1, 409b: "Primus status proprie incipit a spiritus sancti missione: licet et alio modo ceperit a christi iesu predicatione."

90 *Arbor*, V, 1, 409b-410a: "Secundus proprie cepit a persecutione facta sub nerone: quavis et alio modo ceperit a lapidatione Stephani: vel etiam a passione christi. Tertius proprie cepit a tempore Constantini imperatoris ad fidem christi conversi: seu a tempore beati Silvestri: seu a tempore Niceni concilii contra arrianam heresim celebrati. Quartus cepit a tempore magni Anthoni: seu a tempore Pauli primi heremite: vel secundum Ioachim a tempore Iustiniani augusti: sub quo habemus magna culta. Quintus vero proprie cepit a tempore Caroli magni. Sextus vero iniciatus est a tempore seraphici viri Francisci. . . . Septimus autem uno modo inchoat ab interfectione illius antichristi quem iudei recipient."

91 *Arbor*, V, 1, 410a: "In primo eminet principatus prelationis et cura pastoralis. In secundo onus passionis et pugna triumphalis. In tertio sonus predicationis et tuba magistralis. In quarto ornatus sanctitudinis et vita singularis. In quinto zelus rectitudinis et ira iudicialis: ac vita condescensiva et conventualis. In sexto forma christi formatoris ecclesiam reformans. In septimo vero gloria deiformis ipsam felicitans et consummans."

excel in the first period, the warriors of the Christian army operate in the second, and so on until the sixth period, which sees the arrival of the reformers of the evangelical life.[92]

Of course, Ubertino goes into greater detail in his discussion of church history in the *Arbor*; but the point here centers on the intersection between his apocalyptic ideas and his reform ideology. This intersection is to be found in the special place of the fifth and sixth periods. As noted above, he describes the fifth period as a time of condescension when the church increasingly pursued temporal possessions. Ubertino believes that the decadent status of the church at the end of the fifth period resulted in the appearance of Francis and Dominic, along with their followers, who fought the horrible "leprosy" then infecting the church. Their coming marked the end of the fifth period and the beginning of the sixth.[93] Concomitant with Francis' arrival is the coming of the Antichrist, followed in a short time by the reappearance of Christ to do battle with him. The result of such a battle will be the defeat of the Antichrist and the damnation of his followers, along with the elevation of the righteous, who will reside in the New Jerusalem. It is in this context that Ubertino speaks of the special place of Franciscan poverty in the end times.

Before analyzing the coming of the New Jerusalem and the place of the Spirituals in the city, Ubertino takes up a discussion of the poverty of the Spirituals and its relevance for the end times, expressed in terms of the elect found in Rv 14. This chapter speaks of the appearance of Christ accompanied by the army of the elect numbered at 144,000 to do battle with the two beasts of Rv 13. Despite its large number, Ubertino associates this army with the Spirituals. In order to confirm his association, he says that it is necessary to refute certain errors which arise over the size of the army. There are some, he notes, who say that the evangelical life of Francis in his renewed *Rule* was not meant for large numbers of people because it could not be properly observed. Ubertino holds that those who make such arguments are really trying to excuse their own evils.[94] Christ, through his angel Francis, will declare them liars.[95] He continues that when the number 144,000 is understood in a literal sense, it

[92] *Arbor*, V, 410a: "Propter quod in primo preeminent pastores ecclesie catholice. In secundo pugiles christiane militie. In tertio precones christiane sapientie. In quarto observatores vite celice. In quinto iusti zelatores et pii regularis sanctimonie. In sexto reformatores vite evangelice. In septimo pregustatores eterne glorie."

[93] *Arbor*, V, 2, 421a: "Quia vero plenior malitia huius quinti status maxime apparet in contemptu spiritus dei apparentis in eo in viris perfectis Francisco et Dominico: et eorum virtuosa prole: quam fumus huius pessimi putei horrenda lepra infecit: in quo maxime stat pugna huius quinti cum principio sexti."

[94] *Arbor*, V, 9, 471b: "Et ad confundendam fallaciam transgressorum huius temporis qui ad suam excusandam malitiam dicunt quod evangelica vita per franciscum in regula renovata non fuit data pro tanta multitudine: et quod tali multitudini inobservabilis est."

[95] *Arbor*, V, 9, 471b: "Unde eos iesus per predictum angelum declarabit mendaces."

shows that a great and perfect multitude of believers are converted to evangelical perfection, a fact that serves to reassure the "poor flock" of the Spirituals.[96] There will then be in the time of the elect many more observers of the *Rule,* called the legitimate sons of Francis, than there are now false accusers of the *Rule* who do not observe Franciscan poverty and the *usus pauper*.[97]

Ubertino then sets out to give a more thorough explanation of the characteristics of the elect in order to explain the renovation of which he speaks and the role of the Spirituals in such a renovation. He proceeds by examining seven characteristics enjoyed by the elect and shared by the Spirituals as shown in Rv 14:1-5. The first of these characteristics relates to the conformity of the "society" of the elect to Christ.[98] He says that they stand on top of Mt. Zion, which symbolizes the "high and solid eminence" of the contemplative life.[99] The elect transcend the prominence of other contemplatives. They stand associated with Christ the Lamb, in His innocence and mildness, experiencing the complete consuming fire of the cross, and rapt in highest contemplation.[100] Ubertino adds that the 144,000 is understood to be the army of the Lamb, with the Lamb as their leader. The members of the army, known as "little Jesuses," are said to be transformed in Christ through the renovation of His cross.[101]

After Ubertino has established the relationship between the army of the elect and Christ, he takes up the second characteristic of the army. He says that through a certain and regular comparison of the "perfect number," the army is conformed to Christ's apostolic leaders.[102] The relationship between the army and the apostolic leaders is explained by Joachim of Fiore. Joachim said that the army of the elect corresponds to the elders who surround the seat of God in Rv

[96] *Arbor*, V, 9, 471b: "Sed cum hoc literaliter est intelligendum quod multitudo perfecta et magna ad perfectionem evangelicam convertetur per hunc numerum designata: et hic ponitur ad comfortandum pauperculum gregem."

[97] *Arbor*, V, 9, 471b: "Dum multo plures tunc erunt legitimi filii francsici regulam observantes: quam nunc sunt spurii regulam accusantes et usum pauperem non servantes."

[98] *Arbor*, V, 9, 471b: "Exponendo autem per hac renovatione prima que nunc instat septupla prerogativa hic electorum monstratur: prima est eorum ad christum conformis et individua societas."

[99] *Arbor*, V, 9, 471b: "Nam dicuntur *stare super montem syon* [Rv 14:1] per quem designatur alta et solida eminentia contemplativi status."

[100] *Arbor*, V, 9, 471b-472a: "Et dicuntur *stare super montem* [Rv 14:1]: quia. . . ceterorum contemplativorum eminentiam transcendunt: dicitur autem hic christus agnus cum quo hi stant et cum sua innocentia et mititate et holocaustica immolatione crucis stant in alto contemplationis."

[101] *Arbor*, V, 9, 472a: "Et intelliguntur ista centum xliiii milia esse milia agnorum cum principali agno iesu qui dicuntur iesunculi per renovationem crucis sue in iesum transformati."

[102] *Arbor*, V, 9, 472a: "Secunda est certa et regularis commensuratio perfecti numeri suis apostolicis capitibus conformati."

4:10 through their perfect imitation.[103] As such they represent the Holy Spirit who descends from both the Father and the Son.[104] Ubertino notes that the principal of *concordia*, seen first in terms of the Old and New Testaments, helps explain the relationship between the army of the elect and the elders: the concordance between the patriarchs and apostles is akin to that of the elect and the elders of Rv 4:10.[105] Thus the number 144,000 is truly a symbolic number.

The relationship between the elect and the Lamb is exhibited not only by the special nature of their number; it is also seen in the name of God inscribed on their foreheads (Rv 14:2). Ubertino's discussion of this name illustrates the third characteristic of the elect. God's name implies the faith, love, and contemplation of God the Father and Son.[106] Through His name is expressed the well-known notion that God is love.[107] The name of God is impressed on their foreheads, symbolizing an open and forceful confession of love for God on the part of the elect.[108] Through the name is also expressed the presence of the Holy Spirit.[109]

The fourth characteristic given by Ubertino is related to the song sung by the elect before the throne of God, depicted in Rv 14:3. He says that the song itself has a seven-fold nature.[110] Of particular interest is the fourth element, which describes the quality of the voice that sings the song. Ubertino says that the voice is sweet and joyful.[111] It sounds like the sound of many harpists.[112]

103 *Arbor*, V, 9, 472a: "Nam secundum Ioachim c xliii m faciunt xx legiones correspondentes xxiiii *senioribus* circumstantibus *sedem dei* [Cf. Rv 4:10] et agni ita ut cuilibet seniori respondeat sua legio per imitationem perfectam."

104 *Arbor*, V, 9, 472a: "Et propter hoc datur intelligi quod per istos representatur status spiritus sancti qui concorditer a patre et filio spiratur."

105 *Arbor*, V, 9, 472a: "Sicut et isti concorditer a veteri testamento et novo quasi utriusque concordia et perfectio spirata procedunt scilicet a perfectione xii patriarcharum: et xii apotolorum: tanquam xxiiii seniorum."

106 *Arbor*, V, 9, 472a: "Tertia prerogativa est fidei et amoris et contemplationis dei patris et filii humanati frontalis inscriptio per hoc quod sequitur: *habentes nomen eius et nomen patris eius scriptum in frontibus suis* [Rv 14:1]."

107 *Arbor*, V, 9, 472a: "Per nomen designatur famosa noticia que respectu dei nihil est nisi sit amativa."

108 *Arbor*, V, 9, 472a: "Per frontem aperta et fortis et viva dei confessio."

109 *Arbor*, V, 9, 472a: "Spiritus enim sanctus in ipsa inscriptione intelligitur."

110 *Arbor*, V, 9, 472a: "Quarta prerogativa est precellentia iubilatori cantici istorum perfectorum: quam quidem septiformiter magnificat."

111 *Arbor*, V, 9, 472a: "Sequitur quarta prerogative [Ubertino here means the fourth part of the fourth prerogative] quod hec vox erit suavis et iocunda."

112 While the term *cithara* is literally translated as a lute or lyre, the *New Oxford Annotated Bible* understands the word to be harp. I have chosen to follow this latter translation.

The harp has no sound for the elect unless the box under the strings is empty, which Ubertino understands to mean that the highest and most humble poverty will be in the elect, taking them from all concerns and matters of the world.[113] It is through such poverty that Francis and the Spirituals are connected to the events of Revelation. The form of the harp first appeared on Mt. Alverna at the time Francis was marked with the stigmata; he was thus made a harpist by Christ because he was made free from the cares of the world through his evangelical poverty.[114]

The fifth characteristic of the elect addresses their perfection. Ubertino states that it concerns their perfect and immaculate purity, and that they have been redeemed from the "earth" by the passion and blood of Christ.[115] He continues that they are not "defiled" by women, and thus are virgins, as Rv 14:4 remarks.[116] Ubertino concludes that "holy virginity" will thus be renewed in the elect in both mind and flesh. In fact, the perfect purgation from all past sins and experiences of the flesh is understood by the name "virgin."[117] Examples of elect people are Mary Magdalene and Peter, leader of the apostles, neither of whom was excluded from hearing the song of the Lamb.[118] The natural conclusion is that the Spirituals themselves are perfect, since they too hear the song.

The sixth characteristic mentioned by Ubertino is built upon Rv 14:4, which mentions that the 144,000 follow the Lamb wherever He goes. He says that this following symbolizes the fact that the elect follow Christ in His perfect life.[119] The more they share in His many and higher perfections, the more they

113 *Arbor*, V, 9, 472a-472b: "*Audivi sicut citharedorum citharizantium in citharis suis* [Rv 14:2]: Cithara eis non sonat nisi sit vacua: per quod datur intelligi quod in eis erit paupertas altissima et humilissima eos evancuans ab omni reputatione sui et substantia mundi."

114 *Arbor*, V, 9, 472b: "Huius cithare forma sexto statui danda primo apparuit in hoc sacro monte cum in stigmatibus passionis fundator sexti status franciscus: a christo factus est citharedus."

115 *Arbor*, V, 9, 472b-473a: "Quinta autem prerogativa istorum est puritas perfecta et imaculata pro qua subdit: qui empti sunt de terra: quasi dicat christi passione et sanguine eius."

116 *Arbor*, V, 9, 473a: "Cum dicitur: *Hi sunt qui cum mulieribus non sunt coinquinati: virgines enim sunt* [Rv 14:4]."

117 *Arbor*, V, 9, 473a: "Et licet intelligatur quod in illo statu renovabitur sancta virginitas tam mente quam carne. . . . Nihilominus nomine virginum intelligitur omnis perfecta purgatio ab omni preterita labe et experientia carnis."

118 *Arbor*, V, 9, 473a: "Sicut fuit in benedicta magdalena: et in apostolorum principe petro: qui nequaqua ab agni cantico excluduntur."

119 *Arbor*, V, 9, 473a: "Septima [sic--this seems likely to be a transcription error; from the context of the text Ubertino clearly means the sixth prerogative] prerogativa est indivisibilis ad christum sequella in sua vita perfecta: pro qua dicitur: *Et sequuntur agnum quocumque ierit* [Rv 14:4]."

are said to follow Him.[120] Because they always have a leader to guide them and because they always gaze into the eyes of His soul, they are directed towards His whole being and transformed into it.[121] Thus the Spirituals are transformed into Christ's being through the practice of evangelical poverty in the context of the *usus pauper*.

The seventh and final characteristic of the elect relates to their impact on the reform of the church. This characteristic also reveals Ubertino's strongest thoughts concerning the special role of the Spirituals and how they are responsible for the reform of the church. He starts by saying that the seventh characteristic sees the elect as embodying the universal primacy of a dedicated life and the foundation of the "new church."[122] The elect of this new church have been removed from all things, and more specifically from all men, in the sense that they are separated and redeemed from carnal human life; and the elect are also removed from the general corruption of humankind through the grace of Christ and His most precious blood.[123] The elect become totally transformed through the contemplation of the glory of God, and in the sacrifice of the Lamb; and, therefore, they are the first foundation of the third and final age of the world.[124] Regarding those who stand in the way of the elect, Ubertino refers to them in distinctly Spiritual Franciscan tones. The "religious" of his times are seen as duplicitous and crafty, holding out hypocritical crosses to the world.[125] Ubertino shows that the elect are devoid of such a price; when citing Rv 14:5 he says that they have no lies in their mouths and that they always carry Christ in

[120] *Arbor*, V, 9, 473a: "Quo ergo in pluribus et altioribus perfectionibus participant: vitam eius: ipsum magis sequuntur."

[121] *Arbor*, V, 9, 473a: "Et etiam quia ipsum semper habent ducem sui itineris: et ipsum semper speculantur ante oculos mentis sue: et in ipsum totum suum esse dirigunt et transformant."

[122] *Arbor*, V, 9, 473a: "Septima prerogativa est universalis primatus dedicationis sancte: et fundationis nove ecclesie: que in principalibus coniunctis predicto angelo est fundata."

[123] *Arbor*, V, 9, 473a: "Pro qua dicit: hi empti sunt ex omnibus: sive ex hominibus secundum litteram veriorem. . . . Et est sensus quod a carnali vita hominum: et a generali corruptione humani generis sunt per christi gratia et eius preciosissimum sanguinem singulariter segregati et empti."

[124] *Arbor*, V, 9, 473a: "Quia totaliter sunt transformati in contemplatione glorie dei: et in holocaustum crucifixionis agni: et sunt prima fundamenta tertii status mundi."

[125] *Arbor*, V, 9, 473b: "Alias etiam quia religiosi huius temporis sunt duplices et dolosi hypocritales cruces mundo pretedentes [sic]."

their mouths instead.[126] The Spirituals are blameless before the throne of God, and thus they appear without blame against the hypocrites who attack them.[127]

Ubertino's connection of the Spirituals to the events of Revelation continues when he turns to the mystical significance of Christ's two nights spent in the tomb.[128] He identifies the period between the defeat of the mystical Antichrist and the appearance of the great Antichrist with the Sabbath which intervened between the two nights that Christ spent in the tomb (Cf. Mk 15:46-16:5).[129] In order to complete his identification, Ubertino compares Christ's body in the tomb to the mystical body of Christ, understood by him as the body of evangelical men under attack by the mystical and great Antichrists in the sixth period. The first attack, that of the mystical Antichrist, is reminiscent of Christ's first night in the tomb, while the attack of the great Antichrist reminds one of Christ's second night in the tomb.[130] But Ubertino makes the point that interspersed between the two nights of agony was a time of peace, which he calls the Sabbath. So too in the sixth period was there a Sabbath, a time of peace reserved for the evangelical men, in whom the clarified poverty of Christ can overcome any hardship.[131] Just as Christ was resurrected, so too will the mystical body of Christ be resurrected in the sixth period. Ubertino describes the mystical body of Christ as the body of evangelical men, men joined to the soul of Christ in their faith and devotion.[132]

It is with Ubertino's discussion of the chronology of the seventh period that the place of the evangelical men in the end times is most fully revealed.

[126] *Arbor*, V, 9, 473b: "Ostendit eos ab hoc vitio alienos dicens *in ore eorum non inveniri mendacium* [Rv 14: 5]. . .semper in ore portantes iesum."

[127] *Arbor*, V, 9, 473b: "*Sine macula enim sunt ante thronum dei* [Rv 14:5]. . . et sine macula apparere contra hypocritas qui eos impugnant."

[128] *Arbor*, V, 10, 473b: "Triumphator mortis iesus cuius proprium est super occasum ascendere: et in se et in membris suis de mortis triumphare conflictu: sicut in proprio corpe duabus noctibus iacuit in sepulchro."

[129] A general study of the notion of the Antichrist in the Middle Ages may be found in Richard Emmerson, *Antichrist in the Middle Ages* (Seattle, 1981); for the idea of the double Antichrist in the Middle Ages, see Bernard McGinn, *The Calabrian Abbot: Joachim of Fiore in the History of Western Thought* (New York, 1985), pp. 111 and 121 n.63; the idea of the double Antichrist in Olivi's *Lectura super apocalypsim* is treated in Burr, *Olivi's Peaceable Kingdom*, pp. 132-162.

[130] *Arbor*, V, 10, 473b: "Sic in corpore suo mistico quasi duabus noctibus videtur subiacere mortis imperio: dum sub mistico antichristo quasi sub prima nocte: et postmodum sub aperto quasi sub secunda nocte."

[131] *Arbor*, V, 10, 473b: "Hec sunt due noctes horrende: antichristus misticus et apertus: in quorum medio evangelicis viris relinquitur sabbatismus: in quo christi iesu clarificata paupertas illius possit superare insultus."

[132] *Arbor*, V, 10, 474a:. "Ab hac morte resurgens iesus in spiritu suo tamquam principali malitia magnum cantari alleluia. . . . totum corpus populi in orbe dispersi cum principalibus militibus: qui sunt quasi anima mistici iesu in fide et devotione iungentur."

After the defeat of the great Antichrist, an angel descends from heaven, depicted in Rv 18:1. This angel has a great authority which brightens the earth.[133] Ubertino identifies this angel with a great pope who will put down the "carnal church" (the whore of Babylon) and lead the movement for the reform of the church.[134] Ubertino thinks that those who will receive the benefits of the seventh period, the evangelical poor, are described by Rv 19:17, which relates an angel calling the flock to the great supper of God. In reality, Ubertino thinks they are the highest and most clear contemplative teachers of the time.[135] Finally, they may be found in the camp of the saints mentioned in Rv 20:9. They are a spiritual body and are the primary warriors of the seventh period. As such, they will reside in the "beloved city" of the New Jerusalem, which Ubertino calls the church in general.[136]

The appearance of the New Jerusalem, wherein the elect will reside, marks the culmination of history. To illustrate the significance of this idea, Ubertino explains both the coming of the New Jerusalem and its characteristics. He describes the future city of the elect as rising from the earth and flying towards the heavens bedecked with the poverty of Christ and crucified in His love.[137] The foundation of this city is Christ and His apostles, with the faith of the church resting on His foundation.[138] God's place in the city is detailed in Rv 21:3. In analyzing this verse, which says that "The home of God is among men, and he dwells with them," Ubertino singles out three elements: church, tabernacle, and dwelling with them. Ubertino contends that these three elements suggest three grades or levels of union. The church designates the unity of the city reflected in the groups of the spiritual poor. The tabernacle represents

[133] *Arbor*, V, 10, 476b: "Unde xviii apocalypsim: post bellum antichristi tam mistici qua aperti: dicitur *post hec vidi alium angelum descendentem de celo habentem potestatem magnam: et terra illuminata est a gloria eius* [Rv 18:1]."

[134] *Arbor*, V, 11, 476b: "Et forte iste angelus erit idem summus pontifex de quo supra est dictum vel alius eius perfectionis successor;" *Arbor*, V, 11, 477a: "Tunc autem singulariter tria predicabuntur scilicet iudicium meretricis et omnium habentium characterem bestie et exhortatio ad fugam sui consortii et sequele: et postea invitatio nove sponse."

[135] *Arbor*, V, 11, 477b: "Et status ille figuratus est in angelo illo de quo dicitur Apocalypsim xix[:17]. *Vidi* ait *unum angelum stantem in sole: et clamavit voce magna omnibus avibus que volabant per medium celi. Venite congregamini ad cenam dei magnam.* Iste designat altissimos et preclarissimos contemplativos doctores illius temporis."

[136] *Arbor*, V, 11, 477b: "Possunt etiam merito per *castra sanctorum* [Rv 20:9] intelligi spiritualia collegia evangelicorum pauperum: qui usque ad finem erunt principales milites huius status. Per *civitatem* vero *delectam* [Rv 20:9] ecclesia generalis."

[137] *Arbor*, V, 12, 478b: "Quia in hac tota futura civitas electorum tertii status quasi seraphicatur que scilicet apperebit [sic] ab omni terrenitate levata: et volabit in celum altissime vite christi simul paupercula et amoris in cendio crucifixa."

[138] *Arbor*, V, 12, 479a: "Fundationem autem huius civitatis attribuit christo sive agno: et apostolis eius quia tota fides ecclesie huic fundamento innititur."

Christ's indwelling as in a family. Dwelling with them means that He will be identified with them but will adapt Himself to each individual.[139]

While Ubertino does go into great detail to analyze the physical components of the New Jerusalem, the primary focus here is the place of poverty and how it is related to the Spiritual Franciscan practice of poverty. To begin, the third age, contemporary with the seventh period of church history, is built upon the highest poverty, a poverty which will triumph over all of its attackers.[140] Ubertino figuratively describes the place of poverty in the city in terms of the streets of gold mentioned in Rv 21:21. For him, the streets signify the community of highest poverty, which demands that all property be held communally and indivisibly.[141] The example for the city's populace is provided by the evangelical men, upon whom indeed the streets of the city are built.[142] The evangelical men will live by a vow of poverty which includes the perfect expropriation and most poor use of things, based on the idea of imitating Christ.[143] The whole church, therefore, will be united in the practice of the poverty of the Spirituals.[144] As a result, Ubertino concludes that the true followers of Francis' *Rule* and *Testament* will be vindicated in their long struggle against the forces of evil. Their victory will end in the practice of the highest poverty.[145] Finally, the highest poverty of the Spirituals will lead all

[139] *Arbor*, V, 12, 478b: "Nec descendit de celo propter causas superius sepe dicans. Singulariter in hac *est dei tabernaculum cum hominibus et habitat in eis* [Rv 21:3]. Nota hec tria: civitatem: tabernaculum: et habitare in eis: hi sunt gradus unionis in generali: ecclesia erit quasi unitas civitatis in collegiis spirtualium pauperum: erit iesus in tabernaculo eodem quasi in eadem familia. In perfectissimis vero erit quasi idem cum eis: et hoc cum dicitur. Et habitabit in eis: licet omnia singulis adaptentur."

[140] *Arbor*, V, 12, 481a: "Quis sicut secundi status generalis fuit firmitas in fide dei humanati Iesu. Sic et hic tertius erit firmatus in altitudine paupertatis Iesu: que paupertas tunc triumphabit super omnes suos impugnatores."

[141] *Arbor*, V, 12, 480b-481a: "De *platea autem civitatis* singulariter dicitur: quod *erat aurum mundum: tanquam vitrum perlucidam* [Rv 21:21]. . . sic per plateam civitatis significatur communitas altissime paupertatis. . .quia contemplationi aperta: nec isti vel illi instar domorum appropriata: sed omnibus communis et indivisa."

[142] *Arbor*, V, 12, 481a: "Quia statim viris evangelicis hec platea fundabitur."

[143] *Arbor*, V, 12, 481a: "Quia nullus sinetur dubitare: quin perfectam expropriatio et pauperrimus usus rerum ex ardore imitationis iesu sit ei clarissime assimillari."

[144] *Arbor*, V, 12, 481a: "Pro tota vero ecclesia illius temporis erit horum participium: ut sit ad modum auri solida preciosa et fulgida: et sine duplicitate et fraudulentia ad modum vitri patula: ac per hoc mutua charitate multum erunt unita corda: et sibi invicem clara. In ecclesia vero beatorum omnia omnibus erunt mutuo pura et aperta."

[145] *Arbor*, V, 12, 478b: "Ac per hoc principales horum preliorum victores sunt pauperes evangelici contra utramque funestam bestiam strenue dimicantes: et idcirco in paupertatis altissime vero cultu horum preliorum victoria terminatur."

within the city to a communal life, as a result of which all people may enjoy the peace of conscience and the contemplation of the heavens.[146]

Ubertino's call for the reform of the church is not a program of reform in the strictest sense; he presents no concrete set of actions which will provide for a return to the church's roots. Instead, he exhibits his understanding of reform in terms of Franciscan poverty; and he interprets that poverty in the context of his reading of church history. For him, the predetermined course of history will produce a church that in the end will be reformed. The reform is almost inevitable, and yet it mandates the presence of Franciscan poverty. In order to explain the necessity of Franciscan poverty, he associates it with the poverty which Christ and His apostles founded and practiced. Their poor ways were subsequently lost to the church, requiring a renewal if history was to be fulfilled. This renewal was begun by Francis and his first followers and would help prepare the church for the conclusion of history. But Francis' practice was itself weakened and finally lost to both the greater part of the order and to the church after the saint's death. At the same time, the end of history continued its approach. Thus Ubertino sees an urgent apocalyptic need for a renewed emphasis on the proper practice of Franciscan poverty. He witnesses in the poverty of the Spirituals a means for facilitating that renewed emphasis. It was they who remained true to Francis' wishes, and it would be they who would find a special place in the New Jerusalem. Their special place is proven by their relationship to the elect depicted in Revelation, people who will own nothing and use very little. Their practice of the evangelical poverty of Christ and Francis will allow them to serve as examples for all the righteous who will eventually live in the New Jerusalem and, therefore, fulfill the prophecies. History will be made complete through the close relationship of the Spirituals to God, as expressed by their practice of poverty and predicted in Revelation.

[146] *Arbor*, V, 12, 485a: "In hac ergo civitate requietionis perfecte in altissima paupertate et evangelica perfectione firmata: fac nos interim pie iesu requiescere: et ab insidiis diaboli seducentis nos misericorditer protege: ut securi possimus tremendum iudicium in tranquilla pace conscientie et contemplationis celice expectare."

MILES SPIRITUS SANCTI: THE APOCALYPTIC DIMENSION OF COLA DI RIENZO'S REFORM IDEOLOGY

Thomas C. Giangreco

For the few short months between May and December 1347, Rome was under the control of the revolutionary government of the self-styled tribune Cola di Rienzo (1313-1354). This commoner had risen from obscurity to overthrow the power of the Roman barons and attempted to restore peace, prosperity, and order to a city which, since the departure of the papacy to Avignon in 1305, had fallen into anarchy and economic ruin. His bold plan for reform included civic, economic, political, and apocalyptic dimensions. Ultimately, Cola hoped to restore the economic life of the city, break the destructive power of the Roman aristocracy, and create a federation of the Italian city-republics under Roman leadership. These reform ideas and goals are contained in the *Vita di Cola di Rienzo*[1] as well as in his substantial body of correspondence.[2] Taken together, these two texts represent the main sources of information regarding Cola's life and thought.

The salient events in the life and career of Cola di Rienzo are well known, so only a brief sketch will be provided here. The future tribune was born to humble parents in the Regola district of Rome in either April or May of 1313. His father, Lorenzo, was a tavern keeper and his mother, Madalena, was a washerwoman. At an early age he was sent away to Anagni to be educated. By whom is unknown, and Cola disappears from the record until 1343. The *Vita* is silent about this period in his life. What is clear is that he received training in

[1] The following account of the life and career of Cola di Rienzo is based on the material in *La Vita di Cola di Rienzo.* The *Vita* is part of an anonymous fourteenth century chronicle known as the *Historiae romanae fragmenta,* but since its initial publication in 1624, the *Vita* has been presented as an integral work. The text of the *Vita* used here is Anonimo Romano, *Chronica: Vita di Cola di Rienzo* [hereafter *Vita*], ed. Ettore Mazzali (Milano, 1991). For an English translation of the *Vita,* see *The Life of Cola di Rienzo,* trans. John Wright (Toronto, 1975). References to specific portions of this text have been made where clarification seemed to be in order. References to sources other than the *Vita* have also been noted. While the *Vita* is the most important primary source account of the life of Cola di Rienzo, there are also a number of important secondary works. Some of the most significant biographical studies include: Jean Antoine du Cerceau, *La conjuration de Nicholas Gabrini dit de Rienzi tyran de Rome en 1347* (Paris, 1733); Felix Papencordt, *Cola di Rienzo und seine Zeit* (Hamburg, 1841); Conrad Burdach, *Rienzo und die geistige Wandlung seiner Zeit* (Berlin, 1912); Gabrielle D'Annunzio, *Vite di uomini illustri e di uomini oscuri: La vita di Cola di Rienzo* (Milano, 1913); Paul Piur, *Cola di Rienzo: Darstellung seines Lebens und seines Geistes* (Wien, 1931); Victor Fleischer, *Rienzo: The Rise and Fall of a Dictator* (London, 1948).

[2] The critical edition of Cola's correspondence can be found in *Briefwechsel des Cola di Rienzo* [hereafter *Briefwechsel*], ed. Conrad Burdach and Paul Piur (Berlin, 1912). The Burdach and Piur edition includes not only Cola's letters, but also all the letters written to and concerning him. Their critical edition contains all the documents relevant to Cola's life and career other than the *Vita* which are currently extant. A less comprehensive edition of Cola's letters can be found in *Epistolario di Cola di Rienzo* [hereafter *Epistolario*], ed. Annibale Gabrielli (Roma, 1890; reprint Torino, 1966).

the Latin classics. Cola became known as a scholar and an orator. He was known to wander around the city translating the old Latin inscriptions on the monuments and was often heard to exclaim "Where are those good Romans? Where is their high justice? If only I could live in such times!"[3]

Cola first played a role in Roman politics when in 1343 he was sent as an envoy of the revolutionary government of the "Thirteen Good Men" to Avignon to announce the takeover of the city by the people in a short-lived coup. It was on this occasion that he spoke before Pope Clement VI and Petrarch, whose admiration he won, and Cardinal Colonna, whom he upset sufficiently to find himself destitute on the streets of Avignon. He was only saved by the intervention of Petrarch, who arranged for him to become a papal notary.

On his return to Rome, Cola was made an object of scorn by the great nobles, who would invite him to dinner to hear his verbal attacks on them only to mock Cola afterwards. The noble families did not take Cola seriously until it was too late. On the night of May 19, 1347, Cola gathered his followers together, and after hearing thirty masses of the Holy Spirit, led the people to the capitol under the banners of liberty, peace, justice, and concord. He seized control of the government without opposition or bloodshed.

Once in power, Cola set out to reform the city and set up a civic administration. He formally took the title of tribune in a lavish coronation ceremony on August 15, 1347. It was at this time that Clement VI began to grow suspicious of Cola, whose revolution he had initially favored. In addition, the people were beginning to turn against him as well because of the increasing extravagance and pomp of his public spectacles. The tribune began using more and more elaborate titles in his correspondence, referring to himself as "the severe and clement" and as the "August Tribune," and describing himself as a "white-robed knight of the Holy Spirit," "the liberator of the city," "the zealot of Italy," and "lover of the world."[4]

The step which brought about his fall, however, was his imprisonment of the great nobles. His original intention was to kill them, but at the last moment he relented. Having been given this second chance, they united and attacked Rome on November 19, 1347. The resulting battle at the San Lorenzo gate of the city ended in defeat for the nobles, but it proved to be a phyrric victory for Cola. Faced with opposition from the barons, the church (he was excommunicated in December of 1347), and the people whom he had once led, Cola abdicated on December 15, 1347, and fled into exile into the hills of central Italy.

It was during this period of exile that Cola first came into direct contact with the Fraticelli, who convinced the fallen tribune of his role in the coming apocalypse. He took them seriously enough to venture to the court of the

[3] *Vita,* p. 191, "Deh como spesso diceva: Dove sono questi buoni romani? Dove ène loro summa iustizia? Pòterame trovare in tiempo che questi fussino!"

[4] *Briefwechsel,* p. 101: "Nos candidatus Spiritus Sancti miles, Nicolaus Seuerus et Clemens, liberator Vrbis. zelator Ytalie, amator orbis et Tribunus Augustus..."

Emperor Charles IV at Prague in 1350. From there he was sent by the emperor to Avignon to defend himself before the pope. Clement VI, who had plans to execute Cola, died however, and was replaced by Innocent VI. The new pope granted Cola the title of senator and sent him back to Rome as papal legate to restore order to the city. He returned to Rome on August 1, 1354. However, this second reign was to be even shorter than the first. Outraged by his cruelty, an angry mob dragged Cola out into the street and killed him on October 8, 1354. His body was strung up by its heels for all of his former followers to see, thus ending the short but stormy political career of this apocalyptic visionary and revolutionary leader.

In addition to the practical attempts at political and economic reform made by Cola, his ideology also included a strong element of apocalypticism. This esoteric aspect of Cola's thought colored all of his actions throughout his career. Although overshadowed by the fast pace of events in 1347, apocalyptic ideas were never far from the surface, as can be seen from the numerous references to the Holy Spirit and from the symbolic paintings employed by Cola to communicate his political ideas. While in exile, Cola found refuge among the Fraticelli, who served to heighten and focus his apocalyptic thought. In the last stages of his career, he became convinced that he was helping to bring about a radical apocalyptic renewal of the world.

The nature and extent of Cola's apocalypticism has been the subject of some controversy. However, if one studies the manifestations of Cola's apocalyptic thought throughout his career, one finds a basic consistency to his apocalyptic ideology, the differences being of emphasis rather than of content. While attempting to restore the political and economic life of Rome, Cola saw himself not so much as a populist political leader but rather as the agent of the Holy Spirit, who was helping to usher in a new age of history. Viewed in this light, Cola's reform ideology combines the temporal with the spiritual and the practical with the esoteric. Not all scholars agree that an apocalyptic dimension was consistently present in Cola's thought. The difference in tone between Cola's early and later correspondence can be used to support the argument that Cola only began to manifest apocalyptic ideas after 1347. Such an argument ignores Cola's lifelong devotion to the Holy Spirit and the content of his allegorical paintings, but the obvious difference between Cola's letters of 1347 and those which followed presents a troublesome problem.

Many vexing questions associated with this issue need to be addressed. Among them are: What constitutes apocalyptic reform? When did Cola's thought become apocalyptic? How can the change in the tone of Cola's correspondence be reconciled with a consistent apocalypticism? Does Cola's thought display evidence of being influenced, either directly or indirectly, by the ideas of Joachim of Fiore? What role did the Fraticelli play in the development of Cola's thought? How does Cola's apocalypticism relate to his reform thought as a whole? Such questions need to be answered regarding this difficult issue if a dimension of central importance in Cola's thought is to be properly understood and the conflict surrounding it resolved.

Apocalypticism is often viewed as one of the most eccentric and revolutionary aspects of medieval reform thought; but, far from being a fringe element of Christian theology, ideas of apocalyptic reform were an integral part of the Judeo-Christian tradition since Old Testament times.[5] In its simplest form, apocalypticism is the divine revelation or prophecy of the imminent violent destruction of the world and the salvation of the righteous. Such a concept is a natural outgrowth of a linear view of history; if history has a definite beginning it must therefore have an ending or final revelation of God's universal plan. Apocalyptic reform was the anticipation of this culmination of history, which would give structure and meaning to the whole of time.[6]

Early Christian apocalyptic is best represented by the Book of Revelation, which describes the events of the last days and symbolically chronicles the historical signposts which would herald the second coming and the last judgment. This text became the basic scriptural foundation for subsequent Christian apocalyptic literature. Produced in an environment of hostile opposition to the new faith from both Jews and Romans, the Book of Revelation expressed the hope for the future triumph of the faithful. For these early Christians, this future triumph at the end of history was assumed to be close at hand, and when it became increasingly apparent that the second coming was not imminent, a re-evaluation was necessary. The expected end was put off to an undetermined future date while characters such as the Antichrist, the angelic pope, and the Last World Emperor were added to the story over the centuries. In addition, an outline of the apocalyptic drama took shape; and, while individual writers might differ on the details of the end the history, they held to the basic story: at some point in the future, a great crisis would occur, during which the Antichrist would lead the forces of darkness over the world until defeated by the forces of light, who would then inaugurate one thousand years of peace and prosperity for the faithful until the Second Coming and the Last Judgment brought an end to the world.

With the skeleton of a story and the basic *dramatis personae* in place, it was left to individual authors to flesh out the details in the light of their own times and circumstances throughout the Middle Ages. A plethora of apocalyptic texts of varying qualities exist for this period, each with its own candidates for the starring roles in the drama, reflecting the anxieties and threats facing each era. But, for our present purposes the writer whose ideas were of the greatest significance was the Abbot Joachim of Fiore, perhaps the most famous

[5] The volume of material on the subject of apocalypticism is enormous. A few of the many works available concerning this subject on which the following discussion is based are Norman Cohn, *The Pursuit of the Millennium* (New York, 1970); Bernard McGinn, *Apocalyptic Spirituality* (New York, 1979); idem, *Visions of the End* (New York, 1979); Wilhelm Bousset, *The Antichrist Legend* (London, 1896); Rudolf Bultmann, *History and Eschatology: The Presence of Eternity* (New York, 1962); Mircea Eliade, *Cosmos and History: The Myth of the Eternal Return* (New York, 1959); Walter Schmithals, *The Apocalyptic Movement: Introduction and Interpretation* (Nashville, 1975); David Russell, *Apocalyptic Ancient and Modern* (Philadelphia, 1978); idem, *The Method and Message of Jewish Apocalyptic: 200 B.C. - 100 A.D.* (Philadelphia, 1964).

[6] McGinn, *Apocalyptic Spirituality,* pp. 4-5.

apocalyptic writer in history. It was Joachite and Pseudo-Joachite ideas which were of enormous influence in the fourteenth century and which are evident in the thoughts of many figures of this period, not least of all Cola di Rienzo. It is therefore necessary to understand the basic ideas of Joachim of Fiore in order to understand and put into context many of Cola's reform ideas.

Joachim of Fiore (1135-1202), born in the town of Celico in Calabria, spent almost all of his adult years in the quiet seclusion of the monastic life.[7] After traveling to Constantinople, Syria, and Palestine he entered the Cistercian monastery in Curazzo in 1159 and became Abbot of that house in 1167. He remained in the Cistercian order until 1188, when he left to establish the monastery of San Giovanni in Fiore and founded the Florensian order. He remained at San Giovanni until his death in 1202. Despite this seemingly ordinary life, Joachim possessed an extraordinary reputation for piety, mysticism, and prophecy during his lifetime and exerted a profound influence after his death.

In his writings Joachim produced a progressive, evolutionary, and developmental philosophy of history based on the Holy Trinity. Joachim viewed all history as the history of salvation, in which God's plan is progressively worked out in accordance with a trinitarian structure. He divided all human history into three periods: the age of the Father, corresponding to the time of the Old Testament; the age of the Son, corresponding to the New Testament; and the age of the Holy Spirit, which was the future third age yet to come and which would be the age of reform. Each of these three ages was a progressive revelation and realization of the Trinity in history; a manifestation of the timeless within the temporal. In Joachim's thought, history will end when the Trinity has been fully realized and an absolute perfection comes into being at the end of time. Rather than attempting to reform the present according to the model of an idealized past "golden age," Joachim's apocalyptic reform is the final establishment of perfection itself, the full achievement of spiritual enlightenment which would take place when the Trinity was fully realized in history at the end of the third and final age. Joachim viewed the three ages as progressive steps on the road to spiritual enlightenment, with each stage bringing humanity a further revelation of God's plan.

Joachim saw the world in which he lived as being near the end of the second age and on the verge of the advent of the third and final one, which he calculated would begin in 1260. The transition to the third age would be marked by what Joachim called a "new leader" of the Church, who would be the initiator of the age of the Holy Spirit. He would be helped in leading the Church into the

[7] A great deal of material exists concerning the life, thought, and influence of Joachim of Fiore; some of the more important works on the subject are Bernard McGinn, "Joachim and the Sibyl," *Citeaux* 34 (1973): 97-138; idem, "The Abbot and the Doctors: Scholastic Reactions to the Radical Eschatology of Joachim of Fiore," *Church History* 40 (1971): 30-47; idem, *The Calabrian Abbot* (New York, 1986); E. Randolph Daniel, "Apocalyptic Conversion: The Joachite Alternative to the Crusade," *Traditio* 25 (1969): 127-154; Marjorie Reeves, *The Influence of Prophecy in the Later Middle Ages: A Study of Joachimism* (Oxford, 1969); idem, *Joachim of Fiore and the Prophetic Future* (London, 1976).

new age by a group of "spiritual men". This third age would be marked by a new spiritual understanding and enlightenment, as well as by institutional supremacy brought about by the return of the eastern churches, the destruction of Islam, and the conversion of the Tartars and the Jews. The Church would thus enjoy both a spiritual and a temporal harmony and ascendancy.

Although the primary concern of Joachim was to construct a trinitarian theology of history, his ideas lent themselves well to political applications. Even after 1260 passed without incident, many continued to put forward candidates for the roles of "new leader" and "spiritual men." In the thirteenth and fourteenth centuries diverse groups ranging from the mendicant friars to the flagellants could claim to be the "spiritual men" written about by Joachim. The Franciscans and the Dominicans, however, became increasingly associated with Joachim's two orders. Radical offshoots such as the Franciscan Spirituals and the Fraticelli were even more likely to view themselves in this manner, especially since they were antagonistic to the institutional Church. Groups of flagellants began to appear in 1260, to coincide with the calculated beginning of the third age. They continued on into the fourteenth century, doing public penance and calling for the people to prepare for the imminent crisis. The chaos and disorders of the fourteenth century were easily interpreted by such a group in Joachite terms, since Joachim himself had said that chaos and decline would signal the transition from one age to the next.

Pseudo-Joachite texts also began to appear, whose authors took Joachim's theology further and in directions Joachim himself never intended.[8] These works attempted to make predictions about the transition to the new age and placed contemporary figures in the major roles of the eschatological drama. The Emperor Frederick II was alternately viewed as both the heroic "Last World Emperor" and as the Antichrist, depending on the partisanship of the author. Other political figures, including Cola di Rienzo, could and did find supporting roles for themselves to play in helping to usher in the new age. As for the date of 1260 for the beginning of the third age, that was easily revised by the simple means of modifying Joachim's calculations.

It is understandable how and why Joachim's work could have such far reaching influence. His ideas were compelling, especially in the light of the cataclysms of the fourteenth century. At the same time they were vague enough to lend themselves to modification. Both cynical politicians and true believers could find uses for Joachite and Pseudo-Joachite prophecies to buttress their positions, attack their enemies, or give direction to their actions.

Cola di Rienzo, as a product of the calamities of the fourteenth century, was hardly exceptional or unique in his use of Joachite ideas and he must be numbered among the disciples of Joachimism.[9] From early on in his career,

[8] For a discussion of Pseudo-Joachite texts and ideas, see McGinn, *Visions of the End,* pp. 145-148, 234-238; idem, *Apocalyptic Spirituality,* pp. 149-181.

[9] Interestingly enough, Giovanni di Vico, who was perhaps Cola's staunchest enemy, was also a Joachite, even to the extent of giving his protection to the heretical Fraticelli; see Wright, *Life of Cola di Rienzo,* p. 20.

subtle signs of Joachite influences are discernible in his thought. Much of his elaborate symbolic imagery shows Joachite themes. Even though Cola's Joachimism became even more obvious in his later years, from the beginning apocalypticism was at the heart of his thought and exercised a profound impact on his actions and reform ideology.

During the period between his embassy to Avignon in 1343 and his seizure of power in 1347, one of the favorite methods by which Cola communicated his message to the Roman people was by means of allegorical paintings. A close examination of these paintings reveals apocalyptic themes and Joachite references. Since these allegorical paintings were produced prior to Cola's meeting with the Fraticelli of Monte Maiella, they argue for the consistency of Cola's apocalyptic thought and against the notion that Cola's early and later reform thought are radically different.

The earliest of the allegorical paintings deals mainly with the condition of "widowed Rome" in the mid-fourteenth century and is essentially a call for civic reform.[10] However, on closer examination, there is an apocalyptic undercurrent to the allegory and a striking similarity in imagery to that found in the Old Testament Book of Daniel. In this picture, which Cola had painted on the wall of the Campidoglio, Rome, personified as a black-robed widow, is shown in a rudderless ship being tossed by the sea, praying for salvation. Below the surface of the water are the wrecks of four other ships, masts broken and also rudderless. The four are labeled as Babylon, Carthage, Troy, and Jerusalem, with the inscription reading, "Because of injustice these cities were endangered and fell."[11] Flanking the ship were three islands, one inhabited by a woman representing Italy and the other with four women personifying the four cardinal virtues, while on a smaller island a white-robed woman described as Christian faith laments that without Rome she will have no place to stand. In the sky above were four different groups of animals blowing the winds which were causing the ship to founder. The animals represented the people whom Cola saw as destroying Rome, namely, the barons, their followers, the government officials, and the common criminals. Above all was the Divine Majesty, come in judgment, with two swords coming out of his mouth and flanked by Saints Peter and Paul.

The point of this picture is clear: Rome is being tormented from within and is in danger of being destroyed as were Babylon, Carthage, Troy, and Jerusalem before her. Should this be allowed to happen, a terrible judgment must surely follow, since it is not just the city that is threatened, but Italy, the Christian faith, and the virtues as well. Rome is depicted as the bulwark against chaos and the foundation of Italy and the Christian faith. Without the eternal city, both are in danger of falling in a cataclysmic disaster.

Even more significant, however, are the references to four preceding states, which fell due to their own injustice. In the Book of Daniel, the prophet Daniel relates a dream in which he saw the four winds stirring the sea, out of which came four beasts which represented earthly kings: a lion, a bear, a leopard,

[10] The painting is described in the *Vita,* pp. 192-193.

[11] *Vita,* p. 192: "Queste citati per la iniustizia pericolaro e vennero meno."

and a ten-horned monster.[12] The final beast was destroyed by the Son of Man, who then would establish an everlasting kingdom. In a subsequent vision, Daniel describes an allegory which speaks of a progression of four kingdoms, the Median, the Persian, the Greek, and an unnamed future empire which will challenge the Prince of Princes.[13] All of these kingdoms, despite their power, will ultimately perish because of their own iniquities and be succeeded by the Son of Man, who will come in judgment and establish the final heavenly kingdom which will be eternal.

While the prophecies of Daniel and the allegories of Cola are not without substantial differences in content, what is striking is the similarity in imagery, particularly the four unjust fallen predecessors and the looming Last Judgment. Although the particulars of the two messages differ, the allegorical manner by which the ideas are communicated and the imagery used to express these ideas are quite alike. Granted, Daniel and Cola were saying different things in response to different circumstances but the apocalyptic language they used was very similar.

Confirmation of the apocalyptic nature of Cola's early allegorical images can be found in the second picture which Cola had painted on the wall of the church of Sant'Angelo in Pescheria.[14] This painting depicted a fire consuming the common people and an old woman, who was burned over two-thirds of her body. To the right was a church, out of which came an angel dressed in white with a red cloak, fully armed and carrying a sword. The angel, acting on the commands of Saints Peter and Paul, was pulling the old woman from the fire. In the sky above were falcons, which were being driven into the fire by a dove while a sparrow took a wreath of myrtle from the dove and crowned the old woman. Below the picture was written the caption, "The time of justice is coming, and you await the time."[15]

Again the message concerns the sorry state of Rome. The Roman people and "widowed Rome" herself are being destroyed in the fire while birds of prey fly overhead. The falcons represent the barons, who are destroying the city and its people. The white-robed angel is Cola himself, carrying out his divine orders to save the city. What is most notable however, is the presence of the dove, symbol of the Holy Spirit. The dove serves a dual function: first, to rout and destroy the barons, and second, to bring the crown from heaven with which Rome would be adorned. The dove, of course, was the symbol of the Holy Spirit and, therefore, represented the coming third age of history in the thought of Joachim of Fiore. Cola's painting portrays the Holy Spirit as the liberating force, under whose guidance he will save Rome and restore it to greatness, inaugurating a new age of peace and prosperity. Cola's references to the Holy Spirit indicate a Joachite dimension to his reform ideology. The apocalyptic

[12] Dn 7:1-28.

[13] Dn 8:1-27.

[14] The painting is described in the *Vita,* pp. 196-197.

[15] *Vita,* p. 196: "Veo lo tiempo della granne iustizia eià taci fi' allo tiempo."

aspect of Cola's thought is mingled here with ideas of civic reform, but it is nevertheless clearly present.

The Holy Spirit also figures in a picture found on the walls of the church of Santa Maria Maddalena which was painted after Cola fell from power in December, 1347 but before his exile among the Fraticelli.[16] It was produced while Cola was in Castel Sant'Angelo and represented a vain attempt to rekindle popular support. This painting was the least elaborate of the three, depicting again an armed angel wearing the arms of Rome and carrying a cross over which flew a dove. Underneath the angel's feet were a trampled asp, basilisk, lion, and dragon. Once again Cola himself was represented by the armed angel, a heavenly knight sent by the Holy Spirit to defend Rome and defeat her enemies. While not as rich in imagery as the previous two paintings, this one serves to further demonstrate Cola's devotion to the Holy Spirit. The Holy Spirit occupies a more prominent part of Cola's thought than either the Father or the Son, reinforcing the claim that Cola was a consistent disciple of the apocalyptic theology of Joachim. Cola arguably saw himself as a player in the apocalyptic drama, who would, by his deeds, help usher in the third and final age of history, that of the Holy Spirit.

Such a claim would appear to be tenuous if the only evidence were these three highly symbolic allegorical paintings. However, if one examines the writings of and actions taken by Cola during the tribunate, one sees that devotion to the Holy Spirit was very much in evidence in his words and deeds. The vivid references to the Holy Spirit that figure prominently in Cola's public statements and actions effectively counter the argument that Joachite ideas only entered Cola's thought after his encounter with the Fraticelli following the fall of the tribunate. When taken in conjunction with the allegorical paintings, they confirm the consistent presence of Joachite apocalyptic influences in Cola's reform ideology throughout his life.

As early as 1343, Cola makes reference to the role played by the Holy Spirit in his plans for the restoration of Rome. Writing from Avignon to announce to the Romans the papal proclamation of the Jubilee, Cola expressed his belief that the pope and cardinals were acting in accord with the "divine will of the Holy Spirit" in granting the request of the ambassadors.[17] Admittedly, this is only a brief reference, but it is illustrative of the basic consistency in Cola's thought regarding the influence of Joachite apocalypticism from the earliest period of his public life.

[16] This painting is described in the *Vita,* p. 262.

[17] *Briefwechsel,* p. 6: "Etenim post honorabilis ambaxiate vestre supplicacionem non humano, verum diuino consilio conformatam, prehabita deliberacione matura dominorum cardinalium omniumque Romane curie prelatorum, diuersis ac variis linguis in diuinam consonantibus voluntatem Spiritus Sancti, oracionibus ac missis per vniuersas Auinionenses ecclesias celebratis, die XXVII mensis huius in magna frequencia populi, quasi Romani exercitus, vocem gracie expactantis, solempnissimo, ymmo angelico premisso sermone in voce salutis et leticie decreto apostolico ad futurum quinquagesimum et sic deinceps perpetuo annum promulgauit et reddidit iubileum."

The allusions to the role played by the Holy Spirit in Cola's revolutionary plans become even more pronounced in his writings and actions of 1347. In that year he deliberately chose the day of Pentecost for the insurrection which brought him to power and on the eve of the coup went to the length of hearing thirty masses of the Holy Spirit in the church of Sant'Angelo in Pescheria.[18] In announcing to the world his seizure of power, he was very clear in crediting the "inspiration of the Holy Spirit" for his achievement.[19] Following his coronation and investiture as a knight, Cola began to refer to himself as the "white-robed knight of the Holy Spirit."[20] When summoning the rival imperial candidates and the German electors to Rome, Cola commanded them to appear before him on the next Pentecost.[21] At his coronation ceremony, Cola had himself crowned with six silver crowns which were presented to Cola along with a scepter by the prior of the Holy Spirit in Saxia, saying, "August Tribune, receive the gifts of the Holy Spirit and the spiritual crown with this crown and scepter."[22]

In addition to Cola's letters, the *Vita* records examples of Cola's devotion to the Holy Spirit. When riding through the streets of Rome at the head of a procession, Cola carried a silver mace topped with a gold cross, on which was inscribed "GOD" and "HOLY SPIRIT." Over Cola's head a white standard was held, on which was a golden sun surrounded by silver stars and which was topped by a silver dove carrying an olive branch in its mouth.[23] Before his battle with the barons, in which Cola defeated the Colonna forces at the gates of Rome, Cola gave his men the watchword "knights of the Holy Spirit."[24]

[18] *Vita*, p. 198.

[19] *Briefwechsel*, pp. 17-18: "Annunciamus vobis ad gaudium donum Spiritus Sancti, quod pius pater et dominus noster Ihesus Christus in hac veneranda die festiuitatis pasche Penthecostes per inspiracionem Spiritus sancti huic sancte Vrbi et populo eius ac vobis et omnibus fidelibus populis Christi, qui membra eius consistitis, dignatus est misericorditer elargiri."

[20] This title appears in many letters of 1347; for one example of Cola's use of this title, see *Briefwechsel*, p. 117: "Candidatus Spiritus Sancti miles...."

[21] *Briefwechsel*, pp. 103-104: "...ad festum pasche Pentecostes proxime futurum, quod infra dictum terminum in ipsa alma Vrbe et sacrosancta Lateranensi ecclesia coram nobis et aliis officialibus domini nostri pape et Romani populi debeant cum coram iuribus comparere; alioquin a dicto termino in antea procedemus secundum quod de iure fuerit et Spiritus Sancti gracia ministrabit."

[22] The coronation is not mentioned in the *Vita*, but the program of the coronation is included in an appendix to the Gabrielli edition of Cola's letters. See *Epistolario*, p. 246: "Sexta corona fuit argentea, et sceptrum; fuerunt presentata per priorem Sancti Spiritus in Saxia, dicentem: tribune auguste, suscipe dona Spiritus Sancti cum corona et sceptro et spiritualiem coronam."

[23] *Vita*, p. 207.

[24] *Vita*, p. 231: "Spirito Santo cavalieri."

Such examples of Cola's great devotion to the Holy Spirit are manifold and to chronicle every example would require countless pages. Virtually all of Cola's correspondence from this period make at least some reference to the grace, gifts, or inspiration of the Holy Spirit. Such references are a defining characteristic of Cola's writings, and their sheer volume helps paint a clear picture of the mind-set of the tribune. It becomes clear from these numerous references to the role of the Holy Spirit in his life and thought that Cola understood a divine force to be guiding his actions. He saw himself as the "knight of the Holy Spirit," doing the bidding of powers much greater than himself. Cola had, in short, a sense of mission which he saw as directing his life and giving meaning to his deeds.

The fact that Cola saw himself in this light is not particularly unusual, even if it is somewhat egomaniacal. What is striking, however, is Cola's close association of himself with the Holy Spirit. Although no direct link can be shown to have existed between Cola and the ideas of Joachim of Fiore during this period of his life, such ideas were in the air at this time and almost certainly would have been at least indirectly known to him. It is very difficult to imagine that the Holy Spirit could have been so great an influence on Cola's thought without his having been exposed to Joachite or Pseudo-Joachite ideas.

Cola's subsequent exile from 1348-1350, during which time he took refugee among the Fraticelli, seems to lend at least circumstantial evidence in favor of the argument that Cola was a Joachite throughout his career. Why else would he seek refuge among this group, and why would the Fraticelli protect Cola if he were not already a kindred spirit? Cola may very well have already been familiar with the Fraticelli from early on in his career.[25] However, the radically different tone of Cola's correspondence during his period of exile clouds the issue. It is possible to argue that this period marks a radical break with Cola's earlier thought; but in reality, while the tenor of his writing changes, and while his thought becomes more clearly apocalyptic, it is not as entirely inconsistent with his previous ideas as might be supposed. The apocalyptic dimension of Cola's thought only becomes more prominent because all else has been stripped away.

After Cola's fall from power in December of 1347, he embarked on a seven year odyssey which would take him from Rome, to Monte Maiella, to Prague, to Avignon, and back to Rome. During this period he would go from tribune to exile, to prisoner, and finally papal senator.[26] It was the most difficult

[25] Douie mentions that the Fraticelli were in Rome early in the fourteenth century; see Decima Douie, *The Nature and Effect of the Heresy of the Fraticelli* (Manchester, 1932), pp. 64-65. In addition, Gennaro notes that Fra Venturino de Bergamo and his penitents were in Rome in 1335; see Clara Gennaro, "Venturino da Bergamo e la peregrinatio romana del 1335," in *Studi sul medioevo cristiano offerti a Raffaello Morghen*, 2 vols. (Roma, 1974), 1.375-406. Although this is only highly circumstantial evidence that cannot prove Cola knew the Fraticelli before his exile, it does make it plausible.

[26] *Vita*, pp. 262-264. This period of Cola's life is dealt with only briefly in the *Vita*, but information in his letters helps piece together events.

time of Cola's life; but through it all he still retained his sense of mission, which, if anything, was reinforced and even heightened by his trials. In this regard, the most important encounter in Cola's wanderings for the development of his thought was with the Fraticelli of Monte Maiella in the mountains of central Italy.

The Fraticelli among whom Cola found refuge were an heretical offshoot of the Franciscan order.[27] They were driven by the same reformist impulses as Saint Francis and his earliest followers, but carried these impulses into an extremist form of heresy. Saint Francis originally hoped to lead a life of voluntary apostolic poverty along with his followers, but always within the established church. This was possible in the early days of the Franciscan order when membership was small. However, when large numbers flocked to the new mendicant order, an organizational apparatus became necessary. The expanding order was faced with the difficult problem of what to do about the ownership of property. Francis had wanted to lead a mendicant life in which he and his followers owned nothing whatsoever; but, as the order grew it became impossible to sustain a large and far flung organization without at least some form of corporate property. The resulting debate over the ownership of property split the order, with some arguing that their order should remain as Francis originally envisioned it: as an absolutely poor organization, both individually and collectively. They based their position on the belief that Jesus and the apostles had been without possessions and that, following the spirit of Francis, they should do likewise.

The factions within the Franciscan order that favored absolute apostolic poverty were known as the Franciscan Spirituals, since they favored a purely spiritual order and church. This group, led by Angelo of Clareno (1247-1337), came to be seen as a threat to the church, since their logic would call into question the ownership of property in the church as a whole. Pope Celestine V (1294) had allowed the Spirituals to form their own Order of Poor Hermits; but Boniface VIII (1294-1303) revoked papal permission, and the order was forced into exile in Greece in 1295.

As the Spirituals were falling further away from the established church and were suffering trials and tribulations as a result, they adopted a form of Joachimism in which they saw themselves as the "spiritual men" of whom Joachim had written, who along with the "new leader" would reform the church and bring it into the third age of the Holy Spirit. In this new age the institutional church would pass away, and be replaced by a purely spiritual

[27] Concerning the Franciscans and the Franciscan Spirituals, see Reeves, *Influence of Prophecy;* Cohn, *Pursuit of the Millennium;* McGinn, *Visions of the End;* idem, *Apocalyptic Spirituality;* Franz Ehrle, "Petrus Johannis Olivi, sein Leben und seine Schriften," *Archiv für literatur- und Kirchengeschichte des Mittelalters* 3 (1887): 409-552; Ernst Benz, *Ecclesia Spiritualis* (Stuttgart, 1934); E. Randolph Daniel, "Spirituality and Poverty: Angelo da Clareno and Ubertino da Casale," *Mediaevalia et Humanistica* n. s. 4 (1973): 89-98; idem, *The Franciscan Concept of Mission in the High Middle Ages* (Lexington, 1975); Malcolm Lambert, *Franciscan Poverty* (London, 1961); David Burr, *Olivi's Peaceable Kingdom: A Reading of the Apocalypse Commentary* (Philadelphia, 1993).

church, in which all would live as the Spirituals did. The writings of such prominent Spirituals as Peter John Olivi (1248-1298) and Ubertino de Casale (1259-1328) best express these Joachite ideas of the Spirituals.

Considering their increasing enmity with the institutional church, it is easy to see how the apocalyptic thought of the Spirituals could became a full-blown heresy, in which the institutional church was actually viewed as the Antichrist. The heretical Fraticelli grew directly out of the Franciscan Spirituals.[28] Essentially, they were Franciscans who had made the complete journey from reformers within the framework of the institutional church to heretics who viewed that same institutional church as the great enemy, the servant of Satan on earth. Since according to their own thinking the Fraticelli saw themselves as the "spiritual men," and since the church opposed them, it followed that the church opposed the new age of perfection which they represented and, therefore, that it was not the true church but was rather the Antichrist.[29] The Fraticelli thus represent the ultra-radical extent to which the ideas of Saint Francis and Joachim could be taken, so radical in fact, that they no longer truly represented the ideas of either Saint Francis or Joachim.

Such were the people among whom Cola sought and found refuge.[30] The leader of the Fraticelli of Monte Maiella was a certain Fra Angelo, who was possibly a follower of Angelo of Clareno himself.[31] A natural meeting of minds occurred between Cola and the Fraticelli.[32] Cola remained on Monte Maiella for thirty months, living the life of a penitent hermit.[33] What Cola was told during these thirty months by Fra Angelo undoubtedly had an enormous impact on his subsequent actions. However, it is important to note that while the details were new to Cola, the basic ideas were not. The letter in which Cola describes what he was told by Fra Angelo conveys a sense that his fundamental beliefs were

[28] Concerning the Fraticelli, see Reeves, *Influence of Prophecy;* Cohn, *Pursuit of the Millennium;* McGinn, *Visions of the End;* Gordon Leff, *Heresy in the Latter Middle Ages,* 2 vols. (New York, 1967); Douie, *Heresy of the Fraticelli.*

[29] Reeves, *Influence of Prophecy,* p. 213.

[30] *Briefwechsel,* pp. 191-197. In this letter to Charles IV, Cola tells of his meeting with the Fraticelli of Monte Maiella, and thereby supplements the sketchy account of the *Vita.*

[31] Mario Cosenza, *Petrarch and the Revolution of Cola di Rienzo* (Chicago, 1913; reprint New York, 1986), p. 171 and n. 3.

[32] Ferdinand Gregorovius, *History of the City of Rome in the Middle Ages,* trans. Annie Hamilton, 8 vols. (London, 1894-1900), 6.341, "A bond of secret affiinty brought the Candidate of the Holy Ghost among these mystics; the Tribune of the people was easily transformed into a theologian."

[33] *Briefwechsel,* p. 193: "...vbi in oracionibus vna cum heremitis in montibus Apenninis in regno Apulie constitutis in paupertatis habitu sum moratus - et dum iam per menses triginta quadam arta vita quodammodo laborassem, superuenit frater quidam nomine Angelus de monte Vulcani se asserens heremitam, quem multi heremite, vt asseritur, reuerentur."

elucidated and confirmed by Fra Angelo, and that they fortified his broken spirit, but not that the ideas expressed in the letter were previously alien to him. Cola also appears to have been willing to receive Fra Angelo's teaching with little resistance. In Cola the Fraticelli found a willing disciple and kindred spirit, who under the personal stress of his fall from power could easily make the intellectual journey from an orthodox devotion to the Holy Spirit to an heretical adherence to the radical apocalypticism of the Fraticelli.

During this time, it was explained to him that he had been divinely chosen to play a role in the universal reform which, according to Fra Angelo, had already begun. Cola was told that God had planned to punish the sins of the faithful and the church with mass destruction, but had withheld this judgment because of the work of Francis and Dominic. Now, according to Fra Angelo, God was moving toward the reformation of the church to its pristine state. There would be peace among Christians and between Christians and the infidel. Soon, an angelic pastor would arise whom God had already chosen, who would, along with a new emperor, bring about the age of the Holy Spirit and reform the church.[34] This angelic pastor would be a new Francis, who, along with the emperor, would divest the church of its wealth and make it a purely spiritual institution. When this was accomplished, the angelic pastor would rule as pope, and with Charles IV as Holy Roman Emperor and Cola as Duke of Rome, they would govern Christendom together in imitation of the Holy Trinity. Fra Angelo informed Cola that he should seek out the emperor in Prague and assist him, giving the emperor counsel and serving as his precursor. In addition, Cola was assured that soon both pope and emperor would return to Rome, making it again the *caput mundi*. Having heard all these prophecies, Cola hesitated; but this hesitation was overcome when Fra Angelo showed him prophecies which had already come to pass.[35] Reassured, Cola set off for Prague in 1350 to explain to Charles IV what he had learned and to play his appointed role in the eschatological drama that was about to be played out. Upon his arrival in Prague, Cola went before the emperor and explained to him what was about to happen, seeking to enlist imperial support for this universal reform of both the church and society as a whole.[36]

From Cola's letters to the emperor and the Archbishop Ernst of Prague we can discern what Cola said to the emperor. In two letters dating from August 1350, Cola related to both the emperor and the archbishop the state of Rome and Italy. He described the divisions and bad government under which the Italian people were suffering, for which he blamed the papacy and curia, whom Cola claimed intentionally fostered the conflict between Guelfs and Ghibellines so as

[34] This variation on the idea of the angelic pope and his replacement in the eschatological drama with an angelic pastor cut out of the same mold as Saint Francis can easily be accounted for by the anti-papal feelings of the Fraticelli and is evidence of their influence on Cola.

[35] *Briefwechsel*, pp. 191-197.

[36] Concerning Cola's time in Prague, see *Vita*, pp. 262-263, and *Briefwechsel*, pp. 191-213.

to keep the peninsula divided and weak.[37] According to Cola, it was the emperor who should march into Italy, overrun the peninsula, and seize power from the church and the tyrants and thereby restore good government to Italy.[38]

In these letters, Cola displays an open hostility toward the papacy and decidedly pro-imperial leanings. Nevertheless, his analysis of the conditions in Italy is valid; and his calls for imperial intervention in the peninsula are not new, echoing Dante's similar appeals. What is new is the influence of the Fraticelli which can be discerned in Cola's anti-papal, pro-imperial ideas. The clearest evidence of this influence occurs, however, in a subsequent letter of August 1350 which illustrates just how important an influence the Fraticelli had become in Cola's thought and how many of their ideas Cola had adopted as his own.

The letter entitled *Responsiva oracio Tribuni ad Cesarem super eloquio caritatis* is filled with Fraticelli ideas, including references to one of their particular heroes, Pope Celestine V, the hermit who became pope only to resign and be succeeded by Boniface VIII. In this letter, Cola speaks of a man as holy as Tobias, whose coming was prophesied by Merlin and Joachim. This holy man was deceived into renouncing the papal throne; and although not mentioned by name, he appears to be none other than Pope Celestine. Cola proceeds to relate that it was for this reason that God punished the church by sending the papacy to Avignon, where the clergy are devoid of virtues and consumed with vice. Cola already detested the Avignon papacy for other reasons, but now with the help of the Fraticelli he had another reason to despise it. Cola then proceeded to enumerate the abuses of the clergy and called on the emperor, whom he likened to Moses and proclaimed was the "elect of God," not to punish the clergy, for that was to be in God's hands alone, but rather to support the people, who lived under "the stench of sins and God's anger."[39] The emperor should at once march on Rome and restore the city, which was not just the capital of the Caesars but also of Christ. Cola even identified Rome with the New Jerusalem spoken of in the Book of Revelation.[40]

[37] *Briefwechsel,* p. 236: "Nam falso Ecclesia dicitur corpus Ecclesie enormiter sic diuisum, adeo quod in tantum error iste scismaticus in prouinciis ipsis fuit, quod in aliquibus ciuitatibus grauis sit pena, si vltra duo Gebellini congregati inuicem alloquantur, et in aliquibus non solum ab omni officio et beneficio, verum cum eorum familiis ab incolatu ciuitatum penitus sint exclusi; et sic similiter in aliquibus ciuitatibus fit de Guelfis."

[38] *Briefwechsel,* pp. 198-213.

[39] *Briefwechsel,* pp. 304-305: "Non ego punire habeo, nec a te Cesare postulo eos puniri; sed quia non est qui faciat bonum, peto, vt tu electus a Domino fias vnus bonus populi eius adiutor tantorum sub peccatorum fetoribus in ira Domini laborantis, prout tibi, vt Moisi, diuinis tabulis est consultum."

[40] *Briefwechsel,* p. 326: "Speraueram quidem, quod in aduentu meo Ierusalem noue, Romani videlicet regni tui et Vrbis alme sacerdotalis et regie, que volente dotatore suo domino Ihesu Christo caput est mundi, quesiuisses tribunum, qui vulnera eius nouit et tetigit, de suis infirmitatibus caritatiue ac eciam de vnguentis. Nam

What is apparent in this letter is that the concrete proposals for civic reform which are found in the letters of 1347 had given way to more radical ideas. Whereas during the tribunate Cola had hoped to bring the pope and curia back to Rome and restore the status and prosperity of the city, now he was calling for a clean break with the established order and a complete reformation under imperial auspices. Cola was advocating and hoping to call forth the apocalypse itself. This was not entirely dissimilar to what Cola was attempting in 1347, when he saw his reforms as being inspired and guided by the Holy Spirit. The crucial difference was that, whereas in 1347 Cola had been striving for reform within the basic framework of the existing ecclesiastical, social, and political order, by 1350 he was calling for a reform which would overthrow that order. In a nutshell, Cola, under the influence of the Fraticelli, had progressed from being an essentially conservative reformer to being a radical anti-establishment revolutionary.

On Monte Maiella, Fra Angelo had told Cola that his mission in this regard was to enlist the aid of the emperor in carrying out the total reform of the church and society; and in Prague Cola directed all his eloquence toward this end. The emperor, however, was polite but skeptical. Indebted for his throne to Pope Clement VI, Charles IV was not about to turn against his patron. For his troubles, Cola was imprisoned and turned over to papal authorities in Avignon, where he was to be tried for heresy. Ultimately, as has been seen, Cola was exonerated and sent back to Rome as papal senator.

Having described these various manifestations of the apocalyptic dimension of Cola's thought, how then is it to be assessed? Was it consistent? Was Cola's early thought Joachite? If Cola's thought was Joachite from the beginning, what role did the Fraticelli play in the development of Cola's reform ideology? How does apocalypticism relate to his reform ideology as a whole? These questions have nearly as many different answers as there are commentators on Cola's life and ideas. Various scholars have come to totally different conclusions on this difficult issue.

Guillaume Mollat has argued that, from the first public actions of Cola in 1343, his political and social agenda were Joachite.[41] Perhaps even more significantly, Conrad Burdach and Paul Piur considered Joachite ideas to be an essential part of Cola's program of reform and an important element in his relationship to the Italian Renaissance.[42] All of these scholars have seen in Cola's allegorical paintings and devotion to the Holy Spirit signs of Joachite thought which predate his period of exile.

However, other scholars are skeptical or unsure. Paul Oskar Kristeller dismissed a Joachite influence in the mainstream of Cola's thought, arguing that he only encountered such ideas from the Fraticelli during his Monte Maiella

sanato capite sanabis pocius Christiani populi cuncta membra."

[41] Guillaume Mollat, *Les Papes d'Avignon, 1305-1378* (Paris, 1950), pp. 148-149.

[42] For this interpretation, see Burdach, *Rienzo und die geistige Wandlung seiner Zeit;* Piur, *Cola di Rienzo*.

experience.[43] Marjorie Reeves' views on the subject contain elements of both positions, and are a good example of the confusion which this question causes. At one point in *The Influence of Prophecy in the Middle Ages* Reeves maintained that Cola only came into contact with Joachite ideas from the Fraticelli on Monte Maiella but later in the same work admitted that there was evidence of Joachite influence in Cola's thought from as early as 1343.[44] Reeves later reconciled the two views in *Joachim of Fiore and the Prophetic Future,* but her difficulties with this question are illustrative of the problems involved.[45] Joachite elements can be discerned in Cola's thought from the beginning, but it is also true that the Fraticelli had an enormous influence on Cola's intellectual development. How best to reconcile these two assertions concerning Cola's apocalyptic thought is the challenge for any scholar dealing with this issue.

As seen earlier, there is strong but indirect evidence that Cola's thought from its early stages manifested Joachite influence. Cola's intense devotion to the Holy Spirit is the key element in this regard. The role of the Holy Spirit in the third age of history is a hallmark of Joachim's trinitarian theology of history. It is a defining feature which other apocalyptic writers do not share with Joachim. With this in mind, the numerous references made by Cola to the role played by the Holy Spirit in his reform movement and the apocalyptic imagery of his allegorical paintings illustrate the intellectual foundations of his thought. The prominence of the Holy Spirit in Cola's thought strongly suggests that Joachimism was an integral part of his ideology from the earliest part of his public life.

Nevertheless, even though Cola exhibited Joachite tendencies from the start, his exile among the Fraticelli influenced his life and thought profoundly. The heretical group led by Fra Angelo on Monte Maiella radicalized Cola, exposing him to a militantly anti-papal, pro-imperial ideology. Under their influence, Cola adopted the apocalyptic expectations of the Fraticelli as his own, even to the extent that he traveled to Prague on the instructions of Fra Angelo to carry their message to the emperor. Cola left Monte Maiella for Prague with a renewed sense of mission and purpose that energized and guided the second half of his career. In this sense their influence on Cola's life was profound, but their impact on his thought was not as substantial as it might appear to be on the surface. The radical apocalypticism of the Fraticelli did not create an entirely new train of thought for Cola. Rather, they modified ideas which he already possessed. Intellectually, therefore, their influence is primarily to be seen in the transformation of Cola's thought from being basically orthodox to being clearly heretical.

The argument that Cola was consistent in his apocalyptic thought might still be challenged because of the changes in tone between his earlier and later

[43] Paul Oskar Kristeller, *Renaissance Thought* (New York, 1961), pp. 154-155 and n. 28.

[44] Reeves, *Influence of Prophecy,* pp. 318-319, 420-421.

[45] Reeves, *Joachim of Fiore and the Prophetic Future,* pp. 70-71.

letters. However, these changes can be accounted for if the purpose of the correspondence is taken into consideration. Cola's letters of 1347 were public documents dealing with the concrete problems of government, administration, and civic reform. On the other hand, his later letters are documents meant to preach the radical apocalypticism of the Fraticelli to the imperial court in Prague and lack references to the day-to-day administrative affairs associated with government, with which he was no longer involved. Without civic issues to deal with, Cola concentrated on spiritual matters, and lacking practical issues to address, the spiritual dimension of his thought assumed a disproportionate prominence which accounts for the differences in tone between his early and later letters. It can therefore be said that, while Cola's exile inaugurated a new period in his intellectual development, the change was primarily one of emphasis rather than of basic ideas. The form changed but the substance remained essentially the same.

The apocalyptic dimension of Cola's thought was fundamental to his overall reform program. Everything Cola did in his vain attempt to restore the city of Rome to its former glory was conditioned by this idea that he was the "knight of the Holy Spirit" and by his actions was helping to bring about the apocalyptic fulfillment of history. To minimize the importance of this aspect of Cola's ideology is to fall short of a full understanding and appreciation of both the intellectual basis for his revolutionary movement and the context in which he attempted to implement his reform agenda.

Despite the ultimate failure of his revolution, Cola nevertheless left his mark on history. His bold plan to reform Rome and return the city to its ancient glory, while unsuccessful, struck a cord with later scholars and artists, particularly with the romantics and nationalists of the nineteenth century.[46] In his own time, Cola was viewed both as a visionary hero and as a madman but no matter how one views the tribune and his actions, one tangible result of his revolution was that he succeeded in calling attention to the anarchic state into which Rome had fallen during the period of the Avignon papacy. The tragedy of the story lies in the fact that the man who so clearly perceived and dramatically illustrated the ills besetting Rome lacked the political skills necessary to bring his plans for the reform and renewal of the city to fruition and thereby turn his dreams into a reality.

[46] In particular, note the historical novel by the English author Edward Bulwer-Lytton, *Rienzi: The Last of the Roman Tribunes* (London, 1835), which was the basis for Richard Wagner's opera *Rienzi*.

REFORMING LIFE BY CONFORMING IT TO THE LIFE OF CHRIST: PSEUDO-BONAVENTURE'S *MEDITACIONES VITE CHRISTI*

Lawrence F. Hundersmarck

This paper seeks to articulate the number of ways is which the *Meditaciones Vite Christi*[1] (*MVC*) can be considered as a reform document within the Franciscan tradition. This work, long attributed to Saint Bonaventure (1221-1274),[2] is now thought to have been composed by an Italian Franciscan, possibly John de Caulibus from San Gimignano.[3] The author identifies the *MVC* as a book[4] offered as spiritual direction for a Franciscan religious, specifically a Poor Clare nun.[5] The author tells her that he intends to direct her in an orderly fashion, thus he began the process of jotting down meditations lest he forget their content (61.86-105; 7.48-49). He hopes that his limited expertise will supply her lack of erudition (prologus.87-88; 9.42-44; 74.12-13; 78.153-155) as he offers to her an introduction to the life of Christ.[6] The author intends

[1] *Iohannis de Caulibus Meditaciones Vite Christi olim S. Bonauenturo attributae*, ed. Mary Stallings-Taney (Corpus Christianorum 153; Turnholti, 1997). All references will be to this critical text in the form of chapter and line, so 15.2-7 is chapter fifteen, lines two to seven. On the ways this text differs from that found in *Sancti Bonaventurae opera omnia*, ed. Adolphe Peltier (Paris, 1864-1871), 12.509-630 see Mary Stallings-Taney, "The Pseudo-Bonaventure Meditaciones Vite Christi: Opus Integrum," *Franciscan Studies* 55 (1998): 254-260.

[2] For attributions to Bonaventure in the manuscript tradition, see C. Fisher, "Die 'Meditationes vitae Christi' Ihre handschriftliche Ueberlieferung und die Verfasserfrage," *Archivum Franciscanum Historicum* 25 (1932): 3-35, 175-348, 449-483.

[3] For an overview of the entire issue of authorship see Stallings-Taney, *MVC*, pp. IX-XI, and her earlier doctoral dissertation, Mary Jordan Stallings, *Meditaciones de Passione Christi olim Sancto Bonaventurae Attributae* (Washington, 1965), pp. 3-14; Benedetto da Cavalese, *Prodromus ad Opera omnia S. Bonaventurae* (Bassano, 1767), pp. 698-700. The source for the identification of the author as Iohannes de Caulibus is Bartholomew of Pisa; see *De Conformitate vitae B. Francisci ad vitam Domini Iesu* (Analecta Franciscana 4-5; Quaracchi, 1906-1916), 341; nothing is known about this Franciscan from "Caulibus."

[4] Stallings-Taney, "Opus Integrum," pp. 269-270. So 17.99-100; 50.8-9; 50.74-76; 51.53-54; 57.64-68; 61.88-94.

[5] Stallings-Taney, "Opus Integrum," pp. 270-276. So 12.126-127, 15.163-165 and the use of female Latin endings, 36.30, 73.11, and 78.149. There are specific references to Saint Clare of Assisi (1194-1253), prologus.40-43 and 44.250-254 and Saint Francis of Assisi (1181/2-1226), prologus.63-67 and 73.97-102. The addressee of the work was aware of Italian geography (14.58-62) and, based on a reference to the gate of San Gimignano (77.61-64), it has been argued that her convent may have been in this area; see Stallings, *Meditaciones de Passione*, p. 6 n. 11.

[6] "Nunc autem te in ipsas uite Christi meditaciones aliqualiter introducere cogitaui. Sed uellem quod hoc a magis experto magisque docto acciperes, quia talibus maxime insufficiens sum. Verum iudicans melius fore aliqua ut conuenit dicere quam penitus tacere, experiar impericiam meam et familiariter tecum loquar rudi et impolito sermone: tum ut melius possis que dicuntur capere, tum ut non aurem sed mentem

to state only what is confirmed by sacred scripture or what was spoken about in the words of the saints or in what he terms, but does not define, "approved interpretations" (74.24-26). The author tells her, later in the work (65.105-108), that she can repay him by effectively studying the material, inasmuch as he was pulled away from other duties because of this effort. Indeed, he states that writing this work has brought no lack of distraction to him (65.109-110).

The *MVC* is a work of 108 chapters running 347 pages in the *Corpus Christianorum* critical edition. The work, which stands as one of the first attempts at a complete biography of Jesus, was penned in Latin with occasional Latinizing of Italian words[7]. This massive representation of the gospels is greatly dependent upon the whole of scripture and Bernard of Clairvaux (1090-1153).[8] The *Meditaciones* was written between 1300 and 1364, but the exact date of the work remains unknown.[9]

The Franciscan author of the *Meditaciones* has created a series of images, events, presentations, and dialogues that aim at bringing the gospel account to his Poor Clare reader as meditations that are fully alive and meaningful. The author has a talent for personalizing the text for her instruction. He selects sections of the gospel narratives for extensive presentation because in his judgment they will have the most impact on her spiritual development.[10] If there is a chance to offer traditions not found in the New Testament, it is very common throughout the *MVC* to use whatever is, in the author's opinion, acceptable information to enhance her meditations.[11] As her spiritual director,

studeas inde reficere" (prologus.77-84).

7 Stallings-Taney, "Opus Integrum," pp. 263-264. She gives ten examples of Latinized Italian terms.

8 See Stallings-Taney, *MVC*, pp. 357-379. Bernard is quoted 134 times from 29 of his works. Apparently the early manuscripts of the *MVC* are very close to the critical edition of Bernard; *S. Bernardi opera,* ed. Jean Leclerq et. al. 8 vols. (Rome, 1957-1977). See Stallings-Taney, *MVC*, p. XII. The *MVC* is also dependent, but to a much less degree, on works such as Petrus Comestor's *Historia scholastica* (PL 198), Iacobus a Voragine's *Legenda aurea*, the *Glossa ordinaria* on the Bible, and Guillelmus a S. Theoderico's *Epistula ad fratres de monte Dei* (PL 184).

9 See Edmund Colledge, "Dominus Cuidam Devotae Suae: A Source for Pseudo-Bonaventure," *Franciscan Studies* 36 (1976): 105-107; Livario Oliger, "Le *Meditationes Vitae Christi* del Pseudo-Bonaventure," *Studi Francescani* 7 (1921): 143-183; 8 (1922): 18-47; Luigi Cellucci, "Le *Meditationes Vitae Christi* e. poemetti che ne furono ispirati," *Archivum Romanicum* 22 (1938): 74-93; and Sarah McNamer, "Further Evidence for the Date of the Pseudo-Bonaventuran 'Meditationes Vitae Christi,'" *Franciscan Studies* 50 (1990): 247-248.

10 So the following three receive the most attention: Infancy (chs. 4-18), the Martha-Mary section on the contemplative life (chs. 45-58), and the Passion (chs. 64-80). Events from the public life are given less attention because, as the author states, it would take too long to convert everything Jesus said and did in his public life into meditations (18.1-6).

11 To take but one of a great many examples, see chapter 72, where Jesus informs His mother of His impending death. He writes: "Hic potest interponi

his eye is focused on what can be mined for her growth. Thus, if material, such as the Sermon on the Mount, is too long to lend itself to being transformed into her meditations, he will limit his description and focus only on one theme (ch. 21). For the sake of clarity he will reduce the two multiplications of the loaves into one meditation (ch. 34), or separate interconnected units for the sake of explaining points more clearly.[12] In some places, such as the Passion narrative, the author deliberately focuses the Poor Clare's attention only upon the sufferings of Jesus as presented mainly through the gospels.[13] Elsewhere, because she does not have books (other than scripture) to read (44.115-116), he offers extensive citations from Saint Bernard, identified as a very great contemplative, so that she might practice what Bernard teaches in both words and deeds (36.130-138).[14]

The *Meditaciones Vite Christi* was a very influential work in the history of late medieval piety. It stands as a rich and comprehensive expression of the medieval devotion to the humanity of Christ.[15] It stands too as an important witness to an emerging and immensely popular new genre: the life of Christ, of which the Carthusian Ludolphus de Saxonia's *Vita Christi* is perhaps the most well known example.[16] The *Meditaciones* continued to enjoy a great influence

meditacio ualde pulchra de qua tamen Scriptura non loquitur" (72.1-2). He rarely offers this warning, either because the Poor Clare had the capacity to read the scriptures herself, as is assumed in 31.14-15, or because he has already stated that he intends to offer nothing heterodox (74.24-26). After all, he notes the evangelists did not relate everything (80.13-14; 104.17).

12 Ch. 36, where Mt 14 offers both Jesus' prayer on the mountain and His walking on water.

13 "Verum quia totam passionem Domini Iesu tibi sine auctoritatum interposicione transcurri ne aliquis se ad aliud quam ad ipsam passionem conuerteret, cogitaui uel nunc aliquas tibi referre ut earum leccio mentem excitet ad ipsam feruencius et deuocius meditandam. Accipe igitur Bernardum more solito in quibusdam sic dicentem..." (81.96-101).

14 Elsewhere, "Habes igitur a beato Bernardo more suo melliflua eructante de Domini Iesu passione pulcherrima. Videas ne in uacuum ea recipias. Sed toto corde totoque affectu ipsius auctoritatibus incitata in Dominica passione uerseris, quia ipsius passionis meditacio super omnes alias que de uita ipsius occurrere possunt noscitur eminere" (81.307-312).

15 See Jacques Hourleir, André Rayez, "Humanite du Christ (Devotion et Contemplation)," in *Dictionnaire de spiritualité ascétique et mystique* (Paris, 1969), 7.1053-1095; Alberich Altermatt, "Christus pro nobis: Die Christologie Bernhards von Clairvaux in den 'sermones per annum,'" *Analecta Cisterciensia* 33 (1977): 3-176; A. van den Bosch, "Dieu rendu accessible dans le Christ d'aprés S. Bernard," *Collectanea Ordinis Cisterciensium reformatorum* 21 (1959): 185-205; 22 (1960): 11-20, 341-355; 23 (1961): 42-57; Giles Constable, *Three Studies in Medieval Religious and Social Thought* (Cambridge, 1995). This tradition has a long history and can be traced back at least as far as Rabanus Maurus (ca. 784-856) who pictured the Man of Sorrows in the extreme agony of the Passion as the object of compassion and sorrow; see *Opusculum de Passione Domini* (PL 112.1425-1430).

16 *Vita Jesu Christi e Quatuor Evangeliis* ed. A. Clovis Bolard, Ludovicus M. Rigollot, and J. Carnandet (Paris, 1865). On the relationship and difference of these

as an officially approved alternative to Lollard teachings through its Middle English translation at the hands of Nicholas Love (ca. 1410).[17] The *MVC* was considered by many to be a safer approach to the gospels than that offered by various vernacular translations because, unlike the translations, the *Meditaciones* surrounded the naked text of the New Testament with orthodox explanations.[18] Finally, scholars have studied the immense influence of the *MVC* on the development of medieval drama[19] and art.[20]

What has received little attention are the ways in which the *Meditaciones* offers to the original recipient of the work an elaborate reform treatise. Because she has in her possession what the author calls, "this little book of the humanity of Christ" (50.76), she has the vehicle by which to transform her whole life.[21] Citing Bernard,[22] the *MVC* sees the whole reason for the Incarnation as the desire of God to win back the affections of carnal humanity. It is through an intimacy with the humanity of Christ that the Poor Clare will move ever closer

two works, see Walter Baier, *Untersuchungen zu Den Passionsbetrachtungen in Der Vita Christi Des Ludolf von Sachsen* (Salzburg, 1977), 2.325-338; Lawrence Hundersmarck, "Preaching the Passion: Late Medieval 'Lives of Christ' as Sermon Vehicles," in *De Ore Domini: Preachers and Word in the Middle Ages*, ed. Thomas Amos, Eugene Green, and Beverly Kienzle (Kalamazoo, 1989), pp. 147-167.

17 *Nicholas Love's Mirror of the Blessed Life of Jesus Christ: A Critical Edition*, ed. Michael Sargent (New York, 1992); Elizabeth Salter, *Nicholas Love's 'Myrrour of the Blessed Lyf of Jesu Christ'* (Salzburg, 1974); *Nicholas Love at Waseda: Proceedings of the International Conference*, *20-22 July, 1995*, ed. Shoichi Oguro, Robert Beadle, and Michael Sargent (Cambridge, 1997).

18 Margaret Deanesly, "The Gospel Harmony of John de Caulibus or S. Bonaventure," *Collectanea Franciscana* 10 (1922): 10-19.

19 Alessandro D'Ancona, *Le origini del teatro italiano* (Turin, 1891); Livario Oliger, "Le Meditationes Vitae Christi del Pseudo-Bonavetura (Note Critiche)," *Studi Francescani* 8 (1922): 18-47; Karl Young, *Drama of the Medieval Church*, 2 vols. (Oxford, 1933); and D. Jeffrey, "St. Francis and Medieval Theatre," *Franciscan Studies* 43 (1983): 321-346.

20 Emile Mâle, *L'Art religieux de la fin du moyen âge en France: Étude sur l'iconographie du moyen âge et sur ses sources d'inspiration* (Paris, 1908); Gertrud Schiller, *Iconography of Christian Art*, 2 vols. (New York, 1972); E. S. Varanelli, "Le *Meditationes Vitae Nostri Domini Jesu Christi* nell' arte del duecento italiano," *Arte Medievale* 6 (1992): 137-148; Ise Ragusa, Rosalie Green, *Meditations on the Life of Christ: An Illustrated Manuscript of the Fourteenth Century* (Princeton, 1961); Anne Derbes, *Picturing the Passion in Late Medieval Italy: Narrative Painting, Franciscan Ideologies, and the Levant* (Cambridge, 1996); D. Robb, "The Iconography of the Annunciation in the Fourteenth and Fifteenth Centuries," *Art Bulletin* 18 (1936): 480-526; and Jeryldene Wood, *Woman, Art, and Spirituality: The Poor Clares of Early Modern Italy*, (Cambridge, 1996).

21 Transformation is a basic theme for all discussions of reform. The idea is central to Saint Paul and fundamental to the reform idea throughout western monasticism; see Gerhart Ladner, *The Idea of Reform: Its Impact on Christian Thought and Action in the Age of the Fathers* (Cambridge, 1959), pp. 49-62, 319-340.

22 *Sermones super Cantica*, 20, 6-7, *Sancti Bernardi opera*, 1.118-120.

to an intimacy with the invisible God (107.41-61). In this intimacy her spirit, as an imperfect beginner (50.1-7), will be reformed by God's grace.[23] This gift of God's presence will heal and elevate her (108.32-97).[24] This gift is always to be her goal (107.49-53).[25]

Before, during, and after a meditation upon the life of Christ, the devout Poor Clare must be aware of the dangers of a life without such a goal. The dynamics of meditation, its techniques and goals, become clear only when what stands in opposition to meditation is clearly understood. For the *MVC*, to seek divine attachment requires an earthly detachment, a shift from the temporal to the eternal. Reform is always both toward something and away from something. Throughout the entire *MVC* the author never ceases to remind his reader of those realities that threaten the whole of the religious life. Like an effective preacher, the author seeks to warn as well as encourage, to reject as well as affirm.

We are pilgrims in a world characterized in the *MVC* as perishable and transitory (16.33-50). Life attached to this realm is a life of vanity and vainglory (12.137-144), of idle curiosity (12.124-125) and frivolity (15.196). This earthly realm is filled with the superfluous (8.47; 44.358-368), and so constant vigilance is necessary to be content with what is alone needed (15.197-204). Thus, the *MVC* sets forth the image of Mary Magdalene who, after washing the feet of Jesus with her tears, dries them with her hair. This action is thought utterly appropriate because her hair, which was associated with her vanity, is now being put to humble good use (28.36-40). Mary and all the heroes of the gospels have freed themselves from the weight of worldly affairs because they are not slaves to passing things (21.18-28). No wonder Jesus flees when the crowds seek to make him a worldly king (35.3-9). For the *MVC* this

[23] "Denique Deus caritas est, et nihil est in rebus quod possit replere creaturam factam ad imaginem Dei, nisi caritas Deus, qui maior est illa" (47.81-83); "... coram Deo tuo te humiliauers, indignam te reputans ab omni beneficio suo, certissime credas quod quodcumque pecieris obtinebis" (37.24-26); "Et si ulterius ascendat ut uisitacionem sponsi recipiat eiusque presencia glorietur, nonne tunc recipit plus quam millecplum omnium quecumque fuerint et quomodocumque fuerint que pro eo dimiserat?" (39.16-19); "Non enim habemus quid manducemus nisi ipse det. Et in uia deficimus si nos ieiunos dimittit, et sine ipso non possumus nobis in aliquo spirituali negocio prouidere. Non ergo habemus elacionis materiam cum de manu Domini aliquam consolacionem percipimus uel cum aliquem profectum spiritualis exercicii sentimus. Quia non a nobis sed ab ipso est" (34.28-33).

[24] The source in this passage, chosen to conclude the *MVC*, is Bernard's *Sermones super Cantica*, 15, 5-7, *Opera*, 1.85-87.

[25] See also "Vnde credis quod beatus Franciscus ad tantam uirtutum copiam et ad tantam luculentam intelligenciam Scripturarum, ad perspicacem eciam noticiam fallaciarum hostis et uiciorum peruenerit, nisi ex familiari conuersacione et meditacione Domini sui Iesu? Propterea sic ardenter afficiebatur ad ipsam, ut quasi sua similitudo fuerit. Nam in cunctis uirtutibus quam perfeccius poterat innitebatur eundem, et tandem ipso compellente et perficiente Iesu per impressionem sacrorum stigmatum, fuit in eum totaliter transformatus. Vides ergo ad quam excelsum gradum meditacio uite Christi perducit" (prologus.63-73).

world, because it is transitory, miserable, and shallow, seeks to poison and sicken the soul (106.28-32).

This world is also characterized as the realm of the arrogance of the flesh (15.48), the changing passions of a corrupt body (51.7-10). In the body, pleasures seek their gratification (12.180-181), and a life craving to gratify the pleasures of the flesh is a life incapable of prayer (17.23-29). The advice offered is simply, "under no circumstance should you dare involve yourself in worldly concerns or dealings" (42.16-18).

This Poor Clare nun is told to flee conversations with worldly persons that will fill her eyes and ears with empty fantasies (17.30-45). Indeed, she is not to be concerned with her relatives (20.65-77). Continued conversation with some closely-related lay people may have been a specific weakness for her, thus prompting her spiritual advisor to remind the nun that he has repeatedly warned about exactly this difficulty (56.63-64; 107.27-41). In her religious life verbosity is a vice, hateful and despicable to both God and man, a sign of shallowness (8.52-58). She has consecrated her mouth for the gospel (8.70-72). Thus, as Christ was silent and remained hidden for thirty years, she is taught to humbly remain silent (16.286-307). This is why, he tells her, silence is virtuous and so it is regulated in religious obligations (8.54-58; 55.2-16). This is why the holy fathers of monasticism sought the wilderness in order to pray far from all human traffic (17.30-45).

The dangers of the world, the flesh, and the devil (36.227-242) all express in their own way the one truly great and fundamental danger throughout the *MVC*: pride, the accursed vice (12.188-189), the enemy of all grace, and the beginning of all sin (16.254-260). In pride there is the supreme act of injustice for the proud person attributes all good gifts of God to himself (16.141-143). Pride is at the core of all ambition, and so the ambition for the top grades of ecclesiastical orders ought to be looked upon with dread (35.186-190). Others express pride in their ambitions for knowledge and honor under the guise of winning souls. These clerics deceive themselves as if they might better supervise the salvation of others (35.192-201). The author of the *MVC* seems sensitive to this danger in his role as one with some authority over another's religious life (prologus. 78-90). After all, even Saint Peter needed reminders of his weakness lest he become proud and think himself equal to God (36.154-160).

The goal of the *MVC* is to lead the reader to embrace the eternal as expressed in the life of Christ, to turn from the path of vanity, which embraces all the desires, grounded in pride. Its aim is to pull the intellect and the will away from all that is transitory, a mental and volitional retreat from "the poisoned arrows of a very wicked world" (6.56-61). The Poor Clare is to imitate blessed Cecilia who, because of constant meditation upon the life of Christ, was capable of strengthening and stabilizing the mind against empty and transitory things, even, we are told, in the midst of the vanity and pomp of wedding celebrations (prologus. 22-28). This life of Christ is a school against all vain enticements, tribulations, adversities, temptations, and vices (prologus.14-16). The contemplative must let go of everything if she wishes to be emptied out for God (55.64-66). This means actively seeking to abandon even the residue of the imagination and the fantasies which so impede the activities of contemplation

(55.70-72). Only through contemplation on the gospel story can the intellect be enlightened and the will given its proper orientation (51.21-24).

The enlightenment of the intellect, arousing the emotions and directing the will, captures the intention of the *Meditaciones*. All that is contained throughout the entire work deals with these aspects of intellect, emotion, and will in the Poor Clare's struggle for spiritual perfection. The author advises that she think and feel in a certain way about the life of Christ and will to imitate certain acts contained throughout that life. To the extent she achieves the prescribed quality of mind, emotion, and will she is experiencing a conformation that is reformation. For the *Meditaciones Vite Christe,* to conform to Christ's life is to be reformed. This is for her a love whose sweetness lays hold of the whole heart to the exclusion of every earthly love and carnal attachment (107.27-29). This is a love born of gratitude for every gift of God placed before her in her contemplation of scriptures (63.15-24). This meditation alone gets rid of pride, tones down sensuality, and confounds idle curiosity (12.124-125; 44.43-47).

The author notes that although this sister of the Franciscan Order owns nothing and has accepted with her life in the convent the vow of poverty, nevertheless, there remains within her a cupidity. She has a heart burdened by the weight of greed, concupiscence for the goods of this world (44.26-47). Only when she utterly places herself with total mental, emotive, and volitional attention onto the life of Christ, then, and only then, are all other cares and worries set aside (prologus.103-107). All else, except for this life, is, in a sense, crowded out. All else is distraction (70.52-56). As a contemplative she is to empty herself for God by casting aside every other concern (55.2-16). Only then will she be so inflamed that it will be enough to warm the whole of herself (107.44-45).

The *MVC* is a work ever alert to the dangers of a lack of intimacy with the gospel story. This is the context that gives the work its urgency. For this author, the life of his Poor Clare is either a life conformed to her Lord's life or else her existence remains deformed. Therefore, what remains before us is a discussion that seeks to understand the dynamics of total immersion offered throughout the *Meditaciones*. This is best accomplished by organizing our discussion under three different but interrelated aspects of the person: the intellect (and with it, imagination), the emotions, and the will. All aspects of the Poor Clare's being must be actualized (45.43-56).

The intellect to be fully engaged must enter into the gospel scene enticed by and enveloped within a rich tapestry of events, images, and conversations. The author invites the reader to be present to the gospel scene (85.10-13; 74.12-30). Repeatedly, the *MVC* will remind the reader to meditate assiduously (28.60; 25.9); to pay attention (12.140); to gaze upon (13.115-116); to observe the scene carefully (65.10; 73.34; 79.103; 91.62-65). In essence, the reader was to place before the mind's eye all that was said and done by the characters of the gospel narratives (18.13-30).

Recollection of the gospel narratives, even if accomplished with genuine attention, is only one aspect of the meditative process. The goal for the author is to draw the nun into a situation where she is to conduct herself as if she were both intellectually and physically present within the gospel story (85.10-13). She is told to kneel in order to receive a blessing from the child Jesus, then from Mary, and then Joseph (12.200-206). Elsewhere in the Infancy section of the *MVC* she is invited to take the boy Jesus and mount him on a donkey and, when he wants to dismount, take Him joyfully into her arms (13.71-75). She is called to join the disciples in amiable conversation with Jesus (62.17-24). She is called to be present by the use of her imagination[26] and, as we will discuss later, through the intensity of her emotive response.

To help her enter the scene with the imagination, her guide does not hesitate to present not only the gospel account but also whatever is spoken about in the witness of approved interpretation (74.12-30). By this he appears to mean broadly, "what can be piously believed to have happened" (9.41-42) or what, in his judgment, is not contrary to faith, doctrine, justice, or good morals (prologus.90-107). To help his reader, the author admits he has no intention of recounting every aspect of a harmonized gospel account but only those scenes and deeds that offer the most food for meditation (18.2-11). It would be a great good if she can hold the meditations fast in her memory (15.109; 21.10-11; 73.220-221).

In order to make an impression that lasts, this teacher of the gospels does not hesitate to utilize a whole range of techniques designed to intensify the gospel accounts. His aim is to activate the reader's full fascination and interest, to make an impact by creating mental images that are memorable. To this end he will insert throughout the narrative numerous geographic details regarding the distances of one place from another.[27] Elsewhere we are offered the image of angels kneeling (4.21) and falling to the ground (17.176-183); mother and child embracing (12.11-12); and Jesus and Mary walking together (13.72-75; 20.96-108). Mary offers bread to other women (34.54-57), but is not seated with the other guests at Cana (20.16-26). Jesus sits humbly on the summit of a mountain (21.63-64); and, after the sermon, His disciples follow Him down the mountain as do chicks behind a hen (21.74-81). We are told that the pillar of Jesus' scourging still shows signs of blood (76.36-37) and that the cross was fifteen feet high (77.36-37).[28] The author has seen at the church of the Lateran in Rome the four sided square table of the last supper which he measured himself as having two arms lengths plus three fingers. Thus, three disciples could sit on each side with Jesus at one corner (73.48-57). In chapter 78 there is an elaborate presentation of the method by which Jesus is nailed to the cross. Two different

26 Other examples are to take the boy Jesus by the hand (13.44-46); kiss the feet of the boy John the Baptist, beg for his blessing, and commend herself to him (13.89-91); keep watch over the child Jesus as He sleeps (15.165-186); and enter into conversation with Lazarus, Martha, and Mary (66.1-7).

27 See 7.115-118; 5.5-6; 14.14-16; 17.3-6; 17.97-100; 17.204-205; 20.10-14; 21.2-4; 31.2-4. The author claims that the distances are from those who have visited the Holy Land (17.99-100).

28 Source here for pillar and cross is *Historia scholastica*, PL 196.1634.

methods are described: nailing after he is elevated on the cross and nailing before the cross is elevated. What matters, we are told, is whatever conceptualization is more acceptable for the meditation (78.20-52).

As an articulation of the intense mariological focus of the work, and as a way, one supposes, to enkindle an identification of the work's recipient with Mary, the *MVC* often presents an enhanced role for the mother of Jesus. If the Poor Clare had only the gospel texts she would have been deprived of experiencing the emotions depicted as Jesus tells His mother of His impending death (72.2-34) or of His mother covering her son's nakedness on the cross with her head veil (78.12-20). In the temple, before the Annunciation, Mary embodies all virtues, all piety, and is nourished by food received from the hands of angels (3.70-94). At the Annunciation the entire Trinity awaits her response and consent (4.20-29). The infant John gazes only upon Mary, reluctant to return to the arms of his mother Elizabeth (4.43-52). The whole of the Infancy narrative focus is more often upon Mary than her son.[29] Jesus and His mother are so close that He returns to Nazareth because He wants to do whatever pleases her (14.72-77). Before his public ministry He takes joy in walking her home to Nazareth (20.96-108). After His death He appears to her with the address, "Greeting, holy parent" (82.2-45); while earlier in His life, after His forty day fast in the desert, angels transport to Him the only food He desires, that cooked by His mother (17.120-164). Mary's responses to her son are offered as a model for the Poor Clare's responses. This is also true, to a lesser extent, for the other major female figure of the work, Mary Magdalene.[30] The male disciples are likewise presented as positive role models.[31]

These women have already achieved what all meditation longs to achieve: to gaze upon the holy face of Jesus. This face, while not described in any detail, may serve as the symbol of the goal and simultaneously the difficulty of that goal as the *MVC* imaginatively reconstructs the gospel events. To picture that holy face, the author must admit, is more difficult than anything presented throughout the work (18.13-30). Yet he advises the Poor Clare to gaze upon it

[29] See 7.11-14; 7.22-46; 8.17-19; 8.23-24; 8.37-44; 9.47-63; 10.16-31; 11.13-25. See also George Marcil, "The Image of Mary in the *Meditationes Vitae Christi,*" *The Cord* 41 (1991): 338-345.

[30] See 91.31-40; 105.145-146; 80.26-83; 75.192-194; 28.1-115; 71.7-20; 84.12-23; 72.39-47. Male figures other than Jesus are given little voice in the text compared to these two women. See for Joseph (14.16-23); John the Baptist (17.187-191); Peter (80.167-208); and John the Apostle (79.43-52; 80.101-103; 73.78-88). See also Helen Meredith Garth, *Saint Mary Magdalene in Medieval Literature* (Baltimore, 1950).

[31] When the disciples sleep in the garden, Jesus does not condemn them but watches over them, like a good shepherd, for He is the security permitting their rest (75.132-140). Their flight is understandable, for they are now orphans with intense pain; so Jesus pities them (75.152-153). After the Resurrection they are forgiven with the words, "Rise, my brothers, all your sins are forgiven" (91.10-11). The same words are offered to doubting Thomas (100.14-15). Only Judas is condemned (75.147).

(21.62-67), a face noble and handsome (18.52-57), in order to feed upon the attractiveness of His appearance (73.214-222).

In this encounter with the impossibility of conceptualizing the holy face, the *MVC* reaches the real limits of its meditative method through the use of imagination. This is why we see the text struggle to imagine the incorporeal God in His commands to the angel Gabriel (4.14-22). Perhaps this is why the *MVC*, grounded in the interplay of imagination and scripture, emphasizes the emotive and volitional responses to the recreated gospel accounts. It is to these two aspects of his reader's inner life that we now turn.

The emotive dimension of the meditative activity is clearly evident throughout the *MVC*. In meditation there is the experience of sweetness (18.13-16). This is why the words of Bernard of Clairvaux, words called exceedingly beautiful, are liberally interspersed throughout the work. To ruminate on Bernard's words is to taste their sweetness (36.130-138). These words, but especially the gospel scenes, are presented like courses of food served in order to be tasted, indeed chewed thoroughly and often (6.69-70; 107.7-13).

To savor the sweetness appears to mean not only the intellectual grasp of the event but also the experience of the most compassionate Jesus who always exhibits love and kindness in His zeal to save souls.[32] This mercy toward humanity is what attracts the love of others (28.1-7). Jesus is the gentlest Lord of exceeding love (61.2-3). Thus, the reader is often drawn to that quality of charity without which it is impossible to please God (28.111-115).[33]

Because of this compassion for humanity the Jesus of the *Meditaciones Vite Christi* is the humble one who suffers for humanity. He suffers because He entered as a servant into the human condition (16.14-32). Jesus' human condition is described as an entire life that was labor-laden (31.5-6). It was a life filled with hardships and pains (8.9-44). The hardships are often related to the difficulties derived from the confinement of the material body. Thus, the Franciscan author does not miss opportunities to highlight the pain experienced by Jesus when He chooses to walk barefoot (17.184-186; 17.202-204; 36.144-150). We are told that the Lord's feet are anointed with a costly perfumed ointment because they are bruised from his travels (28.40-44). He lies on bare ground and thus becomes a humble companion of the beasts (17.9-12). Out of love Jesus wills to be baptized by immersing Himself into frigid water in a season that is freezing cold (16.264-270).

In the beginning of His life He is tortured by the cold of the cave of His birth (7.36).[34] At the end of His life, following the text of the gospel of John

[32] "Benignitas" as a descriptive term can be found in: 28.3-11; 73.102-104; 73.121-128; 78.95-98. So we read, "In quo Domini benignitatem et humilitatem solitam et caritatem considera. Aperte enim uides quomodo diligenter, affectuose imprimit; reiterat et recommendat Petro animas nostras" (102.28-31).

[33] See 4.103-107; 5.40-43; 15.188-190; 44.15-20; 56.122-138; 62.10; 66.17-18; 102.29-31; 104.36-39.

[34] This is why, we are told, His mother anointed Him immediately after birth with the milk from her breast, then, wrapping Him in her veil, laid Him in the

18:18, the cold night sends the stripped Jesus into shivering pain (76.57-61). The Jesus of the *MVC* is worn out from His long wakefulness as an adult (36.144-146), just as when He was an infant He suffered extended imprisonment in the womb (6.44-49), the pain of circumcision (8.9-44), and the hardships of travel to Egypt (12.44-81). When the *MVC* turns to the Passion narrative, it presents one long intense portrait of physical suffering.[35] In this passion, He is pictured as supplying a remedy for the world "through the suffering of His own body" (71.1-3). So extreme is His physical suffering that, after His scourging, not only the torturers but also the onlookers are utterly exhausted (76.36-45). His torments are so great that they cannot be fully recounted, only imagined (78.70-71). After He dies, we are told that every aspect of His body experienced suffering (78.145-153).

The physical sufferings of Jesus are given the greater amount of space throughout the *Meditaciones*. However, internal suffering is not ignored. The suffering of the soul is understood to be even more intense than that of the body. The *MVC* claims that, from the beginning of His conception, Jesus was aware that His father was abandoned and dishonored by sinners. The pain of this knowledge was so great that He was willing to endure the physical pain of the passion to alleviate this greater spiritual pain (6.61-68). Overshadowing the joy of the temple feast, the twelve-year-old Jesus is afflicted with an intense heartache over the dishonor shown to His father by so many sins (14.4-9). Before He chooses His disciples Jesus suffers loneliness as He travels alone (16.14-32; 36.146-149). In the passion He is shamed by being forced to collect His stripped clothes (77.11-33); and, when He is crucified, the text notes the shameful dimension of the Crucifixion (78.2-4). When He weeps in the garden, it is because of human malice; while, at the grave of Lazarus, it is because of human misery (71.38-50).[36]

The Poor Clare is offered this image of the humble suffering servant who, throughout His entire life, is afflicted with internal and external torment. The intensity of this image is designed to prompt her full emotive response of sorrow and tears. She is to have compassion for Him. She is to suffer with Him who suffered for her (77.73-74). Compassion, more than delight, is the vehicle by which she is to encounter the Incarnation with her total affections (3.97-100). Her compassion, although primarily directed toward the suffering

manger. To keep the newborn infant from suffering, the ox and the ass knelt positioning their mouths over the manger; and thus with their breath continued to offer Him warmth (7.31-37).

[35] The focus is on pain; see 74.30-54; 76.65-77; 78.4-12; 78.70-73; 78.53-71. All this is described as a long hard war, a funeral bed of pain (74.73-75).

[36] In the same passage we read that His weeping over Jerusalem was sorrow for human blindness and ignorance because His people did not realize the time of His visitation. When He cried as a baby, it was to conceal the mystery of the Incarnation from the devil.

Jesus, ought to also be given to His mother,[37] His foster father (12.200-206; 13.53-56), and the disciples.[38]

The form of compassion most often advised is tears. Jesus may have wept a few times, but the *Meditaciones* is filled with numerous images of weeping and extreme sorrow. In the Infancy narrative Mary cannot stop crying because of the tears of her son (8.9-44). The aged Joseph[39] sheds tears in the midst of the family's struggles on the way to Egypt (14.25-29). When John the Baptist's death is reported, Jesus weeps, as do His disciples, as well as Mary, who lifted John from the ground as a newborn and loved him most tenderly (30.68-71). In the Passion narrative John, Magdalene, and Mary's sisters all cry so bitterly at the foot of the cross that they are utterly shaken and inconsolable (78.84-91; 79.38-39). In terms of emotional intensity no chapters of the entire *Meditaciones* can match the dramatic scene offered at the cross and the tomb (chapters 79-80). There, Mary collapses half-dead when her son's side is opened; and, when her dead son is placed in her arms, she bathes His face with her tears as Magdalene sheds tears on His feet. His mother wishes to die and be buried with her son and so must be pulled away from the tomb. Be compassionate, the author repeatedly tells his reader as he depicts the final death scene. Here the characters of the gospel are suffering the greatest affliction; so the only appropriate response for one who sees is to also feel, to shed the tears of pity and sorrow. In all this the Poor Clare is drawn fully into the gospel events emotionally. She is to bring not only her mind but also the full intensity of her feelings and thus be transformed from a focus on the self to a dynamic self-transcendence into the other.[40]

The author of the *MVC* is happy to remind the recipient of the work that the founder of their tradition, Saint Francis of Assisi, strove to have his whole life serve as a mirror resemblance of Christ's life (prologus.63-73). The desire to clothe the self in virtue (prologus.61-63) is a high priority throughout the

[37] See 7.11; 8.24-34; 12.193-195; 13.53-56; 14.29-31; 15.165-168; 71.51-60; 72.35; 75.210-211; 76.7-16; 76.28-29; 78.84-91; 80.26-39; 80.208-218.

[38] See 30.7-13; 65.25-27; 66.29-31; 71.51-60; 72.36-38; 73.214-222; 79.38-43; 80.26-39; 80.225-234.

[39] Joseph is always presented as very old, a common tradition summarized by Jacobus de Voragine in his *Legenda aurea*. This is a very ancient tradition going back to the *Evangelia Apocrypha*, so the second century *Protoevangelium* 8:3.

[40] Emotional involvement with Jesus' suffering is so important for the *Meditaciones* that other issues that would draw the attention of the Poor Clare away from this experience are avoided. Thus, unlike other Passion narratives in late medieval piety, there is very little attention given in the *MVC* to anti-Judaism themes; see 77.1-11 for brief mention of the Jews. For an overview of other works of the passion; see Thomas H. Bestul, *Texts of the Passion: Latin Devotional Literature and Medieval Society* (Philadelphia, 1996), pp. 69-110. Bestul sees the *MVC* in its depiction of Mary's extreme emotional response as indicative of established ideas about gender relationships; see pp. 111-114.

Meditaciones. Jesus' life is offered for the instruction of humanity (12.11-32),[41] a life filled with examples of many virtues (17.7-9; 44.112-120). His mother's life is likewise offered as an exemplar of virtues, as are the lives of other, less frequently mentioned characters in the gospel narratives.

Throughout this gospel story of divine love the virtue that most embodies this love is humility. This virtue exemplified by the lives of Jesus, Mary, and the disciples, who humbly obey Jesus (35.17-18), is often the focus of the author. This virtue is as celebrated through the use of citations from Bernard[42] as through the examples derived from the *MVC's* harmonization of the gospels. Humility serves as a rejection of pride (21.17-26). This virtue has its core meaning for the *Meditaciones* in the divine condescension where the supreme glory of divinity enters into the realm of human weakness and suffering. In the Incarnation Jesus sought to humiliate Himself most profoundly (16.85-88). Thus, He is called the master and teacher of humility (16.7; 18.31-34; 85.7-10). In Him humility has achieved its highest degree (16.63-75). Its opposite, pride and arrogance, can never be pleasing to God (7.81-88). Only by not fleeing from the path of humiliation can a person achieve humility (15.126-138). Thus, the author never grows weary of celebrating the lowly and humble works of Mary[43] and her son.[44] Using the example of Mary, the Poor Clare is taught the following: be embarrassed when commended by others or in the middle of a jostling crowd; be modest; be gentle; be silent; bear trials; and minister to others. Using the example of Jesus, the Poor Clare is taught: use honor or power to a good end; speak the truth if only to a small group; learn to desire others to despise and consider us worthless; move among others unnoticed; be a servant; and suffer persecution. The author offers through Bernard the connection of humility and virginity (16.193-254). The expression of virginity and humility are examined in the lives of the Virgin Mary (4.79-85) and John.[45]

[41] "Et redeamus ad intuendos actus et uitam Domini Iesu speculi nostri, sicut est principale nostrum propositum. Igitur te omnibus presentem exhibeas, ut sepius tibi dixi" (15.158-160).

[42] See 16.92-109; 16.132-143; 16.173-212; 16.222-254; 27.17-29; 35.181-186; 36.208-216; 61.55-62; 81.116-142.

[43] See 3.37-39; 3.70-94; 4.40-50; 4.79-85; 4.98-107; 4.103-107; 5.5-13; 5.34-43; 6.24-29; 6.34-35; 7.11-14; 7.67-68; 9.61-63; 9.97-100; 10.2-6; 10.16-31; 12.41-81.

[44] See 7.81-88; 8.9-44; 9.111-114; 11.57-66; 13.104-107; 14.9-11; 14.81-85; 14.97-102; 15.83-100; 15.103-106; 16.7-11; 16.14-32; 16.59-62; 16.7; 17.18-81; 20.29-45; 28.3-11; 31.17-26; 35.204-209; 51.2-3; 68.11-13; 73.118-139; 77.11-33; 85.7-10; 90.24-37.

[45] We read that at the wedding feast of Cana, Jesus tells John (the apostle) to leave his wife and follow him because he will be led to a more exalted nuptial. Thus, in that Jesus attended the wedding, He approves of physical marriage, "Sed in hoc quod uocauit Ioannem de nupciis, aperte dedit intelligi quod longe dignius est spirituale matrimonium quam carnale" (20.94-96). In the text John is the bridegroom of the wedding celebration at Cana (20.6). The source for this is Jerome's prologue on the gospel of John; see *Nouum testamentum Domini nostri Iesu Christi latine*, ed.

The relationship between humility and modesty is examined as well (5.13-16; 61.55-74). The fruit of humility is also patience, a virtue often commended.[46]

What is most often commended as the expression of humility is the virtue that Saint Francis called the pathway of salvation: poverty (7.56-59). The author of the *MVC* writes to the Poor Clare that she and he have vowed poverty and it is to be held in great esteem (44.82-85). Their true poverty is not rooted only in the lack of the things of this world, but lies in the fullness of virtue that moves a person to the purity of God. Concupiscence with consent suffices to destroy the merit of the vow, because she would live only in want, not within a virtuous and meritorious poverty (44.26-47). To intensify her commitment to a life of virtuous and meritorious poverty is an important goal of her spiritual advisor. He argues that poverty produces disgrace and contempt from the world. In this life poor people are trampled under foot by all; they are laughed at and despised (44.67-78).[47] She is advised to take poverty as her mother (44.47).

To present the Franciscan ideal of poverty the text inserts numerous extra-scriptural details. Mary, before the Annunciation, gives the food she received from the priests of the temple to the poor (3.91-92). When receiving gold from one of the three kings her son shows His disdain and averts His eyes from the gold. Mary, who is strongly zealous for poverty and understands the will of her son, gives all the gold to the poor within a few days (9.84-88). The mother and child receive alms as paupers (9.94-96). She is a model of poverty (5.13-16), having neither possessions nor money (5.65-70). Her child's clothes are very shabby (7.67-68).[48] Indeed, we are often reminded that the whole family was utterly poor.[49] As a family in Egypt they are supported by Mary's sewing and spinning, while the aged Joseph does what he can as a carpenter. This perfect family struggles by the sweat of their brows and maintains perfect poverty (12.92-205).[50] Once, some rich man felt sorry for this family in poverty and

John Wordsworth and Julian White (Oxford, 1895), p. 485. The author of the *MVC* does admit however that on this point, the text of Jerome is unclear (20.1-6), since the *Historia Scholastica* was unsure whose wedding festivities were being celebrated at Cana; see PL 198.1559.

46 See 3.37-39; 6.34-35; 12.57-66; 17.17-19; 27.9-11; 32.14-17; 43.84-88; 75.148-153; 76.22-28; 77.45. Patience grounded in humility leads to peace (15.126-138).

47 "Et propterea non sunt contemnendi pauperes mundi qui ipsum Dominum representant" (44.80-82).

48 As if to reinforce this and critique the possessions of others, we read, "Et cum tanta esset necessitas, nullam audio pellium fieri mentionem" (7.104-105). The same type of contrast is set forth when Jesus rides into Jerusalem on humble animals, "Conspice nunc bene ipsum et uide quomodo in hoc suo honore uituperauit honorabilem pompam mundi. Non enim fuerunt hec animalia frenis et sellis deauratis et phaleris sericatis ornata, more stulticie mundialis; sed uilibus pannis et duobus funiculis, cum esset rex regum et Dominus dominancium" (71.28-32).

49 See 6.41-42; 7.9-11; 7.49-52; 9.9-11; 13.51-58.

50 This twelfth chapter is filled with specific details regarding the family's poverty. Mary was paid for her sewing and spinning but never more than what was

offered the boy Jesus money for expenses, embarrassing the boy and His mother. Out of His love for poverty He accepts the offering (13.47-53). This becomes the pattern for His entire life because, as an adult, Jesus loves poverty and the poor.[51]

The *Meditaciones Vite Christi* seeks to reform its reader through an intensive and elaborate attempt to conform her life to that of the gospels. In this impulse the *MVC* stands with the entire history of Christianity. However, to fully appreciate the orientation and content of the entire text that aims at religious reformation, it is important to situate the *Meditaciones* within a specific context within the history of Christianity. The context for the *MVC* is the Franciscan tradition about a century after the time of the founder, a time of challenge and difficulty for the order.[52] One scholar has argued that the author of the *MVC* was a committed representative of the fourteenth century's spiritual Franciscan movement because of the text's strong focus on poverty and its common tradition shared with Ubertino of Casale (1259-c.1330) regarding Mary giving the gold of the Magi to the poor.[53] Against this it can be argued that, unlike other Spiritual Franciscans,[54] the author of the *MVC* does not articulate an awareness of, nor does he enter into, the central points of debate regarding the distinctions between ownership and use of money. Nor do we find in the *Meditaciones* a critique of the papacy.[55] Indeed, rather than understanding the

necessary for she loved poverty deeply and remained faithful to it even to death. Her five-year-old son would help her by soliciting work (begging) and, at times, would be abused by the proud, who refused to pay for Mary's completed work. Mary never produced anything but necessities, never any objects of art that would be the occasion for vainglory. Further, in the midst of her labors, Mary never neglected her vigils and prayers.

51 See 15.79-85; 21.15-18; 21.32-38; 44.13-15.

52 See Carolly Erickson, "The Fourteenth-Century Franciscans and their Critics," *Franciscan Studies* 35 (1975): 107-135; 36 (1976): 108-147; John Moorman, *A History of the Franciscan Order from its Origins to the Year 1517* (London, 1968), pp. 307-438. On the earlier history of the order see: Badin Gratien (de Paris), *Histoire de la fondation et de l'évolution de l'ordre des Frères Mineurs au XIIIe siècle* (Paris, 1928).

53 Michael Thomas, "Zum religionsgeschichtlichen Standort der 'Meditationes Vitae Christi,'" *Zeitschrift für Religions–Geistesgeschichte* 24 (1972): 209-226 and "Zum Ursprung der 'Meditationes Vitae Christi,'" *Scriptorium* 33 (1979): 249-254.

54 For an overview of the movement, see Livorlo Oliger, "Spirituels," in *Dictionnaire de théologie Catholique,* vol. 14/2 (Paris, 1941): 2522-2549; Franz Ehrle, "Die Spiritualen, ihr Verhältniss zum Franciscanerorden und zu den Fraticellen," *Archiv für Litteratur-und Kirchengeschichte* 1 (1885): 509-569; 2 (1886): 106-164, 249-336, 3 (1887): 553-623; 4 (1888): 1-190; and Malcolm D. Lambert, *Franciscan Poverty: The Doctrine of the Absolute Poverty of Christ and the Apostles in the Franciscan Order, 1210-1323* (London, 1961).

55 Also, the *MVC* never uses key terms that emerged from the debate, such as Spirituals, Conventuals, Fraticelli, or Michaelists; see also Richard Kieckhefer, "Recent Work on Pseudo-Bonaventure and Nicholas Love," *Mystics Quarterly* 21/2

MVC as a representation of a position in the struggles of the fourteenth century, it can be argued that the author's intention was essentially an attempt to conserve a Christianity taught by Francis and Clare. To conserve a traditional Franciscan Christianity moves the author to, first, reinforce the central elements of monastic community life centered on prayer and liturgical activities; secondly, to emphasize the Incarnational expressions of love and humility through images of suffering, patience, and poverty; finally, to habitually call for a complete union with the gospel in thought, emotion, and will. These three elements were fundamental to the Franciscan movement and serve as a framework that helps in the consideration of how this new elaborate gospel harmonization, the *MVC*, seeks to preserve and reinforce the essence of Franciscan Christianity.[56]

The strong biographical emphasis of the *MVC* and its reconstruction of the gospel story with an eye to enhancing the meditative process have led at least one scholar to severely criticize the work for essentially ignoring the living presence in the liturgy of the Christ of glory.[57] This conclusion needs to be modified. Throughout the *MVC* the contemporary liturgical and sacramental life of fourteenth century Poor Clares is reinforced. Throughout the *MVC*, the spirit

(1995): 41-50. We read in the *Meditaciones*, "Summum uictoriae genus diuinae cedere maiestati, et auctoritati matris Ecclesiae non reluctari summus honor et gloria" (61.50-52).

56 Kieckhefer, "Recent Works," p. 45, has argued that a crucial question is in what sense the *MVC* displays specifically Franciscan themes. He has suggested, rightly, that the issue also necessitates a full study of a wide range of medieval *Vite Christi*.

57 Jaime Vidal, *The Infancy Narrative in Pseudo-Bonaventure's Meditationes Vitae Christi: A Study in Medieval Franciscan Christ–Piety*, Ph.D. dissertation, Fordham University, 1984, p. 399. For Vidal, the fundamental problem of the Infancy narrative of the *MVC* emerges from its inadequate Christology. He writes, "A concept of the Godhead which is almost exclusively imaginative leads us to an anthropomorphic God—a 'superman' figure rather than the 'Wholly Other'—to an image of the Incarnate Christ from which the coincidence of opposites so richly expressed in the final chapters of Bonaventure's *Itinerarium* is totally absent. It is this superficial concept of the Divinity which undermines the whole image of Christ in the *Meditationes*: his humanity is undermined by an almost Monophysite stress on his divinity, but the divinity in turn is undermined by the refusal to deal squarely with its intrinsic otherness and un-imaginability, so that the hypostatic union is superficialized into a notion somewhat like that of a king traveling incognito, or if we may use an irreverent but only too apt comparison, to the relation between Superman and Clark Kent" (p. 385). Vidal also notes the work's sentimentality and its objectification of the subjective in its imaginary reconstructions of gospel accounts (pp. 386-389). For a positive and enthusiastic appraisal of the Christology of the *MVC*, see Robert Worth Frank, "Meditationes Vitae Christi: the Logistics of Access to Divinity," in *Hermeneutics and Medieval Culture*, ed. Patrick Gallacher and Helen D'Amico, (Albany, 1989), pp. 39-50. Frank is impressed with the work's image of a loving God embodied in an image of Jesus who is "unfailingly considerate and loving" (p. 42). As such, "The *Meditationes* also creates a more completely and convincingly human Christ than had ever been seen before;" see ibid. Frank argues this based upon the multiple images of family intimacy throughout the *MVC* (pp. 44-47).

of the liturgical life of the Poor Clares can be found.[58] The value of the sacramental and liturgical life of the community is affirmed by the great many allusions to the liturgical life of the church.[59] Often throughout the *MVC* the author ties an event of the gospel to a particular celebration of the church.[60] He admonishes his reader to be a woman of prayer; for prayer alone instructs the mind, overcomes temptations, bears patiently all adversities, and is the way to keep herself going in the spiritual life (36.30-42).[61] She is to pray for eternal life and the needs of both soul and body. Do not be surprised, he tells her, that he thinks she ought to pray for the goods of the body, for with health she will have the means to serve God. However, her prayer is to be restricted to only what is necessary in the realm of temporal blessings (36.92-106).

It is possible that the author of the *Meditaciones* sent sections of the work to the convent in conjunction with specific feasts of the church year. Repeated references to "the feast of the day" for the Annunciation (4.109-148), the Nativity (7.154-172), the Visitation of the Magi (9.9-30), and the Presentation in the Temple (11.25-45)[62] emphasize for the Poor Clare that "today is the day when...." This focus on the liturgical celebration of the day serves to make the

58 On the life of the "Poor Ladies" of Assisi, see Livario Oliger, "De Origine Regularum Ordinis Sanctae Clarae," *Archivum Franciscanum Historicum* 5 (1912): 181-209, 413-447; Lazaro Iriarte, *Letra y Espiritu de la Regla de Santa Clara* (Roma, 1974); Chiara A. Lainati, "La Clôture de Sainte Claire et des Premières Clarisses dans la législation canonique et dans la pratique," *Laurentianum* 14 (1973): 223-250; H. Böhmer, *Histoire abrégee de l'ordre de Ste. Claire d' Assise*, 2 vols. (Lyons, 1906); Duane Lapsanski, *Evangelical Perfection: An Historical Examination of the Concept in the Early Franciscan Sources* (St. Bonaventure, New York, 1977), pp. 160-171; Wood, *Women, Art, and Spirituality*; Octave d'Angers, "Le Chant Liturgique dans L'Ordre de Saint Francois aux Origines," *Études Franciscaines* 75 (1975): 157-306; Ernest Gilliat-Smith, *St. Clare of Assisi: Her Life and Legislation* (New York, 1914); and Fausta Casolini, "Sainte Claire et les Clarisses," in *Dictionnaire de spiritualité* 5 (1964): 1401-1422. On *The Rule, Letters and Testament of Clare*, see *Regulae et Constitutiones Generales Monialium Ordinis S. Clarae* (Roma, 1941); *Claire d'Assise, Ecrits*, ed. Marie-France Becker et al. (Sources Chrétiennes, 325; Paris, 1985); Regis J. Armstrong, *Clare of Assisi: Early Documents* (St. Bonaventure, New York, 1993).

59 See "Initia Locorum Liturgiae" in Stallings-Taney, *MVC*, pp. 380-389.

60 See 4.108-110; 70153-154; 8.5-6; 9.3-6; 11.25-26. So: "Appropinquante autem hora uespertina, dicit eis Dominus Iesus:" (89.28-29); "O qualis est nunc domuncula ista, et quam gloriosum habitare in ea! Nonne tibi uidetur esse eciam hic magnum Pascha, si aliquid deuocionis habes? Puto quod sic," (91.28-31); "Vidisti quocics hodic habuisti Pascha: nam omnes iste appariciones in die Paschatis fuerunt" (91.45-47).

61 "Sumas oracionem nichilque aliud. Necessariis curis tantum exceptis, te delectet nisi oracio. Quia nichil te tantum delectari debet quantum morari cum Domino, quod per oracionem fit" (36.53-55).

62 All the characters in the gospel scene of the Presentation of Jesus at the temple, "Postea uadunt ad altare processionem facientes que hodie representatur per uniuersum mundum." Simeon and Joseph sing psalms and Mary places her son on the altar with prayers to God the Father (11.25-45).

past present through her daily experience of prayer and sacrament. Indeed, she is told very clearly that the object of her gospel meditations is the very God she receives in the Eucharistic host (73.151-165).[63] At the end of the work she is offered the suggestion that her meditations be organized in accord with the seven days of the week (108.1-31); and some of the Passion material is arranged, in the *MVC*, in accord with the canonical hours (chapters 75-80).[64] In the attention to the importance of the sacramental life the *MVC* stands with Saint Francis who is depicted by his biographers as aglow with love for the Eucharist.[65]

Saint Clare's desire to leave the world and to live the poverty of Christ, in imitation of Francis, is the motivation of her life and that of the other Poor Ladies of San Damiano.[66] They were to practice humility, patience, love, and poverty, freed from the distractions of the world in their cloistered life.[67] This is why the author tells the Poor Clare that she has not been imprisoned for punishment but for protection, that is, placed in a most secure fortress of sacred convictions (6.55-56). This is why he tells her that the spiritual exercises of solitude, fasting, prayer, and bodily mortification will be, as they interact together, very helpful in the spiritual life (17.12-15).[68] She is encouraged to thank God that she is placed in a convent and has vowed poverty (44.27-29); thus, she and her spiritual advisor must hold poverty in great esteem (44.82-85).[69]

[63] "Nichil enim maius, carius, dulcius uel utilius nobis relinquere potuit quam seipsum. Ipse namque quem in sacramento sumis illud idem est qui de Virgine mirabiliter incarnatus et natus pro te mortem sustinuit, et qui resurgens et gloriose ascendens sedet a dexteris Dei ... Ipse sic in hostia tali modica oblatus et tibi exhibitus, ipse est Dominus Iesus de quo loquimur: Filius Dei uiui" (73.156-165).

[64] See *Regula*, ch. 3, for the importance of the divine office and the sacraments in the life of the Poor Clares.

[65] See Thomas de Celano, *St. Francisci Assisiensis vita et miracula*, ed. Edouard d'Alencon (Rome, 1906), *Legenda Secunda* n. 201; S. Bonaventura, *Legenda (Maior) S. Francisci*, in *Opera Omnia* (Quaracchi, 1898), 8.504-564, C.9, N.2. For a more recent critical edition of Celano's *Vita Prima* and *Vita Secunda,* see *Analecta Franciscana* 10 (1926-1941).

[66] See *Regula*, ch. 1, 6, and 8; and *Testamentum*, 5, 6-17, 24-26, 29, 33-38, 46-50. For Francis and Clare the poverty of Christ and that of His disciples is expressed in the texts of scripture: Mt 12:21; Mt 16:24; Lk 14:26; Mt 8:20; Mt 19:21; Lk 9:3; Lk 14:33; Mt 10:8-10; and Lk 13:33.

[67] See *Regula*, ch. 5, 9, 10, and 11; and *Testamentum*, 18-23, 27-28, 39-43, 51-73.

[68] The *MVC* advises, with Bernard, that bodily exercises be done with discretion and reason for a body broken through an excess of mortification would impede spirituality (44.313-344).

[69] "Igitur considerabilis est multum hec uirtus paupertatis, et maxime a nobis qui eam promisimus. Ipsam itaque propterea semper cum omni reuerencia et deuocione obseruare curato" (44.82-85).

The Poor Clare is constantly encouraged in her life commitment. She has chosen "the best part," a life of contemplation (57.93-97). Her life as a contemplative ought to be occupied with God alone (58.3-7). If there are times of difficulty she is to leave everything for God to handle (73.89-96). And if she occasionally experiences a dryness of the soul where it seems as if she is abandoned by God, she is advised to continue to diligently seek the divine through continuous engagements in holy meditations and good works (14.91-96).[70]

Approximately a century before the *MVC*, writing to Agnes of Prague, Clare of Assisi advises a contemplation of God in order to taste the hidden sweetness reserved by God for those who love him.[71] Here the image of a mirror is used, a theme basic to the letters of Clare.[72] To Agnes, Clare offers images of the poverty of the manger and the cross as well as that of Jesus' poor mother.[73] Clare calls Agnes to a full contemplation of Jesus, this mirror of divinity, by suffering and weeping with Him, by dying with Him on the cross of tribulation. Agnes, the noble queen, is to gaze upon Jesus to consider, to contemplate, and to desire to imitate him.[74] In the embrace of the humble one Agnes will, in a life of poverty, leave the things of time and exchange them for those of eternity.[75] In these four letters to Agnes of Prague, Clare desires, above all, to strengthen Agnes in the "holy service which you have undertaken out of a burning desire for the 'Poor Crucified.'"[76]

Near the end of the *Meditaciones* (107.1-13) the author is writing to his dearly beloved daughter reminding her that she is in possession of the life of the Lord Jesus transmitted to her in the form of meditations. He pleads with her to reverently, willingly, even joyfully, open her mind to what is said. She is to be

70 The context here is the search for the lost Jesus in Jerusalem by His mother. The loss of the divine could, we are told (14.94), even happen to the mother of God; but at the end His mother, and this Poor Clare, will find Him once again (14.96).

71 *Epistola Tertia ad Beatam Agnetem de Praga*, 12-14, in *Claire d'Assise, Ecrits*. The four letters to Agnes were written between 1235 and 1253.

72 See Regis Armstrong, "Clare of Assisi: The Mirror Mystic," *The Cord* 35 (1985): 195-202.

73 *Epistola Quarta ad Beatam Agnetem de Praga*, 18-25, 33; see also *Testamentum*, 45: "ut amore illius Dei, qui pauper positus est in praesepio, pauper vixit in saeculo et nudus remansit in patibulo."

74 *Epistola Secunda ad Beatam Agnetem de Praga:* "Sponsum tuum prae filiis hominum speciosum, pro salute tua factum virorum vilissimum, despectum, percussum et toto corpore multipliciter flagellatum, inter ipsas crucis angustias morientem, regina praenobilis, intuere, considera, contemplare, desiderans imitari. Cui si compateris conregnabis, condolens congaudebis, in cruce tribulationis commoriens cum ipso in sanctorum splendoribus mansiones aethereas possidebis" (20-21).

75 *Epistola Prima ad Beatam Agnetem de Praga*, 30.

76 *Epistola Prima*, 13.

unstinting in familiarizing herself with this life, to open to it with care, with complete delight and cheerfulness. This is the life upon which she can build her life; this is the life upon which her life is nourished and brought always to more sublime heights. He speaks to her as did, in essence, Clare with Agnes, or Francis with Clare, "Quia hec est uia tua et uita tua: hoc est fundamentum super quo poteris magnum edificium constituere" (107.5-7). As Clare encouraged Agnes, as Francis encouraged Clare, the Franciscan author of the *MVC* encourages his Franciscan reader to reform her life by conforming it to the life of Christ.

GERSON AND THE CELESTINES

How Jean Gerson and his friend Pierre Poquet replied to various questions of discipline and points of conscience (ca. 1400)

Gilbert Ouy

Since he was especially concerned about the reform of the church, Gerson relied, to support his endeavour, on the two religious orders which he regarded as having preserved their original purity, viz the Carthusians, for whom he proclaimed his love,[1] and the Celestines, an order in which he encouraged two of his younger brothers to make their profession. These two orders he entrusted with the task of circulating his works by dedicating his treatise *De laude scriptorum*[2] to them.

Among the Celestines, he had found both a spiritual guide and a friend in the person of Pierre Poquet,[3] more than twenty years his elder. It was already a well-known fact that the latter had exerted a strong influence on the chancellor, and especially that he had induced him to share his particular devotion to Saint Joseph.[4] But it is only thanks to a manuscript found some fifteen years ago at Saint Petersburg that we know how, at least once, the two friends had jointly held a session of *quodlibeta,* probably at the Celestine convent in Paris, of which Poquet had been the prior before being elected head of the province of France.

Of the questions that they were asked on this occasion, bearing primarily on cases of conscience or points of monastic discipline, and of the answers they gave, not all remained unknown nor even entirely unpublished, but what had been published accounted for less than half of the total;[5] besides, one could not

1 "Amo te, sacer Ordo Cartusiensis . . ." *Super Cantica Canticorum,* ed. Palémon Glorieux, *Œuvres complètes,* 10 vols (Paris, 1960-1973) [hereafter Glorieux], 8.665 n. 422.

2 Ibid., 9.423-434 n. 454.

3 See the excellent notice that Olivier Caudron devoted to him in the *Dictionnaire de spiritualité ascétique et mystique,* 16 vols. (Paris, 1937-1995), 12.1922-1926. Knowing that this young scholar was working on Pierre Poquet, I contacted him upon my return from Russia in 1984 to propose working in collaboration on the presentation of the document that I had just discovered. He willingly accepted, but his nomination at that moment to head the Bibliothèque universitaire de la Réunion prevented him from pursuing the project. After having waited a long time, I resign myself to doing this publication alone. In the present article, I am using various information drawn from our correspondence and the notice in the dictionary cited above.

4 See notably the commented edition of his *Dictamen de laudibus beati Joseph* by Max Lieberman in *Cahiers de Josephologie* 12 (1964) : 5-71.

5 Of the *Quæstiones 4* (Glorieux 9 n. 427), only the fourth question (p. 72) is related to the text published here, being in some sense a resume of its questions 1 to 5. For the *Quæstiones 46* (ibid., pp. 72-83 n. 428) – which, despite the title, are only 45 in number (this could be explained by the fusion of two of the questions in G 33) – here is the concordance between the rubrics of the Glorieux (G) edition and those of the ms. of Saint Petersburg (P) : G 1 = P 105 ; G 2 = P 103 ; G 3-5 = P 106-108 ; G 6 = P 98 ; G 7-8 = P 100-101 ; G 9-11 = P 7-9 ; G 12-15 = P 13-16 ; G 16 = P 19 ; G 17 = P 23 ; G 18 = P 28 ; G 19-25 = P 36-42 ; G 26 = P 44 ; G 27-28 = P 46-47 ; G 29-30 = P

know thet Poquet had taken part in the session, since all the answers were attributed to Gerson alone.

For his edition of the *Quæstiones 46,* Glorieux—as is often the case—contented himself with copying the Du Pin edition of 1706, which itself merely reproduces the text of the Richer edition of 1606, and he evidently took little or no interest in ms. BnF lat. 14905 (ms. NN 9 of Saint-Victor)[6] which he is supposed to have used, since he left two questions unpublished, viz those which appear respectively on fol. 42r of this collection (corresponding to q. 102 of the Saint Petersburg ms.) and on fol. 43r (this one absent from our ms.). Now this Victorine manuscript has a curious characteristic: twice (fol. 42v and 43r), the word *Cancellarius* appears in the left margin before an answer, which looks hardly justifiable since all the responses are attributed to Gerson: we have here a kind of vestige, whose origin can only be understood when one has seen the full *reportatio* of the session during which Pierre Poquet and the chancellor of *Notre-Dame* spoke in turns.[7]

This document figures at fol. 309v-320r of a manuscript preserved at the Public Library (former Saltykov-Shchedrin Library) of Saint-Petersburg with the shelf-mark Lat. Ov II N 1. Like so many others, this volume had been stolen from Paris—almost certainly from the Celestine convent—by the Russian diplomat Piotr Dubrovsky[8] (1754-1816) who appended his *ex-libris* to it, but soon sold it to Empress Catherine. This character is well-known for the way he took advantage of the confusion that reigned in the church of France, around 1791, following the adoption of the *Constitution civile du clergé:* he systematically ransacked the libraries of all Parisian abbeys and convents, beginning with Saint-Germain des Prés, where the venerable manuscripts of Corbie were kept. He himself or his accomplices, after ensuring some collusion on the spot in order to work safely, would withdraw some particularly interesting

49-50 ; G 31 = P 52 ; G 32-33 = P 54, 55+56 ; G 34-36 = P 58-60 ; G 37 = P 64 ; G 38 = P 66 ; G 39 = P 68 ; G 40 = P 70 ; G 41-42 = P 90-91 ; G 43-45 = P 95-96. Finally, the *Quæstiones 3* (ibid., p. 83 n. 429) correspond to questions 76 to 78 of the ms. of Saint Petersburg. Note that these last three questions, which Glorieux edited from ms. 31 of the Musée Calvet of Avignon (f. 145r) should have been completed by a fourth which figures on the other side of the same leaf, corresponding with our question n. 60. As we see, a good fifty questions of the Saint Petersburg ms. remained unedited.

[6] See Danièle Calvot and Gilbert Ouy, *L'œuvre de Gerson à Saint-Victor de Paris* (Paris, 1990), pp. 105-106 n. 18.

[7] In his *Gallicæ Cælestinorum congregationis . . . monasteriorum fundationes* (Paris, 1719), A. Becquet lists the *Quodlibeta* among the works of Poquet, but mentions no manuscript copy. In his precious collective catalogue of manuscripts of the Celestine convents of France (ms. BnF fr. 15290, p. 332), elaborated around 1770, Daire records two manuscripts, one at Amiens, the other at Limay-lès-Mantes, whose title corresponds almost exactly to that of the Saint Petersburg ms., but we do not know what became of those two volumes after the Revolution.

[8] Cf. Tamara Voronova, "Western Manuscripts in the Saltykov-Shchedrin Library, Leningrad," *The Book Collector* 5 (Spring, 1956) : 12-18 ; Michel François, *Pierre Dubrovsky et les manuscrits de Saint-Germain des Prés à Leningrad, Mémorial du XIVe centenaire de l'abbaye de Saint-Germain des Prés* (Paris, 1959), pp. 333-391.

leaves or quires from various manuscript collections, or, more often, would strip a binding of its contents then put it back in its place after filling it with papers of no value, so that the absence of the precious document would go unnoticed for a long time[9].

The manuscript which bears the shelf mark Lat. Ov II N 1 at the Public Library of Saint-Petersburg is a fine little volume made of 363 vellum leaves measuring 187x130 mm. (original foliation in Roman numerals). In a frame (130x88 mm.) traced with black lead, the text (33 lines per page) is written in a neat semi-cursive gothic minuscule by a scribe who was not only very careful, but also intelligent and learned. The very sober decoration is limited to filigree capitals with flourishes, end caps and paragraph signs in red, black and blue. The date—mid-fifteenth century[10]—which looks obvious, is soon confirmed by a seven line colophon written by the same scribe below the right column of fol. 309r; it was erased, but remains mostly readable under the ultraviolet lamp: *Perfectum est hoc opus ultima mensis / Januarii, anno Domini millesimo / quadringentesimo quinquagesimo primo (?) / in conventu fratrum Celestinorum / Parisius, per ordinationem venerabilis / patris Guillelmi*[11] .... */ de p.....* Further on, at f. 361v, another erased colophon – that one rubricated – is less easy to read: *Istud volumen ..../ ...... quod ibidem scribi fecit venerabilis / pater Guillelmus ... de pe.../ sibi donatis (?) adversis personis ...* The shelf mark (*96*) of the Celestine library of Paris appears at the beginning, and various *ex-libris* of the convent, most of them erased, are found in many places, especially at ff. 198v, 307v, 309r, 325v and 351v. The thief has added his own *ex-libris*: *Ex Musæo Petri Dubrowsky* and his coat of arms, as well as a sumptuous binding adorned with lacing of gilt leather.

The main part of the volume (fol. 1-308) is occupied by the *Summa de casibus abbreviata per ordinem alphabeti* of Bartolomeo da San Concordio, accompanied by various tables.

The questions studied here follow immediately (fol. 309v-320r). Then come several *opuscula* of Gerson: *De potestate absolvendi*[12] (fol. 320r-321r); *Circa irregularitatem*[13] (fol. 321r-322v); *De modo excommunicationum*[14] (fol. 322v-323r); *Resolutio circa materiam excommunicationum*[15] (fol. 323v-324r).

9 See *Lettres et mémoires adressés au chancelier Séguier*, ed. Roland Mousnier, 2 vols (Paris, 1964), 1.10.

10 Yet, on the other side of the first flyleaf, a librarian has written: *mss. de l'an 1338.*

11 The prior Guillaume Romain had a fair number of manuscripts copied: see the catalogues of the libraries of the Arsenal and the Mazarine.

12 Glorieux, 9.421-423 n. 453.

13 Ibid., 9.86-89 n. 431.

14 Ibid., 9.92-93 n. 433.

15 Ibid., 6.294-296 n. 290.

We have a complete change of topic with the text at fol. 324v-325v: *Moralitas deorum diversorum quos colebant antiqui,* which is followed by a short treatise on the twelve fruits of tribulation (fol. 326r-328v). At fol. 328v-351v (completed by fol. 363r-v, where an omitted passage was transcribed) we find an abridged version of the treatise *De doctrina cordis* or *De præparatione cordis* often ascribed to the Cistercian Gerard of Liège. This text is followed by some questions raised in Paris in 1269 at the General Chapter of the Franciscan order (fol. 351v-352v).

We return to Gerson with five unedited *conclusiones* about Sunday rest (fol. 352v-353r) which will be published at the end of this article and, after several extracts (fol. 353v-355r), with three *opuscula: De potestate clavium et valore indulgentiaru*[16] (fol. 356v-357r), *De indulgentia peccatorum*[17] (fol. 357r-358r) and *De absolutione defuncti apud Cartusienses*[18] (fol. 358r). But the chancellor did not take part in elaborating the text which follows (fol. 358v-361r), seventeen propositions of the Faculty of Theology of Paris about Sunday rest[19], since he was in Lyon on the date (October, 1426) when the redaction took place. This collection reaches completion with a question (fol. 361v) taken from the *Summa confessorum.*

In that period, theological *quodlibeta* were the usual practice, and we can be sure that, as a student, Gerson attended and even took part in many *disputationes;* but none of his works in this genre have been preserved. This absence is hardly surprising for, in his eyes, these brilliant intellectual jousts were tainted with two of the poisons of the soul which the sin of pride brings in its wake: *curiositas* and *singularitas.* In his treatise *Contra curiositatem studentium,*[20] he clearly defined these vices: *Curiositas est vitium quo, dimissis utilioribus, homo convertit studium suum ad minus utilia vel inattingibilia sibi vel noxia. . . . Singularitas est vitium quo, dimissis utilioribus, homo convertit studium suum ad doctrinas peregrinas et insolitas.*

But, in this case, we are dealing with *quodlibeta* of an altogether different genre, which, however, are much more rarely represented in the manuscripts: most of the questions here submitted to the chancellor and to his friend Pierre Poquet appear to be genuine cases of conscience. This document could therefore be a reliable source of information as to the various types of problems to which, at that period, the monks of the Celestine convent of Paris were seeking answers.

These questions, which I deemed convenient to number continuously from 1 to 108, do not follow a well-defined order. They constitute two unevenly

16 Ibid., 9.654-658 n. 473.

17 Ibid., 9.658-660 n. 474. It seems to be the second part of the preceding text rather than an independent treatise.

18 Ibid., 9.643-644 n.467.

19 *Chartularium Universitatis Parisiensis,* ed. Heinrich Denifle and Emile Chatelain, 4 vols. (Paris, 1889-1897), 4 n. 2283.

20 Glorieux, 3.230 n. 99.

distributed groups: about one hundred to which the chancellor responds alone, and a dozen[21] to which Poquet, then Gerson respond in succession. For the first group, we could say roughly that questions 1 to 35 concern celebration of mass, questions 36 to 69 confession, questions 70 to 75 excommunication, questions 76 to 94 monastic discipline. For the second group, it is hardly possible to find an order; we can only remark that the psychological and moral problems seem to be given more attention than in the first group.

We have to do here, in the true sense of the term, with cases of conscience. There is, for instance, a question (q. 101) concerning the thoughts, some frivolous, some indeed frankly guilty, which occasionally will assail the celebrant during the office. In his response, Gerson has recourse to the formula that he almost always employs when he wants to draw on his personal experience: "I know someone who. . ."

It is interesting to remark that more than a tenth of the questions concern the appropriate action to be taken when the consecrated wine (*sanguis*) or the host (*corpus Domini*) risk being tainted: what is to be done, for instance, if one finds a fly or a spider in the chalice, if the host falls on the ground or if someone vomits after communion? This seems to indicate that the eucharistic materialism against which Berengar of Tours had been fighting in earlier days was still deeply rooted and vivid at that period and could provoke real qualms of conscience for some Celestine monks.

The chancellor himself takes this kind of question very seriously. Thus, when a monk—who probably suffers from bronchitis—asks if it safe to spit one half hour after celebrating mass, Pierre Poquet briefly reassures him: it is not even necessary to wait one half hour but it would be best, out of prudence, to spit in the fire or, failing that, at least to choose an area where nobody might tread. Gerson, intervening afterwards, wants to give a more detailed answer; he also envisages the case of the same person not only after, but before mass as well. Using a vocabulary that denotes a certain proficiency in the medicine of his days, he recommends a light mouthwash, but advises against gargling, since part of the water would flow down to the stomach of the celebrant who, therefore, would no longer have an empty stomach.

In all other domains, however, Gerson never fails to put his interlocutors on guard against exaggerated scruples. He also advises them not to adopt unusual behaviours, but to conform as far as possible to the practices of the place and time (*observetur usus loci et temporis*). Above all, he insists that they should abstain from all acts susceptible of troubling simple souls. Thus, when asked (q. 4) if the broken fragments of an altar may be reused as any other kind of stone, he answers that they may, provided that it does not risk scandalizing the little people who, knowing that they were once consecrated stones, might be horrified to see them treated that way. This constant concern for avoiding *scandalum pusillorum* is indeed consistent with the letter as well as the spirit of the gospel, but we may also view it as a mark of both the affection and the respect that the

[21] Numbers 102 and 104 are not properly speaking responses to questions, but two brief statements about venial sins which Gerson made perhaps because he had been asked by the public to do so.

chancellor felt for that humble country people of which he was born and that he never renounced.

(ST-PETERSBOURG, Bibl. Publ., ms. lat. Ov II n. 1, fol. 309v-320r)

SEQUUNTUR QUESTIONES ALIQUE QUORUM RESPONSIO DATA EST A DOMINO CANCELLARIO ECCLESIE PARISIENSIS, IN SACRA PAGINA PROFESSORE EXIMIO

1. Primo queritur utrum liceat consecrare altare magnum vel parvum factum ex duabus vel tribus aut .iiii.[or] peciis vel amplius.

Respondetur quod non, intelligendo de principali tabula.

2. Utrum liceat celebrare missam super altare fractum.

Respondetur quod non, si sit fractus enormiter, sic quod pecie nullomodo ahereant adinvicem, nec sint aliquomodo continue licet sint contigue. Et nota quod altare, secundum usum communem, bene fit de uno solo lapide sine alio adiuncto, et consecratur, et ita manet consecratum quantumcumque alia extrinseca moveantur aut tollantur, quamvis iuriste antiqui senserint oppositum pro tempore suo.

3. Utrum de peciis altaris fracti liceat facere minora altaria aut portabilia absque benedictione aut reconciliatione iterata.

Respondetur quod non, sicut nec calix fractus manet benedictus ; et nota de vestimentis sacris in *Summa Confessorum*, quomodo licet ea resarcire et quomodo non.

4. Utrum pecias altaris fracti liceret ad aliud opus non sacratum ordinare.

Respondetur quod sic, presertim ubi non timetur scandalum pusillorum qui cognoscunt quod tales pecie fuerunt sacrate et inde habent horrorem si non honorantur.

5. Utrum mappe vel alia huiusmodi non sacrata que iam quodammodo servierunt circa altare vel in ecclesia, et quecumque alia fuerint oblata in ecclesia possint ad alios usus converti.

Respondetur quod sic nisi propter scandalum, ut dictum est in dubio precedenti.

6. Que ornamenta vel vasa ecclesie sunt de necessitate benedicenda ?

Respondetur quod fiat recursus ad usum communem et ad libros episcoporum. Illa tamen sunt magis de necessitate benedicenda que applicantur immediate ad tangendum vel continendum sacramentum altaris, ut calix et corporale et indumenta sacerdotalia pro missa. Et tutius est quod benedicatur etiam cingulum, si non fuerit usus publicus in oppositum : tales enim constitutiones et benedictiones sunt de iure positivo et sunt quandoque de congruitate, non de necessitate, ac pro qualitate temporum mutari possunt.

7. Utrum liceret extrahere muscam vel araneam aut aliud huiusmodi de sanguine cum cocleari parvo aut aliquo alio non consecrato.

Respondetur quod sic, presertim ubi non posset aliquid tale extrahi commode cum digito consecrato vel cum patena aut aliquo tali.

8. Utrum, si caderet aut inveniretur in sanguine musca aut festuca vel pillus aut filum aut aliquid tale quod posset impedimentum aut nocumentum patrare sumenti sanguinem, deberet extrahi, et quid inde fieret.

Respondetur quod posset extrahi, et lavaretur bene, et lotio sumeretur [310r] si non esset venenosa, et musca vel festuca combureretur, aut ipsa vel cinis eius poneretur in loco abdito ut in altari vel piscina.

9. Utrum graviter peccaret ille per cuius neglectum talia invenirentur in calice.

Respondetur quod tutum est facere conscientiam et confiteri ; et est peccatum maius aut minus secundum quod negligens debuit adhibere maiorem cautelam.

De missa, consecratione et communione

10. Primo, qua hora liceat dici missam vel saltem fieri consecrationem ut non prius quam debeat fiat.

Respondetur quod regulariter non debet celebratio misse fieri priusquam crepusculum probabiliter existimetur apparere, nisi ex privilegio et in die Natalis Domini.

11. Utrum in vigilia aut ieiunio possit dici missa post .xii.am horam.

Respondetur quod sic usque nonam, nisi scandalum probabiliter timeatur in populo non assueto sic audire ; etiam in die non ieiunii pro aliqua causa rationabili sic diceretur.

12. Utrum, quando sic tardatur, debeat dici missa de vigilia aut ieiunio sic quod non alia.

Respondetur quod non oportet dici certam missam, nisi quia missa de vigilia magis congruit, et presertim dum celebratio fit in publico.

13. Utrum, quando ponitur primo vinum et aqua in calicem, si – ut sepe contingit–resiliat una gutta vel amplius et remaneant ab intus intra labium calicis et fundum, debeant post consecrationem tales guttule dici consecrate.

Respondetur quod non, presertim si sacerdos non intenderit – nec intendat communiter – consecrare nisi illud vinum quod est in fundo calicis ; potest tamen illa gutta sumi ante ablutionem sub intentione generali, si consecrata est, ut consecrata, si non, ut non consecrata ; et cautum est ut sacerdos sit sollicitus ab initio vigilare circa talia et circa panem ne mice cadant ab hostia, et ne tales gutte remaneant. Si autem sacerdos, dum advertit ante consecrationem tales guttulas, intendit consecrare eas, ipse sunt consecrate ; similiter, si habeat in principio generalem intentionem consecrandi quicquid est consecrabile in calice, tunc totum est consecratum.

14. Utrum, si quis omittat vel dubitet omisisse aliquid in consecratione, an debeat solum reincipere ad id quod omisit vel omisisse se credit, aut si ab initio debeat reincipere ; et quid de illis qui assuescunt reiterationem ?

Respondetur quod non est leviter iteratio facienda, et malum est consuescere; presertim in verbis sacramentalibus, non debet iteratio fieri nisi constet certitudinaliter quod verba non sunt dicta. Si autem sit dubitatio probabilis, tunc fiat reiteratio sub conditione implicita, sicut fit dum dubitatur de aliquo si fuerit baptizatus, ut dicatur sic in corde : "Ego non intendo consecrare hanc hostiam si sit consecrata ; sed si non sit consecrata, [310v] intendo eam consecrare" ; et tunc dicat verba. Et posset alio modo provideri nisi timeretur scandalum : ut sumeretur hostia de novo non consecrata et consecraretur, et alia sumeretur sub intentione generali ante ablutionem, scilicet ut consecrata si sit consecrata, si non ut non.

15. Utrum, si quis sine lumine diceret missam, aut si deesset lumen in media parte misse, et maxime a consecratione usque in finem, incurreretur excommunicatio.

Respondetur quod debent facere conscientiam tam sacerdotes quam ministri ; non est tamen sententia excommunicationis super hoc lata.

16. Utrum necesse est accendere facem seu torchiam in consecratione vel communione populi ; aut si is qui portat corpus Domini aut defert teneatur habere superlicium cum stola, aut si sufficeret stola sola, vel econtra.

Respondetur quod observetur usus loci et temporis. Non puto tamen quod aliquid istorum sit preceptum obligans, nec omissio debet reputari peccatum mortale, nisi fieret scienter ex contemptu vel cum scandalo pusillorum.

17. Utrum necesse est dare pacem in missis que non sunt mortuorum, aut quando in rubrica signatur non dandam esse pacem.

Respondetur quod observetur consuetudo loci et temporis et dicatur sicut in dubio precedenti.

18. Utrum, si ante *Pater noster* frangatur hostia, fient signacula consueta.

Respondetur quod fient cum parte notabiliori ; et si tota hostia ceciderit in calicem, non est necesse illa signacula fieri, sed peniteat qui neglexit.

19. Si hostia sit in modico maculata vel perforata aut detruncata aut non rotonda ut moris est, quid fiet ?

Respondetur quod talis non debet assumi in principio, presertim ubi necessitas non urget et potest alia haberi; sed si sit iam sumpta et non potest alia peti convenienter sine scandalo, dimittatur ipsa et fiat conscientia postmodum de neglectu.

20. Utrum peccet quis, sive sacerdos sive ministri alii, si omiserint accipere stolam vel manipulum aut aliquid huiusmodi.

Respondetur quod peccant secundum qualitatem negligentie. Puto tamen quod non est hic excommunicatio vel irregularitas. Sciatur tamen a iurisperitis si sit statutum positivum ; et dicunt illi a quibus inquisivi quod non.

21. Item quid si ex ruditate aut negligentia ministri vel alterius ceciderit hostia in terram?

Respondetur quod fiat sicut habetur communiter notatum circa defectus misse, quia debet radi terra et poni in piscina ; penitentia vero determinata est in canonibus, sed nunc omnes tales penitentie reputantur arbitrarie, et sic habet usus et auctoritas doctorum.

22. Utrum, si quis dicat horas solus, teneatur dicere : "Dominus vobiscum", vel sufficeret dicere : "Domine, exaudi orationem meam".

Respondetur quod sufficit secundum, ymmo magis videtur congruere quam primum.

23. Utrum, si quis dicat missam ita quod ibi nullus sit nisi is qui iuvat eum, teneatur ad *Confiteor* dicere : "et vobis, fratres" vel : "misereatur vestri", etc.

Respondetur quod sic, quia ille [311r] unus gerit vicem totius populi.

24. Utrum liceat communicare quemquem post .xii.am horam, preter infirmos.

Respondetur quod sic, sicut licet etiam celebrare, nisi timeatur scandalum, et si communicandus sit ieiunus.

25. Item qui vel quando tenentur communicare, et sub qua pena ?

Responsionem latiorem quere in *Somma Confessorum*. Puto tamen quod omnis, dum ad annos discretionis pervenerit, teneatur nisi possit aliunde excusari. Et vocantur anni discretionis communiter in puero circa .xiiii.cimum annum et in puella circa .xii.cimum quoad actus civiles et legitimos ; sed, quantum ad actus nostre religionis, ille vel illa qui possunt habere sufficientem reverentiam ad sacramentum eucharistie, tam ex doctrina parentum quam ex bonitate ingenii et iudicii rationis, per que suppletur etas, consulerem quod reciperent quia, sicut dixit quedam mulier devota suo filio adolescenti formidanti communicare : "Scias, o fili, quoniam ad sacramentum hoc nunquam accedes quin plura peccata tunc commiseris quam fecisti".

26. Utrum epileutici aut qui quodammodo perderent sensum, aut etiam leprosi et qui patiuntur fluxum debeant promoveri ad sacros ordines vel iam promoti ministrare.

Responsionem quere ut prius. Puto tamen quod primi et secundi sunt arcendi ab utroque, leprosi vero a primo, sed nec ipsi nec quarti a ministrando nisi scandalum timeatur.

27. Utrum, quando sacerdos debet communicare aliquos in altari, debeat sumere ablutionem calicis antequam communicaverit illos ; quia, si contingeret remanere super corporale vel in patena particulas hostiarum et ipse vellet eas colligere et assumere eas post ablutionem, iam, secundum aliquos, videretur non ieiunus sumere corpus Domini.

Respondetur quod tutius est quod differat ablutionem propter causam tactam, quia aliter non posset sumere illas particulas, sed posset servare eas in vase deputato pro hostiis sacratis, vel illas dare ieiuno.

28. Item quantum spatium requiritur post perceptionem <sacramenti> ad digestionem eius ita quod, si ex infirmitate vel alias homo evomeret, iam non esset necesse colligere quod evomuit tanquam ibi adhuc essent species sacramenti, et an sufficeret modicum dormisse post perceptionem sacramenti, sive ante talem dormitionem sumpserit alium cibum vel non ?

Respondetur quod citius aut tardius fit digestio secundum qualitatem complexionum ; sed est certa regula quod, si appareant species in vomitu, ille debent colligi et sumi, vel tanquam corpus Domini in vase mundo servari ; alioquin, si nullomodo appareant species, ponatur vomitus in piscinam vel comburatur.

29. Utrum ministri altaris, scilicet sacerdos et dyaconus, subdiaconus et clerici, teneantur semper calciari caligis cum sotularibus vel solummodo calsariis, et hoc pro monachis.

Respondetur quod teneatur consuetudo religionis et loci ; nec oportet in [311v] transgressoribus esse semper peccatum mortale, nec est excommunicatio.

30. Utrum is qui legit evangelium in populo vel, apud monachos, in choro, in matutinis aut super infirmum, et alii qui cappis induuntur et qui ministrant in superliciis, alibi quam in altari similiter teneantur calciari.

Respondetur ut prius.

31. Utrum, si quis predictorum inciderit in pollutionem, teneatur prius confiteri quam ministret.

Respondetur quod probabile est quod sufficiat contritio cum proposito confitendi nisi dum vult celebrare, quia confiteri tenetur, secundum interpretationem Ecclesie et doctorum, dum habet conscientiam de peccato mortali certam vel probabilem, secus de solis scrupulis levibus.

32. Utrum is qui legit evangelium, ut dictum est prius, teneatur semper habere superlicium vel albam cum stola, aut sufficiat stola sine illis, aut si illa sufficiant sine stola.

Resp. Teneatur consuetudo de qua informetur per seniores.

33. Utrum liceret ponere calicem cum sanguine vel patenam cum corpore Domini super mappas sine corporali subtracto, aut si liceret ea ponere super altare nudum consecratum ; aut si hoc facere liceret super altare non consecratum vel aliquid aliud.

Respondetur quod non, presertim in missa, nisi ubi consuetudo est in oppositum, sicut dum fertur vas ad infirmos in quo est corpus Christi. Puto tamen quod talia observanda sunt regulariter magis ex congruitate quam ex precepti necessitate.

34. Utrum, si celebratur missa de mortuis, benefactum sit dicere ultimam orationem de vivis. Item, si dicatur de vivis, an ultima oratio debeat dici de mortuis.

Resp. Teneatur consuetudo de qua scietur per seniores vel per usitatos in consuetudinibus sui loci.

35. Utrum beneficiati seu religiosi qui tenentur ad officium canonicum teneantur etiam ad officium misse dicendum.

Respondetur quod non, nisi aliunde consurgat obligatio quam ex hoc precise quod sunt tales beneficiati et religiosi et ad officium canonicum obligati.

36. Quam potestatem habet abbas de iure in absolvendo subditos suos ?

Respondetur quod habet potestatem ordinariam plenariam, nisi pro quanto superior suus, scilicet papa vel episcopus, inveniatur limitasse eam per iura scripta vel aliter ; potest insuper potestatem suam subdelegare.

37. Utrum abbas possit absolvere novitios sicut professos.

Resp. Puto quod sic.

38. Utrum illi qui adhuc sunt in layco habitu antequam habeant habitum novitiorum vel antequam habeant consensum quod recipiantur pro novitiis, possint absolvi ut supra.

Resp. Puto quod sic, si habeant propositum tentandi religionem [312r] sine fraude. Ista tamen questio et precedens spectant magis ad eos qui sciunt statuta positiva et consuetudines in religionibus approbatis observatas.

39. Utrum abbas possit delegare suam potestatem, et usque ad quem numerum descendendo.

Respondetur quod potest delegare quibuscumque vult ; potest etiam illis quos delegat dare quod eligant et nominent tot et tales quot et quales voluerint, et ipse auctoritate sua delegat eos; et hoc stat cum illa regula quod subdelegatus subdelegare non potest ; verum est itaque auctoritate sua.

40. Utrum vicarius abbatis in absolvendo habeat similem potestatem sicut abbas.

Respondetur quod sic si sibi contulerit, licet ipse directe subdelegare non possit.

41. Utrum priores, et maxime in illis religionibus que non habent nisi unum abbatem qui toti religioni presit, habeant potestatem sicut abbates, et utrum possint delegare, et quibus.

Respondetur quod priores habent potestatem ordinariam sicut curati parrochiales, sed illam potestatem habent limitatam sepe per suum abbatem vel episcopum vel papam ; possunt tamen subdelegare in illis casibus qui eis auctoritate ordinaria relinquuntur.

42. Utrum sacerdotes seculares, eo iure quod sunt sacerdotes, possint absolvi ab aliis sacerdotibus secularibus quibuscumque, scilicet de casibus communibus.

Respondetur quod non secundum iura scripta ; sed consuetudo invaluit in oppositum, scientibus prelatis et tolerantibus ; et ita videntur consentire et dare licentiam. Sed de religiosis secus est, quia non possunt audire seculares sine licentia suorum maiorum.

43. Utrum ebrietas dicatur et sit peccatum mortale.

Responsionem pleniorem quere in *Somma Confessorum*. Dico tamen quod ebrietas non dicitur regulariter peccatum mortale nisi proveniat ex consensu et deliberatione, sic scilicet quod homo sciens et volens tantum bibit propter crapulam et delectationem quod inde perdit iudicium rationis et exponit se periculis multis aliorum peccatorum.

44. Utrum sit celandum quicquid dicitur in confessione sub sigillo confessionis.

Respondetur quod peccata et eorum circumstantie et ea per que posset haberi cognitio peccatorum sunt de sigillo confessionis et de necessitate celanda. Alia etiam sunt celanda tanquam secreta si dicuntur bona fide et intentione nec tendunt ad subversionem, sed edificationem.

45. Utrum, si aliquis professus in aliqua religione, utputa Celestinorum, recordetur se aliquando fecisse votum dum secularis erat de ingressu alterius religionis, utputa Cartusiensium, teneatur dimittere religionem suam quam primo professus est, et ingredi aliam

Respondetur quod non tenetur exire, ex quo est iam professus, secus si esset novitius. Et hoc expresse dicit sanctus Thomas in *Secunda Secunde*, quest. c[ma].lxxxix[a]: *Utrum liceat de una religione transire ad aliam* etc. [312v]. Ait enim votum solenne quo quis obligatur minori religioni est fortius quam votum simplex ex quo quis astringitur maiori religioni. Post votum enim simplex si contraheret quis matrimonium, non dirimeretur sicut post votum solenne ; et ideo ille qui iam professus est in minori religione non tenetur implere votum simplex quod emisit de intrando maiorem vel artiorem religionem.

46. Utrum confitens possit dare licentiam confessori revelandi quidquam quod ab eo audierat in confessione, sive tangat confitentem aut alium quempiam, sive etiam pro pace aliquorum adinvicem reformanda aut pro admonitione alicuius seu correctione aut huiusmodi.

Respondetur quod proprie loquendo non potest dare licentiam quod confessio reveletur, sed potest dicere extra confessionem ; et adhuc cautela magna servanda est in tali revelatione, et expedientius est quod ipsemet confitens dicat quod dicendum est, et presertim si sit dicendum in publico. Rursus, dum tangit peccatum alterius, secretum confitens nullomodo debet revelare nisi ad bonum ipsius, sicut vellet sibi fieri, et quod dicatur tali et taliter quod prodesse debeat, non obesse.

47. Utrum, pro periculo vel dampno corporali aut magis spirituali confitentis aut confessoris aut alterius persone singularis aut plurium vel unius aut totius communitatis evitando, posset aliquid sub sigillo confessionis auditum revelari, dato saltem quod confessor diceret confitenti quod talia non reciperet sub sigillo confessionis; aut quid super hoc sit faciendum.

Respondetur quod nullomodo, etiam pro salvando uno regno, licitum est confessionem revelare, quia non sunt facienda mala etc. Nec sufficit dicere post auditionem confessionis quod confessor non capit in confessione ea que iam audivit, secus si a principio diceret sic : "Noli michi confiteri, quia non volo tenere secretum illud quod dixeris" ; et tunc iam non erit confessio sacramentalis, de cuius ratione est quod sit secreta, nisi aliter vel aliunde sciatur.

48. Utrum, si quis ficte religionem petat, sepe iterans peccata priora, vel si fantasias patitur aut huiusmodi, sive sit novitius qui talibus laborans repelli posset aut deberet manifestatus, aut si sit professus, cui remedium adhiberi posset ; aut si contra Dei maiestatem peccaret, sicut de quodam legitur qui missam celebrabat nec tamen erat sacerdos, quem, ut audivi, unus papa fecit revelari.

Respondetur quod tales debent induci, quantum possibile est, quod cessent a talibus et se corrigant aut manifestent extra confessionem ; et confessor, si non speret de correctione, debet cessare ab audiendo eum in confessione, ut in ultimo casu faciendum est. Nec puto quod aliquis papa potuerit dare licentiam revelandi unum talem, nisi dentur alie circumstantie, quia papa nichil potest contra ius divinum. [313r]

49. Utrum, si quis peccaverit occulte sic quod tale peccatum tangat vel scandalizet communitatem, sive peccatum sit grave sive leve ; utrum peccans teneatur seipsum publicare, et hoc tangit religiosos.

Respondetur quod si peccatum sit de se publicum, sicut hic supponitur, licet persona sit occulta, tunc, si per prelatum interrogetur de dicendo veritatem, ipse debet illam dicere, tam de se quam de aliis, in casu tali ; et in hoc non prodit se, sed obedit Legi Dei et suo superiori qui cogunt se revelare vel alios. Potest tamen talis culpabilis prelato suo interroganti in publico coram aliis sic dicere : "Domine, ego quid scio paratus sum dicere vobis ad partem". Si autem factum esset occultum de se et persona aliqua esset publice diffamata vel accusata, ipsa similiter dum interrogatur a superiore tenetur dicere veritatem. Si autem factum sit occultum et persona non sit diffamata, tunc talis persona interrogata per suum superiorem non tenetur se revelare et potest dicere : "Domine, non debetis me super talibus interrogare ex quo non sum diffamatus vel denuntiatus". Si autem superior vigeat per iuramentum et sub pena excommunicationis, ipse non tenetur obedire nec penam timere. Scd si per tales evasiones et responsiones ipsa persona veniat in suspicionem superiorum vel audientium quod ipsa aliquid sciat, hec est maior difficultas. Et plane si sit res cognita in confessione solum, dicunt doctores quod potest absque scrupulo dicere et iurare : "Domine, ego nichil scio de istis", et hoc sic intelligitur quod nichil scit tali modo vel scientia quali modo superior potest et solum debet interrogare. Si autem possit similiter in aliis pure secretis ita respondere sine mendacio ego non audeo diffinire ; videretur tamen alicui par ratio et par verbi intellectus.

50. Utrum in casu predicto possit prelatus precipere, si quis sciverit, accuset eum, aut si talis teneatur obedire.

Respondetur sicut ad priorem in omni casu. Et addo quod superior in tali inquisitione pure secretorum graviter peccaret et esset puniendus, quoniam excedit methas officii sui et violat quantum in se iurisdictionem Dei, que sibi soli secreta reservavit punienda.

51. Utrum expediat quod prelatus vel curatus reservet sibi semper confessiones sibi subditorum.

Respondetur quod non ; ymmo sepe esset fatuum et scandalosum et labor stultus, nisi sit talis paucitas quod ipse possit semper omnes audire.

52. Utrum, si quis malitiose accedat ad prelatum confitens peccatum de quo credit se non posse publice puniri quia ei secreto confessus est ; si vero ante confessionem peccati vel post venerit ad notitiam prelati tale peccatum per confitentem vel per alium, possit prelatus ipsum peccatum revelare ; et - quod amplius est - utrum possit publice punire peccantem, et precipue si publice accusetur.

Respondetur quod sic ; sed observet prelatus ne scandalum oriatur, et hoc faciet ostendendo prius qualiter scit, modo [313v] publico vel ante confessionem vel post peccatum confessum, celando tamen quod aliquid sciat in confessione, ymmo pretendendo oppositum, quantumcumque accusatus hoc dicat quod confessus est ; ymmo, si per hoc innuat quod prelatus revelat confessionem, ipse est gravissime puniendus.

53. Utrum prelatus possit sibi reservare absolutionem talis peccati occulti sibi ignoti.

Respondetur quod sic, sed non ut capiat vindictam publicam vel quod deducat in publicum.

54. Utrum, si maior solus aut unus vel duo alii soli sciant peccatum alicuius, an possint aut debeant adducere tale peccatum ad publicum iudicium.

Respondetur quod oportet ad minus esse duos testes, et qui sciant ex certa cognitione, non ex solo auditu ; vel quod ipse reus confessus sit publice. Potest etiam in hoc casu per iuramenta et aliter molestari ille qui publice est diffamatus de aliquo facto, vel ubi factum est publicum licet persona sit occulta, quatinus publice veritas cognoscatur.

55. Utrum revelator confessionis remittendus sit ad superiorem, et ad quem, et si in omni casu, id est semper.

Respondetur ut hoc tutius est ut remittatur ad terrorem maiorem, quoniam peccatum est enormissimum et pessimum, et reputarem minus malum appostatare decies ab una religione professa, licet non sit talis pena in canonibus statuta.

56. Si quis hoc publice fecerit, id est revelaverit confessionem, et exprobrando, qua pena multandus erit ?

Respondetur quod hodie pena erit arbitraria et vix potest dari sufficiens. Iura tamen instituunt quod talis retrudatur in artum monasterium etc., non quod iura cogant profiteri religionem, sed cogunt carcerem talem pati vel penitentiam.

57. Si publice quis revelaverit, non exprobrando sed lusorie aut surreptione ?
Respondetur quod levius peccabit, sed tamen puniendus est, quia Non patitur ludum fama, fides, oculus ut, in tali casu, homo non excusaretur si alium occideret vel occidendum preberet.

58. Utrum, si quis non publice sed singulariter, exprobrando tamen, et hoc extra confessionem vel etiam in confessione, peccatum dixerit in confessione auditum, sit, et quomodo, puniendus.
Respondetur quod ex caritate et in confessione potest sibi obicere peccatum confessum, servata discretione ; sed sepe non expedit, ubi confessus scandalizaretur et male caperet, et forte retraheretur a confessione alias facienda. Extra vero confessionem nunquam fiat exprobrando nec etiam amonendo, nisi forte in quodam generali, et hoc adhuc vix potest bene fieri. Propterea tutius est dimittere et semper ostendere quod de peccatis confessis nichil sciat aut cogitet. Reperiatur alia via monendi quam ista, et cogitet quilibet quid sibi vellet fieri aut non fieri in hac parte.

59. Utrum, si confitens obliviscatur penitentiam, debeat iterum confiteri.
Respondetur quod talis debet confiteri de penitentia oblita ; et quia penitentie nunc sunt arbitrarie, videtur quod [314r] non oportet confiteri peccata priora, licet doctores antiqui dixerint oppositum.

60. Utrum, si quis non compleat penitentias iniunctas ex negligentia et torpore vel ex mala voluntate aut forte quia nimis graves sunt, sufficiat se iterum confiteri, et non iterum facere primas penitentias.
Respondetur quod confessor potest secundum suam discretionem relaxare, presertim in penitentiis datis pro peccatis occultis, non ita de publicis ; nec videtur recurrendum esse de necessitate ad priorem confessorem aut superiorem, et presertim quando tales penitentie date sunt non per superiorem, sed per equalem ; alioquin tutum est recurrere ad superiorem vel equalem pro relaxatione aut commutatione, et hoc quoad penitentias adhuc faciendas ; sed de iam omissis puto quod confessor qui habet potestatem absolvendi potest secundum arbitrium suum dare novam penitentiam et non iniungere completionem illius que omissa est.

61. Utrum, si quis ex oblivione non compleat penitentias quia credit se fecisse ...
Respondetur quod complebit hoc vel in purgatorio secundum iudicium Dei ; hic etiam casus cadit in confessionem de peccatis oblitis.

62. Utrum quis statim post confessionem teneatur complere penitentiam quantum in se est, utputa si dicat confessor: "Dic *Miserere*" et non addat : "quando volueris aut potueris", et non ponat horam vel terminum.

Respondetur quod bona equitas et conscientia illius qui habet dicere penitentiam de hoc habet iudicare ; tamen tutius est "statim" dicere nisi commoditas maior rationabiliter expectetur vel quod, dum datur penitentia, querat a confessore ipse confessus horam et tempus dicendi quando voluerit. Et notetur hic quod nullus debet iniungere penitentiam, nec etiam recipere, nisi probabiliter credat quod possit aut debeat impleri ; et hoc intelligatur de penitentia pro peccatis occultis.

63. Utrum, si quis contra prelatum aut curatum vel alium confessorem murmuraverit in corde suo aut eum iudicaverit aut quidpiam contra eum occulte fecerit, an expediat quod talis confiteatur tali prelato aut curato vel confessori, si tamen timeat eum posse scandalizari aut contra eum indignari, vel si magis expediat accedere ad alium confessorem petendo licentiam a suo prelato vel curato.

Respondetur quod potest confiteri illi suo prelato, sed nullomodo expedit quod nominet eum, nec hoc requiritur, sed sufficit dicere : "Murmuravi contra aliquos maiores meos aliquando et patres spirituales". Et si prelatus velit inquirere tempus et personam, debet respondere : "Domine, sufficiat vobis", quia nec ad veritatem hoc est requirendum, nec oportet quod, si prelatus sit maioris auctoritatis, quod propter hoc in casu predicto nominetur, ymmo nec expedit quod alteri cui fiet confessio nominetur : nam in hoc casu iam esset quedam infamatio sua.

64. Utrum expediat sepe aut omnibus confiteri eadem peccata, scilicet aut propter pleniorem indulgentiam acquirendam que ex maiori confusione causari potest, aut propter maiorem humilitatem, aut propter maiorem familiaritatem acquirendam.

Respondetur quod hoc bene potest [314v] fieri modeste propter aliquam causarum tactarum aut aliam similem, utpote propter habendum consilium ; et caveatur in tali narratione curiositas, et specialiter in peccatis carnis ; caveatur etiam circa tertiam causam, de familiaritate contrahenda, ne sit suspecta de adulatione vel complacentia sensuali vel de perditione temporis per garrulationes superfluas et curiosas.

65. Utrum, si peccata mea preterita secundum aliquam apparentiam sint causa peccatorum presentium, confessus sum tamen preterita generaliter aut specialiter, ego confitendo presentia tenear dicere : "Incidi in tale peccatum propter tale preteritum" specificando illud preteritum, aut si sufficeret dicere generaliter : "Incidi in tale peccatum propter peccata mea preterita".

Respondetur quod hoc ultimum sufficit ex quo de preteritis certus est se fuisse confessum.

66. Utrum, si quis commiserit plura peccata similia eiusdem generis aut speciei que tamen non inducunt ad alium peccatum grave, id est que non habent circumstantias graves, utrum sufficiat de quolibet genere aut specie generaliter confiteri, et non in speciali de omnibus.

Respondetur quod sufficit, presertim si dicatur numerus peccatorum dum scitur aut, dum nescitur, explicetur taliter quod confessor possit satis cogitare multitudinem peccatorum, ut dicendo: "per unum annum" vel "per mensem incidi in tale peccatum totiens quotiens tentabar" etc., quia quoad quodlibet speciale descendere non oportet nec sepe expedit propter audientem et loquentem et temporis amissionem.

67. Utrum possit revelare quis peccatum secretum pro emendatione peccantis, et hoc saltem ei qui potest corrigere aut ei qui potest et vult collaborare peccanti ad salutem.

Respondetur quod sic, dum tamen ille cui revelatur teneat in secreto nec corrigat inde alium nisi secrete, ita quod ille velit et possit prodesse, non obesse vel prodere. Et hoc expresse iubetur fieri in Regula sancti Augustini, quoniam et quilibet deberet velle ita sibi fieri pro medela corporali, quanto amplius pro spirituali.

68. Utrum, si plures non simul, sed unus post alium aut duo tantum simul, viderint quempiam peccare, possint eum ad publicum iudicium adducere.

Respondetur quod si duo simul viderint idem factum et eodem tempore et eodem loco, possunt testificari ut in publicum veniat, secus si sint diversa tempora et diversi actus successive et unus vidit post alium et non simul etc., quia tunc non sufficit testimonium ad convincendum.

69. Utrum pro quolibet tempore teneamur ad correctionem fraternam iuxta illud: "Si peccaverit in te frater tuus, vade et corripe eum ... " etc.

Respondetur quod sic, observatis aliquibus conditionibus : prima, dum probabiliter speratur quod proximus emendabitur, quia si inde debeat deteriorari, melius est silere ; item, si spero quod aliter potest per alium corrigi, non obligor ; item, si sum occupatus in melioribus ; item, si expecto tempus [315r] magis ydoneum; deinde, si nolit corrigi et peccatum sit manifestum, dicam Ecclesie, secus si semper sit secretum.

70. Utrum propter presentiam heretici, scismatici vel alterius excommunicati debeat quis cessare ab oratione vel in missa sistere, in quolibet passu fuerit, vel in officio divino.

Respondetur: Si talis assistens sit notorie excommunicatus et denuntiatus et hoc constat illis de choro vel ecclesia, talis celebrans debet cessare et significare palam causam sue cessationis, et hoc nisi excusetur per timorem cadentem in constantem virum. Si autem excommunicatio sit occulta nec fuerit denuntiatio facta, talis non debet cessare a celebratione publica, presertim iam inchoata, quia nec debet alium propalare.

71. Utrum, si quis recordetur se incidisse in sententiam excommunicationis ex tempore preterito, sive tunc sciret sive non, et non est absolutus quia oblitus erat, interim autem in oblivione illa ingessit se ad divina ; utrum sit irregularis, et utrum sic mortaliter peccaverit.

Respondetur quod, si se discusserit cum illa diligentia que communiter solet adhiberi, non apparet quod talis peccaverit mortaliter novo peccato ; item nec est irregularis, quia non contempnit claves Ecclesie. Attamen expedit quod in qualibet confessione confessor intendat absolvere ab omni sententia excommunicationis a qua potest, sive fiat confessio expressa sive non, et tunc confitens est vere absolutus ab excommunicatione ; quia, nisi sic, ipse non esset absolutus ab aliis peccatis. Debet tamen postmodum confiteri et absolvi si recordetur in speciali. Addo quod sufficit forma communis absolutionis, dicendo : "Ego absolvo te", si per hoc confessor intendit absolvere ab excommunicatione, quoniam in hoc nulla requiritur certa forma, sed sufficit quod intentio sit qualitercumque explicita.

72. Utrum, si quis noviter inciderit in sententiam excommunicationis, et forte non habet tempus vel oportunitatem confitendi, habet tamen propositum, interim posset se coniungere aliis ad psallendum vel ad colloquium aut ad cibum aut huiusmodi.

Respondetur per distinctionem, quia vel excommunicatio secreta est totaliter, et in hoc casu non obligatur fugere consortium aliorum taliter quod se prodat vel notificet excommunicatum ; sed si potest querere aliam occasionem se separandi, hoc bonum est et humile et tutius. Si autem excommunicatio sit publica, tunc debet se separare, nisi interim per confessorem suum daretur sibi licentia, et tempus ydoneum prefigeretur quo posset ire ad illum qui potest absolvere.

73. Item quid si incidit, non tamen querebat immediate oportunitatem confitendi, quia forte nesciebat hoc esse necessarium antequam se coniungeret aliis aut iungeret se divinis, attamen se ingessit ?

Responsio satis patet ex precedenti, addendo quod ignorantia potest esse talis quod excusat a toto ne fiat irregularis, ut si errabat invincibiliter in hiis que sunt [315v] facti, vel si habebat ignorantiam iuris probabilem, secus si ignorantia erat quodammodo voluntaria, hoc est quia talis non quesivit veritatem tanta sollicitudine sicut potuisset et sicut in talibus fieri communiter solitum est per illos qui solliciti sunt de salute sua.

74. Item, si quis cum aliquali indignatione percutit vel impellit aliquem, quia forte impedit eum alicubi ire aut aliquid facere, non tamen proprie vellet ei nocere, utrum incidit talis in sententiam excommunicationis.

Respondetur quod non, quia textus dicit : "Si quis, suadente dyabolo, id est certo proposito ..." etc.

75. Item, si quis iocose aut quasi corrigendo percussit alium, non tamen ad eum pertinet omnino illius correctio ; ille tamen irascatur et non accipiat ad iocum, aut sicut vidi aliquem qui dicebat : "Revoco ad animositatem ; vos estis excommunicatus" ; utrum propter hoc talis debeat dici excommunicatus.

Respondetur quod non, nisi iterum talia attemptet post hec verba, dum percipitur ira alterius; poterit tamen in omni eventu queri absolutio, et reconciliatio fiat cum illo socio.

76. Utrum, si quis ex aliqua oblivione aut aliqua quavis causa vel negligentia aut occupatione dixerit unam horam ante aliam, utputa tertiam ante primam, teneatur redicere secundum ordinem aliarum horarum, aut sufficiat confiteri de hoc.

Respondetur quod expedit repetere si habeatur magna oportunitas repetendi totum, quatinus evitetur necessitas confitendi et scrupulositas de peccando. Si autem desit oportunitas propter alias occupationes meliores et urgentiores, non oportet repetere totum nec tali ordine, sed sufficit de negligentia confiteri, et poterit omissum in aliud commutari.

77. Item, si quis, cogitationibus vagis intentus aut negligentia vel somnolentia vel utroque simul victu, non intellexerit aut non dixerit unum vel duos psalmos aut lectiones, responsoria, orationes vel huiusmodi, utrum teneatur reincipere vel solum que omisit redicere antequam diceret missam vel horam que secuntur post illam negligentiam.

Respondetur quod in servitio communi quod fit in ecclesia, tales negligentie non sunt de necessitate corrigende per novam repetitionem illorum que omissa sunt ; et quantum ad illa in quibus evagatio est nec attentio actualis, non est sepe necessarium, ymmo quandoque noxium reiterare, prout alibi tractatum est.

78. Item si pro tali negligentia predicta, pro evitando scrupulositatem reiterandi officium, sufficeret aut magis expediret dicere duos vel tres alios psalmos.

Respondetur quod arbitrium confessoris determinare sufficiet sicut volet.

79. Item si verum est quod irregularis, ut dicunt aliqui, nec audeat solummodo induere superlicium ad ministrandum in altari vel in choro.

Responsio queratur a iuristis, quoniam si talis austeritas servari debeat, hoc non est ex libertate [316r] Legis Christi, sed ex pondere imposito iugi positivi. Invenio quod etiam ipsi iuriste circa hoc et similia iudicanda vel interpretanda sic variantur adinvicem quod vix haberi potest aliqua certitudo, nisi quod dicunt post multas allegationes : "hunc vide, tene certum, dimitte incertum" ; sed per hoc plane non alleviant iugum.

80. Si semper tenentur inimici reconciliari adinvicem antequam offerant vel communicent, sive sint prope sive sint longe.

Responsio habetur plane in *Somma Confessorum*, et patet ex sequenti.

81. Item si in predicto casu sufficeret si satisfaceret vel per litteras vel per nuntium, et hoc si faciat ex corde et bona voluntate.

Responsio sufficienter habetur in *Somma Confessorum*. Et constat quod hoc habunde sufficeret, ymmo nec requiritur talis actualis satisfactio nisi secundum preparationem animi, id est quod sit paratus in corde satisfacere, habita loci et temporis oportunitate, et sic talis vadit reconciliari prius fratri suo pedibus affectionis et caritatis, etsi non pedibus corporis.

82. Item, si quis non potest omnino vincere cor suum ut veniam petat vel indulgeat petenti, utrum saltem sufficiat hoc facere verbis aut signis aut, ut dictum est, litteris vel per nuntium.

Respondetur quod oporteret hic multa dicere qui vellet plane satisfacere. Dico tamen quod si talis dolet secundum iudicium rationis quod non vincit aliter cor suum, scilicet sensualem motum ire et indignationis, et vellet ac satagit quod hoc posset, et agit que ponuntur in hac questione, ipse non peccat, ymmo meretur multum et sufficienter agit secundum rationem, que libera est, licet sensualitas nolit sequi aut non statim possit propter commotionem spirituum circa cor aut aliunde : exemplum est in aliis tentationibus.

83. Item, quid si alter respondeat quod non indulgebit nisi aliter iste satisfaciat, aut respondeat quia se vindicabit ?

Respondetur quod ille qui sic respondet portabit onus suum, et iste qui se offert ad satisfactionem rationabilem iuxta arbitrium sui superioris vel alicuius boni viri liber est a peccato, ymmo humiliando se meretur.

84. Utrum Ecclesia teneatur ministrare necessaria illis qui recipiuntur in libertate Ecclesie, et que sufficiunt, id est ad que tenetur.

Respondetur quod non, nisi in extrema necessitate, quando scilicet moritur ille si non ei statim succurritur. Item debent illi tamdiu recipi et tolerari quamdiu manet causa quare querunt libertatem. Item, qui fraudulenter et scienter ageret aliquid ad eiciendum tales, ut si iudex negaret eis quod possent habere victum per quemcumque, etc., talis esset fractor immunitatis ecclesiastice. Potest tamen ministrari talibus illud solum quod est ad necessitatem pro victu et loco, et quod hoc faciat per amicos si potest.

85. Utrum vir vel mulier ad alterutrum, mater et pater filiis et econverso, prelatus [316v] subditis, id est abbas fratribus et econverso, et sic de singulis qui sibi correlative in necessitatibus procurandis iunguntur vel tenentur in necessitate, id est in periculo mortis, succurrere teneantur, id est providere omnia necessaria pro evadendo mortem et recuperando sanitatem corporis, etiamsi contra consuetudinem Ecclesie vel religionis, aut contra votum per se vel per personam infirmam agere deberent, vel si ex hoc ad paupertatem devenire deberent et ad es alienum se obligare.

Resp. Quicquid dixerint aliqui quod votum religionis absolvit a succurrendo parentibus, dico plane cum Christo quod mandatum quodcumque hominum vel votum voluntarium nullomodo potest irritum facere mandatum Dei de iure divino et naturali quod est de honorando parentes et quod parentes thesaurizent filiis, etc. Item extrema necessitas cogit ad sibi subveniendum sub pena peccati mortalis apud eos qui possent subvenire et dimittunt perire. Attamen homo debet plus sibi providere de necessariis quam alteri ; sed usque ad necessitatem exclusive tenetur succurrere parentibus et aliis ut in casu quovis, nec frangit talis votum si implet.

86. Novitius religionem petens in ea confitetur et absolvitur auctoritate qua possunt abbas vel eius vicarii aut priores ; si vero, aliqua tentatione pulsatus, recedat, vel causa rationabili exigente vel alias licentietur et non profiteatur, utrum debeat iterum confiteri, non valente priore confessione, et specialiter de casibus reservatis.

Respondetur quod ex quo talis fuerit bona fide confessus et absolutus, ipse nullomodo tenetur iterum confiteri.

87. Item novitius petit professionem ex consensu deliberato, aut forte non cum consensu sed ficte, et hoc tamen in communi. Conventus vero, credens hoc eum facere ex puro corde, consentit, quia forte non vidit quare renui deberet. Antequam autem sumat habitum et fiat solennitas consueta fieri, penitet aut penitere se simulat. Utrum talis possit recedere securus, ita quod non teneatur reus, voti vel professionis, saltem quoad Deum ; et hoc intelligitur si per annum fuerit probatus.

Resp. Pro ista questione et .iiii.[or] sequentibus oportet aliqua presupponere. Presupponitur primo quod novitius non intendit preoccupare tempus professionis quin per totum annum maneat liber ad exeundum. Et ita presupponitur secundo quod per hoc quod petit consensum ante annum probationis elapsum, non intendit se obligare voto vel professione pro tunc, sed ipse facit talem petitionem ut liberius possit disponere de rebus suis et securius, dum videt affectionem Ordinis. Presupponitur 3° quod similiter Ordo non intendit se ligare ad recipiendum talem novitium quin semper remaneat sibi libertas durante toto anno ad repellendum eum, sicut etiam novitius habet libertatem ut dictum est. Istis presuppositis, si concedantur, patet responsio ad istam questionem. Si autem dicatur quod novitius per talem petitionem intendebat se ligare voto, tunc palam est quod obligatus est apud Deum intrare religionem, etiam ubi in ista non reciperetur. Similiter, si conventus intendebat se obligare ad [317r] recipiendum, ipse peccat non recipiendo. Videtur tamen quod conventus, secundum constitutiones suas de probatione per annum, non debuerit fecisse talem obligationem, sicut nec debet tempus professionis preoccupare. Et in signum huius petitur, ut intellexi, a novitio dum vult profiteri si vult discedere, licet prius consensum conventus habuerit. Presupponitur ergo quod possit egredi libere, alias frustra fieret hec petitio.

88. Item, si in casu predicto inveniatur talis egisse aliquid pro quo sit dignus repelli, scilicet post petitionem et consensum professionis, utrum, ipso nolente vel reclamante vel etiam ipso consentiente, possit repelli, sic quod consensus ad professionem nichil valeat.

Responsio patet per premissa, quod potest talis repelli etiam invitus.

89. Item, si quis novitius petit professionem priore absente, et pars conventus sibi assentit, altera vero non nisi conditionaliter, id est nisi prior vel abbas absens expectetur, aut nisi ipse prelatus consentiat ; nichilominus tamen prior pars importat sic quod datur consensus novitio illi se disponendi et negotia sua et, quod amplius est, etiam iuvatur a fratribus aut sociatur in eundo ad disponendum : utrum prior vel abbas superveniens possit eum repellere et impedire a professione, nulla tamen causa quam que prius apparebat imminente.

Respondetur quod hec questio dependet ex consuetudinibus Ordinis et ex potestate quam habet conventus sine priore, vel prior supra conventum.

90. Item, si quis petens probationem religionis invenitur tunc strabo aut debilis aut inscius aut in aliquo inhabilis, et hoc bene tunc notatur, permittitur tamen sic per annum; post hoc petit professionem et nullum habet aliud impedimentum quam prius : utrum propter illa impedimenta priora possit repelli.

Responsio patet, quod sic potest recipi, etiam gratis, non assignata ratione.

91. Item novitius, interrogatus an habeat aliquod impedimentum pro quo non possit profiteri, respondet se non habere et mentitur, et sic consentitur professioni, ymmo de facto profitetur ; invenitur tamen postea quod impedimentum habebat : utrum talis professio valeat.

Respondetur quod talis novitius ligatus est intrare religionem istam vel aliam; sed de conventu maior est difficultas, quia presupponitur quod non consentit nisi sub conditione quod novitius non haberet aliquod tale impedimentum quod expresse nominatur et in statutis Ordinis ponitur ; et ita videtur quod non stante tali conditione consensus non tenet. Sunt tamen argumenta ad oppositum de conditionibus appositis matrimonio que dimitto ; consulerem tamen quod talis iam professus exterius et diu toleratus non expelletur nisi necessitas urgeret, et hoc propter scandalum vitandum et caritatem nutriendam.

92. Quomodo intelligitur illud quod in aliquibus regulis et constitutionibus monachorum legitur aut dicitur : "gravis inobedientia" aut "coniuratio gravis" ?

Respondetur quod illa debet dici inobedientia gravis que fit ex contemptu precipientis et quodammodo in eius despectu, quasi dicendo : "quia sic precipis ego non faciam", vel dicitur gravis inobedientia quia fit contra regulas Ordinis explicitas. [317v]

93. Item, si quis non contempnit, sed procrastinat obedire prelatis, querens semper occasionem non faciendi aut evadendi, et hoc ex cautela, volens inducere prelatum ad seipsum; utrum talis possit dici obediens vel inobediens.

Respondetur quod talis non videtur iudicandus plane inobediens inobedientia que sit peccatum mortale, et presertim nisi iungatur scandalum et si talis sit paratus tandem obedire.

94. Si dispensator aut procurator monasterii vel alius cui forte date sunt pecunie pro emendo aliquid pro communi aut pro quavis alia causa communitatis, ipse emat pro se vel pro alio cultellum vel graffium aut filum vel acum absque licentia generali aut speciali aut permissu presidentis; utrum talis faciat contra votum paupertatis et reputetur proprietarius, peccaveritque mortaliter tanquam transgressor voti ; et similiter dico si dederit vel acceperit ab extraneis.

Respondetur per distinctionem, quia vel talis procurator estimat probabiliter et rationabiliter quod superior suus vellet bene si sciret quod illa fierent de quibus queritur, et in hoc casu non videtur talis procurator proprietarius vel transgressor voti ; si autem credit aut credere debeat probabiliter et rationabiliter quod si superior talia sciret non approbaret sed displiceret sibi, et hoc displicentia gravi, tunc talis est fur et transgressor voti.

QUOLIBETA DETERMINATA PER REVERENDUM PATREM PETRUM POQUETI CELESTINUM, VISA PER DOMINUM CANCELLARIUM PARISIENSEM ET PER EUM AMPLIATA

95. Et primo queritur utrum quis renuere debeat officium quodcumque iniunctum a maiore propter aliquod impedimentum ipsius officii.

Respondetur quod, revelatis excusationibus suis maiori suo, si idem persistat in sua voluntate, obtemperet sibi, confitendo de divino adiutorio ; et hoc etiam habet ex Regula quod si impossibilia iniunguntur, aliter ... etc.

Cancellarius ecclesie Sancte Marie Parisiensis addit quod sequitur : Presupposito tamen quod non habeatur rationabilis existimatio de maiore quod ex imperitia vel malitia precipiat illud, et quod illud quod iubetur sit de illis que pertinent ad Regulam et ad que se extendit potestas maioris ; alioquin non oporteret obedire. Dicitur autem rationabilis existimatio quando rationes probabiliores habentur ad sic credendum quam ad oppositum, dummodo non fabricet sibi tales rationes inordinata vel indisciplinata affectio.

96. Item queritur quomodo intelligitur illa auctoritas beati Thome de Aquino quod consensus delectationis mortalis peccati est mortale peccatum.

Respondetur quod si quis tentatus fuerit de aliquo peccato mortali et delectetur in eo delectatione morosa, et placeat sibi illa delectatio ratione deliberante ita quod non vellet quod tentatio recederet ut delectatio duret amplius, posito quod non vellet actualiter committere peccatum – hoc est exercere peccatum suum ad extra – peccat mortaliter.

Cancellarius : Et hec responsio probata est, et in [318r] multis casibus aliis habet locum eadem auctoritas. Propterea cautissimum est statim abigere tales recogitationes operum carnalium, tam aliorum quam suorum, quamvis sit aliquando in tali recogitatione vitium cuiusdam curiositatis noxie quam non oportet esse peccatum mortale potius quam sit delectatio carnalis ; et hec curiositas consequens est apud quemlibet ex sensibus, ut oculus non saturatur visu nec auris auditu, etc. Et potest magis dici delectatio huiusmodi sensualis quam carnalis aut libidinosa.

97. Item queritur utrum post celebrationem misse per dimidiam horam habundans quis in fleumate audeat spuere sine scrupulo.

Respondetur quod ante dimidiam horam adhuc potest, quia non multum remanent species ; sed consulitur quod spuatur in ignem ut consummantur sputa; quod si in promptu non est, spuatur in locum honestum non conculcatum ab hominibus.

Cancellarius : Quia autem homo pronior est ad spuendum crassum sputum ex gutture proveniens quando sumpsit ablutionem, hoc provenit propter excitationem nature ex tali sumptione.

Idem : Nota quod non est cautum ut homo celebraturus in abluendo os suum ponat notabilem quantitatem aque in ore, sed potius digito intincto purget os suum; nec videtur securum quod exponat se ad faciendum gargarismos – id est quod levando caput dimittat aquam decurrere usque ad guttur – quamvis retinere conetur ne ultra deglutiat, quia vix evenit quod non fluat aqua per modum cuiusdam potus usque ad stomachum, et hoc percipitur dum sentitur frigiditas aque vel aliquid simile, secus ubi iam aqua quasi conversa est in salivam dum facit homo ablutionem primo modo.

98. Queritur item utrum quis non habens specialem missam dicendam debeat celebrare pro toto populo indistincte, aut pro sibi coniunctis specialiter. Quod si pro toto populo, quibus plus proficiat, an sibi coniunctis aut ceteris.

Cancellarius respondit quod hec questio habet plures angulos distinctionum et vix potest explicari <nisi> multis verbis. Nichilominus, debet sufficere caritati celebrantis et inquisitioni quod bene agat, sine scrupulosa tali nimia inquisitione quid plus prodest, hoc vel illud : scit enim Deus ponderare meritum suum et omnem actionem. Habeatur pro regula quod, ubi celebrans magis elevat intentionem suam caritativam in Deum et in proximum, illic, ceteris paribus, plus proficit, ac si diceret : "Domine, miserere omnium sicut scis et potes, et sicut me scis et vis orare debere". Denique prefigi regula non potest generalis quin aliquando plus afficiatur homo dum orat pro uno, quandoque plus dum orat pro pluribus. Item nulla est missa que possit aut debeat celebrari quin omnes comprehendat quos Ecclesia comprehendit ; quod si contraxerit valorem ad aliquos particulares, hoc debet facere non preiudicando huic Ecclesie constituto. Demum, ceteris paribus, salubrius est conari ad orationem generalem ad Deum [318v] convertendo se ad Deum quam in particularibus fantasiis circa homines occupari.

99. Item queritur utrum quis non sentiens multum inflammari per misse frequentationem, nec etiam se minus reverentem, sed quasi in eodem statu se semper sentiens, auderet celebrare quotidie si non haberet impedimentum aliunde.

Respondetur supponendo duo : primo quod nos ordinati sumus ad exhibendum honorem Deo et reverentiam et latriam ; secundo quod non est nobilior actus latrie quam in celebratione misse. Istis suppositis, respondetur quod sic, unicuique suggerendo ut hoc dicat in corde suo et sic sentiat : "Domine, non sum dignus tale vel tantum officium exercere ; verumtamen, quia ad hoc ordinatus sum ut te laudem et pro populo orem, confidens de tua misericordia et non in virtute mea presumens, hoc sacrificium tibi offero, primo ad reddendum gratiarum actiones pro beneficiis tuis, secundo in salutem omnium vivorum et defunctorum". Et sic faciens cum humilitate secure absque scrupulo potest accedere.

Cancellarius : Et hoc est pium consilium, supponendo quod celebraturus non sentiat probabiliter impedimentum aliud quominus celebret, preter tepiditatem premissam.

100. Item queritur utrum in *Memento* in missa sit tutum facere memoriam specialem pro pluribus, propter cogitationes que possent oriri ex personarum recordatione.

Respondetur consulendo pro tutiori quod melius esset, antequam accedat quis ad altare, quod faceret suum *Memento* speciale, hoc est quod dicat in corde suo quod intendit orare pro tali et tali ; et tunc, quando erit in suo *Memento* in missa cum hiis que continentur in *Memento* missali, sufficit cordialiter dicere : "Memento, Domine, horum pro quibus teneor et decrevi orare et horum qui pro me orant", nisi sit aliquis frater mortuus pro quo oportet facere *Memento* in speciali.

Cancellarius : Et hoc est tutum consilium, etiam ubi non fecisset homo pro illo die vel recenter aliquod memoriale pro amicis, sed haberet sufficienter in habitu, presertim ubi celebrans est in publico et ubi probabiliter estimat quod per tale *Memento* dearticulatum non inflammaretur ad devotionem spiritualem, sed potius inquietaretur et ad reliqua dicenda in missa minus esset ydoneus.

101. Item queritur de cogitationibus vanis aut noxiis que superveniunt in canone aut in *Memento*, utrum ibidem resistendum est illis.

Respondetur quod non debet tunc se occupare quis circa illas, sed ultra procedere.

Cancellarius : Hoc est tutissimum et necessarium consilium, etiam ubi cogitationes viderentur esse de commodis rebus et expedientibus, quia debet eis tunc dici, saltem facto : "Venitis importune : non habeo nunc horam et locum respondendi vobis ; expectate tempus aliquod dum vacabit". Porro quoad cogitationes fedas, noxias et blasfemas, sive sit homo in missa sive alibi, ille potius vincuntur contempnendo nec respondendo eis quam pugnando. Scio quemdam qui ad occursum talium solitus est in animo subridere quasi subsannans nec curans immissiones istas fedas per angelos [319r] malos, que inde protinus evanescunt.

102. *Cancellarius* : Item nota hic quod nullus tenetur confiteri peccata venialia Lege divina, nisi sit ad hoc specialiter obligatus per votum vel particulare statutum, quale non debet leviter fieri; et quandoque magis expediret cessare a confessione talium quam nimiam incurrere sollicitudinem, que plus impediret aliquando quam fructus confessionis iuvaret; alioquin de ipsa etiam confessione facta oporteret sepe statim iterum confiteri, et sic deinceps sine termine, attento quod vix facimus aliquid ubi non possimus rationabiliter formidare de peccato veniali. Nota hic quod non sufficit ieiunium Ecclesie ad celebrationem, sed requiritur ieiunium nature, et generaliter impedit omnis sumptio cibi vel potus, etiam causa medicine et in parva quantitate.

103. Item queritur utrum iunior ambulans in via aut equitans cum seniore debeat sibi obtemperare in omnibus.

Respondetur quod simpliciter et sine aliqua interrogatione iunior debet obtemperare suo seniori in omnibus, nisi manifeste precipiat contra precepta divina.

Cancellarius : Supponitur quod iunior merito reputet seniorem memorem salutis sue et quod sufficienter advertat ad id quod facit et quod habeat recordationem eorum que habentur in Ordine, secus ubi deesset aliquid istorum, quia posset humili verbo vel signo reducere hoc ad memoriam vel advertentiam senioris.

104. *Cancellarius* : Nota quod dupliciter dici potest peccatum veniale : nam aliud est veniale solum ex genere, sicut verbum otiosum aut mendacium iocosum ; aliud est veniale ex hoc quod non fit cum deliberatione perfecta, sed est in primo motu vel quadam surreptione, quemadmodum nullum est peccatum adeo mortale quin per defectum perfecti consensus possit remanere infra metas solius venialis et econverso. Ad ista peccata venialia verissima est Regula beati Augustini, videlicet quod nullum peccatum adeo veniale est quin fiat mortale dum placet. Sed de primis venialibus non oportet ; ymmo sanctus Thomas dat pro regula quod consensus in actum venialem – supple : de genere – non est nisi venialis, sicut mentiri iocose, etiam ex deliberatione, vel frangere silentium quod solum impositum est per modum discipline ; et delectari in istis non est nisi veniale. Si autem delectatio ferretur super hoc quod est esse peccatum, id est quod quis delectaretur in hoc actu sub hac ratione quia prohibetur et displicet Deo, tunc ipsa delectatio peccatum mortale esset ; sed hoc esset dyabolica placentia, qua quamvis posset forte sine peccato mortali quis in hoc casu delectari, in hoc quod habet talem libertatem sic agendi nesciente suo superiore, vel alia tali ratione.

105. Queritur item quando committitur peccatum mortale in voto obedientie.

Respondetur quod maiores precipientes aliquid subditis suis non intendunt ligare animas eorum nec debent ; et ideo, si quis aliquid sibi iniunctum a maiore ex negligentia aut incuria non sic adimpleret, aut differret, non propter hoc peccaret mortaliter.

Cancellarius : Secus si hoc ageret ex contemptu. [319v] Dicitur autem quis proprie peccare ex contemptu quando facit aliquem actum motus principaliter ex hoc quod iniunctum est sibi oppositum, ac si diceret : "Quia michi precipitur hoc, ego in contemptum precepti faciam illud" ; quasi scilicet vellet ostendere suam falsam libertatem et habere illam velamen malitie.

106. Queritur rursus utrum sit utilius fratri in cella residenti vacare lectioni quam orationi vel meditationi aut e converso.

Respondetur quod non solum attendendum est ad illud quod magis proficit pro presenti quam etiam ad illud quod disponit ad futuros profectus. Et quia assuescere meditationi forti et vehementi plus proficit in futurum propter habitum quem acquirit homo, ut postmodum faciliter meditetur, ymmo etiam contempletur quando voluerit, etiam solus, etiam in officio, etiam sine libris, consulendum est omnino quod frater assuescat meditationi ne semper oporteat eum habere libros ante oculos suos, sed sint ipse cogitationes solide libri sui.

107. Item queritur utrum quis habere possit certificationem quod Deus remiserit ei peccata sua, saltem quoad culpam; et si non habet certificationem, quanto tempore oportet eum deflere.

Respondetur quod de hoc nullus certus esse potest nisi per revelationem, quia scriptum est : "Nemo scit an amore aut odio dignus sit". Sed quando quis confessus est pro parvo posse et dolet de peccatis suis et proponit deinceps non peccare, iste creditur esse in statu gratie, et de pietate divina pie confidere potest quod ei Deus remiserit peccata, saltem quoad malum culpe ; et in tali statu existens potest accedere ad communionem aut missam celebrare.

De secundo respondetur quod quis in religione existens, ex quo secundum modulum suum et posse confessus est peccata sua que fecit quorum recordabatur, et contritus satisfecit ad voluntatem Ecclesie – id est maioris sui qui specialiter curam eius habet – et proponit amplius non peccare, tutius est ut de cetero non reflectat oculos suos ad peccata sua singulariter consideranda, et maxime carnis, que ei possent plus obesse quam prodesse ; sed, confidens de misericordia Dei et bonitate, studeat proficere de die in diem ascendendo de virtute in virtutem ut tandem possit videre Deum Deorum in Syon. Cum vero ab elatione tentatur, tunc ad eius memoriam reducere potest generaliter peccata sua non discurrendo per singula, ut inde humilietur et gratias referat Creatori suo qui eripuit eum de tot ac tantis periculis in quibus aliquando extitit et permansisset nisi eum bonitas divina, que neminem vult perire, sublevasset et liberasset.

Cancellarius : Apud Patrum narrationes data est varia responsio ab uno patre, modo uni, modo alteri, secundum quod prospexit quod iste ex recordatione preteritorum <peccatorum> humiliaretur et ferveret in amore, alter, non satis adhuc purificatus, tentaretur et rediret ad carnem.

108. Queritur, si alicui fratri perturbato aut occupato in diversis preceperit aliquid senior, et ex surreptione responderet ei iunior : "Sinite me ; ego nichil faciam pro vobis" ; verumtamen statim compungitur dolens et adimplet [320r] preceptum senioris quod paulo ante dura responsione renuerat ; queritur, inquam, an sic respondendo mortaliter peccet.

Respondetur quod pro una vice aut duabus aut tribus non peccat mortaliter; sed si ex consuetudine habeat sic frequenter respondere, peccat mortaliter, quia debet resistere consuetudini male ; sed, ex quo frequenter recidivat, sic signum est quod tali vitio est habituatus, et non cadat ex surreptione.

Cancellarius : Respondent in simili doctores theologi quod, sicut prima ebrietas non est peccatum mortale, ita nec secunda nec tertia nec centesima, nisi addatur circumstantia in una ebrietatum sequentium que convertat eam in peccatum mortale : puta quod nunc advertit inebrians se periculum mortale quod incidit ex ebrietate, et tamen deliberat quod se inebriabit. Applicatur ad propositum.

(ST-PETERSBOURG, Bibl. Publ., ms. lat. Ov II n. 1, fol. 352v-353r)

SEQUUNTUR ALIE CONCLUSIONES TRACTE ET DETERMINATE
PER DOMINUM CANCELLARIUM PARISIENSEM

Prima conclusio : Observatio sabbati quoad circumstantias temporis et modi et loci pro maxima parte relicta est determinationi prelatorum que cognoscitur tum ex eorum institutis, tum ex consuetudinibus per eos legitime toleratis. [353r]

De operibus servilibus non exercendis in diebus dominicis et festivis *2a conclusio* : Plus ut frequenter determinat consuetudo loci et personarum a prelatis tolerata quam alia lex scripta.

Tertia conclusio : Consuetudo exercendi opera servilia, hec ab istis, hec ab illis, in diebus festivis tunc maxime esset dicenda corruptela quando totaliter a servitio Dei et cultu festorum, et maxime ab auditu misse revocaret ; quando preterea hec servilia magis ex cupiditate quam pia necessitate reipublice pertractantur.

4a conclusio : Ioci et alie recreationes corporales apud vulgus diebus festivis, quamquam sepius habeant amixtas malitias contra Dei Legem, non tamen per directum obviant ecclesiasticis institutis.

5a conclusio : Opera servilia plerumque fructuosius fierent, si non ea prohiberet Ecclesia, quam illa que vulgares in festis exercent. Propterea prelatorum interesset intendere circa festivitatum multitudinem ne sit illa ad cumulum peccati potius quam ad cultum Dei.

THE RHETORIC OF REFORM: NICOLAS DE CLAMANGES' IMAGES OF THE END[1]

Christopher M. Bellitto

Ecclesiastical reform efforts were often couched in terms of expectations that the End Times had come. In assessing the apocalyptic writings of the eleventh and twelfth centuries, Bernard McGinn identifies two related strands in these works as applied to reform and the End. What he terms "Antichrist language" occurred when a writer used apocalyptic images primarily as a rhetorical device, while "Antichrist application" employed the Christian tradition to locate current events within salvation history, including an apocalyptic End. But McGinn concludes that these approaches were not mutually exclusive, "[P]eople who used apocalyptic imagery both expected the end and used endtime symbols for their own present purposes. The process of understanding present conflicts in terms of symbols of the end can have apocalyptic significance even in the absence of definite prediction about the imminence of the last things."[2] Can this marriage of Antichrist language and application also be found in the late Middle Ages when the Church's institutional chaos was accompanied by a wave of dire societal circumstances? Famine, plague, a series of civil wars throughout Europe, as well as "international" conflicts such as the Hundred Years War, and economic and demographic contraction easily opened themselves to an *ex eventu* interpretation that placed contemporary figures and developments within an apocalyptic context, and frequently did. Heiko Oberman has referred to this apocalyptic lens as the basic posture or "climate of thought" at work in the late Middle Ages which lent urgency to discussions of reform as it blended pessimism about the current states of affairs and a coming judgment with optimism for a heavenly reward for the stalwart. It can, therefore, be difficult to discern if a late medieval writer or preacher actually thought that Antichrist had been born or whether apocalyptic imagery was being employed largely rhetorically to render a call for reform more compelling.[3] To pursue this matter, the writings of Nicolas de Clamanges (1363/1364-1437), Parisian humanist and Avignon papal secretary, are instructive. They offer a prism through which we might see how a late medieval writer rhetorically called for reform, that is, used Antichrist language. But it does not appear that Clamanges was seeking to provide a vision of the End that comprehensively applied an Antichrist scenario to every event and figure of the late Middle Ages. What an examination of

1 Aspects of this article were explored in conference papers at Western Michigan University and Columbia University. My thanks go to Heiko Oberman and Robert Lerner for their comments on those presentations in addition to Louis B. Pascoe, S. J. for advice on initial research.

2 Bernard McGinn, *Antichrist: Two Thousand Years of the Human Fascination with Evil* (San Francisco, 1994), pp. 119-121 with quotation at p. 120. For a survey of medieval apocalyptic themes and genres, see idem, *Visions of the End: Apocalyptic Traditions in the Middle Ages* (New York, 1998).

3 Oberman to author, 13 September 1995. On the variety of late medieval attitudes toward the End, see the essays collected in *L'Attesa dell'età nuova nella spiritualità della fine del medioevo* (Todi, 1962).

Clamanges' writings reveals is a rhetoric that, while relying on apocalyptic imagery for much of its emotional force, ultimately focused itself on reform goals.

Clamanges' summons for men to purify themselves and address the state of church and society was rendered stark by his use of apocalyptic imagery and themes, especially those describing the Antichrist and the End Times, within the context of the need for reform. He illustrated how the Schism and poor religious behavior, the French civil war, and Muslim advances in Europe could be seen as destroying individual Christians, the church, and society, thereby paving the way for Antichrist. Clamanges saw Antichrist's goal of conquering Christian Europe as more plausible if church and civil leaders failed to take the opportunity to reform. Unlike other late medieval authors, however, he did not identify particular popes, antipopes, or secular rulers as Antichrist or the forces opposing Antichrist.[4] Since Clamanges' goal was not to provide an apocalyptic scenario for its own sake but mainly to encourage Christians to reform themselves, he generically used an *ex eventu* approach to present the End as an opportunity for reform and not necessarily to predict the moment of Antichrist's coming, although in his last writings he would offer some indications of Antichrist's imminence. He viewed the chaos of his times through an apocalyptic lens even if he did not consistently believe that the End was coming on an exact date and time.

Because a call for reform was Clamanges' main purpose in writing, it is not surprising that his apocalyptic writings were not as detailed or even as lengthy as his other works. His was a derivative apocalypticism: not a line-by-line exegesis of the Book of Revelation but an attempt to place easily-recognized apocalyptic themes at the service of his fundamental goal of reform. His relevant writings included principally a short treatise, *De Antichristo et ortu eius, vita, moribus et operibus*, and another brief work in which he made a number of more inspirational comments related to the End, *Exhortatio ad resistendum contra Machometicos*. Clamanges wrote both of these little treatises about 1430. He also discussed the End in his unfinished commentary on the Book of Isaiah, *Expositio super quadraginta septem capitula Isaie*, completed ca. 1426 but planned or perhaps even begun as early as 1413. These late dates, however, do not mean that Clamanges only turned to apocalyptic imagery toward the end of his long life. The apocalyptic focus of these three works does not represent a final and detached stage of his reform thought. He expressed apocalyptic imagery often throughout his career, beginning with his first such allusions in several letters dating to the 1390s and continuing until he gathered these thoughts together in a more comprehensive and finalized fashion ca. 1426-1430 in his *Expositio*, *De Antichristo*, and *Exhortatio*.[5]

[4] For examples of such late medieval identifications, see McGinn, *Antichrist*, pp. 143-199, and Raoul Manselli, "Papes et papauté entre Christ et Antéchrist: approches religieuses du Schisme," in *Genèse et débuts du Grand Schisme d'Occident* (Paris, 1980), pp. 591-598.

[5] I rely on two unpublished critical editions of Clamanges' works produced as dissertations which update the faulty *Nicolai de Clemangiis Opera Omnia*, ed. J.

In describing the need for personal and societal renewal within the context of the End Times Clamanges portrayed himself as a reforming prophet, a role that is not unusual in the history of church reform. In his own era Clamanges joined the company of Bridget of Sweden, Catherine of Siena, and Vincent Ferrer in exercising this function. Phillip H. Stump also found that in Advent sermons during the Council of Constance preachers similarly turned to eschatological themes to point the delegates optimistically toward that time when their reforms would be achieved, even as they ominously cautioned their colleagues to be wary of impending judgment.[6] Clamanges appears to have considered himself akin to biblical prophets given his frequent use of—and sometimes identification with —Jeremiah, Ezekiel, and Isaiah. Like his biblical precursors, saintly contemporaries, and the Constance preachers, Clamanges adopted the role of prophet to warn that men will be caught in their own iniquities on the day of the

Lydius, 3 vols. (Leiden, 1613; reprint ed, Farnborough, 1967). They are "L'epistolario di Nicolas de Clamanges," ed. Dario Cecchetti, Università degli Studi di Torino, 1960, and "Nicolas de Clamanges. Opuscules," ed. François Bérier, 2 vols., École Pratique de Hautes Études, 1974. Hereafter, Cecchetti will be cited as C with page and line numbers; Bérier, as B with volume, page, and line numbers. References to the Lydius edition, included here because these two dissertations are mostly unavailable, will appear as L with volume and page numbers.

De Antichristo is found in B 2.177-181 (L 2.357-359) and the *Exhortatio* in B 2:182-186. Cecchetti also edited these as letters: C 657-661 (*De Antichristo*) and 661-665 (*Exhortatio*). The Bérier and Cecchetti transcriptions are virtually identical: the more recent edition of Bérier has been preferred. Palémon Glorieux cast doubt on Clamanges' authorship of these two brief treatises; see "Notations biographiques sur Nicolas de Clamanges," in *Mélanges offerts a M.-D. Chenu*, ed. André Duval (Paris, 1967), p. 310. Bérier, however, attested to their authenticity based on the manuscripts while admitting that their style was not up to Clamanges' typically high standards of elegance; see B 1.xli-xli*. The *Expositio* is Clamanges' only treatise that remains completely unedited; it appears in a single manuscript of 247 folios: Paris, Arsenal, MS. lat. 137, hereafter Ars. 137, followed by folio number. On the *Expositio*, see Alfred Coville, *Le Traité de la ruine de l'Église de Nicholas de Clamanges et la traduction française de 1564* (Paris, 1936), pp. 91-106; François Bérier, "Exégèse et ironie: À propos de l'*Expositio super quadraginta septem capitula Ysaye* de Nicolas de Clamanges (ca. 1425)," *Recherches et travaux. Université de Grenoble Bulletin* 41 (1991): 17-35; idem, "Remarques sur l'*Expositio super quadraginta septem capitula Isaie* de Nicolas de Clamanges: Genèse de l'oeuvre, datation, méthode et contenu" in *L'Hostellerie de pensée*, ed. Michel Zink and Danielle Bohler (Paris, 1995), pp. 41-49; and idem, "Remarques sur l'evolution des idees politiques de Nicolas de Clamanges," in *Pratiques de la culture écrite en France au XVe siècle*, ed. Monique Ornato and Nicole Pons (Louvain-la-Neuve, 1995), pp. 109-125.

[6] Yves Congar, *Vraie et fausse réforme dans l'Église*, 2nd ed. (Paris, 1968), pp. 179-207; Marjorie Reeves offered an introductory treatment in "History and Prophecy in Medieval Thought," *Mediaevalia et Humanistica*, n. s. 5 (1974): 51-75. Étienne Delaruelle noted a shared call for penitence and moral reform among late medieval writers in "L'Antéchrist chez S. Vincent Ferrer, S. Bernardin de Sienne, et autour de Jeanne d'Arc," in *L'Attesa dell'età nuova*, pp. 39-40. For prophecy in the context of the Schism, see Marjorie Reeves, *The Influence of Prophecy in the Later Middle Ages: A Study in Joachimism* (Oxford, 1969), pp. 416-428; on the Constance sermons, see Phillip H. Stump, *The Reforms at the Council of Constance (1414-1418)* (Leiden, 1994), pp. 218-219.

Lord. He touched on this theme in the very first sentence of his first full-scale treatise on reform, *De ruina et reparacione Ecclesie* (1400/1401), where he took as his starting point 1 Pt 4:17, "It is time for the judgment of God to begin." This line, Clamanges wrote, shook him and led him to consider the church's many problems within this larger teleological framework in the rest of this treatise. He closed the *De ruina* with the same threat of impending judgment, promising that however bad situations may appear presently, worse was yet to come. Clamanges continued to exercise this self-appointed prophetic role throughout his career, as in a 1403/1404 letter written against theologians who sought only worldly glory instead of service, a moral life, and their salvation. He stressed there that God gives free will to people who then often set their own doom, fall into the holes which they themselves dig, and eat the fruit of their actions. In another letter, written about a decade later, Clamanges compared Paris to Babylon and noted that some inhabitants of Paris, like their biblical counterparts, sought no counsel, remedy, or help for their salvation. Men who had no fear of the imminent divine retribution, Clamanges declared, were truly insane.[7] Near the end of his career, as seen in the first lines of *De Antichristo*, Clamanges still identified himself not as a scholastic theologian but a humble reader of scripture, especially the prophets and their commentators, to whom had been revealed critical information about the End. He saw himself bound by duty and loving faith to share this information with fellow Christians. Like Ezekiel Clamanges was motivated by the threatened penalty of being responsible for the fate of others if he failed to admonish them to turn from their evil ways. He repeatedly informed his readers that he realized the harshness of his reprimand, but he promised them that the chastisements he offered were for their benefit. By way of example, he pointed to the Old Testament prophets who had tried to cleanse the Jews by warning them of coming tribulations and calling for their repentance. Clamanges then explicitly asserted that his own goal, like theirs, was to signal a time of testing in order to purify, strengthen, and make them worthy of salvation at the End, just as gold was tested in fire.[8]

[7] Bérier notes that, in his commentary on Isaiah, Clamanges followed Jerome in using the prophet's words as a springboard for commenting on current events; see "Exégèse et ironie," pp. 29-31. Coville particularly noted Clamanges' use of Jeremiah in the Isaiah commentary in *Le Traité*, pp. 94-97. For the opening and closing of *De ruina*, see ibid., pp. 111 and 154-156; the passages from Clamanges' letters may be found at C 200.162-201.180 (L 2.119-120), following Sir 15:14, Ps 7:16, Prv 1:27 and 31; C 459.198-460.205 (L 1.177), commenting on Is 48:20.

[8] B 2:177.2, 4-12 (L 2.357): "Cogor...quantum ex sedula lectione propheticarum litterarum illorumque qui Prophetas vigilantius scrutati sunt intelligere concessum est, aliquatenus aperire. Licet enim nec speculator sim nec digna super specula constitui, illa tamen uerba Domini ad Ezechielem directa magnum, quotiens ea relego, michi terrorem incutiunt: Si, dicente me ad impium: morte morieris, non annunciaueris ei ut auertatur a sua via mala et viuat, ipse in iniquitate sua morietur, sanguinem autem eius de manu tua requiram (Ez 3:18)." B 2.178.30-37 (L 2.357): "[O]pere precium putaui que de cladibus acerbissimis super latinam Ecclesiam instanter affuturis ex Prophetarum eloquiis, illorumque qui Prophetas in his que tempora ista respiciunt liquidius enuclearunt, colligere potui, ad catholice religionis vtilitatem ad salutemque electorum qui, uelut aurum in fornace, in temptatione ista

Clamanges laid down his basic description of the End Times, full of destruction and assault but also hope through penitence, in his *De Antichristo* and in his treatment of Isaiah's apocalypse (Is 24-27) in the *Expositio*. He predicted two judgments with a delay between them. Jesus would come at the second judgment, signalling the end of the world; Jesus' arrival would immediately be preceded by a period of purgative testing and assault against Christianity. This assault would be led by a beastly prince: apparently Antichrist himself at the head of an army riding on horses with hooves like flint. Secular leaders would be powerless to resist and there would be turmoil from all sides. Railing against God, Antichrist would be restrained by an unnamed armed man but just for a time because only God could completely conquer Antichrist. The armed man may have been a reference to a conquering Last World Emperor who is the Church's champion. This common apocalyptic figure, however, appears nowhere else in Clamanges' writings on the End--another example of his lack of extended interest in explicating every detail of the Last Events.[9] Under the guise of being the Messiah, Antichrist would lead the Jews to the Promised Land, a deception that had become a standard element of late medieval apocalyptic scenarios and one to which Clamanges also referred in his *Expositio* written about the same time. He quoted Paul in saying that, ultimately, Jesus would come and destroy Antichrist with the breath of His mouth and by His coming. With intriguing specificity, Clamanges added that this would take place in the Alps.[10]

There would be signs that these End Times were coming. Citing Paul's letters to Timothy, Clamanges noted as early as 1400/1401 in *De ruina* that hypocrisy and faithlessness would increase during the End Times. This would naturally produce great confusion among the faithful, a point he repeated in a 1410/1411 letter to Jean Gerson where he again turned to Paul while complementing his epistles with the synoptic gospels' predictions. As Jesus foretold, many would be deceived and led into error at the End by false miracles, signs, illusions, and prophets claiming to speak in His name. His overview of Isaiah's apocalypse in the *Expositio* added that nations will fight each other, tyrants and demons will target and tempt Christians, false prophets will claim to be from God, and idolatry will increase. All of these events will lead to the

proculdubio probabantur, quantum Dominus suggerere dignatur, in medium proferre (Wis 3:6, Sir 2:5, Prv 17:3, Is 48:10)."

9 B 2.178.44-49 (L 2.357-358); B 2.178.53-179.64 (L 2.358); B 2.179.79-180.90 (L 2.358), following Ps 121:4, Is 5.27-28, Mt 25:5; B 2.180.97-181.112 (L 2.358-359), following Hb 1:10, Dn 7:25 and 11:36, 2 Thes 2:6-7. For legends of the Last World Emperor including their beginnings with Pseudo-Methodius in the seventh century and continuing with versions contemporary to Clamanges, see McGinn, *Visions of the End*, pp. 70-76, 246-252.

10 B 2.181.112-114 (L 2.359), following 2 Thes 2:8; B 2.181.116, 119-123, 130-133 (L 2.359); Ars. 137, fol. 130vb. On the deception of the Jews, see Andrew Colin Gow, *The Red Jews: Antisemitism in an Apocalyptic Age 1200-1600* (Leiden, 1995), pp. 93-130 and especially appendix C, "Antichrist and the Jews at the End of Time," pp. 351-381, where he traces the development of this idea in Latin and Middle German texts.

tribulations of war, sedition, and faithlessness represented by the seven heads and horns of the apocalyptic beast. Antichrist will lead the unfaithful nations, Clamanges predicted in several very dark passages, but he added that the rewards of glory and salvation would be granted to those who keep the faith and act penitently even though shaken violently by these events. Punishment in an inferno, on the other hand, would be doled out to those who were persistently wicked.[11]

To press his goal of promoting reform, Clamanges elaborated on this portrait of the End with an *ex eventu* approach. He particularly saw the Schism as weakening the church from within and preparing the way for Antichrist, as did his mentor Pierre d'Ailly who also turned to apocalyptic imagery with some frequency to point out the need for reform instead of to lay down a precise chronology of the End Times.[12] Throughout *De ruina* Clamanges maintained that the split in ecclesiastical leadership would surely lead to the desolation of the church. In a poem he composed during the Schism, *Deploratio calamitatis ecclesiastice*, Clamanges presented a picture of a church that would be in complete confusion if broad reforms were not undertaken. Although he did not explicitly use End Time imagery here, Clamanges repeated similar comments which elsewhere he made in an apocalyptic context: within and without, the church would be attacked, harassed, oppressed, weakened by opposition, and threatened by utter destruction. The church's position was further undermined by rampant simony and faithlessness. In his 1412 treatise on simony, *Contra prelatos symoniacos*, Clamanges identified the behavior of simoniacal prelates as a clear sign of the forces of Antichrist at work within the church. He linked the simony of his contemporaries with the challenge of Simon Magus to Peter, portraying both acts as examples of heretical and faithless opposition to the divine law which should not be abandoned, changed, or dissolved. Clamanges declared these actions to be hallmarks of Antichrist.[13]

Clamanges factored heresy into his rhetorical calls for reform, as well. In *De Antichristo* he declared that the approach of the conquering beast from the sea described in Revelation would be hastened by lapses in the orthodox faith among heretics, whom he frequently described as Antichrist's allies. In both the

[11] Coville, *Le Traité*, p. 141, following 1 Tm 4:1-2 and 2 Tm 3:1-2, 6-7; C 282.50-54 and 283.87-91 (L 2.175), following 1 Tm 4:1; Mt 24:4-5, 11, 24; Mk 13:22; Lk 21:8; Ars. 137, fol. 126rb-143vb.

[12] D'Ailly's position is treated in Louis B. Pascoe, "Pierre d'Ailly: Histoire, Schisme et Antéchrist," in *Genèse et débuts du Grand Schisme d'Occident*, pp. 615-622; see also Laura Ackerman Smoller, *History, Prophecy, and the Stars: The Christian Astrology of Pierre d'Ailly, 1350-1420* (Princeton, 1994), pp. 85-101.

[13] Coville, *Le Traité*, pp. 153-154. For the *Deploratio calamitatis ecclesiastice*, see C 645-648, especially 646.27-36; this poem may also be found in idem, *Recherches sur quelques écrivains du XIVe et du XVe siècle* (Paris, 1935), pp. 261-264, especially pp. 261.24-262.33. On simony, see B 2.143.213-218 (L 1.163-164): "Antichristi hec erit doctrina, qui Legem Dei euacuare, mutare ac dissoluere conabitur, de qua vnus non potest apex preterire (Mt 5:18, Lk 16:17). Si male fidei possessor nullo vnquam potest tempore prescribere, quo pacto infidelis contra fidem, Antichristus contra Christum, Simonis heres contra Petrum prescribet?"

Expositio and *De Antichristo* he particularly pointed to heretics in Italy and Germany, naming the Italian heretics "Patarini" several times in the *Expositio* and, in one place, even more specifically calling them Lombard Patarini. Considering that Clamanges wrote these two works in the first third of the fifteenth century, the German heretics are easier to identify than the Italian: the former are probably members of the Hussite factions fighting for their independence in Bohemia. The general references to Italian heretics may allude to participants in the continuing Franciscan battle among Conventuals, Observants, and splinter groups in the Fraticelli tradition; he may also have been referring to remnants of the *flagellantes*, Beguine, Beghard, or Free Spirit groups. His specific use of the word "Patarini," especially as Lombard Patarini, is curious. Strictly speaking, the Patarini were a Milanese group with roots in the orthodox reform efforts of Gregory VII; their name came to be used generically for all heretics, especially Cathars, in Italy in the wake of the Third Lateran Council (1179) even after the first real Patarini had disappeared. But while Cathars lasted in Italy a bit longer than elsewhere in Europe, they had ceased to be a major threat to orthodoxy by the first part of the fourteenth century, nearly a century before Clamanges wrote these two apocalyptic treatments. The reference to Lombard Patarini, then, may be another indication of Clamanges' rhetorical use of apocalyptic imagery to serve his more important goal of reform.[14]

Clamanges added the Muslim threat to that of the German and Italian heretics. Throughout the Middle Ages Muslims had appeared in apocalyptic writings whenever they threatened European forces or territory, beginning with Pseudo-Methodius' fears concerning Islam's initial expansion in the seventh century. In the late Middle Ages Muslims were especially seen as the great enemy of Christian Europe as the Ottoman Empire became a stronger presence with its capital firmly established at Adrianople by 1366 and its conquest of Constantinople in 1453. During this period the Muslims had successfully invaded and occupied the Balkans while their stubborn resistance in Spain remained worrisome despite the advances of the Reconquest. Following the account in Revelation, in *De Antichristo* Clamanges painted the Muslims in terms of the Whore of Babylon who would corrupt the earth with her prostitution. He predicted in his *Exhortatio* that Muslim armies would pour into Europe from the east via the Mediterranean Sea to exterminate the Christians in Italy, including those in Rome. Other Muslims would move from Africa into Spain and France; still more would invade northern and eastern Europe. One of

[14] B 2.180.90-96 (L 2.358), "Huic autem crudeli bestie, in nostrum interitum de mari protinus surrecture, coniungenda est insuper et alia bestia in Christiane similiter religionis extinctionem de terra consurgens (Rv 13:1-18), varii scilicet heretici in partibus Ytalie Germanieque constituti, qui vniuersi vno impetu contra Christum et fideles suos in illius infausti temporis articulo conspirabunt..."; Ars. 137, fol. 133ra, 134rb, 134va. For the persistence of the Fraticelli and other movements to which Clamanges may have been referring, see Gordon Leff, *Heresy in the Later Middle Ages*, 2 vols. (Manchester, 1967), 1.255, 1.347-352, 2.493. On the Patarini, see Malcolm Lambert, *Medieval Heresy: Popular Movements from Bogomil to Hus* (New York, 1977), pp. 40-41, 84, 383; and Christine Thouzellier, *Hérésie et hérétiques* (Rome, 1969), pp. 204-221.

Clamanges' points in using the Muslim threat was to reiterate his call for steadfast faithfulness and morality during these tumultuous events that would comprise the End Times. He feared that the many intolerable sins of Christians and heretics would actually open the way for the innumerable armies of Muslims. Sinners must be wary of allowing the Whore to corrupt them and so usher in their own destruction, especially since Christians would be assaulted, he warned in the *Expositio*, by the cruel beasts and dogs with the worst bite of the Muslim sect.[15]

Clamanges also linked the French civil war to his apocalyptic imagery by explaining that it produced just the sort of chaos which would make victory easier for Antichrist. His 1411/1412 letter to theologians at the Collège de Navarre in the University of Paris laid the blame for societal discord at the feet of the protagonists of the French civil war. He compared France's situation with the confusion of the Tower of Babel and implied that the sins of the French were piling up just like the Whore of Babylon's. The main thrust of the *Exhortatio*, indeed, was a plea for Christian princes to cease their factionalism and unite against the common enemy of the Muslims. Christian princes must be of one body if they were to resist Antichrist and its advance guard, the Muslims. Efforts to wrest power from each other left these princes diverted from their task of protecting Christian Europe. Just as the unreformed church would be distracted by the Schism and left incapable of fending off Antichrist and its forces, secular leaders would similarly be unable to resist Antichrist because of civil war. Princes should fight their common enemy with one heart and one mind in order to save both the faith and the faithful from defilement. The enemy, expecting division among its foes, should instead find united opposition.[16]

Clamanges sharpened the urgency of his counsel to reform as soon as possible with his belief--or at least his rhetorical flourish--that the coming of Antichrist was fast approaching. In the *Expositio*, finished about 1426, he first declared the End to be without doubt near, adding more precisely in the same text that the final calamity was about four years away. Just about that time, in 1430 when he wrote the *De Antichristo*, he saw Antichrist arriving within two to three years. Despite these predictions, in *De Antichristo* Clamanges did not fail to note the well-known New Testament principle that the exact time and hour when the Father will place power in His Son cannot be known.[17] It should be

[15] Norman Daniel, *The Arabs and Medieval Europe*, 2nd ed. (London, 1979), pp. 312-322. B 2.179.64-71 (L 2.358), following Rv 19:2; B 2.182.14-183.27; Ars. 137, fol. 140va, 142ra, and especially 142va: "...crudeles bestias atque canes mordacissimos secte machometice..."

[16] C 387.5-11 (L 2.230); C 388.39-45 (L 2.230), following Gn 11:1-9; C 388.61-389.72 (L 2.231), following Rv 17-18; C 389.85-93 (L 2.231); B 2.183.29-35, 38-41; B 2.184.56-69, following Acts 4:32; B 2.184.71-77.

[17] Ars. 137, fol. 109va, identified by Bérier, "Remarques sur l'*Expositio*," p. 47 n. 20; the reference to four years is at Ars. 137, fol. 142rb, where Clamanges commented on Is 27 and the description there of the punishment and winnowing on the coming day of the Lord. The *De Antichristo* timetable of two or three years after 1430 is at B 2.178.40-44 (L 2.357); Clamanges repeated the imminence of the End in

noted that these dates and predictions appear in Clamanges' last writings near the end of his life. François Bérier, who is preparing a critical edition of the *Expositio*, has provided evidence that Clamanges' concerns with the End grew heavier and more burdensome as he came to the end of his own life. Clamanges feared the violence of the End and his personal end were simultaneously impending. This dark view of his own approaching end surely joined with the lasting effects of the Schism and the French civil war to color the dour portrait of current events that is found throughout Clamanges' unfinished commentary on Isaiah, where he seemed consistently to take for granted the fact that the End Times loomed.[18]

He contended that reform should be occurring all the time but especially if the End was imminent, even if the exact final moment could never be known with certainty. He stressed in *De Antichristo* that there would be two chances for personal reform and salvation during the End Times. The first opportunity would occur during the delay between the two tumultuous judgments already described in his basic timetable. He believed that this delay between the two judgments would afford a time of personal contrition and renewal. This interval would be a tranquil period free from the turmoil of war, like the sabbath Paul had identified. In the tumultuous assault on Christianity led by Antichrist which would conclude the delay and immediately precede the second judgment, those opposing or failing in the faith would have still one more opportunity to turn from their dangerous errors and rejoin the Church, just as a wild olive branch may be grafted onto a tree. They would then await the coming of the Lord and the End of the world in a final moment of quiet and tranquility. In the *Expositio* he identified the time before Jesus' arrival in traditional terms as a period of one thousand years, but in the *De Antichristo* he did not describe the delay between the two judgments as a millennium. In his *De Antichristo* Clamanges also did not link either the delay between the two judgments or the final time of tranquility to a common apocalyptic idea that there would be a period of forty-five days just before the End known as the refreshment of the saints (*refrigerium sanctorum*), calculated from the apocalyptic prophecy in Dn 12:10-12. The fact that Clamanges did not use the familiar medieval phrase and scriptural citation concerning the *refrigerium sanctorum* explicitly is another indication that his purpose in using images of the End Times was principally to issue a call for reform and not to provide a comprehensive apocalyptic scenario or an exegesis of apocalyptic scriptural texts that addressed every aspect of the Last Events as did other, more complete medieval accounts. The focus is always on the goal of

the opening lines of the *Exhortatio*, dating also to about 1430, at B 2.182.2-6. For Clamanges' statement that ultimately the exact moment of the End is not knowable, see B 2.178.52-53 (L 2.358), following Mt 24:36, Mk 13:32, Acts 1:7.

[18] Bérier, "Remarques sur l'evolution des idees politiques," pp. 122-123, citing especially Ars. 137, fol. 103va; on Clamanges' pervasive theme in the *Expositio* that the times were bad at the end of his life, see also idem, "Remarques sur l'*Expositio*," pp. 43-46, and Coville, *Le Traité*, pp. 103-105. Both Bérier and Coville note that Clamanges discussed the coming destruction of Babylon (Is 13) within the context of the similarly dark tribulations of his own era.

reform--promoted through the means of an apocalyptic perspective--and not on the End of the world *per se*.[19]

Clamanges also frightened and threatened his readers into taking up the opportunity for their personal reform, as when he turned to the vitalistic parable of weeds planted among wheat (Mt 13:24-30, 36-43). At the harvest both would be collected but then separated, with the wheat going into storage and the weeds burned. In explaining the parable, Jesus noted that the harvest represented the End when the faithful would be judged worthy of heaven or hell. Clamanges referred to this parable's message a number of times in the early part of his career: in his 1394 and 1402 letters to France's Charles VI as well as in a letter to d'Ailly ca. 1398-1403.[20] Another warning of a coming judgment to spur reform is found in Clamanges' somber 1410/1411 letter to Gerson. There Clamanges lamented that the times in which they lived were extremely bad and stressed that vindication would come. God, he promised Gerson, would know who had acted faithfully for the Church and had not deserted her; disaster would not befall these faithful Christians who had earned their election. Those who extolled themselves, however, would be crushed by the powerful hands of Christ and condemned by their own actions even while they were ignorant of the fact that they were contributing to their doom. Clamanges repeated the threat of Christ's coming judgment a few years later in another letter where he again noted that Christians would be held accountable for the sins by which they put themselves in danger. Therefore, if love of God did not entice a man to God, should not fear of God as judge at least cause him to tremble? Clamanges relied on this fear of threatening judgment to plead his case that people should reform themselves by changing their ways. With a divine judgment and an End of the world assured why did people delay, ignore penance and reconciliation, resist divine counsel, and persist in blasphemy? A harsh judgment awaited when the king and judge comes, Clamanges promised, unless people relinquished their old ways.[21]

Clamanges was mostly concerned with what people should do to avail themselves of the opportunity for reform offered by the coming judgment at their end or the world's End. This goal is especially evident from the manner in which he exploited scripture to indicate a course of action for his readers. Clamanges pressed them to take action to correct their culpable behavior and so avoid the promised tribulations. The consequences of the failure to reform were made clear

19 B 2.178.53-179.64 (L 2.358), following Heb 4:9, Rom 11.17-24; Ars. 137, fol. 130va. Robert E. Lerner has provided a complete discussion of the *refrigerium sanctorum* in "Refreshment of the Saints: The Time After Antichrist as a Station for Earthly Progress in Medieval Thought," *Traditio* 32 (1976): 97-144.

20 C 3.43-46 (L 2.3); C 114.500-501 (L 2.69); C 178.103-111 (L 2.106). The last reference does not explicitly mention this parable but does describe an eternal separation of good and bad that clearly echoed Jesus' explanation of the weeds and wheat.

21 C 282.56-283.61 and 283.92-284.101 (L 2:175); C 452.106-453.154, 164-168 (L 2:274-275), especially ll. 142-144: "Si amor vos ad eum non allicit, saltem timor trahat. Quis iudicem contremiscere non debeat?"

through his recourse to the judgment and destruction of Sodom and Gomorrah (Gn 18:16-19:29) as well as to Ezekiel's story of the two evil sisters Oholah and Oholibah that had foretold punishment for the Israelites (Ez 23). Clamanges linked Ezekiel's theme to that offered in Revelation's account of the fate of the Whore of Babylon (Rv 17-18).

In *De ruina* and several letters Clamanges pointed to Sodom and Gomorrah's destruction to prod his readers into reforming themselves before they were likewise consumed by their own iniquities. He used the story of Sodom and Gomorrah to make two points. First, the immorality of the current church was as bad as it had been during the worst moments of the past. The second point followed from the first: the destruction of God's disobedient people which is recorded in the Old Testament threatened also the church of Clamanges' era. But Clamanges also used Sodom and Gomorrah to offer optimism and hope. In his 1398 letter to Benedict XIII he slightly softened the pessimism that characterized much of his other apocalyptic treatments with the hope that a destruction similar to that sent down upon Sodom and Gomorrah as punishment for the actions of the cities' citizens could actually be avoided in their own times. Clamanges expressed this hope by invoking Abraham's question to God whether He would spare Sodom if Abraham found ten just men there. His prophetic message that destruction awaited but there was still time to repent was made even clearer in his 1411/1412 letter to the Collège de Navarre. There he complained about the lack of order and peace, reminding his Parisian friends of God's disgust with the many sins of Sodom and Gomorrah. But, as if to encourage them to seize a final opportunity for reform, Clamanges again noted that in the case of Sodom and Gomorrah God had investigated the citizens' conduct before destroying their cities. This hopeful sense that there was still time for change was repeated two years later in another letter he devoted to the recent sack of Soissons during fighting connected to France's civil war. What had happened to the city was only a portent of what could come: like Sodom and Gomorrah, Soissons would be completely destroyed by God's fire at the End unless its inhabitants repented. It was possible, however, to stave off imminent ruin if they lived rightly.[22]

Continuing in his role as a reforming prophet, in *De ruina* Clamanges also invoked the allegorical story from Ezekiel of Oholah and Oholibah, sisters who were prostitutes in Egypt and represented the Israelites' faithlessness. Oholah and Oholibah were eventually consumed by their own iniquity: they were repaid according to their sins and destroyed by foreign forces. Concluding *Contra prelatos symoniacos* a decade later, Clamanges warned against the dangers into which simoniacs placed themselves by once more referring to the harlot sisters who were repaid according to their crimes. As the prophet Ezekiel had done, Clamanges employed the story of the harlot sisters to rouse his listeners to reform their ways before it was too late. He enlivened this admonition by linking the fate of the sisters to that promised to the Whore of Babylon. The Book of Revelation foretold that the Whore would also be consumed by her own iniquity, which is precisely what had happened to Oholah and Oholibah.

[22] Coville, *Le Traité*, p. 156; C 91.311-313 (L 2.55), following Gn 18:32; C 388.53-58 (L 2.231), following Gn 18.20-21; C 482-486 (L 2.287-290).

Clamanges combined these Old and New Testament accounts to advise those within the Church that if they failed to heed his warnings about the peril into which they placed themselves, they would meet a fate similar to that which had befallen the sisters and would be visited upon the Whore of Babylon.[23]

* * *

Having examined the images of the End Clamanges utilized to stress his calls for reform in the church and especially among individual Christians, it is important to locate him more fully in the tradition of apocalyptic imagery. Clamanges' perspective was more properly eschatological and patristic than apocalyptic. The words "eschatology" and "apocalyptic" are of course imprecise and still subject to debate, particularly when they are joined in the phrase "apocalyptic eschatology", as they frequently are. While eschatology refers to the Last Things in the broadest terms, it can usefully be taken to focus on an individual's spiritual state at the end of his own life, a perspective typically urged on Christians by the fathers. Their writings on the topic were marked by a rejection of literalism and an *ex eventu* approach in favor of concern for personal reform through purgative suffering, asceticism, and an interiorized understanding of the End's ultimate meaning. By contrast, "apocalyptic" more often implies an imminent, cataclysmic End of the world that in the Middle Ages was often fairly strictly linked to a literal interpretation of current events.[24] Recalling McGinn's thesis that Antichrist language and application are not always mutually exclusive and that one need not believe the End to be imminent to talk about the Last Things, we identify in Clamanges' writings a late medieval use of Antichrist language which appealed to the emotion and imagery of Antichrist application but was almost always put to the service of focusing the individual Christian on his own end. Clamanges' rhetoric of reform about the End allows us to apply McGinn's assessment of the marriage between Antichrist language and application to the late Middle Ages in addition to the Gregorian Revolution. Moreover, we see in his writings precise evidence of the simultaneously optimistic and pessimistic climate of apocalyptic thought identified by Oberman in the fourteenth and fifteenth centuries.

Clamanges' rhetoric of reform renewed the fathers' emphasis on the individual's spiritual state at his own end, whether or not that event coincided with the end of the world. This description rings true despite his stated reliance on the most influential of the literally-minded medieval apocalyptic authors, Joachim of Fiore, whose work was available to Clamanges in libraries at

23 Coville, *Le Traité*, pp. 146-148; B 2.147.325-327 (L 1.165), following Ez 23:35, 49. What follows the story of the two sisters in Ezekiel is a reference to the Babylonian exile of the Israelites: Ez 24:1-3.

24 On the definition of these terms see McGinn, *Antichrist*, pp. 2, 12-16; idem, *Visions*, pp. 3-4; and idem, *Apocalyptic Spirituality* (New York, 1979), pp. 4-7. McGinn treats the patristic period, from which this description is excerpted, in *Antichrist*, pp. 57-82.

Avignon and the Collège de Navarre, his home in Paris.[25] But we have seen that Clamanges' literal approach was not very comprehensive or consistent. It is his attention to personal reform that distinguishes his writings on the End Times. In this personal emphasis Clamanges was in step with others of a similar mind who attended to an individual's end more than the world's. Barbara Nolan has identified this as a "gothic visionary perspective": after the twelfth century and reaching into the late Middle Ages, visions of the End were seen in much more personal terms, particularly via meditations on the heavenly city as imagined in the Book of Revelation. The Christian's attention was laid on his or her own place within the course of history, a microcosm within a macrocosm. The spiritual journey to move closer to God was a pilgrimage of penance and grace toward the culmination of one's own life.[26] Such a personal, non-literal interpretation mirrored that of the fathers who, even while noticing in the collapse of the Roman Empire signs of terrible times, were not strictly wedded to an imminent apocalypse. In fact, Clamanges' perspective during the Schism, the Muslim advance, and the French civil war recall and were perhaps informed by Gregory the Great's writings on the End within his own tumultuous context, particularly his *Moralia in Job*, which was in the Collège de Navarre library, and his homilies on Ezekiel, which Clamanges personally owned.[27] Gregory believed in a vague way that the End was approaching--that is, that the world was old and dying--but never fixed a precise date for the event. As would Clamanges, Gregory took the opportunity of dark times to advocate personal renewal built on self-reflection and purgation. The End was the proximate context for personal reform for Gregory: since the Last Things approached, albeit

[25] Bérier believes that Clamanges relied on Joachim of Fiore for his general portrait of the End Times, noting that Clamanges himself claimed Joachim had explained everything one needed to know about such matters; see "Remarques sur l'*Expositio*," p. 47; idem, "Remarques sur l'evolution des idees politiques," p. 123. Clamanges could have come into contact with Joachim's work in the Avignon papal library during his two periods of service as secretary to Benedict XIII (1397-1398, 1403-1408) and/or in Paris, first during his student and professor days (ca. 1375-1397), and then again when he returned to resume study and teaching (ca. 1423-1437). Joachim's writings were in the Avignon library according to *La bibliothèque pontificale à Avignon et à Peniscola pendant le Grand Schisme d'Occident et sa dispersion: Inventaires et concordances*, ed. Marie-Henriette Jullien de Pommerol and Jacques Monfrin (Rome, 1991), pp. 146-147. Isabelle Chiavassa-Gouron found Joachim's writings listed in a Collège de Navarre inventory; see "Les lectures des maîtres et étudiants du collège de Navarre: Un aspect de la vie intellectuelle à l'Université de Paris (1380-1520)," M. A. thesis, École Nationale des Chartes, 1985, p. 194.

[26] Barbara Nolan, *The Gothic Visionary Perspective* (Princeton, 1977), pp. 132-133.

[27] Chiavassa-Gouron, "Les lectures des maîtres et étudiants du collège de Navarre," pp. 103, 189, 198. Gregory the Great could not have been Clamanges' source for the exegesis of the harlot sisters Oholah and Oholibah from Ezekiel, however, because the pope did not comment on Ez 23 where that story appears.

generally, Christians were clearly being corrected for their fiery final judgment, for which they must urgently prepare.[28]

Clamanges' appeal to apocalyptic imagery, it may be concluded, was an example of form following function: the vivid and familiar imagery of the Last Events allowed him to invigorate and make even more urgent his primary message of the need for reform. His rhetorical use of apocalyptic ideas represents not merely an effective use of evocative imagery, however, but also an important ideological perspective within which he envisioned and pressed his reform program. While never an apocalyptic visionary, he used the easily-recognized imagery of the apocalyptic genre to make his point via historical circumstances that the time was ripe for the reform of Christians, the church, and Christian society. That is not to say, however, that Clamanges' apocalyptic imagery was merely a stylistic choice. Pressed on the matter, he may have responded that the End could occur given the current state of affairs and the need for reform within the church, as he seemed to indicate in his own final years. The important point is that the concerns and anxieties which accompanied Clamanges' rhetoric throughout his career were another indication of his primary intent: to offer a convincing call for the Christians of his day to work for reform immediately in their troubled times.

[28] Carole Straw, *Gregory the Great: Perfection in Imperfection* (Berkeley, 1988), pp. 1-2, 14-15, 184-185; Brian E. Daley, *The Hope of the Early Church: A Handbook of Patristic Eschatology* (Cambridge, 1991), pp. 211-215; and McGinn, *Antichrist*, pp. 80-82

PETER OF CANDIA AT PADUA AND VENICE IN MARCH 1406

Thomas E. Morrissey

A. The Context

The opening years of the fifteenth century were filled with unrest, uncertainty, great hopes, fears and disappointments. This was true in affairs of both church and state. The interminable fighting between England and France in the Hundred Years' War had been lulled by a truce signed in 1396 which was however violated by spasmodic violence in the intervening decades down to 1415 and the new invasion.[1] The long years of discontent in the Holy Roman Empire had reached a critical point in 1400 when the electoral princes, discouraged and disabused of any hope of progress and action from King Wenceslaus of Bohemia, had deposed him as Emperor-Elect and had chosen Ruprecht of the Rhine Palatinate as the new King of the Romans.[2] Florence and the Roman papacy had joined in an alliance against Milan, while Francesco il Novello de Carrara in Padua called on the newly elected Ruprecht to use this opportunity against the power of the Visconti in Milan and to regain the powers of the emperor that had been usurped.[3] These manuevers were only a part of the complex of shifting arrangements that Italy saw in these years. Ruprecht had then attempted to intervene as Emperor-Elect in the tangled and bitter quarrels of Northern Italy.[4] Confident in his expectations of an easy and swift victory over the forces led by Giangaleazzo Visconti from Milan that would be followed by a triumphant march to Rome and imperial coronation by the pope of the Roman line of obedience, Boniface IX, Ruprecht had instead experienced a humiliating defeat and in ignominious retreat limped back to Germany.[5]

1 Christopher Philpotts, "The Fate of the Truce of Paris 1396-1415," *Journal of Medieval History* 24 (1998): 61-80.

2 Johannes Glanz, in *Deutsche Geschichte in 12 Bänden,* ed. Heinrich Pleticha, vol. 5, *Die ausgehende Mittelalter 1378-1517* (Gütersloh, 1982-83), pp. 32-37; see also, Thomas E. Morrissey, "The Crisis of Authority at the End of the Fourteenth Century: A Canonist's Response," *Mediaevalia* 9 ([1986 for] 1983): 251-267 at p. 253; Ernst Schubert, *Einführung in die Grundprobleme der deutschen Geschichte im Spätmittelalter* (Darmstadt, 1992), pp. 152-153.

3 G. Romano, "La pace tra Milano e i Carraresi del 1402," *Archivio storico lombardo* 8 (1891): 841-857 at p. 842; Hans Baron, *The Crisis of the Early Italian Renaissance,* rev. ed. (Princeton, 1966), p. 130.

4 Glanz, *Die ausgehende Mittelalter,* pp. 37-38; for a good account of this tangle of Italian, French and other interests in North Italy that had a long history and would continue beyond this era, see Paolo Brezzi, "Lo Scisma d' Occidente come Problema Italiano," *Archivio d. R. Deputazione Romana di Storia Patria* 67, n. s. 10 (1944): 391-450.

5 John Julius Norwich, *A History of Venice* (New York, 1982), p. 266; W. Carew Hazlitt, *The Venetian Republic, its Rise, its Growth and its Fall A.D. 497-1797,* 2 vols. (London, 1915; New York, 1966), 1.783-784. See also now Benjamin G. Kohl, *Padua Under the Carrara, 1318-1405* (Baltimore, 1998), esp. chap. 10, "Ambition and Destruction, 1392-1405."

Perhaps nowhere more than in Italy were there cries for and need for the three desiderata of that era: peace, unity and reform. Political leaders, canonists, theologians, saints, conciliarists, papalists and common folk could all agree in the need for all three of these as the century began. The messy and rapidly shifting series of alliances and power grabs in North Italy appeared to be moving now in an inevitable slide into an expansive and threatening Visconti realm.[6] All of Giangaleazzo Visconti's dreams and plans seemed to be going his way and all of the worst fears of his opponents appeared to becoming realities,[7] when suddenly all was changed overnight and Giangaleazzo Visconti was no more, done in not by war or assassination but by disease in late 1402.[8] Instantly the whole configuration of power groupings was overturned and scores were settled by long standing enemies. The duchess of Milan, Giangaleazzo's widow, sought peace with the Carrara ruler in Padua who had stood by Florence in this time of danger and thrown in his lot with Ruprecht. Francesco il Novello's terms were strict: Vicenza, Belluno, Feltre and Bassano were all to be returned to Carrara rule and a payment of eighty thousand florins was exacted.[9]

In December 1402 the Carrara future seemed assured (in their eyes at least) and they were riding on the crest of a wave of fortune. But the moment of glory was only too fleeting, and the subsequent fall was catastrophic as the relations of Padua and Venice rapidly deteriorated.[10] The gifted but unreliable Francesco il Novello de Carrara in Padua soon paid the price for his choosing the wrong side in allying with Milan against the Venetian Republic; and, when he lost the war, the Carrara lost everything, their realm in Padua, Padua's independence, and ultimately, for Francesco and his two sons their very lives were forfeit.[11] The

[6] Norwich, *History of Venice,* pp. 266-267, points out that, after the defeat of Ruprecht, Giangaleazzo rapidly added Bologna to his conquests and had Pisa, Siena and Lucca in his control when he turned toward Florence; see also Brezzi, "Lo Scisma d' Occidente," pp. 426ff.

[7] Daniel Waley, *Later Medieval Europe from St. Louis to Luther,* 2nd ed. (New York, 1985), p. 178; also Norwich, *History of Venice,* p. 279.

[8] Frederic C. Lane, *Venice: A Maritime Republic* (Baltimore, 1973), p. 228 attributed Giangaleazzo's sudden death to an outbreak of the plague in Milan. Norwich, *History of Venice,* p. 266 reports that "on 13 August 1402, he [Giangaleazzo Visconti] was struck down by fever; and three weeks later he died." Brezzi gave the date of Giangaleazzo's death as September 3, 1402, in "Lo Scisma d' Occidente," p. 427.

[9] Romano, "La pace," pp. 843-844.

[10] Romano, "La pace," pp. 844-852; Kohl, *Padua Under the Carrara,* pp. 329-334.

[11] Hazlitt, *The Venetian Republic,* 1.798-799, reported that on January 17, 1406 Francesco il Novello, and on the next day his two sons, were strangled in the Venetian prison. It was then reported that they had died of disease, and so they were given proper burial. Norwich, *History of Venice,* pp. 267-268, gave the date as January 17, 1405 and only mentioned one son, Jacobo. See also Ernst Bernheim, "Eine Episode aus der venezianischen Geschichte, der Sturz des Hauses Carrara," *Zeitschrift für Geschichte und Politik* 4 (1887): 102-123.

wily and somewhat disreputable Pope Boniface IX would also soon disappear from the scene by natural causes in 1404 to be followed by the brief reign of Pope Innocent VII (1404-1406).[12]

In these same years there was a shift in papal policy, especially that carried out by Baldassare Cossa later Pope John XXIII who then was papal legate in Bologna, which showed remarkable activity compared with the weakness of the papal regime in Rome dominated by the Neopolitan faction at the curia.[13] Cossa allied with both the Florentine bankers and the family of Este in Ferrara.[14] The Este family would soon find its own situation untenable; and, from a marriage alliance with the Carrara, was forced into acquiescence and submission by Venice. Meanwhile papal rule in Rome, even after the death of Boniface IX in 1404, was crumbling and was now dominated by the forces of Ladislaus of Naples. The new pope, Innocent VII, saw an attempt at a bloody coup by his nephew, Ludovico Migliorati, on August 6, 1405 against the popular government in Rome dominated by Ladislaus and his adherents. But this was only an ephemeral occurrence, and Innocent was only able to re-enter the city and try to negotiate peace with Ladislaus a year later in the summer of 1406.[15]

As we have seen above, it is within this context that we can place the journey north and the mission of Peter of Candia who was sent as a papal envoy

[12] Boniface IX died in October 1404; and, on October 17, 1404, Cosimo Migliorati was elected and chose the name Innocent VII; see P. Brand, "Innocenzo VII e il delitto di suo nipote Ludivico Migliorati," *Studi e Documenti di Storia e Diritto* 21 (1900): 179-215 at p. 185. See also August Kneer, "Zur Vorgeschichte Papst Innocenz VII (1404-1406)," *Historisches Jahrbuch* 12 (1891): 347-351. For the career and reputation of Boniface IX see Brezzi, "Lo Scisma d' Occidente," pp. 412ff; Arnold Esch, "Simonie-Geschäft in Rom 1400: 'Kein Papst wird das tun, was dieser tut,'" *Vierteljahrschrift für Sozial- und Wirtschaftgeschichte* 61 (1974): 433-457. For Innocent VII's negotiations at this time in the north, see M. Maillard-Luypaert, "Une lettre d' Innocent VII du 2 octobre 1405 à propos du retour de Liège à l'obedience romaine," *Revue d' histoire ecclésiastique* 62 (1977): 54-60. It should be noted that in his earlier career Cosimo Migliorati had studied at Perugia, Padua and Bologna; he had received his doctorate from Johannes de Legnano at Bologna and had gone with Legnano on a trip to the Roman Curia after the outbreak of the Great Western Schism, which was the exact time period when Franciscus Zabarella was at Bologna to study law with Legnano. Migliorati had then subsequently served in the Roman Curia, been bishop of Bologna in 1386, archbishop of Ravenna (1387 to 1400) and had been created a cardinal in 1389 by Boniface IX; see Kneer, "Zur Vorgeschichte Papst Innocenz VII," p. 347. Finally, one of Zabarella's friends and legal scholars, Petrus de Ancharano, a famed canonist in his own right, had been a student of Migliorati when he was at Bologna.

[13] Peter Partner, *The Lands of St Peter: The Papal State in the Middle Ages and Early Renaissance* (Berkeley, 1972), p. 386.

[14] Partner, *Lands of St Peter,* p. 387.

[15] Partner, *Lands of St Peter,* p. 387.

to the various territories of North Italy by Innocent VII.[16] One must also see the mission in the perspective of what had come about between Padua and Venice in 1404-1405. Once the threat of Milan had been defused, Venice under its new doge, Michele Steno who had come to office in December 1401, went through a stormy reorientation of its policies, specifically in regard to mainland Italy. By 1403 Venice had defeated a Genoese fleet off the coast of Morea.[17] On March 22, 1404 Venice signed an agreement with France which granted compensation for damages done to Venice.[18] Only a few days after this, on March 27, 1404, the Carrara regime had formed a series of alliances. But this was seen as a challenge and a direct provocation to Venice, and so war followed between Padua and Venice.[19] In Venice's eyes the northeastern states in Italy, which the Republic was determined to subdue and occupy, were already accustomed to foreign rule from the previous actions of Giangaleazzo Visconti.[20] During this period while Venice decided to build up a *terra ferma* state, Florence incorporated her neighbor, Pisa, which also paid the penalty for siding with Milan and so appearing as a threat to Florence.[21] Venice now no longer needed nor trusted Padua as an ally and so began to close in on that city.

The effects on Padua were devastating, especially to its university and circle of scholars. The Carrara regime in 1404-1405 stopped all payment to scholars in order to concentrate funds on the war. Humanists such as Giovanni Conversino da Ravenna left Padua. Conversino went to Venice and completed his work there.[22] In March 1405 the Este regime was compelled to make a humiliating peace with Venice. In July 1405 Verona capitulated; and, during that summer Padua was in a horrible state, ravaged by war, pestilence, famine and drought.[23] Terms of peace were proposed in September 1405 and initially accepted by il Novello but then foolishly rejected. Venice's views hardened with the discovery of plots that were traced back to Padua; and, finally in November 1405, Padua fell. Its era of independence was over. As stated above, Francesco il

16 The peace concluded on August 13, 1406 between Pope Innocent VII and Ladislas, king of Naples, should be seen as part of the whole program by the pope; see Brand, "Innocenzo VII," p. 211. See also Etienne Delaruelle, Edmond-Rene LaBande and Paul Ourliac, *L'Église au temps du Grand Schisme et de la crise conciliaire* (Histoire de l' Église, ed. Augustin Fliche et Victor Martin, vol. 14; Paris, 1962), pp. 122ff.

17 Hazlitt, *Venetian Republic:* p. 778.

18 Hazlitt, *Venetian Republic,* p. 782.

19 Hazlitt, *Venetian Republic,* pp. 785-786.

20 Hans Baron,"A Struggle for Liberty in the Renaissance: Florence, Venice and Milan in the Early Quattrocento," *American Historical Review* 58 (1952-53): 265-289 and 544-570 at p. 545.

21 Baron, "A Struggle for Liberty," pp. 559 and 545.

22 Baron, *Crisis of the Early Italian Renaissance,* p.135.

23 Norwich, *History of Venice,* p. 267.

Novello and his two sons, Jacopo and Francesco, were brought to Venice and eventually executed in January 1406 in an atmosphere of alarms, supposed plots and arrests.[24] Shortly before their execution Padua had formally surrendered in a ceremony before Doge Steno, who soon afterwards acted to restore order and stability, as well as subsidies for the university and strong support for it from Venice.[25]

In this time Pope Innocent VII, as mentioned, was working to implement change and reform that was much needed after the long reign of Boniface IX, who had seemed interested only in administrative control over and raising money from the church.[26] Innocent VII and a man he chose to work for the implementation of his policies, Peter Philargus of Candia, were both well known to Venice and favorably viewed in these circles. A generation earlier Innocent, then known by his family name, Cosimo Migliorati, had been sent as papal legate and envoy to mediate between Milan and Florence-Bologna in a dispute in Spring 1390. He was often at Venice and, as Dieter Girgensohn has recently shown, even received the right of Venetian citizenship at this time.[27] After becoming pope, Innocent VII created several new cardinals, who included Angelo Correr (who later, as Gregory XII, would be the first Venetian elected to the papacy), and Peter Philargus. The latter, known to historians as Peter of Candia from his birthplace on the island of Crete, was a former subject of Venice on that account. He had by then been linked for a number of years with Milan and, before being made a cardinal, had held the position of archbishop of Milan. Back in 1390, when the future Innocent VII had been sent as papal legate on the journey of mediation mentioned above, Peter of Candia was also in Venice for many weeks.[28] Later he had been empowered by Giangaleazzo Visconti to negotiate a peace with Venice and achieved this in May 1398. He had also spent many months in 1401 and 1402 in Venice; and thus, in the view of the government of Venice, Peter was an ideal candidate to work for peace as an essential prerequisite for the further goals of unity and reform in the church which all desired. Venice's trust in Peter of Candia is seen in an instance from these months.

In the year after Giangaleazzo's death Venice had sent envoys on 13 April 1403 to the Roman curia of Boniface IX to negotiate peace between Florence and Milan, and these envoys had been instructed to work with Peter of Candia.[29] Now in late 1405 Peter came into Lombardy and arrived shortly after Christmas, and then stayed in Venice for more than two months. This mission of Peter was

24 Hazlitt, *Venetian Republic,* 1.793.

25 Norwich, *History of Venice,* p. 285.

26 Karl Augustin Frech, *Reform an Haupt und Gliedern* (Untersuchung zur Entwicklung und Verwendung der Formulierung im Hoch- und Spätmittelalter; Frankfurt am Main/New York, 1992), p. 307.

27 Dieter Girgensohn, *Kirche, Politik und adelige Regierung in der Republik Venedig zu Beginn des 15. Jahrhunderts,* 2 vols. (Göttingen, 1996), 1.97.

28 Girgensohn, *Kirche, Politik und adelige Regierung,* 1.98.

29 Girgensohn, *Kirche, Politik und adelige Regierung,* 1.98.

very likely part of the overall policy of Innocent VII, who earlier had called for a conference of prelates, princes and representatives to act on the schism that was dividing the church. Venice, on August 3, 1405, had decided to send representatives; but only a few days later the pope had been forced to flee from Rome and this whole project had collapsed. Among those contacted by Innocent at the time with his proposal had been Ruprecht in Germany.[30] Venice was now in a position to make a difference. The Serene Republic was determined to have a safe and peaceful land border around her. She had taken steps to ensure that there were friendly bishops in these neighboring lands, first in Verona in 1405,[31] and then selected a new bishop for Padua from among the ruling families in Venice, Albano Michiel.[32] Only a few months after the formal surrender of Padua, Venice, in order to show her warm regards for Peter of Candia and to strengthen her ties with him, on January 28, 1406 granted to Peter *in commendam* the possession of the cloister of S. Michele de Candiana, located just south of Piove di Sacco in former Paduan territory.[33] Moreover, when Peter came to Lombardy and then Venice on this mission for peace, he was accompanied by an ambassador from Venice, Fantino Dandulo,[34] who had studied with and received his doctorate in civil law at Padua with Franciscus Zabarella in 1401.[35]

Peter Philargus of Candia on Crete, who then was being welcomed to Padua and Venice, was a Franciscan and had had a successful career as a professor of theology in a variety of schools.[36] He had come to the attention of the

[30] Franz Bliemetzrieder, "Die Konzilsidee unter Innozenz VII. und König Ruprecht von der Pfalz," *Studien und Mitteilungen aus der Benediktiner-Ordens* 27 (1906): 355-367.

[31] Girgensohn, *Kirche, Politik und adelige Regierung,* 1.111.

[32] Thomas E. Morrissey, "'Ecce Sacerdos Magnus': On Welcoming a New Bishop, Three Addresses for Bishops of Padua by Franciscus Zabarella," in *Nicholas of Cusa on Christ and the Church: Essays in Memory of Chandler McCuskey Brooks for the American Cusanus Society,* ed. Gerald Christianson and Thomas M. Izbicki (Leiden, 1996), pp. 57-70.

[33] Girgensohn, *Kirche, Politik und adelige Regierung,* 1.99.

[34] Margaret L. King, *Venetian Humanism in an Age of Patrician Dominance* (Princeton, 1986), p. 357.

[35] King, *Venetian Humanism,* p. 359. For further details on Zabarella's activities at this time as professor of law at the University of Padua and his connections with the Dandulo family, see Thomas E. Morrissey, "Ein unruhiges Leben. Franciscus Zabarella an der Universität von Padua (1390-1410): Die Welt, die Nikolaus von Kues vorfand," *Mitteilungen und Forschungsbeiträge der Cusanus-Gesellschaft 24* (1998): 5-40.

[36] Louis Salembier, *The Great Schism of the West,* trans. M. D. (London, 1907; London, 1968), p. 256; F. Gray, "Peter of Candia," in *New Catholic Encyclopedia* (Washington, D.C., 1967), 2.213. On Peter of Candia's career, see also Thomas E. Morrissey, "The Humanist and the Franciscan: A Letter of Giovanni Conversino da Ravenna to Peter Philargus of Candia," *Franciscan Studies* 52 ([1996 for] 1992): 183-189.

Visconti family in Milan, and, through its influence, was appointed archbishop of Milan in 1403 after having served as bishop in a number of dioceses.[37] Then the new pope, Innocent VII, had called him from that position to join the ranks of the cardinals of the Roman line.[38] Now, as cardinal and papal legate, Peter came to Padua in the late winter of 1406.[39]

The Padua Peter visited had seen remarkable change and painful times over the previous couple of years. The effects of the war between Padua and Venice could not have been ignored along with the long siege and final capitulation.[40] Only a few weeks before his arrival in Padua the formal ceremony of surrender

[37] Gray, "Peter of Candia," p. 213. See also Pius B. Gams, *Series episcoporum Ecclesiae Catholicae quotquot innotuerunt a beato apostolo* (Regensburg, 1873) and Konrad Eubel, *Hierarchia Catholica medii aevi* (Münster, 1898-1901). Arnold Esch pointed to Pietro Philargus (Candia), Branda Castiglione and Carlo Brancacci as among the leaders in the intense negotiations between the Roman papacy and Milan in 1402 and to the view that this group was seen as the Milan party in the curia; see "Das Papsttum unter der Herrschaft der Neapolitaner: Die führende Gruppe Neapolitaner Familien an der Kurie während des Schismas 1378-1415," in *Festschrift für Hermann Heimpel,* 3 vols. (Veröffentlichungen des Max-Planck-Instituts für Geschichte 36/I-III; Göttingen, 1971), 2:713-800 at p. 749.

[38] Salembier, *The Great Schism,* p. 256.

[39] Peter of Candia had gone to Lombardy in 1405 for peace negotiations with Milan and had been accompanied by Fantino Dandulo, a student of Zabarella's at Padua. For Dandulo's presence with Peter of Candia see King, *Venetian Humanism,* p. 357. Dandulo would later in his life serve as Archbishop of Candia (1444-1448) and then as Bishop of Padua (1448); ibid., p. 358. According to Andrea Gloria, *Monumenti della Università di Padova (1318-1405),* 2 vols. (Padova, 1888), 2:387, #2164, Dandulo had received his doctorate in law at Padua on August 8, 1401, but we also find that Zabarella delivered the address on the occasion of his receiving the insignia for his degree; see Vienna, Österreichische Nationalbibliothek, Cod. Lat. 5513, fol. 94v-95r and 170r-170v; Stift S Paul in Lavantthal, pap. 31/4, fol. 124v-125r; and Padua Biblioteca Universitaria, Ms. 201, fol. 17v-19r. Both Fantino and his brother Peter were present for the degree in canon law on this occasion on July 14, 1407. One of those present at the awarding of the degree in canon law to Fantino Dandulo in August 1401 was Zacharia Trevisan who was now present in March 1406 to greet Peter of Candia in his official post of Captain of Padua (*Capitaneus*) for the Venetian government.

[40] For the conditions in Padua as a consequence of the war, see Hazlitt, *The Venetian Republic,* 1.790-791. Then as now in tight times university budgets were made victims of cuts; see Giovanni Calo, "Nota Vergeriana (Il *De ingenuis moribus* e il supposto precettorato del Vergerio all corte di Francesco Novello)," *La Rinascità* 2 (1939): 226-252 at p. 248, where Calo noted that the stipend for one of the humanist teachers at Padua was reduced, and one can presume other faculty had similar experiences. Zabarella himself summarized the conditions in his address to the Doge in the formal act of surrender on January 4, 1406 as reported by A. Pino-Branca, "Il Comune di Padova sotte la Dominante nel sec. XV: (Rapporti amministrativi e finanziari)," *Atti del reale Istituto Veneto di Scienze, Lettere ed Arte* 93 (1933-1934): Part II, pp. 325-390, 879-940, 1249-1323 at p. 329 where Zabarella had asked for relief for the city and university in those hard times. Pino-Branca did, however, give the date as January 3, 1406.

had taken place in Venice on January 4, 1406.[41] Among those speaking on that earlier occasion was the man, Franciscus Zabarella, who delivered another formal address now of welcome to Peter of Candia which is presented here. Zabarella welcomed the visitor on behalf of his own city (and he was always very proud of Padua),[42] but also on behalf of and in the name of the people who now held the real power in Padua, the Venetian government. He referred to several of these by citing their official titles without however giving their names in the address. Thus he said that he spoke on behalf of the lord of Venice (*veneciarum domini*), which could only refer to the Doge of Venice, Michele Steno, who succeeded to that position on December 1, 1400.[43] Steno, as Doge of Venice, at the formal ceremony on January 4, 1406 had accepted the symbols of transfer of power and listened to the addresses of the representatives of Padua,[44] and had given his assurances for the security of the citizens of Padua and his support for the university there.[45] Zabarella also in this welcoming address to Peter of Candia said that he was acting in his capacity as public orator to fulfill the command of the heads of the government in Padua and referred to the two titles, the *Podestà* and Captain of the city (*potestatem et capitaneum*). We know that the man who was the first to hold the position of Captain for the

[41] Zabarella's address on this occasion has been preserved, but it was published in a not very easily accessible edition. The text can be found in the following codices: Milan, Biblioteca Ambrosiana, Lat. Cod. D 462 inf. fol. 202r-208v; Padua, Biblioteca Universitaria, Cod. 2231, fol. 77-83; Padua, Museo Civico Biblioteca, B.P. 1013:xix; B.P. 133:xvi (= Ms. 117); B.P. 5 (= Ms. 1418), fol. 1-20; B.P. 802:xvii, fol. 199-222. See also Dieter Girgensohn, "Francesco Zabarella aus Padua: Gelehrsamkeit und politisches Wirken eines Rechtsprofessors während des grossen abendländischen Schismas," *Zeitschrift der Savigny-Stiftung für Rechtsgeschichte*, Kan. Abt. 79 (1993): 232-277 at pp. 261-263 for a discussion of this address.

[42] As an expression of local pride and interest in the records of Padua there is documented for June 27, 1398 the establishment of a chapel in the Franciscan house in Padua by the Zabarella family, including, if not foremost, Franciscus Zabarella; see Gloria, *Monumenti della Università di Padova,* 2.329. In addition in the address now under consideration Zabarella very confidently refers to "this noble city of Padua" (*huius inclite urbis patavi*) and to "this magnificent city" (*huius magnifice urbis*).

[43] Norwich, *History of Venice,* p. 279 gives the date for Michele Steno's election.

[44] Norwich, *History of Venice,* pp. 283-284.

[45] Brian Pullan, *A History of Early Renaissance Italy from the Mid-Thirteenth to the Mid-Fifteenth Century* (New York, 1972), p. 271; Norwich, *History of Venice,* p. 285; Luigi Rizzoli, "L' Università dell' Arte della Lana a Padova," *Bollettino del Museo Civico di Padova* 20 (1927): 166-229; 21 (1928): 1-118 at pp. 192-193 reported Zabarella's address and that Doge Michele Steno issued on January 30, 1406 the famous "Bolla d'oro" which guaranteed support for Padua as Steno's response to this petition. In a letter on April 17, 1406 Doge Steno wrote to Zaccaria Trevisan on the depopulation of Padua (a result of both outbreaks of the plague and of the wars); see Percy Gothein, *Zaccaria Trevisan il Vecchio: La vita e l'ambiente* (R. Deputazione di Storia Patria per le Venezie. Miscellanea di Studi e Memorie, vol. 4; Venezia, 1942), p. 49 and n. 1.

Venetian government in Padua was Zaccaria Trevisan the Elder, who occupied that office from 1405 to 1407. The other position was held at this time by Marinus Caravello.[46]

One author in discussing the reaction of the Venetian government to a plot that had been discovered which appeared to threaten the city noted that on January 7, 1406 a warrant had been granted for the apprehension of Jacopo Gradenigo and Pietro Pisani, the former an ex-*Podestà* of Padua. It appears that Gradenigo had held this office under the Carraresi regime and was suspect for his close ties with the Carraresi. One of the confusions of language at this time was that August Kneer referred to Marinus Caravello as holding the position of *praetor* and Zaccaria Trevisan as *capitaneus* at this time.[47] It seems likely that these two terms *praetor* and *podestà* (one from the days of the Roman Republic and the other from medieval Italian history) were used interchangeably. Our suspicion is reinforced by such usage cited by Percy Gothein, who spoke of Trevisan going to Illyricum where he was designated as *podestà*, "qui in Illiricum profectus erat Iasdae Praetor (Potestas) ab extremo anno 1409 designatus."[48]

The address by Zabarella then is a document that reflects a moment of substantial change in North Italy and in the church. Venice was now supreme in this area politically and militarily, and the hopes for peace and tranquility might shine brighter. The long festering Great Western Schism might even be dealt with at long last now that some semblance of peace seemed possible and reform could also be brought to the fore. Peter of Candia was certainly a man who was laboring for peace, union and reform. Before the year was over Venice had even more reason to be confident and hopeful for, when Innocent VII died, one of her

46 For the career of Zaccaria Trevisan, see King, *Venetian Humanism*, pp. 436-437 and the work by Gothein mentioned above. How the various prominent figures of this era were interconnected can be seen in a letter that Zabarella would later write to his friend, Pietro Marcello, who would become bishop of Padua in 1409. This letter is one of consolation on the death of Zaccaria Trevisan in 1414 at the early age of not yet forty-four. Trevisan was related to Marcello by marriage and both were friends of Zabarella. On Marcello, see King, *Venetian Humanism*, pp. 397-398.

There is a bit of confusion as to who was *Podestà* in Padua in early 1406. Hazlitt, *Venetian Republic*, 1.797, in discussing the reaction of the Venetian government to a plot that had been discovered, noted that on January 7, 1406 a warrant was granted for the apprehension of Jacopo Gradenigo and Pietro Pisani, and that the former was ex-*Podestà* of Padua. Was Joseph Gradenigo the ex-*Podestà* just recently, or had he held this position under the Carrara regime? Percy Gothein, "Zaccaria Trevisan," *Archivio Veneto*, series 5, vol. 21 (1937): 1-59 at pp. 3, 8, and 21, pointed to Trevisan as the first *Podestà* in 1405-1406. King, *Venetian Humanism*, p. 436 has Trevisan holding the posts of both Captain and Vice-Captain. Gothein in his book *Zaccaria Trevisan il Vecchio*, p. 46, has a certain Thomas Mocenigro as vice-podesta and Trevisan as vice-captain when Venice took control of the city. This Mocenigro had just served as duke of Candia for Venice from 1402-1405 and would become doge of Venice in 1414; see Norwich, *History of Venice*, p. 642.

47 Kneer, *Kardinal Zabarella*, p. 39.

48 Gothein, "Zaccaria Trevisan," p. 18.

sons, in fact the first of Venice's sons, Angelo Correr, was elected to be pope of the Roman line as Gregory XII in December 1406.[49]

These hopes and confidence were misplaced as Venice and the rest of the Christian West soon learned that, in spite of all his promises, Gregory XII was just as obstinate and obstructive as any of his predecessors.[50] He and the pope of the Avignon line, Benedict XIII, fulminated against each other and appeared to be in collusion to prevent the very steps toward unity that each had promised to take.[51] Some even referred to them by a play on their names, Correr and de Luna as "Errorius" and "Lunarius" to indicate the low level of their reputation. Another writer spoke of them as being the aquatic animal (Benedict XIII) versus the land animal (Gregory XII), who could never get together,[52] and so the disunity of the church was doomed to continue so long as they had to wait for these two to cooperate in a joint venture for unity, and so reform was also apparently a mere hope or dream.

Soon, by 1408, the cardinals of both obediences had enough; and, breaking with both popes, they called for a general council to meet at Pisa to act to unify and reform the church.[53] It was during these years, between 1403 and 1408, that the orator whose address is presented below, Franciscus Zabarella, composed his tract *De schismate,* in which he justified the Christian

[49] Delaruelle, LaBande and Ourliac, *L' Eglise au temps du Grand Schisme,* p. 127; Innocent VII died on November 6, 1406; see Brand, "Innocenzo VII," p. 211; see Angelo Correr became Gregory XII on November 30; see Brezzi, "Lo scisma d' Occidente," p. 437. See also Eduardo Piva, "Venezia e lo scisma durante il pontificato di Gregorio XII," *Nuovo Archivio Veneto* 6 (1897): 135-158.

[50] Venice soon sent an embassy to the new pope; prominent among this group was Zaccaria Trevisan, who delivered an oration on that occasion that "made him famous." See King, *Venetian Humanism,* pp. 206-207. For the growing disappointment in Gregory, see Norwich, *History of Venice,* pp. 285-288 and Salembier, *The Great Schism,* pp. 232ff.

[51] Delaruelle, LaBande and Ourliac, *L' Église au temps du Grand Schisme,* pp. 130ff.

[52] Esch, "Das Papsttum unter der Herrschaft der Neapolitaner," pp. 749-750; also *Rerum Italicarum scriptores praecipui,* ed. Lodovico A. Muratori et al. (Milano, 1723-1751), 19.916 citing Leonardo Aretino. Delaruelle, Labande and Ourliac, *L' Église au temps du Grand Schisme,* p. 132 n. 39, which cites Bartolomeo da Montececchio who played on a version of "Gregorius" to call him "Digregorius" (disperser) as opposed to "congregorius" (congregator) to describe Gregory's role in the attempt at unity; see also p. 134 and n. 47. C. M. D. Crowder, *Unity Heresy and Reform 1378-1460: The Conciliar Response to the Great Schism* (Documents of Medieval History, 3; New York, 1977), p. 49 n. 32 cited the word play common at that time whereby "correrius" was made into "the contrived word *errorius*" and DeLuna lent itself naturally to "lunarius" or lunatic. George J. Jordan, *The Inner History of the Great Schism of the West: A Problem in Church Unity* (London, 1930), p. 114 cited the view of a writer at that time that both Gregory and Benedict accepted the idea of two popes, for Gregory ruled on land and Benedict at sea.

[53] Delaruelle, Labande and Ourliac, *L' Église au temps du Grand Schisme,* pp. 136ff.

community's right and duty to act for its own salvation without and even against the will of the pope when this was necessary.[54] When the council did meet at Pisa in 1409, the council fathers defended themselves and the council by appealing to the judgement of the legal profession and, in so doing, explicitly referred to just two voices, the famed University of Bologna's law faculty and Franciscus Zabarella.[55] Finally despairing of the two papal claimants, the Council of Pisa held a joint conclave made up of the cardinals of the two obediences who then chose as pope none other than the papal legate who was greeted at Padua by Zabarella in March 1406, Peter of Candia.[56] So once again this address foreshadows how events and fate made the lives and careers of Candia and Zabarella intertwine.

B. The Address

The text of the address is very brief, about two folio sides in the codices where I have found it. The copies that I have identified and used were respectively: Munich. Bayerische Staatsbibliothek. Clm 504, fol. 297^{v}-298^{v}[57] [= M]; Munich. Universitätsbibliothek. Cod lat. 2^{0} 607 fol. 3^{r}-4^{r} [= U]; Vienna. Österreichische Nationalbibliothek. Cod. Lat. 5513, fol. 88^{r}-88^{v}[58] [= W]; Stift S. Paul in Lavantthal (Austria). Cod. pap. 31/4, fol. 197^{v}-198^{v}[59] [= S]; Zeitz. Stiftsbibliothek 2^{0} 48 fol. 229^{v}[60] [= Z]; Eichstätt. Staats- und

[54] Morrissey, "The Crisis of Authority" p. 253; also idem, "Cardinal Franciscus Zabarella (1360-1417) as a Canonist and the Crisis of His Age: Schism and the Council of Constance," *Zeitschrift für Kirchengeschichte* 96 (1985): 196-208 at p. 201, and "Papacy, Community and the Limitations upon Authority," in *Reform and Authority in the Medieval and Reformation Church* ed. Guy F. Lytle (Washington, D. C., 1981), pp. 37-54, and "Cardinal Zabarella on Papal and Episcopal Authority," in *Proceedings of the Patristic, Medieval and Renaissance Conference* [Villanova University] 1 (1976): 39-52.

[55] Johannes Vincke, *Schriftstücke zum Pisaner Konzil: Ein Kampf um die öffentliche Meinung* (Bonn, 1942), p. 136.

[56] Delaruelle, LaBande and Ourliac, *L' Église au temps du Grand Schisme,* p. 153.

[57] For a description and information on this codex, see *Catalogus codicum manu scriptorum Bibliothecae regie Monacensis,* tom. 1, pars 1: Codices Latinos complectens 1-2329 (München, 1868; Wiesbaden, 1968).

[58] This manuscript is described in *Tabulae codicum manuscriptarum praeter Graecos et orientales in Bibliotheca Palatina vindobonensi asservatorum,* ed. Academia Caesarea Vindobonensis, nova editio, vol. III-IV, cod. 3501-6500 (Wien, 1965), p. 146.

[59] Johannes B. Schneyer, "Konstanzer Konzilspredigten: Eine Ergänzung zu H. Finke's Sermones- und Handschriftenlisten," *Zeitschrift für die Geschichte des Oberrheins* 113, N. F. 76 (1965): 361-388 at pp. 377ff and 386.

[60] Philipp Wegener, *Verzeichniss der befindlichen Handschriften der Zeitzer Stifts-Bibliothek* (Zeitz, 1876) lists some fourteen works of Zabarella and his circle from Padua in this manuscript. In actual fact, as I learned in a visit in early June 1995

Seminarbibliothek. St. 218 p. 322a-324a [= E]; Pommersfelden. Graf von Schönborn Schlossbibliothek. Ms. 168, fol. 173v-174r [= P].

The address by Zabarella is pretty straightforward and contains the usual and expected laudatory words that public orators, then and now, always lavish on the subject whom they wish to praise. Quite typically it expressed the hesitancy of the orator before the great virtues and qualities of the guest of honor.[61] Writing as he was in that period when the late Middle Ages were passing over to the Renaissance, Zabarella was well acquainted with both worlds. He had a continuous friendship with the early humanist circles of the generation after Petrarch and included among his friends and associates Coluccio Salutati, Peter Paul Vergerio, Gasparinus Barzizza, to mention just a few.[62] It is not surprising then that in his only literary allusion in the address Zabarella puts in parallel appposition two phrases of praise for Peter of Candia. The first is cited from the Genesis with the words of the Egyptians to Joseph, "Our salvation is in your hands,"[63] and the second is a quotation from *The Aeneid* of Vergil (whom Zabarella referred to simply as Maro), "In you is the highest safety."[64] For Zabarella the world of the Bible and the world of humanism were in full accord with each other.

A little surprising to the modern ear is one expression Zabarella chose in order to praise Peter of Candia. He noted that the pope had called Peter from his position in Milan to serve among the cardinals; and Zabarella went on to say that among these cardinals Peter of Candia was "shining out like a Lucifer" ("tamquam Lucifer effulgies"), a perfectly apt phrase it seems for his time but

to the library there, the manuscript contains some sixty-nine works attributed to Zabarella. I wish to express my gratitude to Frau Nagel, the librarian in Zeitz, for her assistance to me in that visit.

61 Zabarella naturally expressed trepidation at speaking before such an august presence "absque timore ... quod cum cogito nimium terreor." He pointed out the qualities of the honored guest "maiestas inter homines supereminet ... tua inestimabilis sublimitas ... tua incomparabilis humanitas ... tuam angelicam pocius quam humanam effigiem ... te alterum Petrum." There is an interesting wordplay in his praise of Candia. Zabarella sets in parallel that Christ had sent out the Apostle Peter to convert and save the nations, and so now the Vicar of Christ (the reigning pope Innocent VII) had sent Candia as another Peter to stabilize in faith and to save the Catholics of this region. The switching is of course ironic in that the pope who sits on the chair of Peter sends out another Peter (Peter of Candia) for this purpose. From our perspective it is ironic that Peter of Candia would in a few short years himself sit on the throne of Peter when elected as Pope Alexander V at Pisa in 1409.

62 As mentioned earlier, among the leaders in the new government installed by Venice in Padua were prominent men who were both from humanist circles and friends of Zabarella, e.g., Trevisan and Marcello. Coluccio Salutati's association with Zabarella went back to Zabarella's years in Florence (1383-1390), while Vergerio was a student and colleague of Zabarella at Padua and Barzizza was one of his proteges, as their correspondence records.

63 Gn 47:25 in *Biblia Sacra iuxta Vulgatam versionem,* ed. Robert Weber et al., 3rd ed. (Stuttgart, 1969), p. 72.

64 Virgil, *Aeneid,* XII:653, ed. and trans. H. Rushton Fairclough, 2 vols. (Cambridge, Massachusetts, 1986), 2.344.

one that to our ears has a different ring.[65] A final note is that Zabarella, although speaking as a public orator for his city and its government from Venice and so in a context of welcoming in the civil sphere, could not let this chance go by without making a point on canonistic doctrine. Thus, when he has the pope summon Peter Candia to join the cardinals, Zabarella explicity refers to the cardinals as the brothers of the pope ("fratrum suorum").[66] In that era so much history already existed of the debate over the relationship between the pope and the cardinals.[67] One of the key issues of the day for some time had been what as the pope was obliged to take into consideration in regard to his duties toward the college of cardinals,[68] and the converse. i.e., what the rights, powers, and duties of the cardinalate were in regard to the pope, or, as soon became evident, even without or against the pope.[69] I do not think that this insertion was a mere

65 "In numerum fratrum suorum cardinalium inter quos tamquam lucifer effulgens." Zabarella clearly was only employing the word "lucifer" in its literal and original sense, as "light-bearer." For a look at how this term and others have changed, been appropriated and misappropriated, see Jeffrey B. Russell, *A History of Witchcraft: Sorcerers, Heretics and Pagans* (London and New York, 1980) and the sources indicated there.

66 "Fratrum suorum cardinalium" - Zabarella throughout his legal commentaries referred to the cardinals as brothers (*fratres*) in relation to the pope and as a "*collegium*" with certain defined powers, e.g., Comm. ad X 1.6.54 and 3.4.2, both in the Venice 1502 edition.

67 For the literature on this topic see Morrissey, "Franciscus Zabarella (1360-1417): Papacy, Community and Limitations upon Authority," pp. 43-45, esp. n. 28, and also Charles Lefebvre, "Le Cardinalat e la *Communio,*" in *Comunione Interecclesiale: Collegialità - Primato Ecumenismo* (Acta conventus internationalis de historia sollicitudinis omnium ecclesiarum Romae 1967 curantibus Iosepho d' Ercole and Alphonse Stickler, Communio 12-13; Romae, 1967), 2.983-1001 and the literature and sources cited there.

68 One view on this relationship was that of John Watt, "The Constitutional Law of the College of Cardinals: Hostiensis to Johannes Andrae," *Mediaeval Studies* 33 (1971): 127-157, who said of the relationship that the cardinals had a merely moral authority to advise the pope but no real authority to limit, restrict or infringe on the papal prerogatives nor to compel the pope in any way. This was not at all what Zabarella taught. For example, Zabarella, in his Comm. ad X 3.4.2, had stated that, in a serious matter, if the pope acted without the advice of the cardinals (*sine consilio cardinalium*), it was to be presumed that the pope was acting in bad faith.

69 In his various canonistic writings Zabarella was very clear on what he saw as the prerogatives and duties of the cardinals but also on the limits of their position and the limits that their college placed on papal power. Zabarella in 1406 was in the midst of a five year period during which he produced his *De schismate,* which would justify the calling of the Council of Pisa in order to end the schism. His ideas on the authority of the community, i.e., the whole body of the faithful, would be influential in the next generation in the evolution of Nicholas of Cusa's ideas on the consent of the community; see Thomas E. Morrissey, "Cardinal Zabarella and Nicholas of Cusa: From Community Authority to Consent of the Community," *Mitteilungen und Forschungsbeiträge der Cusanus Gesellschaft* 17 (1986): 157-176. Zabarella elsewhere also wrote of the episcopate as being brothers of the pope (*fratres papae*); see Comm. ad X 1.6.4.

accident but a deliberate act of Zabarella to express his views, however controversial they may have been, and to encourage this cardinal to be resolute in carrying out his duties for peace, unity and reform.[70] Zabarella was too good a lawyer not to have realized what he was doing and we know from other instances how carefully and seriously he took language and how much he insisted on precision in language.[71] This opinion is reinforced by the fact that he was in the midst of composing his tract *De schismate,* which he had begun a few years ealier and would finish two years later in its final version. His words then appear hardly an accidental addition; and so what could have been merely a formal and empty address of welcome became also a statement of principle by Zabarella and an encouragement to the former Franciscan, one time archbishop and now prominent figure in the church as cardinal and papal legate, Peter of Candia, to act for the good of the church in unity and reform. Given Candia's role in the subsequent events down to his election at the Council of Pisa as Pope Alexander V and then his all too early death in 1410, it seems the word was well taken.

[70] For one example of Zabarella's willingness to speak bluntly, he wrote in his tract *De schismate* "consider the case as has sometimes happened that the pope would be a heretic" (finge enim sicut aliquando accidit quod papa esset hereticus). Luigi Zanutto, "Pier Paolo Vergerio Seniore e le sue aspirazione al decanato Cividalese," *Nuovo Archivio Veneto,* n. s. 21 (1911): 101-127 reported that in 1409, when the episcopal see at Padua had become vacant, Gregory XII voided the election by the local chapter, which had chosen Zabarella for this position. He used the opportunity to take care of a nephew and to block Zabarella, whose views Gregory considered dubious because of what Zabarella had written.

[71] For Zabarella's outspokenness on critical issues, see his quarrel with Emperor Sigismund, after intially working closely with him and supporting him before and in the earlier period at the Council of Constance; see Thomas E. Morrissey, "Emperor-Elect Sigismund, Cardinal Zabarella and the Council of Constance," *The Catholic Historical Review* 69 (1983): 353-370. For his refusal to read the final version of *Haec Sancta* and his objection to its wording, see Morrissey, "The Decree 'Haec Sancta' and Cardinal Zabarella: His Role in its Formulation and Interpretation," *Annuarium Historiae Conciliorum* 10 (1978): 145-176 and his role in the priority dispute (unity or reform) at Constance, "'More Easily and More Securely': Legal Procedure and Due Process at the Council of Constance," in *Popes, Teachers and Canon Law in the Middle Ages: Festschrift for Brian Tierney,* ed. James Ross Sweeney and Stanley Chodorow (Ithaca, New York, 1989), pp. 234-247.

The Text

In visitacione Petri[72] de Candia, cardinalis et legati apostolici[73], in partibus Ytalie[74].[75] [Coram Petro de Candia. Cardinali et legato apostolico][76] [Pad. 6 Martii 1406][77] [Francisci Zabarellis].[78]

De rebus[79] maximis reverendissime pater neminem[80] sepe videmus contingere ut assistente multitudine loqui absque timore possit quod cum cogito nimium[81] terreor[82] in exequendo[83] mandatum illustrium[84] dominorum[85] patrum[86] meorum potestatis et capitanei tociusque[87] universitatis civium huius inclite urbis patavi[88] hic[89] coram astancium et iubencium[90] ut eorum nomine atque in primis nomine et vice serenissimi[91] nostri veneciarum[92] domini tuam

72 Petri - Domini Petri in U.

73 et legati apostolici - not in U.

74 in partibus Ytalie - in M and U; in patribus Ytalie - in W; in Italia - in Z.

75 In visitacione Petri ... in partibus Ytalie - not in S.

76 [Coram Petro ... apostolico] - in S and P.

77 Pad. 6 Martii 1406 - in S and P.

78 Francisci Zabarellis - only in W.

79 De rebus - de re in U.

80 neminem - in S, P and W; nemini - in M and U; nemine - in Z.

81 nimium - in S, P, W, Z and U; minus - in M.

82 terreor - in Z; terror - in S, P, U, E and M; terreo - in W.

83 in exequendo - in exsequendo in Z.

84 illustrium - in S, P, and U; illustrorum - in W; illustrissimorum - in M; illustrissimi in Z.

85 dominorum patrum meorum potestatis et capitanei tociusque universitatis civium huius inclite urbis patavi - not in Z.

86 patrum - not in U and E.

87 tociusque - tocius in M.

88 huius inclite urbis patavi - huius orbis [sic] inclite patavi in U.

89 hic - in S, P, M and U; et hic - in Z; hoc - in W.

90 et iubencium - atque iubencium in U.

91 serenissimi - serenissime in U; serendissime in Z.

92 veneciarum - veneciarum tuarum in W.

excellenciam[93] salutare[94] seque tibi[95] commendare studeam id quod[96] verbis[97] per paucis tua namque maiestas tantum[98] inter homines[99] supereminet[100] ut de ipsa dignum quippiam non modo exprimere brevi sermone ymo vix cogitare[101] diuturna[102] meditacione posse confidam. Sed quantum a dicendo me revocat tua inextimabilis[103] sublimitas, tantum tua incomparabilis humanitas invitat. Huic[104] igitur[105] innixus[106] exequor invictum[107] illud autem ante omnia videtur hys[108] dominis meis et michi ante ponendum ut publice recognoscamus summas gracias quas debemus[109] celorum regi qui dignos nos fecit[110] in nostris laribus inspicere tuam angelicam pocius quam humanam effigiem; angelus nempe grece, latine nuncius. Sicuti vero in ecclesie primordiis redemptor noster Petrum apostolorum[111] principem misit ad convertendas et salvandas gentes, sic et nunc in ipsius ecclesie successoribus[112] variis ipsius nostri redemptoris vicarius dominus noster summus pontifex te alterum Petrum summum inter sacrosancte Romane ecclesie cardinales tanquam angelum nuncium et legatum fecit in has[113]

[93] excellenciam - et clementiam in W; excellentissimam in M and U.

[94] salutare - salutarem in E.

[95] tibi - in M, P, W and U; sibi - in S and Z.

[96] id quod - idque in P, Z, and U.

[97] verbis - nominis in Z.

[98] tantum - tam in Z.

[99] homines - omnes in M.

[100] supereminet - eminet in E.

[101] cogitare - cogitarem in S and P.

[102] diuturna - assidua in U.

[103] inestimabilis - in M, W and U; inextimabilis - in Sand P; extimabilis - in Z.

[104] huic - hinc in U.

[105] igitur - ergo in U and M.

[106] innixus - nixus in S and E; muneris - in Z; innixus munus - in P.

[107] invictum - invinctum in W and P.

[108] hys - hys not in M.

[109] debemus - deus in W.

[110] fecit - fecerit in U and E.

[111] apostolorum - apostolum in U.

[112] successoribus - successibus in S, P, and W; succoribus in Z.

[113] in has - in hac in M.

et in alias[114] plurimas regiones ad catholicos heu nimium[115] iam labentes instituendos et conservandos in fide. nos[116] itaque pars populi tibi crediti salutem nostram commendamus tue clementie dicentes cum egiptiis[117] ad Ioseph illud[118] quod est in genesi[119] 'salus nostra in manu tua est', simul[120] et illud Maronis in xii[121] 'in te suprema salus'. Reliquum esset ut nostra gaudia orta ex adventu tuo[122] sanctissimo[123] recensentes aliquod[124] fando[125] memoraremus[126] de summis virtutibus ac meritis tuis amplissimis sed huic tante rei nec[127] nos sufficimus nec temporis te in alia maiora vocantis[128] patitur incommoditas ipsa preterea res de se notissima suadet hoc sileri cum nemini sit obscurum[129]. Quis[130] est enim cui[131] non insonnuerit[132] clarissimum nomen tuum[133] quod[134]

114 et in alias - in U and P; the others have only: et alias.

115 heu nimium - heu nuncium in S.

116 nos - nam in M and also in U but this was then crossed out.

117 egiptiis - egipciis in E and P.

118 illud - id in S.

119 in genesi - Liber Genesi 47:25.

120 similiter - in M and W; simul - in S and P; simile in U; sunt - in Z.

121 maronis - Vergil's *Aeneid* XII:653.

122 adventu tuo - adventu suo in S.

123 sanctissimo - fanstissimo in E.

124 aliquod - aliquid in E and P.

125 fr - illegible in several texts; fando in E and P.

126 memoraremus - memoremus in E.

127 nec - ut in Z.

128 vocantis - vocatis in S.

129 obscurum - obscuris in Z.

130 quis - cuius in S.

131 cui - cum in Z.

132 informavit - in M; informevit in S; informerit - in Z; informeritur - in W; insonuerit - in P, U, and E.

133 nomen tuum - non tuum in Z.

134 quod - quam in Z.

dudum inter scolasticos cum[135] docendo cum et libros[136] edendo mirificos retulisti. Quis insuper non[137] audivit te a scolis[138] egressum in rerum publicarum gubernaculis[139] inter summos viros principem existimari[140] cuius eciam rei[141] testimonium amplissimum[142] est quod sanctissimus dominus noster de tua non inscius[143] immensa sapiencia te de tua pontificali sede mediolanensi[144] ultro[145] accersivit[146] atque ascripsit in numerum[147] fratrum suorum cardinalium inter quos tanquam lucifer effulgies[148]. Si ergo cultus et honor[149] in tuos iucundissimo adventu per hos dominos meos potestatem et capitaneum universumque clerum atque[150] populum huius magnifice urbis exhibitus minor extitit quam[151] deceret, suppliciter[152] obsecramus[153] ut illud[154] imputes[155] non nostre voluntati que promptissima[156] fuit sed tue sublimitati

[135] cum ... cum - in S; dum ... cum - in Z; tam ... tam - in U and M; tantum ... tantum - in W; tum ... tum - in E and P.

[136] et libros - in libros in M and U.

[137] non - nos in S.

[138] a scolis - et a scolis in U.

[139] gubernaculis - in S, P, and U; gubernaculum - in Z; gubernacula - in M and W.

[140] existimari - extimari in U.

[141] cuius eciam rei - cuius rei eciam in U.

[142] amplissimum - amplissimem in S.

[143] de tua non inscius - de tua vero in W.

[144] mediolanensi - medeolanensi in Z.

[145] ultro - ultimo in Z.

[146] accersivit - accersuit in M; accersunt - in E.

[147] in numerum - inter numerum in Z.

[148] effulgies - in M; effulgens - in S and Z; effulges - in W, P, and U.

[149] honor - honos in P.

[150] atque - et in M and W.

[151] quam - quoniam in Z.

[152] suppliciter - simpliciter in Z.

[153] obsecramus - exoremus in M.

[154] illud - id in P.

[155] ut illud imputes - ut id imputes in P, Z, and W; ut imputes - in U and M.

[156] promptissima - promptissime in S.

quam nequerit[157] humanus honor attingere denique ipsos dominos meos nosque clerum[158] ac populum paduanum pro tua summa humanitate suscipere[159] commendatos.[160] Amen.[161]

Apparatus

M = Munich Staatsbibliothek Clm 504
U = Munich Universitätsbibliothek Cod lat 2⁰ 607
S = Stift S Paul in Lavantthal Cod pap 31/4
W = Vienna Österreichische Nationalbibliothek Cod lat 5513
Z = Zeitz Stiftsbibliothek Cod 2⁰ 48
P = Pommersfelden Ms. 168

157 nequerit - nequit in Z; nequivit in P, U, and E.

158 clerum - tuum clerum in M; tuos clerum in P, E, W and Z.

159 suscipere - suscipe in P, U, and E.

160 Amen - not in E.

161 F. Zabarellis 1406 - added in E and P.

REFORM AND OBEDIENCE IN FOUR CONCILIAR SERMONS BY LEONARDO DATI, O. P.

Thomas M. Izbicki

At the Council of Constance (1414-1418), one figure, the Dominican Master General Leonardo Dati,[1] stands out for his willingness to present a viewpoint cautiously favorable to the papacy. He did this in a series of three sermons, each of the later ones pointing backward - in the versions preserved for us - to its predecessor. His sermon for the feast of the Circumcision in 1417 pointed back to one given on the feast of Francis of Assisi (October 4, 1416). It, in turn, looked back to a sermon given at the beginning of Lent (March 8) in that same year.[2] The sermon for the feast of Saint Francis even inspired a polemical exchange in the form of memoranda.[3] These sermons deserve attention not just as indications of how low the papacy's prestige had sunk by the late years of the Great Schism but as indications of how the issue of reform played out among the Friars Preachers, from whose ranks the greatest papal apologist of the Restoration Papacy, Juan de Torquemada, would be drawn.[4]

Dati, brother of the Florentine diarist Goro Dati,[5] has left behind a respectable body of sermon texts.[6] Certain of these texts are studded with

[1] On Dati as master general, see Daniel A. Mortier, *Histoire des maîtres généraux de l'Ordre des frères précheurs*, 8 vols. (Paris, 1902-1920), 4.85-140; Paolo Viti, "Dati, Leonardo," in *Dizionario biografico degli italiani*, 49 vols. (Roma, 1960-1997), 33.40-44.

[2] For a poor edition of the Lenten sermon, see Christian W. Walch, *Monimenta medii aevi*, 2 vols. (Göttingen, 1757-64; London, 1966), 1/4.3-45; it is printed under the name of Dietrich von Münster in Johannes B. Schneyer, "Konstanzer Konzilspredigten: Texte," *Zeitschrift für Osterreichsgeschichte* 118 (1970): 134-155. Excerpts from the sermon for the feast of the Circumcision appear in *Acta concilii Constantiensis* [hereafter, Finke, ACC], ed. Heinrich Finke et al., 4 vols. (Münster, 1896-1928), 2.480-481. Editions of the two later sermons are being prepared by Chris L. Nighman and the author.

[3] Finke, ACC, 2.705-729. See also Brian Tierney, "Divided Sovereignty and Constance: The Problem of Medieval and Early Modern Political Theory," *Annuarium Historiae Conciliorum* 7 (1975): 238-256.

[4] For the term Restoration Papacy, see J. A. F. Thomson, *Popes and Princes, 1417-1517: Politics and Polity in the Late Medieval Church* (London, 1980). For Torquemada, see Thomas M. Izbicki, *Protector of the Faith: Cardinal Johannes de Turrecremata and the Defense of the Institutional Church* (Washington, D. C., 1981). Torquemada was by no means the most unqualified Dominican papalist of his time; see Jeffrey A. Mirus, "On the Deposition of the Pope for Heresy," *Annuarium Historiae Pontificiae* 13 (1975): 231-248.

[5] Gene Brucker, *Two Memoirs of Renaissance Florence: The Diaries of Buonaccorso Pitti and Gregorio Dati* (New York, 1967). Leonardo Dati also had ties with the Florentine Signoria at the time of the Council of Constance; see Walter Brandmüller, *Das Konzil von Konstanz 1414-1418*, 2 vols. (Paderborn, 1991-1997), 1.41, 83, 165.

[6] Thomas Kaeppeli, *Scriptores Ordinis Praedicatorum Medii Aevi*, 4 vols. (Roma, 1970-1993), 3.73-77.

references to classical and patristic texts, many of them hard to identify from Dati's impressionistic use of sources. He also made reference to the authors Petrarch and Boccaccio.[7] Some of these homiletic texts, among them the sermon for the feast of the Circumcision, offer opportunities for research about topics other than papal power.[8] These three sermons, however, need to be read in the light of an earlier effort at preaching in a conciliar context. Dati was chosen to preach the sermon for the opening of the Council of Pisa (25 March 1409); his themes included reform and the restoration of ecclesiastical unity under one pope. Furthermore, with its references to Cicero, Macrobius, Peter Damian, Remigio dei Girolami and Coluccio Salutati, this sermon's display of erudition foreshadows the use of literary sources noted above with reference to Dati's preaching at Constance.[9]

When Dati delivered his sermon at Pisa, the council, summoned by the cardinals of both obediences in the schism, was meeting without a pope; writers like Jean Gerson and Franciscus Zabarella were propounding arguments why an assembly could proceed toward ecclesiastical union without being authorized by a Roman pontiff.[10] Nor was there any reason to believe that such a council necessarily would achieve its purpose.[11] Eventually it would depose Avignon's Benedict XIII and Rome's Gregory XII; but its pope of union, Alexander V, died shortly after being elected. Nor would his successor, John XXIII, appeal to those who still adhered to the more entrenched claimants. This would necessitate the holding of another council, that at Constance, before a solution was found to the Schism.[12]

Dati's message to the newly assembled council was carefully nuanced to avoid any inflammatory declarations. He described the council as gathered for three reasons: to defend the truth; to cure the sickness of souls; to reform

7 For a similar problem with sermons delivered at Constance, see Chris L. Nighman, *Reform and Humanism in the Sermons of Richard Fleming at the Council of Constance (1417),* Ph.D. diss., University of Toronto, 1996.

8 Thomas M. Izbicki, "Leonardo Dati's Sermon on the Circumcision (1417)," [forthcoming].

9 See Kaeppeli, *Scriptores*, no. 2841. The text cited hereafter will be a transcription from Göttweig MS 479 [GG], fol. 148v-160v corrected against Paris BN 12543 [PS], fol. 85v-95v.

10 John B. Morrall, *Gerson and the Great Schism* (Manchester, 1960), pp. 76-93; Walter Ullmann, *The Origins of the Great Schism: A Study in Fourteenth-Century Ecclesiastical History* (Hamden, Connecticut, 1972), pp. 191-231; Brian Tierney, *Foundations of the Conciliar Theory: The Contribution of the Medieval Canonists from Gratian to the Great Schism*, new ed. (Leiden, 1998), pp. 199-214.

11 Only recently has this council been studied at length, and Dati's role goes almost unmentioned; see Aldo Landi, *Il papa deposto (Pisa 1409): l'idea conciliare nel grande scisma* (Torino, 1985), p. 283 n. 17.

12 Joseph Gill, *Constance et Bâle-Florence* (Paris, 1965), pp. 27-34.

religious orders.[13] No immediate mention was made of the Schism, although the Council of Pisa was to strive to end it. Instead, speaking of the defense of the faith, Dati alluded to that day's feast, that of the Annunciation, arguing that the truth of the Incarnation was revealed first to Peter. Christ delegated to His vicar and his successors the duty of transmitting this truth to the members of the church together with that of bringing the erring back to the true faith by means of counsel and correction.[14] This placed the papacy at the center of the church, both promulgating and safeguarding the faith.

It was at this point that Dati introduced the topic of the Schism. Schismatics were described, in words derived from Thomas Aquinas, as both refusing to submit to the pope and as refusing to communicate with the members of the church. Dati also linked schism, as Jerome had, with heresy.[15] In this context, a schism starting with the papacy, with two claimants rending ecclesiastical unity, was truly dangerous to the welfare of the church. This situation opened the way for evil men to despoil the church. Furthermore, Dati blamed this situation on the corruption of the church's pastors.[16] He could find nothing worse than those who should take care of others spreading a disease which imperils their souls.[17]

Without immediately naming either Benedict or Gregory,[18] Dati denounced their failure to bring peace to the church. He compared them and their supporters to the evil angels who desired the glory of God and so fell away from their proper allegiance.[19] The council was able to act against them—as the leading universities had declared—as "inveterate nourishers of schism" and as "fallen into heresy." (Dati adroitly mentioned universities located either side of

[13] GG, fol. 157r-v. Both manuscripts say: "ob reformationem religionum."

[14] GG, fol. 158r: "Hanc autem fidei ueritatem primo Petro suisque successoribus iure hereditario delegauit ut ab eo in alios uelut a capite dereuaretur in membra atque deuiantes ab eadem uel consulendo uel corripiendo reduceret Glo. Crisostimi super illo Luce Confirma fratres tuos."

[15] GG, fol. 158r.

[16] GG, fol. 158v: "Ex hoc enim ecclesiasticus status uniuersale periculum propter summum sacerdocium a se inuicem resiliuit atque ad dei omnipotentis iniuriam cum unus sit papa in apostolico solio constitutus alter apparuit. Ex hoc est ut ipsa quoque ecclesias uiolenti homines rapiant atque predia uel bona sacri iuris inuadant."

[17] GG, fol. 159r: "Quod perniciosius tanto ecclesie nocere percipitur quanto ipsius impietatis morbus ab illis qui ceteros curare habent sub salutis spe pertinaciter defensatur."

[18] Later in the sermon (GG, fol. 163v), Dati called, by name, for the removal of "sediciosos homines Petrum de Luna et Gregorium Corrarium...."

[19] GG, fol. 159r: "Hii sunt qui excellencia dignitatis allecti uelut peruersi angeli gloriam dei conuertere cupientes in sua promisse fidelitatis federa deo persoluere contempserunt."

the boundary between the obediences of Avignon and Rome, thus avoiding giving offense of former followers of either claimant.)[20]

Dati was presented, however, with the necessity of showing how the fathers of the council had power to act in such a case. Following one of the several options medieval and early modern polemicists could choose between,[21] he chose to say that the apostles had shared the plenitude of power with Peter.[22] This permitted him, following Remigio dei Girolami, to argue that the bishops had residual power to act for the welfare of the church when the pope was lacking (*deficiente*) or was "reasonably" disqualified from acting.[23] Dati hastened to add, however, that the power inherited by the bishops from the apostles was equal to that of the pope not ordinarily (*simpliciter*) but only in a case of necessity, when the welfare of the church was threatened.[24]

So that the church would not lack aid when the bishops were not assembled, the pope had the cardinals to help and advise him.[25] To them, when Peter's see was vacant, fell both election of a successor and work for the hurch's cwelfare; they were to confer "opportune remedies."[26] When they could not act

20 GG, fol. 159r: "Infideles in deum, profani in deum sacra, mendaces in promissis, sediciosi in clero, crudeles in populis, pertinaces in uerbis, ingrati ad beneficia, indeuoti ad fidem, propter quod denegantes pacem quam Christi gregi dare de facili potuerunt non solum uirga oris uestri percutiendi sunt, ut predixit propheta, id est, potestate uestre sapientie, declarandi inueterati scismatis nutritores, ut Boniniensis scola determinauit, prolapsi in heresim, ut Parisiensis et Wiennensis peritus proficetur." Dati went on (fol. 159r-v) to quote the opinion of the University of Prague that the council should act against them as those who "incorrigibly scandalize the church."

21 See, for example, the discussion by Cajetan of this issue in *Conciliarism and Papalism*, trans. J. H. Burns and Thomas M. Izbicki (Cambridge, 1997), pp. 8-17.

22 GG, fol. 161r.

23 GG, fol. 161r: "Sic eo deficiente aut rationabiliter illegittimato eidem ecclesie illi ex debito prouidere eamque tutare tenentur quibus ex delegata potestate fuit similiter a primo pastore concessum Remigius Florentinus tractatu de potestate pape."

24 GG, fol. 161r: "Ex quibus, ni fallor, apperere iam potest unde moti sunt sancti, unde sacri canones illas duas potestates simul cum Petro ceteris apostolis coequare, ut uidelicet non simpliciter sed in casu necessitatis ecclesie periculis emergentibus, circa eamdem eorum apostolici successores ad prouidendum eidem pro executoribus auctoritatis apostolice habeantur."

25 GG, fol. 161v-162r. On the relationship of the cardinalate to conciliarism, see Francis Oakley, *Council Over Pope?: Towards a Provisional Ecclesiology* (New York, 1969), pp. 61-74. On the larger question of the cardinals' pretensions to a divine right to share in the plenitude of power, see Giuseppe Alberigo, *Cardinalato e collegialità: Studi sull'ecclesiologia tra l'XI e il XIV secolo* (Firenze, 1969).

26 GG, fol. 162r: "Ubique assistere in ecclesiasticam Ierarchiam secum peritus gubernare, uacante sede, successorem eligere ac fluctuanti gubernare ecclesie opportunis remediis uniuersis prouidere...."

well enough for the good of the church, as when two men were contending for the papacy, they could convoke a council to end a schism. Then the council could decide who was true pope.[27] The cardinals had to see that one man was chosen to rule, since plurality of princes (*pluralitas principum*)— according to Aristotle—is useless.[28] Dati, addressing the assembled fathers directly, exhorted them to act with their authority, "like imitators of the apostles," to grant the church peace, concord and unity.[29]

Reform, however, does not appear as a clear agenda item in Dati's sermon. He spoke of repairing the damage done by the Schism. And he borrowed from Bernard of Clairvaux, whose *De consideratione* would be for a time a favorite source for pro-papal writers, a description of the ideal Roman pontiff as, among other things, "the terror of evildoers" (*metum malorum*).[30] Only in one brief passage did the friar urge the council to reform the deformed ecclesiastical city and build up the fallen (*collapsam*) church.[31] He urged cures opposite to the evils of the day to rebuild the Augustinian city built not with hands but with good morals.[32] Elsewhere, however, he called for the correction of deformed morals to return the ecclesiastical city to its ancient beauty, an echo of ideas that the primitive church was more perfect than was the current state of affairs.[33]

27 GG, fol. 162r: "Ac per hoc, correlario inferendo, concluditur quod ad ipsos R. dominos Cardinales, tamquam ad principaliores in ecclesia, maxime ubi de papatu est contentio inter duos, spectat generalis concilii conuocatio; ad ipsumque concilium cause decisio." He went on to quote Thomas Aquinas to the effect that the proper end of those who rule is the unity of the subjects of the regime.

28 GG, fol. 162v: "Ita sit unum totius ecclesie caput. Equidem uolunt entia male disponi pluralitas principum inutilis. Unus ergo princeps concludit philosophus in fine xii metaphisice." Actually, the text cited is *Metaphysics* XI,10, which usually is quoted by Dominicans as saying "plurality of principates"; see *Conciliarism and Papalism*, p. 167 nn. 67-68.

29 GG, fol. 162v, "Ea propter, R. domini, spiritu labiorum uestrorum procedentes auctoritate, scilicet legis et sapientie.... uelut apostolici imitatores precipui optatam pacem diuque prostratam gregi Christi donate, procurate concordiam, concludite unitatem...."

30 GG, fol. 163v. On papalist use of Bernard's work, see Thomas M. Izbicki, "Dominican Papalism and the Arts in Renaissance Rome," in *Iberia and the Mediterranean World: Studies in Honor of Robert I. Burns, S. J.*, 2 vols. (Leiden, 1995-1996), 1.270-289.

31 GG, fol. 165r: "Talibus itaque succedentibus, o sacrum diuinumque concilium, fide clari, caritate feruidi, uirtute conspicui, uosque qui genus electum, regale sacerdotium, gens sancta, populus acquisitionis, i. Petri ii c., deformatam hanc ciuitatem reformate collapsam ecclesiam erigite."

32 GG, fol. 165r: "Hec patriam, hec regnum, hec ciuitas nostra est non manibus sed moribus. Ciuitas ista corruit. Contraria contrariis curantur."

33 GG, fol. 165v-166r. For Jean Gerson's ideas about the primitive church, see Louis Pascoe, *Jean Gerson: Principles of Church Reform* (Leiden, 1973); idem, "Jean Gerson, the *Ecclesia primitiva* and Reform," *Traditio* 30 (1974): 379-410.

Dati's exhortation that the religious orders be reformed was brief, but he promised improvement in both life and studies among reformed religious.[34] He also tied decline in the religious orders to the Schism, since good example and sound doctrine both were lacking, while bad example and rebellion were not.[35] Dati urged the fathers to rise up in their zeal and curb the evils resulting from letting disobedience, insolence, and vice go unpunished.[36]

While Dati's sermon at Pisa was papalist, it was not adverse to some general concept of reform; but he would distinguish himself at Constance for a less irenic viewpoint, although one which still sought harmonization of papal power with the authority of the church and the council.[37] His greater wariness might be explained by the greater prominence at Constance of Jean Gerson, whose hostility to the mendicants was quite pronounced, or by an awareness that some present at the council thought reform of the church in head and members should include restricting the privileges of the friars.[38] Any effort to understand his motivations must include the too-often neglected study of Dati's thought on reform.[39]

The earliest of the three sermons by Dati to be treated here was given in 1416, when the Council of Constance was in between its efforts to secure the resignations of Gregory XII and John XXIII and its later actions against Benedict XIII. Although discussions of reform were proceeding only slowly, Dati's evident worry that this issue might mask other, less worthy motives among the fathers suggests that we may not have documentation of all the proposals aimed at curtailing the privileges granted the mendicants by the popes which were circulating in Constance at that time.[40] The Dominican Master General certainly showed a great desire to curb excessive proposals for the reform of the Church without, however, denying the need for a remedy in an emergency involving the papacy.

At the beginning of his sermon, Dati quoted the epistle for the First Sunday of Lent, *Ecce nunc dies salutis* (2 Cor 6:2). Although he expressed a sense of urgency befitting the text on which he was preaching, Dati,

[34] GG, fol. 166v.

[35] GG, fol. 166v.

[36] GG, fol. 166v-167r.

[37] Giuseppe Alberigo, *Chiesa conciliare: Identità e significato del conciliarismo* (Brescia, 1981), p. 203 n. 29; Paul de Vooght, *Les pouvoirs du concile et l'autorité du pape au Concile de Constance: Le décret Haec Sancta Synodus du 6 avril 1415* (Paris, 1965), pp. 61-67.

[38] See, respectively, Thomas M. Izbicki, "The Council of Ferrara-Florence and Dominican Papalism," in *Christian Unity: The Council of Ferrara-Florence 1438/39-1989*, ed. Giuseppe Alberigo (Louvain, 1991), pp. 429-443, and Phillip H. Stump, *The Reforms of the Council of Constance (1414-1418)* (Leiden, 1994), pp. 245-249.

[39] Some mention of this theme appears in Brandmüller, *Das Konzil von Konstanz*, 2.199-223.

[40] Stump, *The Reforms of the Council of Constance*, pp. 26-31, 245-249.

nonetheless, lashed out at those whose interest in reform masked their own bad intentions and ill-governed passions. He accused the reformers of being a mob from every nation motivated by their own interests rather than those of Christ. He also accused them of writing many pages on reform without changing their deformed way of life.[41] Dati argued that fathers, as recorded in the deeds of the ancient councils, built up the church more by example than through teaching.[42]

Dati offered a vision of the Church which emphasized dependence of the body on the head. He compared the church with the moon, receiving its light from the sun of Justice, Christ.[43] Dati also compared it with a natural body, with its several members depending on its divine head. It was, in Pauline terms, the body of Christ.[44] Within the body there were different powers. The sacramental power of holy orders had been conferred equally on all priests. The power of jurisdiction—and the role of feeding the flock with wisdom and doctrine —also was conferred by Christ on all of the apostles, but it was given especially to Peter and his successors. Citing canon law texts to support him, Dati said that the apostles were given by Christ power equal to Peter's not ordinarily but only in case an emergency, when a pope became a heretic or a scandalizer of the church, required the successors of the apostles to act for the good of the church. Moreover, although Christ conferred the power, the pope divided up territories within which it would be exercised.[45] In such a case—and here Dati made specific mention of the assembly to which he was preaching—the council succeeded to the power of the pope. It was able to undertake such acts as confirming episcopal elections.[46]

Dati, however, did not limit himself to speaking about institutional issues. He called urgently for the eradication of vice and combat against the devil.[47] He also urged that virtues be cultivated as arms against the spiritual foe. Only thus could the victory be obtained.[48] He even held up to the assembly as an example of these qualities King Sigismund, who shone with the virtues of the ancients. Here Dati turned for examples not to the martyrs or the fathers, or even to Christian monarchs, but to the pagan ancients, among them Diogenes, Scaevola, Pompey and Socrates.[49]

A few observations must suffice to pull together these themes. Dati offered no program of institutional reform, although he did permit the council to

41 Schneyer, "Konstanzer Konzilpredigten," p. 138.

42 Ibid., pp. 139-140.

43 Ibid., p. 143.

44 Ibid., pp. 143-144.

45 Ibid., pp. 144-145. This passage paraphases the one quoted in n. 24.

46 Ibid., pp. 145-146.

47 Ibid., p. 148.

48 Ibid., p. 149.

49 Ibid., p. 150.

act for the welfare of the church in settling the Schism and keeping the institution in order until a single pope would be in place. Otherwise reform was left to the moral sphere, making prelates better able to do their work by offering a truly Christian example to the faithful. Vices were to be rooted out, and virtues were to be cultivated; but even the reform of the orders notable in the sermon at Pisa has no place in this sermon. Those who wrote memoranda on institutional reform were dismissed as deformed of life, trying to hide their own wickedness.

The sermon which Dati gave on the feast of Francis of Assisi in October of 1416 returned to certain of these themes. Because of the saint of the day, the Dominican Master General also had to address topics related to the religious life. Here Dati made use of Cicero's *Dream of Scipio,* as transmitted by Macrobius, to praise councils and other assemblies joined together by law. The law pertinent to the faithful in this case was threefold, divine, spiritual and human.[50] The first of these pertained to the unity of the just, the supreme unity, based on faith and charity. The second pertained to the internal unity of the perfect, based on religion and wisdom. The third, however, was the visible unity of a people, in this case the external unity of the Christian faithful.[51] The Church Militant was the way to the Church Triumphant, the external unity of the faithful living by faith and charity being needed to arrive at the other, higher forms of unity.[52] Here, as in his other sermons, Dati pointed to good works as significant signs, in this case as the sign of divine election.[53]

It was into this context of unity and good conduct that the preacher inserted Saint Francis. He was the means by which the Spirit could promote

[50] Lübeck SB 59 [LB], fol. 103va-111ra at fol. 104ra-b: "...uerbis utor affricani superioris, a Cicerone introductis 4to de re p. libro sub hac forma, 'Nichil est enim illi principi deo, qui omnem mundum regit, quod quidem in terris fiat, accepcius quam Concilia cetusque homini iure sociati.' Ex quibus uerbis, prout triplici iure homines uiuunt, quoniam diuino caritatis et fidei, spirituali religionis et sapientie, humano equitatis et iuscicie, Cassiodorus super illo psallmo, Ecce quam bonum et quam iocundum habitare fratres in unum, psalmo 132." This manuscript, once thought lost [Kaeppeli no. 2846], has been returned by the Russian government. The author was informed of its return by Chris L. Nighman.

[51] LB, fol. 104rb-va: "Tercio, ex predictis affricani uerbis, potest fidelibus conuenienter reserari, que unitas est populorum, que sit unitas externa, quali nexu colligatur, quia 'Concilia cetusque hominum iure sociati,' Iure scilicet 'humano equitatis et iusticie,' ut Cassiodorus inquit."

[52] LB, fol. 104va-b: "Iustorum unitas ac superna conformiter dici debent. Ex quo fundamento militancium ecclesia habet unitas nuncupatur. Cum sit ecclesia huiusmodi, multitudo fide et caritate uiuencium, Ut Gregorius scribit xix moralium ca.o xxo, que ideo iustorum et superna ponitur, quia ipsius membra, compaginata fide et caritate formataque, iustos efficiunt, ut dicit glossa super illo Iustus ex fide uiuit, Habac. 2o. Ei si mole corporis sunt in terra horum, tum conuersacio in celis est, Ut scribit apostolus ad phil. iii c.o."

[53] LB, fol. 105ra: "Elegit deus eos qui in eterno ac secretissimo sue maiestatis speculo iam fulserunt, quia alto gradu sanctitatis decorati pestiferis humani generis erroribus sua securitate submotis gregem suum in fructu bonorum operum iam fragrante facerent duplicare, Cassianus ad cesarium de eleccione sanctorum."

unity, not so much through doctrine as by his example. Quoting Bernard of Clairvaux, Dati spoke of the conduct and deeds of the saints as giving direction to our life.[54] Francis had in himself, by a divine gift, the virtues found in several different saints - including the obedience of Noah.[55] Looking at the state of the divided church, Dati argued that division and schism arose from the neglect of good works.[56]

Here Dati, quoting Thomas Aquinas, noted the dependence of unity among the members of the body on their head. The members turned not just against one another but against the head, separating themselves, ultimately, from God.[57] Here, as in the Lenten sermon cited above, Dati questioned the motives of certain men who talked about bringing peace to the church despite the fact that their works contradicted their words.[58] He contrasted with them no small number of the assembled fathers who wished to reform things deformed, stir up the lax and gather together and unite the divided in the church.[59] These made up a council united by the law, *Sollicitous*, in the words of the theme of the sermon, *to serve the unity of the Spirit in the bond of peace* Eph 4:3.

Looking toward the external manifestation of internal unity in the worship of the one God, Dati pointed to two things which bound the faithful together in this worship, the precepts of the Decalog and the counsels of Christ. These latter counsels led believers to works of charity, even to renunciation of life in the world.[60] They were led, once secular occupations have been renounced,

54 LB, fol. 105rb: "Exemplo plusquam uerbo opere pocius quam doctrina, mirum in modum huiusmodi spiritus promoueret unitatem. Sic enim mores et gesta sanctorum nostre uite sunt directiua, Bernardus ad fratres de monte dei."

55 LB, fol. 105vb: "Hec ergo singulaque in ceteris sanctis sparsim et per partes respersa sunt in almo confessore francisco superno numine congesta uidemus."

56 LB, fol. 106ra: "...diuisiones et scismate que in ecclesia solent contingere ac inter ecclesiasticos actu contingunt ex negligentia sancti operis prouenire."

57 LB, fol. 106ra: "Et quoniam unio membrorum maxime ad caput attenditur, ut dicit sanctus thomas 4o contra gentiles ca.o xxxi. Exinde in peccata penam non seruantes, que secundum statum proprium seruare debent, ac per hoc non Solliciti seruare unitatem spiritus, non solum inter se ignominose diuisiones incurrere, sed etiam respectu ad caput sibi creandum perperetes discordias habituros, diuisio enim huiusmodi ex diuisione oritur quam habent cum deo, Ait Cris' super Math. Omel. xii."

58 LB, fol. 106rb: "Non ergo tales optatam pacem diuque prestolatam gregis Christi donare unitatem spiritus concludere uolebunt. Nam quod uerbis predicant operibus impugnant, ut dicit Gregorius in primo pastoralis sui."

59 LB, fol. 106rb: "Et ergo, exsurgant, exurgant timorati, deum hominibus proponentes, de quibus in hac congreacione Concilii copia non deest, quorum sit sermo, edificacio non ludibrium, quorum sit uita iusticia non iniquitas, quorum sit presencia gratia non odium, et, ut sit eorum memoria in benediccione, ut scribit petrus damiani in sermone de scismata, deformata in ecclesiam reforment, laxam erigant, dispersam congregare ac unire fascinent."

60 LB, fol. 106vb: "Dupliciter uero cultui diuino homines religantur, quia per precepta decalogi atque Christi concilia, Ut declarat beatus Augustinus in libello de decem cordis, Et beatus thomas in libello de perfeccione uite spiritualis in plerisque

to "the state of apostolic perfection that consists of doing and teaching." Here, as in his other statements on reform, Dati pointed toward the doing of good works; but he did not hesitate to warn against those who undertake the religious life without wisdom or who seek wisdom without religion. Both, he affirmed, quoting Lactantius, are necessary for perfection.[61]

Next Dati returned to the saint of the day, whom he described as a renewer of the religious life, one in a glorious sequence. First he pointed to the perfection of religion shown by Christ and the apostles. Looking to the history of the Western Church, the preacher enumerated as its teachers Augustine, Benedict, the father of monks, and Bernard. Then, turning to the mendicant orders, Dati gave an apocalyptic dimension to the founders of the Friars Preachers and Friars Minor by comparing them, in Joachite terms but not those derived from the book of Revelation, to Joshua and Caleb, who led the chosen people into the promised land.[62]

Dati treated the two great founders of mendicant orders like certain other great pairs, Moses and Aaron, Peter and Paul. These two founders had come late in time "to renew this Christian religion in a wondrous way with merits and doctrines."[63] Seeking the evidence of good works in the followers of these saints —and especially among the Franciscans—the preacher pointed to those who displayed various outstanding qualities, including popes and cardinals, who had originated in that religious family. These men were rooted in "the glorious athlete of Christ," Francis, whose example recalled many from error and directed them toward heaven.[64]

locis. Inde prope religio accipienda est, prout quis sub ipsis Christi consiliis "ad aliqua opera caritatis se obligat, quibus specialiter deo seruitur uite abrenuncians seculari," ut declarat idem sanctus Thomas in libello contra impugnantes religionem ca.o primo."

61 LB, fol. 107ra: "Sed homines ideo falluntur, quia aut religionem suscipiunt obmissa sapientia, aut sapientie student obmissa religione. Cum alterum sine altero perfectum esse non possit, Ut sibi concludit firmianus lactantius Institucionum libro primo capitulo xi."

62 LB, fol. 107ra: "Hec ergo perfecta religio illa est que sub Christo et apostolis Primo inchoata; deinde quo ad ecclesiam latinam per Augustinum et Benedictum elucidata; tandem per Bernardum roborata; Nouissime per dominicum et franciscum renouata uita pariter et doctrina, hanc unitatem spiritus perficit atque nutrat, de qua finali innouacione Calabriensis uatos libro super xii prophetiarum parte prima ita predixit. Ciues admodum, ait, deficientibus patribus in deserto, sub Iosue et Caleph terram sunt filii promissionis ingressi."

63 LB, fol. 107ra-b: "Hii ergo duo euangelisantes sunt duo sacri ordines predicatorum, scilicet, et minorum, qui iuxta euangelium Iohannis documenta in libro de concordia utriusque testamenti, ad instar moysi et aaron sub lege patris, petri et pauli sub lege filii, uelut sub lege spiritus sancti extremo tempore destinati homines miro modo meritis et doctrinis toto orbe terrarum hanc renouarunt Christi religionem."

64 LB, fol. 107rb-va: "Subticeo honore atque cultu plures dignissimos Romane ecclesie pontifices summos precellentis fame ac sapiencie eiusdem Romane ecclesie Cardinales, patriarchas atque presules, uiros doctissimos cum tanta doctorum eminencia, ut ex hiis hec religio nec primam uisa est, nec habere sequentem. Et ergo,

Nor did Dati refrain from going on to address the controversial topic of the preaching mission of the friars. He linked effectiveness in preaching to poverty, as was true of Christ, who had nowhere to lay his head.[65] Dati admitted that prelates were supposed to be preachers; but he accused them of giving up their office, with its need for poverty, for riches. Francis and Dominic had risen to the challenge of filling the gap left by the withdrawal of the prelates from poverty to pursue things temporal by giving up all possessions for the pursuit of supreme poverty. As documentation of this, Dati pointed to Francis' rule and to the canon law texts which lauded Franciscan poverty.[66]

Having held before the fathers the example of Francis, including his renunciation of worldly goods, Dati moved on to denounce the ill effects, the deforming influence on the mendicants, of abandoning the vow of poverty for the pursuit of vanities. Furthermore, he described this as leading not just to loss of charity but to ambition among the greater members of the order and rebellion among the lesser ones. Nor did he hesitate to denounce friars who dared to use papal bulls to pursue the dignity of "master" that gave them special privileges.[67] Dati urged the fathers to take action against such abuses, declaring that fixing this problem would lead to the entire reformation of the mendicants.[68]

quia quidquid bonitatis in fructu est non ex ramo primo sed ex radice, deriuatur, Ut dicit Citius super illo Arbor bona bonos fructus facit, Math. vii, Quantum gloriosus athleta Christi franciscus ecclesie profecerit quot suo exemplo ab erroribus reuocauerit, quot animas ad celestia direxerit, ex effectu concluditur."

65 LB, fol. 107vb: "Tum ut predicator fieret ueritatis tam pauper esse uoluit, ut neque ubi caput reclinaret, haberet, luc. ix."

66 LB, fol. 108ra-b, "Illud ideo generaliter non exercent, quia paupertate etiam uoluntaria reiecta, adsumptus eiusdem ecclesie et corporalia et corporalia quodammodo student, prout plane declarat Gregorius xxii moralium super illo Iob xxxi, Fructus terre comedent absque pecunia. Unde, correlatiue per locum a maiori, concludi oportet quod, si predicatores uerbi dei generaliter pauperes esse debent, multo magis professores altissime paupertatis, et hanc de qua loquor spiritus unitatem ob hanc causam apostolici uiri dominicus et franciscus, percipientes opere possessiones in communi ac per hoc diuicias materiam potissimum fore relaxacionis huiusmodi, Christi religionis spiritu conceperunt causam remouere defectus ac per hoc suos ordines absque temporalibus possessionibus et redditibus in summa fundauerunt. Et altissima paupertate potissimeque beatus uir franciscus, qui eam singulari modo amplexus est, ut ex sua regula et extra de uerborum signioficacione Exiit qui seminat [VI 5.12.3] Et in clementinis eodem titulo Exiui de paradiso [Clem. 5.11.1]." For the problems raised by these affirmation, especially by *Exiit*, see Brian Tierney, *Origins of Papal Infallibility, 1150-1350* (Leiden, 1972).

67 LB, fol. 108va: "Ita relaxata sunt regularia maximeque in uoto paupertatis Ut ille domum alius agrum multi quoque redditus sibi uere dicantur animales. Unde sequitur disparitas in uestitu, in uictu uarietas. Ita quod in eadem congregacione habundanciam uestram aliqui Ceteri uix uero tegumentum habebunt. Unus quidem esurit; alius auterm ebrius est. Exinde inobedientia, contemptus, rebellio ad maiores. Exinde ad honores ambicio maximeque ad magisterii dignitatem quam, quia uirtute habere nequeunt, interuentu pecunie cui diebus currentibus obediunt omnia et bullarum apostolicarum suffragio habere conantur."

68 LB, fol. 108va: "Et ergo iustissimi iudices orbis, si hanc unitatem spiritus hos ordines reformare curatis, ut debetis, huiusmodi proprietatibus opportunis

Having dealt with the internal unity of the faithful, and especially with the reform of the mendicants, a theme already addressed by him at Pisa, Dati turned to the external unity of the faithful. Here he argued that peace could not be restored to the church without justice. And, just as Augustine had declared of cities and peoples, he linked both with the preservation of order. The members, as Cassiodorus had said, had to be decently arranged; and, citing Eustachius' comment on Aristotle's *Ethics*, he described justice as the imposition of order. Once order was achieved, peace would follow.[69]

Dati mentioned several examples of peace, including the peace achieved by bringing order to the appetites. However, it was civil peace which Dati sought for the church, and this too involved order. The preacher connected peace, whether of a household or of a city, with obedience. Moreover, he expected the celestial city—after which the church was patterned—to be the most ordered and most harmonious of all.[70] This discussion of peace pointed directly to Dati's vision of the ecclesiastical polity, which involved the preservation of order and the obedience of inferiors to superiors, likewise the subjection of things temporal to things spiritual, the profane to the sacred and the temporal sword to the spiritual one. Any other order of things would lead to churches being despoiled and sacred things being trespassed upon. This was the vision of peace and of its contrary which Dati held before the assembled fathers, reminding them of the flocks whose welfare they were supposed to promote.[71]

Achievement of this peace, however, required that they accept order. He warned them that departure from this proper order of things, established by God, would confound the church, not bring order to it. He argued further that the

remediis obuietis hos ad quietatem reducere satagatis. Et ecce reformata sunt omnia."

69 LB, fol. 109ra: "Sic ex summis et mediis ordinibus quadam, scilicet proposicione iusticie per ipsos ordinatis concordia efficiatur populi et ciuitatis, ut declarat Aug' 2o de ciuitate iiio calo. Tunc enim totum corpus reipublice optime disposiciones specie uenustabitur; tunc decentis pulcritudinis decorem induit, si singula queque membra suum locum teneant sortita decenter, Cassiodorus suarum uariarium libro primo xviii cao. Ex quibus illatiue concludi oportet quod si iusticie est practice ordinem rebus imponere, Ut probat Eustachius 2o ethicorum commento 22o, ex ordine uero pax sequatur in rebus, ut dicit Ancelmus quod ubi ordo non est pax esse non potest."

70 LB, fol. 109rb: "Pax domus ordinata in parendi obediendique concordia cohabitancium. Pax ciuitatis ordinata in parendi atque obediendi concordia ciuium. Pax celestis ciuitatis ordinatissima et concordiissima societatis fruendi deo et uincere in deo."

71 LB, fol. 109rb: "Si uos pastores pacem populis Christi iugo subiectis dare qui cupitis ac in uinculo pacis greges uestros unire hanc unitatem spiritus solliciti seruare, ut, scilicet, ecclesiastice policie, sic ordo seruetur in cuntis ut ne subdantur superiora inferioribus, spritualia temporalibus, sacra prophanis. Sicque spirituali gladio temporalis gladius sit subiectus. Ne sicut hucusque simulacione magna simulatum sic est ei impune detur facultas ecclesias spoliandi, sacra inuadendi, propter enim contra populos deus suscitat gladium et bellum, ut pacis bono non fruantur indigni, Cassiodorus super 1o pso."

church would be deformed rather than reformed through disobedience.[72] Here Dati's themes of reform, mostly directed to individual conduct or the mendicant orders, and obedience come together. Furthermore, here he embarked on the most controversial aspect of his preaching, a set of four assertions about the spiritual sword which was intended to show the right order of the ecclesiastical institution to the assembled fathers. One notes here too that Dati still left the door open to measures intended to resolve the Schism, as long as the right order of things went untouched.

The first of these assertions reads:

> The supreme power of the ecclesiastical sword resides in the church inseparably as far as jurisdiction; separably, however, as far as execution.[73]

There is nothing controversial about this assertion that the papacy cannot lose its power whatever becomes of the pope until one reads Dati's assertion, resonant of his Lenten sermon, that the church did not have the execution of this power unless there were no reigning pope or he had become illegitimate or been deposed.[74] The second assertion was less controversial, since it declared the supreme power in the church separable from the pope. Here Dati referred specifically to a pope's ability to lose power by becoming illegitimate or being deposed:

> This is clear because a pope who becomes illegitimate or has been deposed lacks both [jurisdiction and execution], as is clear in that case.[75]

The third assertion touched directly upon the locus of authority in the visible church, denying that the council could share supremacy with a legitimate pope:

> Supreme power of the spiritual sword is in a pope legitimately presiding and residing totally as far as the execution of this sword,

[72] LB, fol. 109va: "Non enim hoc esset ecclesiam ordinare sed confundere, Non reformare sed deformare."

[73] These propositions, but not their explications, are edited by Finke, who used the versions cited in the texts criticizing Dati's ideas; see ACC 2:705.

[74] LB, fol. 109vb: "Pro 2a parte uero patet quoniam talis potestatis plenarie execucionem ecclesia non habet nisi ea papa carente, aut papa illegitimato uel deposito, ut diffuse declaraui in sermone quem feci dominica Inuocauit, qui incipit Ecce nunc dies salutis, in loco Sessionis, ad quem me remitto."

[75] LB, fol. 109vb: "Ista patet quoniam papa illegittimato uel deposito utraque caret, ut in casu patet." Here Dati seems to hesitate between the idea of Huguccio that a pope can lose his see and the alternative view of Alanus Anglicus that the pope must be judged; see Tierney, *Foundations*, pp. 58-65; idem, "Pope and Council: Some New Decretist Texts," *Medieval Studies* 19 (1957): 197-218.

> and in no way, in this case, in a general council.[76]

This assertion lay at the heart of the polemical exchange which the sermon on Saint Francis occasioned. It threatened to deny the council the power to go beyond dealing with the Schism to the reform of the church "in head and members," and so conciliar apologists were quick to claim for the assembly a share in the supreme power of ecclesiastical governance.[77]

The fourth assertion was directed specifically toward the conduct of a council, claiming that the pope alone could define or decide in a general council. He made it clear that this was true even in the relationship between the church, which the council claimed to represent, and any legitimate Roman pontiff.[78] In support of this assertion, Dati argued that the whole was greater than the sum of its parts only when the part depended on the whole for its power. Here Dati, like Cajetan after him,[79] pointed to kingdoms and communities as representing this principle. Nonetheless, he denied the applicability of the principle to the church. The pope's power had been established by God, and so it was not derived from the church as a whole.[80] Dati's idea of a general council was one in which the pope decided and the fathers assented, an argument he based on the form of assent used in councils. He warned the fathers at Constance against flatterers who might advise them differently, saying that heeding them would detract from the work of unity.[81]

[76] LB, fol. 109vb: "Gladii spiritualis suprema potestas est in papa legittime presidente et residente totaliter quoad execucionem ipsius gladii, et nullomodo, eo casu, in concilio generali."

[77] See above n. 3.

[78] LB, fol. 109vb: "Gladii spiritualis suprema potestas sic est in papa legittime residente et presidente, ut approbanda et reprobanda solus papa habet diffinire, et non Concilium generale."

[79] Thomas M. Izbicki, "Cajetan's Attack on Parallels Between Church and State," *Cristianesimo nella storia* [in press]; Katherine Van Liere, "Vitoria, Cajetan and the Conciliarists," *Journal of the History of Ideas* 58 (1997): 597-616.

[80] LB, fol. 110ra: "Et si contra obicitur eo quod potestas Concilii generalis uidetur esse maior quam pape absolute, quia potestas tocius maior est quam potestas partis. Nosse debent taliter arguentes hoc tantumodo ueritatem habere quando potestas partis dependentiam habet a potestate tocius, sicut forte esset de potestate regis respectu regni aut domini alicuius respectu sue communitatis. Sed, quoniam potestas pape a deo dependet non ab ecclesia, argumentum ea faciliter soluitur qua probatur."

[81] LB, fol. 110ra-b: "Patet modo quo ad hoc tantum uiri ecclesiastici surgere habent in iudicio generalis Concilii non autoritate finalis iudicii, sed approbatione et concilio, prout forma hactenus in Conciliis obseruata manifeste demonstrat, qua pontifices siue in diffiniendo diffinienda usi sunt, dicentes, Nos sacro approbante Concilio etc. Et ergo uiri iustissimi qui iudicatis orbem, si in pacis uinculo hanc unitatem spiritus seruare cupitis, perturbato res huiusmodi ordinis compescere satagats prurientes auribus adulatores imitescere faciatis."

In conclusion, Dati held up Francis as an example of obedience and peace. The saint had promoted peace by adhering to the just order in all things.[82] This included having the right order in himself, treating the flesh as the handmaid of the spirit. In this way he achieved that which is "the end of all human appetites."[83] The council, in turn, was to achieve peace, including by binding dissidents "with a supernatural gift in the bond of peace,"[84] that same peace which included observance of the established order. Small wonder that Dati's preaching on obedience and peace, which left scant room for reform imposed on the curia, left many of his hearers, those most supporting conciliar supremacy, convinced that the Dominican Master General had to be answered, since he denied their power and questioned their very integrity, calling them flatterers.

Dati had one last chance to address the assembled fathers, on January 1, 1417. His sermon for the feast of the Circumcision of Jesus dwelt at length on the role of Jewish rites in the order of salvation, but it also offered an opportunity to mention Paul's rebuke of Peter for refusing to eat with uncircumcised converts (Gal 2:11). This text was well known to Dati's auditors, including as a text useful for arguing that the power of the pope was circumscribed with evident limits.[85]

Dati argued conventionally about circumcision, saying that it was valid and life-giving for a time but superseded by the promulgation of baptism as the rite of salvation. Since that time it, like the other sacraments of the Old Law, had been replaced; and this once-potent sign had become death-dealing to those who still employed it after the gospel had been proclaimed.[86] It was in this context that Dati placed Paul's rebuke of Peter. Peter had not retained faith in this superseded sign, which would have made him a heretic; but he had condescended to those who observed the old legal precepts and wished to coerce others into observing them. He seemed to be their supporter and so had become

[82] Dati makes this observation in connection with the imposition of the stigmata on Francis' body; see LB, fol. 110vb: "...ut mereretur quod paucis concessum esse in Christi corpus quasi corporaliter transformari eius, scilicet plagas et stigmata ab ipso Christo sensibiliter in eius membris recipiendo habuit tandem ordinem iusticie respectu proximi pro eius salute se totaliter impedendo."

[83] LB, fol. 110vb: "Nam huius mortalis uite decursu feliciter consumato ad ipsam translatus est pacem que finis est omnium appetituum humanorum."

[84] LB, fol. 111ra: "Tercio quod uniantur diffidentes. Copulentur dissidentes supernaturali munere in uinculo pacis."

[85] For a conciliarist use of this text, see Paul Tschackert, *Peter von Ailli* (Gotha, 1877), pp. [28]-[29]. See also the sermon on Peter and Paul delivered at the Council of Basel by Thomas de Courcelles in Vat. Palat. lat. 596 fol. 64v.

[86] British Library, Royal App. 7 [BL], fol. 55r-68v at fol. 58r: "Sacramenta omnia ueteris legis ac legalia esse terminata, ita quod, sicut sub lege ueteri erant salutifera et de neccesitate salutis, sic sub lege baptismatis sunt dampnabilia et mortifera utentibus eis, ut deducitur Act. xv c."

worthy of rebuke. Although not a heretic, Peter could be accused by Paul of not walking according to the truth.[87]

Here Dati embarked on explaining the council of the apostles and elders held in Jerusalem that is described in Acts 15. Although not a heretic, Peter was vehemently suspect; and so James the Lesser presided in his place. The decree ruling that the things of the law no longer were to be observed, thus quashing a new error undermining the church's trust in baptism, was issued not under Peter's name but in the name of the whole council.[88] Here Dati, interpreting the texts of Galatians and Acts, accepted very wide limits on the authority of any pope suspected of heresy "or of any other crime on account of which the church is notoriously scandalized." This was a conciliatory stance measured by the standards of Dominican papalism. In such a perilous situation, convocation of a council to hear the case belonged not to the pope but to "the successors of the apostles" or the cardinals, acting on their behalf. In this case, Dati observed, even a legitimate pope who did not lose his see could not preside or judge. Judgment belonged to the council alone. Otherwise the pope would be judge of his own case.[89]

Dati hastened to remind his readers that, in all other cases, the pope remained the only prelate able to convoke a council. Moreover, he alone was able, in the ordinary course of things, to "judge and define," especially about a

[87] BL, fol. 58r: "Sic enim et Paulus Galatis arguebat, Si circumcidamini, Christus uobis nichil proderit ad Gal. v°. Quinimmo ex ista causa Petro idem Paulus arguebat, non quidem quia crediderit Petrus absque obseruatione legalium salus dari non posse, nam fuisset ex hoc hereticus, quod post receptionem spiritus sancti asserere non est sanum, sed, quoniam ut Augustinus dicit super epistolam ad Galatos, credentibus illud et obseruantibus legalia ac alios seruare cogentibus nimium condescendebat ita ut eorum fautor notorius et creditor uidetur. Propter hoc enim ei restitit in faciem, id est publice reprehendit eum, quia reprehensibilis erat. Non enim recte ambulabat ad ueritatem ad Gal. ii c."

[88] BL, fol. 58v: "Ob hanc causam arbitrantur quidam concilium fuisse congregatum Ierosolimis ab apostolis et senioribus act. xv, ut et nouello errori contra fidem exorto baptismatis obuiaretur salubriter et imponeretur forma futuris casibus qualiter, errante capite, deberet per ecclesiam prouideri. Et quoniam Petrus de illo errore erat uehementer et notorie suspectus, quamquam caput esset ecclesie, non tamen ut caput in illo concilio resedit, neque in causa iudicauit, sed Iacobus minor auctoritate concilii; neque decretum super cessatione legalium et epistola nomine Petri misse sunt, sed nomine totius concilii, ut patet ibidem in fine capituli [Act. 15:23]."

[89] BL, fol. 58v-59r: "Ex hoc facto, ex quo ius oritur, aliqui pro iure habent diuino quod, si papa est de heresi uehementer et notorie suspectus, quamquam etiam non uere, siue de quocumque alio crimine propter quod scandalizetur ecclesia notorie, incorrigibilis, quod eo casu conuocacio concilii generalis ad papam non pertinebit, sed ad successores apostolorum, uel, quia per orbem ad regimen gregum Christi dispersi facile conuenire non possunt, ad sacrum collegium cardinalium in hoc eorum uices gerencium, qui communiter sunt in unum. Similiter iudicium et decisio cause solius erit concilii generalis, et non pape, quoniam si in dicto casu papa legitime in ecclesia resideat, cum propter hoc non sit papatu priuatus illegitime, cum residet in concilio, quoniam non ut iudex in causa propria potest residere, sed ad hoc tantumodo interesse ut ad purgationem sue fame profiteatur fidei aut innocentie ueritatem, sicut in concilio Ierosolimis celebrato Petrum fecisse legitur, ubi supra Act. xv."

matter of faith.[90] In these cases the council was not the judge; but it could counsel, offer information, and assent to the reasonable and just judgments of the pope.[91]

Referring to his sermon of Saint Francis, Dati argued that his statements in this context supported what he had said before about the power of the pope. He carefully applied his claims for the pope, however, only to a legitimate Roman pontiff. A heretic pope did not preside legitimately in the church, "since he had ceased by the very fact to be the head of the Mystical Body"; and he had to be judged no longer to be pope.[92] Dati added a reference which he did not dispute to theologians who believed that a pope who knew himself to have adhered pertinaciously to a doctrinal error should declare himself deposed or resign, even if the church still regarded him as true Roman pontiff. Dati said, however, that the church could not foresee all contingencies. He gave the example of Pope Liberius, who was accepted as true pope although he had adhered to Arianism for six years.[93]

Looking at other cases involving the papacy, Dati argued that a schismatic pope had his jurisdiction curtailed. He also denied contenders for the papal throne any claim on legitimate jurisdiction, especially to presiding in a council trying to resolve the resulting schism. He listed several other cases of suspension of papal power, including madness and captivity among infidels. In all of these cases, the council was left to judge, to defend the faith and to preserve the *status ecclesiae*.[94] He did, however, warn that, even during a vacancy

90 BL, fol. 59r: "In aliis autem casibus generaliter tenent conuocationem concilii generalis ad solum papam pertinere, ut di. xvii per totum cum suis annotatis, quemadmodum, ut dicunt, approbanda uel reprobanda in ecclesia solus papa habet iudicare et deffinire maximeque in materia fidei...."

91 BL, fol. 59r: "Unde sicut in dicta materia fidei et aliis statum ecclesiaticum concernentibus, generaliter solius concilii generalis est consulere et iudicare iudicio, scilicet cognicionis secundum quod unusquisque bene iudicat de hiis que nouit, ut dicit philosophus, similiter et iudicio approbationis, quod idem est, quod assensus quidam uel consensus eorum, que rationabiliter et iuste per papam diffinita sunt...."

92 BL, fol. 59v: "Sed, ut dixi, procedendo per sensum a contrariis, eciam ex hiis casibus, quoniam, si papa est hereticus, tunc non legitime in ecclesia presidet, cum eo facto corporis mistici desinat esse caput, ac per hoc pro non papa sit iudicandus, Io. 3, Qui non credit iam iudicatus est, esse, scilicet, extra ecclesiam et extra statum salutis, glo. sancti doctoris super eodem."

93 BL, fol. 59v-60r: "In hoc enim casu dicunt theologi quod, si papa sciat se alicui errori contra fidem pertinaciter adhesisse, debet se ipsum depositum reputare et renunciare papatui, quoniam scire se debet a iure diuino esse depositum, quamuis ecclesia uniuersalis, quantum ad illud quod est facti, reputauerit eum papam. Errorem enim facti ecclesia preuidere non potest, sicut contigisse notum est quando Liberium, postquam perfidie Arriane sex annis consensit, credidit esse papam fidelem, et quando pro uero papa tenuit mulierem, ut ex pontificum cronicis habetur."

94 BL, fol. 60r: "Si papa est scismaticus notorie, non legitime residet in concilio, quia habet iurisdictionem alligatam. Si papa est contendens cum alio de papatu, non legitime residet in concilio generali, quia est dubitatus in alterius obedientia. Si est furiosus effectus, si est apud infideles in captiuitate detentus, si est

or when a pope was unable to exercise his office, a council was well advised not to exercise power in individual cases.[95]

Dati concluded this portion of his sermon by recounting the case of Pope Marcellinus, who, according to Gratian's *Decretum*, offered incense to idols out of fear, not out of a loss of belief, which would have been tantamount to a lapse into heresy. Having recounted this case, which the bishops had refused to judge, telling the pope to judge himself, Dati offered for discussion the hypothetical case of a pope captured by Jews, who decided out of fear to embrace the rites of the Old Law and be circumcised. The preacher argued that, were such a case to occur and become notorious, a council indeed could judge concerning that pope.[96] Thus Dati concluded his discussion of the limits of papal power with an admission that, under certain circumstances, a pope might be investigated and judged for incurring suspicion of Judaizing, as Peter had been investigated by a council in Jerusalem. Thus room was left for removal of a pope under the right circumstances, but an undoubted pope could not be coerced into any acts contrary to his own judgement. No room was left for the imposition of reforms, including the curtailment of the privileges of the mendicants, on a legitimate Roman pontiff.

Little homiletic evidence survives from the Council of Pavia-Siena (1423-1424), and none shows papal apologists trying to deal with the reform issue while maintaining the supremacy of a pope not tainted by heresy or some other heinous offense.[97] This inquiry, then, will have to be carried over to the Council of Basel (1431-1449), although the number of pro-papal sermons available for study is limited. Most notable, however, there is Juan de Torquemada's sermon for the feast of Saint Ambrose (December 7, 1432) that will have to be examined

mente captus, si est fascinatus, si est ecclesiastice politie destructor notorius, non legitime residet in concilio, quia habet iurisdiccionem suspensam in hiis enim casibus et similibus, ubi racionabiliter argui potest illegitima in concilio pape residencia. Concilium generale potestatem habet executiuam determinandi et sententialiter iudicandi, et ea que sunt fidei et ea que pro conseruacione status ecclesiastici uidebuntur expedire." On the concept of *status ecclesiae*, see Yves Congar, "Status Ecclesiae," *Studia Gratiana* 15 (1972): 1-31. The term could be applied broadly or strictly, papalists keeping the focus on disruption of the ecclesiastical apparatus; see Izbicki, *Protector of the Faith*, pp. 92-94.

[95] BL, fol. 60v: "Ex quibus sequitur quod, si concilium generale, papa legitime residente et sede non uacante, habet plenariam et executiuam potestatem in multis casibus, similiter, papa non legitime presidente uel sede uacante, habet potestatem in omnibus casibus, quamquam illa potestate uti in singulis non expediat, prout alias dixi, allegando uerbum apostoli dicentis, Omnia michi licent, sed non omnia expediunt 1 Cor. vi."

[96] BL, fol. 60v-61r: "Sic in simili dicendum esset si papa recte credens captus a Iudeis timore mortis legalia seruaret aut permiteret se circumcidi. Constat enim quod in illo casu ubi factum esset notorium quod inquirere de qualitate actus et iudicare de papa ad concilium pertineret." On the case of Marcellinus, see Tierney, *Foundations*, pp. 38, 57; idem, *Origins of Papal Infallibility*, p. 152.

[97] William P. Hyland, "Reform Preaching and Despair at the Council of Pavia-Siena (1423-1424)," *The Catholic Historical Review* 84 (1998): 409-430.

for its handling of these themes.[98] In Dati's case, however, we find him reluctant to address reform in its widest dimensions, even in his sermon at the Council of Pisa. The Constance sermons recessed even farther from this theme, dwelling increasingly on the limits of the power of a pope without addressing reform of pontiff or curia. Reform became, in these sermons, more a club with which to beat those reformers who turned their eyes toward the pope without removing from themselves all stain of vice or misconduct. Given such a reception, advocates of reform must surely have felt alienated and driven to attempt binding the supreme pontiff to accept conciliar decrees curtailing the revenues and powers belonging to him and his court.

98 See Vat. Palat. lat. 976, fol. 24v-30r; Izbicki, *Protector of the Faith*, p. 4.

ANNATES AND REFORM AT THE COUNCIL OF BASEL

Gerald Christianson

Few historians have had more profound effect on the "idea of reform" in our generation—during the very time when his student Louis Pascoe won many friends and admirers for his own work—than Gerhart Ladner.[1] As Father Pascoe has shown, the notion of reform derives from *reformatio,* seen especially as restoration to earlier and better times, most notably in an idealized *ecclesia primitiva.*[2] To Ladner reform means personal renewal, a return to the ideal that we are created *imago dei*. The challenge for medievalists, he thinks, is to determine how this ideal, proclaimed in the Christian gospel and refined in the patristic period, expresses itself in ever new contexts.

At the heart of Ladner's vision stands a medieval civilization whose fabric and structure were informed by the notion of *reformatio melior.* Two important figures represent turning points in this ideal: Gregory I, who emphasized personal renewal, and Gregory VII, who set about reforming church and society with the battle cry of *libertas ecclesiae,* the freedom of the church. To carry out its mission in the world, Gregory and his reform party articulated a vision of a church free from lay interference, especially in the election of clergy and appointments to benefices. In place of lay interference, the freedom of the church entailed clerical celibacy to reduce entangling alliances, and above all a unified church under leadership from the bishop of Rome.[3]

This essay deals with how Ladner's concept of reform in medieval society worked itself out in a single context: the struggle over annates between the papacy and one of the 15th century "reform councils," which met at Basel (1431-1449). It proposes to take Ladner a step farther and suggests that the shift in the late Middle Ages is from an assertion of *libertas* by the papacy over against "the temporal arm" to an assertion of *libertas* by the papacy over against the church itself as represented in a general council.

[1] The foundational work is Gerhart Ladner, *The Idea of Reform: Its Impact on Christian Thought and Action in the Age of the Fathers,* rev. ed. (1959; reprinted New York, 1967). See also idem, *Images and Ideas in the Middle Ages: Selected Studies in History and Art,* 2 vols. (Rome, 1983) for several significant essays on particular aspects of the theme; and his memoirs in idem, *Erinnerungen,* ed. Herwig Wolfram and Walter Pohl: *Sitzungsberichte der Österreichischen Akademie der Wissenschaften,* Phil.-Hist. Kl. 617 (Vienna, 1994). I am grateful to Constantin Fasolt, David Crowner, and my long-time collaborator Thomas M. Izbicki for their helpful suggestions.

[2] See Louis Pascoe, "Jean Gerson, the *Ecclesia primitiva* and Reform," *Traditio* (1974): 379-409; idem, "Religious Orders, Evangelical Liberty and Reform in the Thought of Jean Gerson," in *Reformbemühungen und Observanzbestrebungen im Spätmittelalterlichen Ordenswesen,* ed. Kaspar Elm (Berlin, 1989), pp. 503-514; and in general, idem, *Jean Gerson: Principles of Church Reform* (Leiden, 1973).

[3] For an excellent summary of Ladner's thesis, set in the context of his intellectual development, see John Van Engen, "Images and Ideas: The Achievements of Gerhart Burian Ladner, with a Bibliography of His Published Works," *Viator* 20 (1989): 85-115; and the essay by Phillip Stump in this volume. These stand as a fitting tribute to a great teacher and scholar.

Outside of Ladner's conceptual framework—part of his war-torn generation's concern for the nature and fate of Western civilization—we have few, if any, comprehensive treatments of the reform question from 1300 to 1500. The enterprise is hindered by a lack of clarity about definitions and a readiness to substitute polemical notions. While Renaissance studies have benefitted from definitions of humanism proposed by Charles Trinkaus and Paul Oskar Kristeller, other critical areas are not so fortunate. What, for instance, should we make of the socio-economic situation with its series of unprecedented disasters such as the Black Death and frequent social revolts? Ladner and others refer to the "crisis" of the late Middle Ages. Originally this term was used to describe a decline in agricultural production. Later it came to be applied to the whole process of historical development in the period. Joseph Lortz adapted the term to describe what he saw as a decline in the church after the high scholasticism of the 13th century. Still others try to locate a consciousness of crisis in the sources themselves and detect a feeling of pessimism or anxiety, a notion which owes much to Johann Huizinga.[4]

What, then, is one to make of the "reform councils" themselves? Are they proof of anxiety and decline or optimism and piety? Are they crisis or continuity? Such questions put late 20th century historians on guard against single-minded generalities or anachronistic perspectives, even the broad interpretive themes of a Gerhart Ladner and their need to invoke a late medieval "crisis." Some scholars—one thinks of Jaroslav Pelikan in the history of doctrine and Steven Ozment in the history of the church—take another direction, and elevate reform as a leading theme for the entire period between 1300 to 1600, even though this period covers 300 years or more.[5] Following the lead of Heiko Oberman's pioneering work on late medieval nominalism, Ozment's methodology has proved especially helpful as a framework. Within the larger context of reform impulses (as in Ladner's "idea of reform"), one can measure continuities and discontinuities with past and future.[6]

To help make this methodology useful for our discussion of the annates controversy at Basel, we also need to expand our perspective beyond an exclusive emphasis on individual or national self-interest, and even beyond clashes over

4 Johannes Helmrath, *Das Basler Konzil, 1431-1449: Forschungsstand und Probleme* (Köln, 1987), pp. 328-330. Helmrath provides a comprehensive survey of the literature.

5 Jaroslav Pelikan, *The Christian Tradition: A History of the Development of Doctrine,* 5 vols. (Chicago, 1971-1989), esp. vol. 4, *Reformation of Church and Dogma;* Steven Ozment, *The Age of Reform (1250-1550)* (New Haven, 1980).

6 Heiko Oberman, "Introduction," *Forerunners of the Reformation* (New York, 1966; reprint Philadelphia, 1981). Oberman's methodology of measuring continuities and discontinuities can also put Basel's supposed radicality or novelty in clearer perspective; e.g. Stieber, *Pope Eugenius IV* (n. 56 below) and Stump, *Reforms of the Council of Constance* (n. 12 below) argue that Basel continued the Constance reform program, whereas Antony Black, *Monarchy and Community* (Cambridge, 1970), esp. p. 16, maintains that Basel took a new course and was therefore discontinuous with Constance. Both positions have something to contribute to a complete picture.

theories of reform, to include conceptions of the church and its role in reform, whether expressed by "papalists" or "conciliarists."

H. J. Sieben has supported Ladner's interpretation by demonstrating that the twin terms, reform and councils, go back to the beginning of Christian history;[7] but Hubert Jedin has also shown that the two did not create a close alliance until the outbreak of the Great Schism (1378).[8] What form this alliance took is best expressed by Johannes Helmrath's suggestion that from this point on the demand for reform is coupled with "a conciliar confession."[9] Whereas the older literature spoke of reform councils with little reference to doctrine, one now perceives that a struggle for faith was at the heart of the conciliar movement, that "faith" means, primarily, ecclesiology, and that ecclesiology includes both the urgency for and the power to enact reform.

Although the issues related to the annates at Basel are exceedingly complex, the story itself has not advanced far beyond Richard Zwölfer's detailed description (1929-1930) following the general outlines laid down by Johannes Haller (1911) and an intervening dissertation by Edmund Bursche (1921).[10] These studies show that, despite continuous charges to the contrary, the Council of Basel took its reformatory task seriously and, in the period from its 12th session in July 1433, to the 23rd Session in March 1436, issued a series of carefully wrought reform decrees on elections and reservations (to which, as we will see, the papacy had strong objections), regular diocesan and provincial synods, the establishment of university chairs in biblical languages as well as

[7] H. J. Sieben, *Die Konzilsidee des lateinischen Mittelalters, 847-1378* (Paderborn, 1984), pp. 320-321, 353-354; see also his *Traktate und Theorien zum Konzil* (Frankfurt, 1983).

[8] Hubert Jedin, *A History of the Council of Trent,* 2 vols. (St. Louis, 1957-1961), 1.1-75. The formula "reform equals councils," however, may be an oversimplification. Not all reformers were active in the council, and not all "conciliarists" were reformers, as Johannes Helmrath observes in "Reform als Thema der Konzilien des Spätmittelalters," in *Christian Unity: The Council of Ferrara-Florence, 1438/39-1989,* ed. Giuseppe Alberigo (Louvain, 1991), pp. 75-152, here p. 146.

[9] Helmrath, *Das Basler Konzil,* p. 331.

[10] Richard Zwölfer, "Die Reform der Kirchenverfassung auf dem Konzil zu Basel," *Basler Zeitschrift für Geschichte und Altertumskunde* 28 (1929): 141-247; 29 (1930): 2-58; Johannes Haller, *Papsttum und Kirchenreform* (Berlin, 1903); Edmund Bursche, *Die Reformarbeiten des Basler Konzils* (Lodz, 1921). See also Alexander Patschovsky, "Der Reformbegriff zur Zeit der Konzilien von Konstanz und Basel," in *Reform von Kirche und Reich: Zur Zeit Konzilien von Konstanz (1414-1415) und Basel (1431-1449),* ed. Ivan Hlavácek and Alexander Patschovsky (Konstanz, 1996), pp. 7-28. One should especially add Werner Krämer, *Konsens und Rezeption: Verfassungsprinzipien der Kirche im Basler Konziliarismus* (Münster, 1980), which caused a stir upon its publication, possibly because of its highly positive appraisal of Basel's reform and ecclesiology; see esp. pp. 318-363.

Arabic and Chaldean, the restriction of Jews, the regulation of worship, the reform of the college of cardinals, and the election of a pope.[11]

These decisions were surrounded by considerable discussion. In one case, the decree on the annates, discussion led to heated debate and division. Yet, division was already evident at the Council of Constance (1414-1418).[12] What prompted so much contention? The annates and its twin, the *servitia*, were taxes on ecclesiastical benefices. Sometimes known as "vacancies," these two became the largest single source of papal income in the pre-Constance period. Theoretically, they were the fruits of an incumbent's first year (*annus*), but the rule was not consistently applied.[13] The need for taxation increased sharply when the papacy abandoned the Papal States for Avignon and became acute following the financial disaster of the Schism. The curia then began to grant offices for amounts greater than the annates by means of payments which were "thinly disguised as 'love gifts,'"[14] a fact one should bear in mind when

11 The most important sources are provided by the council's historian, John of Segovia, in *Monumenta conciliorum generalium seculi decimi quinti,* ed. Frantisek Palacky, et al., 4 vols. (Vienna and Basel, 1857-1935 [hereafter MC]), esp. 2.402-405, 447-448, 255-256, 525-528, 757-760, 773-774, 781-782, 801-805, 847-855; and the secretarial protocols in *Concilium Basiliense,* ed. Johannes Haller, et al., 8 vols. (Basel, 1896-1936 [hereafter CB]), esp. 1.111-112, 2.424, 3.294, 336, 350. See also the documents collected in *Sacrorum conciliorum . . .*, ed. Johannes D. Mansi, vols. 29-31 (Florence and Venice, 1758-1798; reprint Paris, 1903-1906 [hereafter Mansi], esp. 29.61-64, 74-77, 280-281, 382-385, 30.550-590. A modern edition of the formal decrees can be found in *Conciliorum oecumenicorum decreta,* ed. Giuseppe Alberigo et al. (Bologna, 1973) [hereafter COD], esp. pp. 464-472 (Session 12), 473-476 (Session 15), 483-485 (Session 19), 485-488 (Session 20), 488-492 (Session 21), 494-505 (Session 23). For general surveys, see Helmrath, *Das Basler Konzil,* pp. 332-347; Krämer, *Konsens und Rezeption,* pp. 12-68; and Gerald Christianson, *Cesarini, the Conciliar Cardinal* (St. Ottilien, 1979), pp. 125-148, all with further literature.

12 For the Constance reforms, the important work is by a Ladner student, Phillip H. Stump, *The Reforms of the Council of Constance, 1414-1418* (Leiden, 1994), here esp. p. 104. Stump challenges the charge that the Constance reforms were "merely cosmetic." See also Walter Brandmüller, *Das Konzil von Konstanz, 1414-1418,* 2 vols. (Paderborn, 1991-1997), the first modern treatment of the entire council. For the literature, see also Ansgar Frenken, "Die Erforschung des Konstanzer Konzils (1414-1418) in den letzten 100 Jahren," *Annuarium Historiae Conciliorum* 25 (1993). Also useful for the sources is *Quellen zur Kirchenreform im Zeitalter der grossen Konzilien des 15. Jahrhunderts,* ed. Jürgen Miethke and Lorenz Weinrich, vol. 1, *Die Konzilien von Pisa (1407) und Konstanz (1414-1418)* (Darmstadt, 1996).

13 Phillip H. Stump, "The Reform of Papal Taxation at the Council of Constance (1414-1418)," *Speculum* 64 (1989): 65-105 at p. 84, to which I am much indebted. While extending the story to Basel, the present essay comes to similar conclusions. See also John Gilchrist, *The Church and Economic Activity in the Middle Ages* (London, 1969), esp. pp. 94, 219; Helmrath, "Reform als Thema," pp. 82-83; and Jean Favier, *Les finances pontificales à l'epoque du Grand Schisme d'Occident, 1378-1409* (Paris, 1966), pp. 205-208. Favier also links the papacy's financial needs in time of crisis with the installation of unpopular fiscal measures.

14 Stump, "The Reform of Papal Taxation," p. 99.

considering the opposition at Basel to any kind of love offerings that would offset losses from vacancy dues.

The emotion generated by this otherwise apparently technical financial matter arose from the attachment of annates to the sin of simony, the sale of offices in the tradition of Simon Magus who tried to buy the power of the Holy Spirit from the apostles Peter and John (Acts 8:9-25). Objections to simony in the late Middle Ages found impassioned expression both outside and inside the councils and the curia. John Hus and Jean Gerson, among several others, wrote treatises; and Bishop Juan González of Cádiz contributed a written opinion to the debate at Basel.[15]

Thus, when the Council of Constance met, some of the French urged the abolition of annates (October 1415) but found little support from the other "nations." Even after the election of Martin V, the council's reform Commission could reach no solution, so the new pope temporarily took matters into his own hands by allowing a reduction in taxation in order to alleviate financial burdens and their attendant grievances. Perhaps little could be accomplished until the papacy had reclaimed the Papal States and their considerable income.[16]

Five years after Constance, the subject was brought to the table again by the French at the Council of Pavia-Siena (1423); but the council closed abruptly without further action.[17] In 1429 vacancy dues were also the subject of a cardinals' reform commission, a body which included a Padua-trained lawyer, Giuliano Cesarini, who would later become papal legate and president of the Council of Basel. The commission urged that an incumbent no longer pay the annates before he entered a benefice and that, if possible, the tax be eliminated altogether, provided that a substitute could be found.[18]

By the time the Council of Basel opened in 1431 the situation had changed. Not only did the return of the papacy to the Papal States alter affairs; so, too, did the re-establishment of a unified papacy. Now the "decisive battle would be fought out" between a reform-minded council and a single, undoubted pope.[19] New complaints about annates arose as early as August, 1432, when the council drew up the duties of a treasurer,[20] and again on December 13 when it received a memorandum on the subject. This was followed by a plea from the

15 See Helmrath, "Reform als Thema," pp. 83-84 n. 24, for references to the literature. On González, see Erich Meuthen, "Juan González, Bischof Cádiz, auf dem Basler Konzil," *Annuarium Historiae Conciliorum* 8 (1976): 250-293.

16 For fuller details on the debate at Constance see Stump, "The Reform of Papal Taxation," pp. 65-99. See also Peter Partner, *The Papal State Under Martin V* (London, 1958).

17 See Walter Brandmüller, *Das Konzil von Pavia-Siena 1423-1424,* 2 vols. (Münster, 1974).

18 Zwölfer, "Die Reform der Kirchenverfassung," pp. 198-205; Jedin, *The Council of Trent,* 1.119-120. The commission's proposal, CB 1:163-168; for Cesarini's role, ibid., pp. 108-110.

19 Jedin, *The Council of Trent,* 1.17.

20 MC 2.220-221; CB 2.188-189.

bishop of Cádiz to avoid hasty measures until the council found alternate compensation for the papacy.[21] Erich Meuthen suggests a connection between González's tractate (1433) and a significant conciliar decree, known as the *decretum irritans,* which prohibited papal reservations to benefices except for just cause.[22] Even the possibility of this connection points toward a divisive issue underlying the entire discussion of simony, finance, and reform in general. "In a very real sense," concludes Francis Oakley, "the institution of the benefice was the obstacle on which late-medieval attempts at churchwide reform 'in head and members' came to grief'."[23]

At the same time, the bishop put his finger on the more immediate issues the council now faced. Although the story of this debate often appears dense with clashes over principle and maneuvers over self-interest, as well as long digressions to resolve other priorities, three related topics emerge in over-lapping stages: simony, annates, and adequate compensation for the papacy.

The council's deputation on reform set up a sub-committee to deal with the annates on March 20, 1433,[24] but other matters intervened—especially a conference with the Hussites—and debate on a decree was postponed. Then a simony decree was submitted on October 3, 1433.[25] It would dominate the field for a considerable period of time.

Heated debate followed, especially on what constituted simony, on whether the pope could be a simoniac, and whether he could at least receive "love gifts" when granting benefices.[26] These were not idle academic speculations. The papacy apparently thought itself above the charge of simony.[27] At the same time, opposition arose from another quarter. The prelates carried a built-in resistance to eliminating taxes from which their offices benefitted. Considering themselves "heads" of the Church in their dioceses, just as the pope was head of the universal Church, they not only collected taxes but levied them as well, and some of the most ardent reformers in the council, such as the archbishop of Lyons, received considerable revenue from the use of their seal and other

[21] CB 2.294, 1.111.

[22] Meuthen, "Juan González," pp. 257-261. See also Zwölfer, "Die Reform der Kirchenverfassung," pp. 169-170; Mansi 29.61; COD, pp. 469-472. Juan de Torquemada also responded to this decree, Mansi 30.550-590.

[23] Francis Oakley, *The Western Church in the Later Middle Ages* (Ithaca, New York, 1979), p. 219.

[24] CB 2.377, 406-407; MC 2.359.

[25] CB 2.458, 493-494.

[26] MC 2.524, 552-554.

[27] Barbara Hallman, *Italian Cardinals, Reform, and the Church as Property, 1492-1563* (Berkeley, 1985).

"customary services." Often at odds on other issues, the papacy and many of the prelates now joined forces to oppose change.[28]

On November 25 the members appointed another committee to discuss the simony decree, and this committee gave its recommendations to Cardinal Cesarini who worked out a draft.[29] Cesarini's comprehensive proposal, a flat denial of the practice, went well beyond the general disapproval of simony by Constance (March 21, 1418). Cesarini included the specifics: all forms of vacancy taxes; services and annates; the sale of sacraments or offices; payment for palliums; dispensations; indulgences. Urging the council to follow the footsteps of Christ, who drove the money-changers from the temple, the cardinal explicitly endorsed the tradition that joined simony and heresy.[30]

Yet, as debate continued, Cesarini showed a willingness to compromise, and drew up a revised form which he submitted on March 30, 1434.[31] The new form provided indemnification for pope and cardinals. Several ranks objected: the prelates to the rejection of their "ancient customs" and the extra financial burden they would bear; the papal envoys to the withdrawal of income; and ambassadors to the denial of secular authority to collate benefices.[32] The president's proposal eventually died in committee,[33] but in the process it did declare that the pope was not immune to the charge of simony.[34]

Despite Cesarini's plea on May 20 that the prelates would suffer the consequences if the church failed to reform, stalemate dragged on for another year[35] until a dramatic change occurred on May 30, 1435. The annates question, lost in the noise of the simony debate, returned abruptly to the fore. The committee of twelve proposed a motion, but this proposal was forgotten when

28 MC 2.558-559; Zwölfer, "Die Reform der Kirchenverfassung," 28.215-216. Stump, "The Reform of Papal Taxation," pp. 87-88, compares the relative positions of bishops and other ranks at Constance and notes that, in contrast to the university graduates, prelates were "on the whole much less ardent" about abolition. On Amadée de Talaru of Lyons and the French delegation see the substantial study by Heribert Müller, *Die Franzosen, Frankreich, und das Basler Konzil (1431-1449),* 2 vols. (Paderborn, 1990), esp. 1.27-220.

29 MC 2.552.

30 MC 2.554.

31 MC 2.676-677; CB 3.53.

32 MC 2.629-630 (the archbishop of Lyons); MC 2.677; CB 3.74 (Jean Beaupére); MC 2.678-679; CB 3.76 (the abbot of Bonneval); MC 2.680; CB 3.76 (the bishop of Tours). Compare Constance in Stump, *Reforms of the Council of Constance,* pp. 25, 104.

33 MC 2.681, 683. For a crucial and evenly divided vote (although prelates and non-prelates were generally on opposite sides), see MC 2.684-693. Segovia gives his own vote, MC 2.693-696.

34 MC 2.683-684.

35 See the various attempts to overcome the divisions among prelates, papal representatives, other members, and the president in MC 2.696-698, 713; CB 3.128, 136-137, 193, 237.

Cesarini introduced his own draft decree on the practice. It prohibited payment both to prelates and popes for confirmation, ordination, or the granting of benefices in the form of annates, seal-money, or bull-money, even on the basis of ancient custom. The council's historian, John of Segovia, thought the cardinal's decree a God-sent inspiration: "What human infirmity could not achieve after months of anxious labor was perfected in a moment by virtue of divine assistance."[36]

In any case, the president achieved success at once. By June 3 all the deputations and a general congregation had approved.[37] Cesarini's co-president, John Berardi, angrily objected that the decree provided no compensation for pope and curia; and when the decree was put to a vote, he and a colleague left amid shouts, "Let the doors be opened, and the slanderers who disturb the work of the Holy Spirit be sent out."[38] The council gave final approval at the 21st session on June 9, 1435. Cesarini presided alone.[39]

What had happened to turn four years of frustrating debate over simony in general into the sudden decision to condemn a particular form of simony? Zwölfer offers two reasons: a secret agreement between the French and the Germans, who together formed a majority in the council, and Cesarini's blunt portrayal of the decree's opponents as opponents of reform, which finally stung the prelates into action.[40]

Subsequent research has made a significant advance over Zwölfer's analysis. Johannes Haller had already discovered in Codex 168 of the Cusanus Hospital at Bernkastel-Kues a manuscript containing 27 items from the early years at Basel. These are not copies, but the originals delivered to someone of importance in the council. While Zwölfer was aware of Haller's discovery, not until 1935 did Heinrich Dannenbauer identify the seal and handwriting in the margins and on the backs of the documents as Cardinal Cesarini's. In effect these constitute the president's own "notebooks" on reform. They help flesh out an incident which otherwise remains mostly a skeleton.[41]

From the council's early days Cesarini had called for reform and offered personal invitations to submit proposals. Several of these remain in his dossier. Apparently, however, he had come to realize by the beginning of 1435 that the council would generate no more than fragmented proposals—especially during the time-consuming simony debate—unless it had a comprehensive plan that would bring together the council's greatest concerns and offer a coherent agenda

[36] MC 2.797-798.

[37] MC 2.799; CB 3.401-402, 404, 408.

[38] MC 2.799-800; CB 3.408-409, 5.135.

[39] MC 2.801; COD, pp. 488-489.

[40] Zwölfer, "Die Reform der Kirchenverfassung," p. 233.

[41] Heinrich Dannenbauer, "Die Handakten des Konzilspräsidenten Cesarini," in CB 8.3-31.

for a reformed church.[42] Thus, on February 24, 1435, he requested a three-week "sabbatical" in which to develop his project and went into retreat at the Carthusian monastery across the Rhine in Little Basel.[43] The cardinal's project does not survive, and the few scattered references give no indication of its content.[44] Ulrich Stoeckel reported to his monastery in Tegernsee on April 4 that Cesarini had finished a plan in seven parts which dealt respectively with the curia, prelates, priests, canons, religious, laity, and other common problems. Stoeckel also relates that the president began to submit his program to the deputations bit by bit but never revealed the entire plan at one time.[45]

While not the final project, the manuscript identified by Dannenbauer does contain the dossier which Cesarini took with him during his brief sabbatical and which later passed into the hands of his friend, Nicholas of Cusa, who deposited it in his library at Cues. Cesarini's collection contains memoranda, proposals, and drafts of decrees, often with his own handwritten notes. The items represent a wide variety of interests, ranging from papal administration and taxation, the color of prelates' robes, world peace, and Sabbath-breaking, to drunkenness, a crusade against the Turks, universities, and the number of sponsors at baptism.[46] The legate's task was to choose the most significant, shape them into proposed decrees, and nurse them through the council. Several of the final reform decrees show the marks of Cesarini's sabbatical project, in particular those on the college of cardinals, the papacy, and the regulation of worship.[47] The latter decree arose from his own statutes for the canons of Basel cathedral, who had frequently opposed his interventions since his arrival in the city.[48] In regard to simony, the president abandoned his controversial decree and, apparently, decided to rescue what he could, a condemnation of the annates.

The discovery of the dossier, which touches on a considerable number of the council's final reform decrees, adds to Cesarini's stature as statesman and

[42] E.g., CB 2.354-355, 358, 388; 3.326.

[43] MC 2.781; CB 3.324-325.

[44] E.g., CB 3.336, 350, 356; MC 2.781.

[45] CB 1.89, 92.

[46] CB 8.33-186.

[47] See Christianson, *Cesarini,* pp. 132-136, 147-148; Helmrath, *Das Basler Konzil,* pp. 93-98; idem, "Reform als Thema," pp. 112-116; all with references to the sources.

[48] CB 8, no. 22. See MC 1.115; CB 2.16; MC 2.728; CB 3.117. Helmrath, "Reform als Thema," p. 141 n. 245, feels that *Cesarini,* pp. 128-129, gave too little attention to monastic reform. I did, however, stress its importance for the cardinal, and more recent research has helped to fill the gap; for example, B. Neidiger, "Statregiment und Klosterreform in Basel," in Elm, *Reformbemühungen,* pp. 539-570; and Pascal Ladner, "Kardinal Cesarinis Reformstatuten für das St. Leonhardstift in Basel," *Zeitschrift für Schweizerische Kirchengeschichte* 74 (1980): 125-160. See also Dieter Mertens (n. 70 below).

reformer,[49] especially when we consider his capacity to guide his proposals through the thicket of conciliar debate and negotiation. More important, these discussions and the resulting decrees, seen together with Cesarini's overall plan, demonstrate that Basel took the enterprise seriously and did not simply attack the problem in fragmentary fashion.[50]

Nevertheless, at the moment of their triumph the council and its president divided immediately over the question of compensation for pope and cardinals in lieu of the annates. Opening the third and final phase of our story, Cesarini endorsed compensation and, on June 10, the day after the council approved the annates decree, he called for a commission to propose a suitable method.[51] The commission met and put forward a proposal, but nothing was ever adopted. The German clergy, not much affected by the annates, feared that compensation would add new *servitia* and thus new servitude. At length they persuaded the French to abide by an earlier agreement that the question of compensation await evidence that the pope would adhere to the decree.[52]

In fact, the pope simply ignored it. The test came quickly. Cesarini and the council asked Eugenius to send the pallium for the archbishop of Rouen, but the curia refused until it had received the vacancy dues.[53] Later, both the Germans, in 1433, and the French, in 1436, complained that the papal Camera collected the fruits during vacancies, despite conciliar decrees to the contrary.[54] Also contributing to an atmosphere of distrust were the pope's opposition to the council, his reluctant submission, and his attempt to pack the presidency with his own candidates.[55]

49 See his correspondence with Pope Eugenius during 1432 in Mansi 29.279-281; MC 2.95-107, 109-117, 203-209.

50 For evaluations see Francesco Santovito, "Il cardinale Giuliano Cesarini (1398-1444)," *Nicolaus: Rivista di teologia ecumenico-patristica* 7 (1979): 187-192; A. Strand and K. Walsh, "Cesarini, Giuliano," in *Dizionario biographico degli Italiani,* 49 vols. (Roma, 1960-1997), 24.188-195; Christianson, *Cesarini,* pp. 36-51, 57-62; and Krämer, *Konsens und Rezeption,* pp. 125-165.

51 MC 2.800-801; CB 3.409-410. See also MC 2.1131-1132 for Cesarini's visits to every deputation in order to secure the subsidy.

52 Stump, "The Reform of Papal Taxation," p. 104. Zwölfer, "Die Reform der Kirchenverfassung," 28.237-246, gives full details of this episode. Heribert Müller, "Lyon et le Concile de Bale (1431-1449)," *Cahiers d'Histoire* 28 (1983): 33-57 at p. 55 observes a remarkable homogeneity among the French delegation which finally bore fruit with the Pragmatic Sanction in 1438: "Ce qui impressionne à Bâle, c'est la compacité des Français, leur charactère de 'pressure group'. . .," (p. 34).

53 MC 2.814; Mansi 30.956-957.

54 CB 1.201, 409. Stump, "The Reform of Papal Taxation," p. 102, wonders whether Eugenius had even "appropriated fruits during vacancies for his own use."

55 See Gerald Christianson, "Nicholas of Cusa and the Presidency Debate at the Council of Basel, 1434" in *Nicholas of Cusa on Christ and the Church,* ed. Christianson and Thomas M. Izbicki (Leiden, 1996), pp. 87-103, with further literature.

The annates decree and its test case signaled a decisive renewal in papal-conciliar hostilities. When two papal presidents, Cardinal Albergati and John Berardi, returned to Rome in June 1435, Eugenius apparently decided to turn hesitant negation into an all-out offensive.[56] The result was a set of instructions for envoys to the princes, called the *Libellus apologeticus* (June 1436), in which the pope objected to the withdrawal of annates and, for the first time, invoked the "numbers game." This was later given the widest possible dissemination by Aeneas Sylvius Piccolomini (Pope Pius II) that the council was an "ignoble mob" and a "confused crowd" where the vote of a cook was equal to that of a prelate.[57]

Such actions hinted strongly that Eugenius would not obey the annates decree. Nicholas Gee, in a document found in Cesarini's dossier, noted that "reform begins in the head; the rest follows easily," and urged that the council make its reform decrees strong enough to withstand papal dispensation.[58] Basel followed such advice when Eugenius transferred the council to Ferrara (1437) in violation of the Constance degree *Frequens*. The council responded by declaring its twin decree, *Haec sancta* on the superior power of council over pope, as a "truth" of the Christian faith, and thus raised the related issues of reform and ecclesiology to a realm from which no pope could dispense. On these grounds it deposed Eugenius in June 1439.[59]

Nevertheless, this new battle remained unsettled for years to come. We now know that the annates decree and many of the council's other reforms, far from being viewed as the hostile product of a radical assembly, were adopted by large segments of the church, most notably in France and Germany. The Pragmatic Sanction of Bourges (1438) incorporated some 23 conciliar reform decrees, and the German princes adopted a similar number in the *Instrumentum acceptationis*, known as the Acceptation of Mainz (1439).[60] These remained in

[56] Joachim Stieber, *Pope Eugenius IV, the Council of Basel and the Secular and Ecclesiastical Authorities in the Empire* (Leiden, 1978), pp. 27-29.

[57] See Gerald Christianson, "Aeneas Sylvius Piccolomini and the Historiography of the Council of Basel," in *Ecclesia Militans: Studien zur Konzilien- und Reformationsgeschichte*, ed. Walter Brandmüller et al., 2 vols. (Paderborn, 1988), 1.157-184. Erich Meuthen, "Ein 'deutscher' Freundeskreis an der romischen Kurie in der Mitte des 15. Jahrhunderts," *Annuarium Historiae Conciliorum* 27/28 (1995/1996): 487-542, is especially helpful for background on Aeneas, as well as Cesarini and Cusanus. It also includes a useful bibliography.

[58] CB 8.171.

[59] Thomas M. Izbicki, "The Council of Ferrara-Florence and Dominican Papalism," in idem, *Friars and Jurists: Selected Studies* (Goldbach, 1998), pp. 3-17 (originally in Alberigo, *Christian Unity*, pp. 429-443).

[60] John Broderick, "The Sacred College of Cardinals: Size and Geographic Composition (1099-1986)," *Archivum Historiae Pontificae* 25 (1987): 7-71 at pp. 42-43.

force until defeated in a long and costly papal campaign to win over the princes.[61]

The question of how to estimate the cost,[62] along with the equally difficult question of how to evaluate Basel's reform program, are loaded with overtones, ranging from confessional interests to general perspectives on the course of Western civilization. These include the charges that Basel intended to destroy the fiscal apparatus of the church,[63] that it wanted to reform the head but not the members,[64] that it concerned itself with the machinery but not the substance of reform,[65] and that the results were only piecemeal.[66]

Some, if not all, of these now demand serious revision; but our concern here—to return to the beginning of this essay—is more specific: concentrating on a single controversy, the annates, what can be said about the "crisis" of the reform idea during the late Middle Ages? We need first to reflect on the respective reform theologies of each "party," papal and conciliar, as they groped for self-definition even as they polarized, and then relate these to Ladner's concept of crisis.

Pope and council held some notions in common. For instance, both shared an assumption, articulated by John of Segovia, that the struggle for reform was a struggle for a right understanding of the church and its mission, so that matters of faith and ecclesiology play a prominent role in the discussion of reform.[67] Many also shared a conviction of Pseudo-Dionysian inspiration that reform moved from top to bottom through a hierarchy of being. For Nicholas of Cusa this meant a "trickle-down" effect in which firm leadership must be asserted from the top; but for Nicholas Gee, the council must first expend efforts on the head.[68]

61 The important general study is Stieber, *Pope Eugenius IV.* See also Helmrath, *Das Basler Konzil,* pp. 346-352; idem, "Reform als Thema," pp. 121-131; Müller, *Die Franzosen,* pp. 823-827.

62 For example, Jedin, *The Council of Trent,* 1.21, observes: "Thus the Papacy had triumphed over the conciliar movement—but at a heavy price. The chief beneficiary was the modern state . . .".

63 Zwölfer, "Die Reform der Kirchenverfassung," p. 234: The "entire financial system of the Curia" is overthrown; see Joseph Gill, *Eugenius IV: Pope of Christian Union* (Westminster, Maryland, 1961), p. 85.

64 Aeneas Sylvius Piccolomini used this argument; see Helmrath, *Das Basler Konzil,* p. 334; Christianson, "Aeneas Sylvius," pp. 166-168.

65 Mandell Creighton, *A History of the Papacy from the Great Schism to the Sack of Rome,* rev. ed., 6 vols. (London, 1914), 2.231.

66 See Helmrath, "Reform als Thema," p. 149.

67 Helmrath, *Das Basler Konzil,* p. 352.

68 For Gee, see n. 58 above. For Cusanus, see Morimichi Watanabe and Thomas M. Izbicki, "Nicholas of Cusa, *A General Reform of the Church,*" in Christianson and Izbicki, *Nicholas of Cusa on Christ and the Church,* pp. 175-202, with a translation of Cusanus' *Reformatio generalis.*

Nor were the papacy and its representatives at Basel indifferent to the matter. Before he became pope, Eugenius was a member of an ascetic order, St. George in Alga; and even after his election supported the observant movement in Italian religious houses. His leading advocate in Basel and thereafter, the Dominican Juan de Torquemada, actively participated in the deputation on reform and the committee on simony. Like Torquemada, at least ten of the leading exponents of papal sovereignty in the years after Basel were Dominicans and all tended to follow his lead.[69]

Among the reasons for the Dominican role in formulating a reform theology centered in papal sovereignty, one first recalls that the order stood in a heritage of allegiance to the papacy which dated back at least to Thomas Aquinas. Furthermore, their independence rested more with popes than bishops which meant dependence on the papal largesse for privileges and preferments. A third reason is the long-standing conflict between the mendicants and the secular clergy. Whereas the monastic orders were deeply involved in reform during the investiture era of the 11th century and the mendicants likewise involved after their founding in the 13th, the observance movement among religious houses played an important part in the conciliar era of the 15th. Now the issue shifted to how, if at all, reforming councils could impose renovations from the outside.[70]

Prompted by such impulses, Torquemada and the Dominicans helped fashion a distinct papal reform theology and sustain it into the 16th century.[71] This reform program had two major themes. On the negative side, a pope was

[69] Jeffrey Mirus, "On the Deposition of the Pope for Heresy," *Archivum Historiae Pontificiae* 13 (1979): 231-248. Mirus, who offers a thorough treatment of the papal counter-attack against Basel which began in the 1430's, thought it continued up to the Fifth Lateran Council of 1512, but Thomas M. Izbicki, "Papalist Reaction to the Council of Constance: Juan de Torquemada to the Present," in *Friars and Jurists,* pp. 81-94 (originally in *Church History* 55 [1986]: 7-20), extends the development beyond the 16th century, especially through the influential figure of Robert Bellarmine.

[70] For a general survey see Kaspar Elm, "Introduction" in Elm, *Reformbemühungen;* and for Basel see Dieter Mertens, "Reformkonzilien und Ordensreform im 15. Jahrhundert," ibid., pp. 431-458; and idem, "Monastische Reformbewegungen des 15. Jahrhunderts: Ideen-Ziele-Resultate," in Hlavácek and Patschovsky, *Reform von Kirche und Reich,* pp. 7-28. See also Helmrath, *Das Basler Konzil,* pp. 129-132; idem, "Reform als Thema," pp. 131-146; Stieber, *Pope Eugenius IV,* pp. 92-113; and for a particular case of reform, see Michael Bailey, "Abstinence and Reform at the Council of Basel: Johannes Nider's *De abstinencia esus carnium,*" *Medieval Studies* 59 (1997): 229-235.

[71] See Torquemada's interventions on behalf of papal rights in Basel, e.g., *Utrum in omni lege licita,* Mansi 30.550-590; *Contra avisamentum quoddam Basiliensium quod non licet appellare a concilio ad papam,* Mansi 30.1074-1093; *Responsio in blasphemam et sacrilegam invectivam,* Mansi 31.69-75; see also Mansi 30.31, 109, 1060-1071. On Torquemada's life and thought, see Thomas M. Izbicki, *Protector of the Faith: Cardinal Johannes de Turrecremata and the Defense of the Institutional Church* (Washington, D. C., 1981). See also *Juan de Torquemada: Disputation on the Authority of Pope and Council,* intro. and trans. idem (Oxford, 1988), which presents a revealing debate between the Dominican and Cesarini arranged by Pope Eugenius at Ferrara.

immune from a council's decrees, including simony, since it lacked the power to impose on a superior. Yet, popes also affirmed the importance of reform; but, having limited the extent to which reform could bind the papacy, they placed the stress on personal and local reforms rather than reforms of the Holy See or the church as a whole.[72]

In the complexities of competing interests during the 15th century, this may be all the popes thought they could expect.[73] As Christendom, the *unitas Christiana,* gave way to princely states, new circumstances demanded new alliances with the princes, who eventually were persuaded that cooperation with Rome was in their best interest. The Concordant of Vienna in 1448 culminated years of negotiation and allowed Emperor Frederick III to retain significant control over ecclesiastical appointments. In return it allowed the papacy at long last to collect the annates, and—beyond this—to maintain a substantial grip on the system of benefices.[74] To play the prince, however, popes had to exploit the revenues of the Papal States and develop new "spiritual resources" such as the indulgence, a practice which became the focal point for Luther's attack in 1517.

While critics often charge that Basel either failed to carry out a wholistic reform program or lacked the spiritual dynamic to do so, the Reformation in Germany had both. Still the issue was not resolved, only exacerbated, in large measure because Luther's primary concerns were the nature of the gospel, justification, and the sacraments, subjects which were not high on Basel's agenda.[75] The same cannot be said for ecclesiology; and here the dialogue may have proved interesting, perhaps fruitful, had not the subject appeared settled when Luther was interviewed by Thomas de Vio, Cardinal Cajetan, the leading Dominican theologian of his day, in 1518, and debated John Eck at Leipzig in 1519.[76]

Can Ladner's "idea of reform," so brilliant in definition and description of its early history, still do service for this story of papal-conciliar conflict and its late medieval context? Popes had often led reform, but at Basel the council assumed this role, while the papal party considered reform councils as dangerous

72 Helmrath, "Reform als Thema," pp. 149-150. Alberto Melloni, "L'Istituzione e la Cristianità: Aspetti dell'ecclesiologia latina nel retrotterra delle discussioni del Concilio di Ferrara-Firenze," in Alberigo, *Christian Unity,* pp. 471-489, aptly contrasts this "microcosmic reform" with the "macrocosmic reform" envisioned by Gerson, Cusanus, and Basel.

73 Helmrath, "Reform als Thema," p. 150. John Nider thought that total reform had little or no chance but still held out hopes for partial reforms (ibid.).

74 A good general survey is J. A. F. Thomson, *Popes and Princes, 1417-1517: Politics and Polity in the Late Medieval Church* (London, 1980). See also Stump, "The Reform of Papal Taxation," pp. 104-105.

75 Helmrath, *Das Basler Konzil,* p. 352.

76 See Ulrich Horst, *Zwischen Konziliarismus und Reformation: Studien zur Ekklesiologie im Dominikanerorden* (Rom, 1985), esp. chs. 1 and 13 on Cajetan and ch. 4 on Sylvester Prierias; and Thomas M. Izbicki, "Cajetan's Attack on Parallels between Church and State," *Christianesimo nella storia* (in press), with further literature.

experiments or emergency measures. Furthermore, popes had rallied the church to the reform idea with the cry of simony during the investiture controversy, but what they had applied to the proper relationship between *regnum* and *sacerdotium* they now hesitated to apply to the relationship between pope and church. Barbara Hallman's work on the Italian cardinals suggests that by the 16th century the papacy had come to regard itself as incapable of simony, part of a larger trend toward distancing itself from all regulation based on the old Gregorian moral agenda.[77]

To account for the crisis of the reform idea, Ladner resorted to the received tradition of his time and heritage. The major factor in the demise of medieval civilization, he thought, was declining confidence in the divine order brought about especially by the rise of the *via moderna* with its emphasis on God's unpredictability. Given the corrective scholarship of Ozment, Oberman and others, this view has now become far less certain, if not untenable.[78]

These scholars reflect a growing discomfort with the picture of the late Middle Ages as an age of crisis. Although no new interpretation has yet emerged with the force of Huizinga or Ladner himself, we can make two observations from this brief study which, while not new, deserve emphasis as foundational for interpreting late medieval reform.

First, despite their quarrels with the papacy, the "reform councils" of the 15th century were dedicated to an institutional polity which—as Ladner demonstrated—reflected principles formulated by the papacy since at least Gregory VII in the 11th century. Second, while its role as the undoubted head of the ecclesial institution remained undiminished even after a long and disastrous Schism, the papacy was no longer the subject but the object of reform. These two considerations in a dramatically changing context put the significant reforming impulses of Constance and Basel into a contradiction which the reformers were unable to overcome.

Similarly, one also senses a contradiction which Ladner's great interpretive design cannot sustain. Nevertheless, we can still apply the term "crisis," in its strict sense of a culmination of conflicting positions or ideologies, to the annates controversy. What is remarkable about this collision of ideas and interests is a subtle, but evident, shift in the perception of the reform ideal. The Renaissance popes surrendered their leadership of reform, once thought to guarantee the *libertas* of the church in the world, in order to preserve the *libertas* of the papacy in the church.

77 See Hallman, *Italian Cardinals*.

78 See notes 5 and 6 above, and Oberman's early work on nominalism, *The Harvest of Medieval Theology* (Cambridge, Massachusetts, 1963; 3rd ed. Durham, North Carolina, 1983). Francis Oakley, "The Absolute and Ordained Power of God in Sixteenth- and Seventeenth-Century Theology," *Journal of the History of Ideas* 59 (1998): 437-461, esp. pp. 444-449, gives a succinct summary.

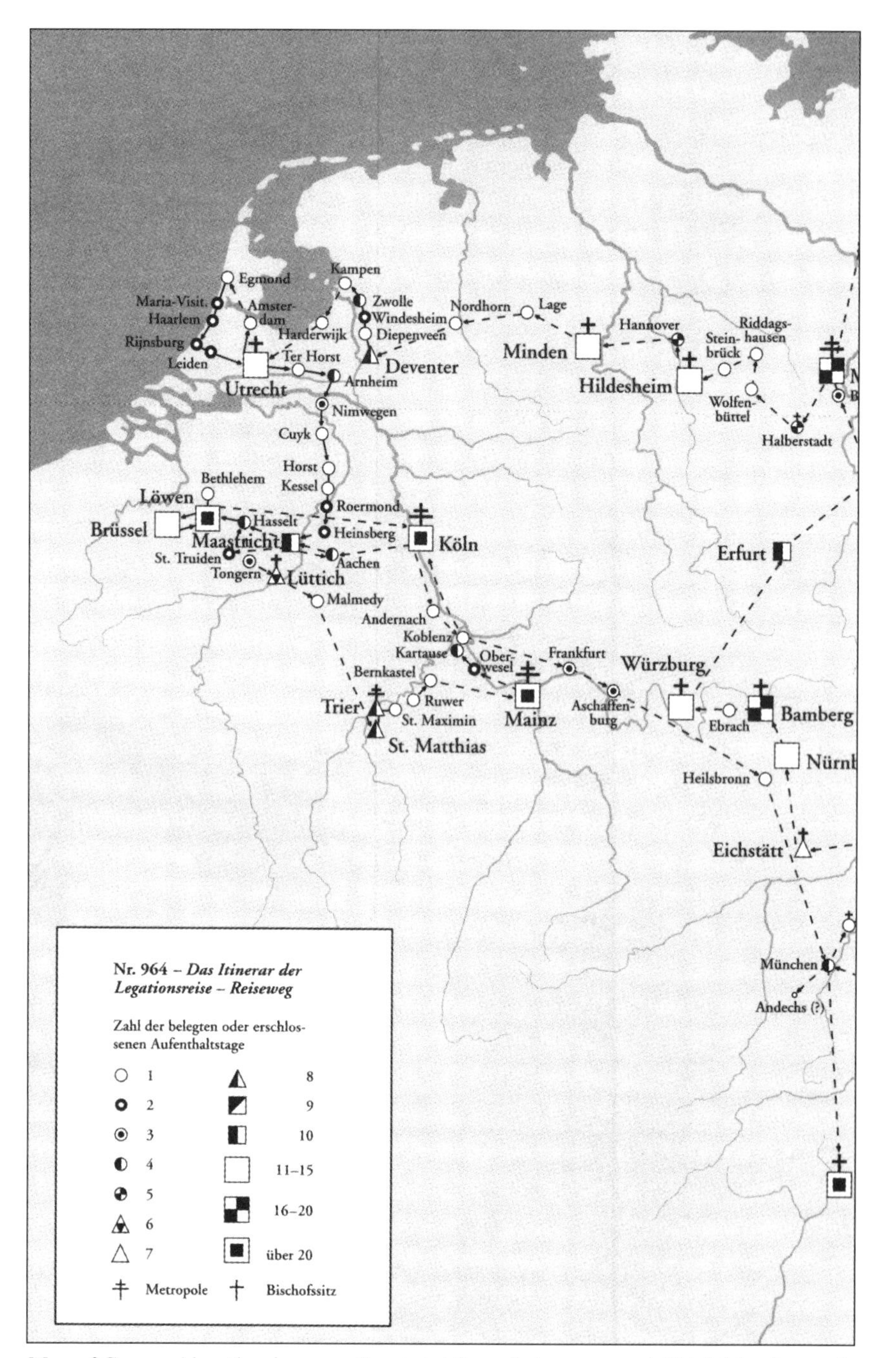

Map of Cusanus' legation journey; Reprinted from Acta cusana, ed. Erich Meuthen and

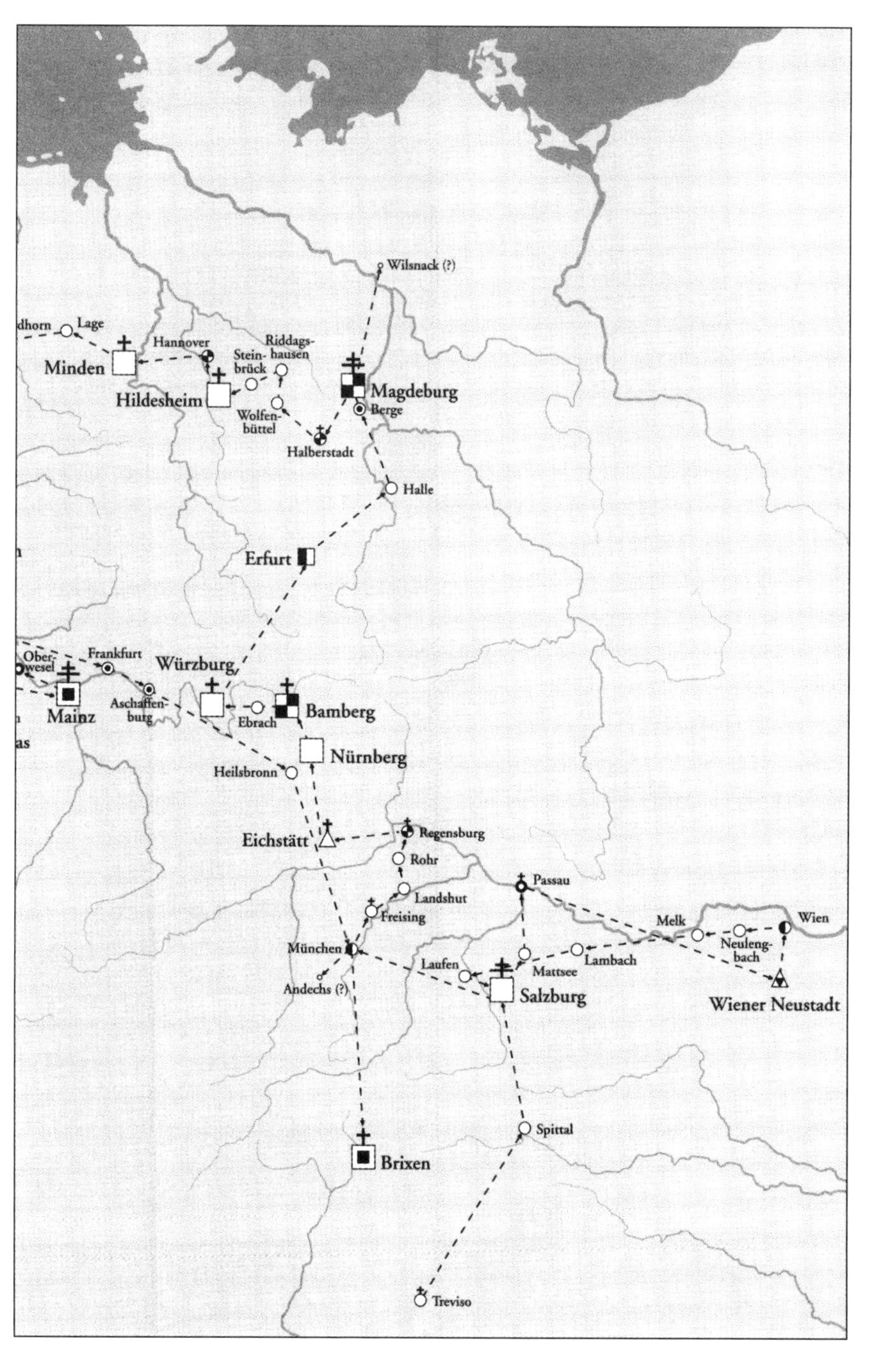

Hermann Hallauer, 1/3 (Hamburg, 1996) with the permission of Felix Meiner Verlag.

THE GERMAN CHURCH SHORTLY BEFORE THE REFORMATION: NICOLAUS CUSANUS AND THE VENERATION OF THE BLEEDING HOSTS AT WILSNACK

Morimichi Watanabe

Preface

Why the Reformation started not in other European countries but in Germany is a complicated question which is still worth pondering. According to Bernd Moeller, the famous German historian of the Reformation, Germany in the Middle Ages was an "especially medieval" country.[1] If he implies that the Reformation began not in less medieval countries but in a more medieval country called Germany, his logic must be examined with great care. In his famous article, entitled "The Essence of Late Medieval Germany," Heinrich Heimpel, one of the most famous German medievalists, characterized Germany as a "particularly medieval country."[2] Apparently, Moeller followed Heimpel's argument. But how do their interpretations relate to the beginnings and nature of the Reformation?

The purpose of this article is to examine reaction to and handling of the problem of the veneration of the bleeding hosts at Wilsnack in the archdiocese of Magdeburg by Nicolaus Cusanus (1401-1464), who went to Germany and the Low Countries from 1451 to 1452 to dispense the Jubilee indulgence and to reform the churches and monasteries in the German territories on orders from Pope Nicholas V (1447-1455). Through Cusanus we shall be able to understand better what the general and spiritual condition of the late medieval German churches was some sixty years before the Reformation and what some of the important issues were for them at that time.

I. Cusanus' Legation

Although Cusanus supported the theory of conciliar supremacy over the pope in the *De concordantia catholica,* which he submitted in 1433 or 1434 to the Council of Basel (1431-1449) as Ulrich von Manderscheid's counsel, he moved from the conciliar majority to the papal minority of the council in 1437 as the question of where to hold a reunion council of the Roman and Greek churches split the council into two parties.[3] Thereafter, he went to

1 Bernd Moeller, "Frömmigkeit in Deutschland um 1500," *Archiv für Reformationsgeschichte* 56 (1965): 29-30.

2 Hermann Heimpel, "Das Wesen des deutschen Spätmittelalter," *Archiv für Kulturgeschichte* 35 (1953): 38.

3 As good, standard studies of Cusanus' life and thought, see Edmond Vansteenberghe, *Le cardinal Nicolas de Cues (1401-1464): L'action - la pensée* (Paris, 1920; reprint Frankfurt am Main, 1963); Erich Meuthen, *Nikolaus von Kues 1401-1464: Skizze einer Biographie*, 7th ed. (Münster, 1992). On his *De concordantia catholica*, see Paul E. Sigmund, *Nicholas of Cusa and Medieval Political Thought* (Cambridge, Massachusetts, 1963); Morimichi Watanabe, *The Political Ideas of Nicholas of Cusa with Special Reference to his De concordantia catholica* (Geneva, 1963); Claudia Lücking-Michel, *Konkordanz und Konsens: Zur Gesellschaftstheorie in der Schrift 'De concordantia catholica' des Nikolaus von Kues* (Würzburg, 1994).

Constantinople as one of the delegates of Pope Eugenius IV (1431-1447), and in the 1440s made serious efforts at imperial and regional diets to persuade German princes, who had taken a neutral position in the conflict between the pope and the council, to return to the papal camp. As a result, his friend Aeneas Sylvius Piccolomini, who later became Pope Pius II (1459-1464), called him the "Hercules of the Eugenians."

Although Pope Eugenius IV named Cusanus a cardinal *in petto* probably on December 16, 1446, it was on December 28, 1448, that Nicholas V elevated him to the cardinalate, announcing this publicly on January 3, 1449. One year later, on March 23, 1450, the pope appointed Cusanus bishop of Brixen (Bressanone) in the Tyrol. The same year he sent Cusanus to the German lands as papal legate, not only to proclaim and distribute indulgences for the Jubilee year of 1450 but also to reform churches and monasteries in the area. At a time when Jakob von Sierk, archbishop of Trier, went to Rome in 1450 accompanied by 140 knights,[4] Cusanus left Rome on December 31, 1450 and started his wintery journey modestly on a mule, accompanied by about thirty co-travelers, including the Scotsman Thomas Livingston.[5] His great journey, which lasted 15 months from January 1451 to April 1452 and which extended about 2,800 miles from Rome to Brixen, can be called, as Josef Koch stated, the "peak in Cusanus' life."[6] In a recent lecture, Erich Meuthen, the foremost authority on Cusanus' legation journey, concluded that "seen from its impact and from his contemporaries' memories, the journey has always been regarded as one of the great events in the history of Germany."[7]

From Rome, Cusanus and his party reached Spittal not by way of Verona and Brixen, as was believed in the past, but, according to a recent discovery, via Treviso and across the Alps.[8] After visiting the Austrian towns such as Salzburg, Wiener Neustadt and Vienna, they entered Germany where, moving

[4] Ludwig Pastor, *The History of the Popes,* ed. Frederick Ignatius Antrobus, 7th ed., 36 vols. (London, 1949), 1-2.91.

[5] Josef Koch, *Der deutsche Kardinal in deutschen Landen: Die Legationsreise des Nikolaus von Kues (1451/52)* (Trier, 1964), p. 11. Pastor says in his *The History of the Popes*, 1-2.109, that Cusanus was accompanied "only by a few Romans." On Thomas Livingston, see Morimichi Watanabe, "Nikolaus von Kues - Richard Fleming - Thomas Livingston," *Mitteilungen und Forschungsbeiträge der Cusanus-Gesellschaft* 6 (1967): 175-177; idem, "Thomas Livingston," *American Cusanus Society Newsletter* 10/2 (1993): 6-8. Livingston was a member of Cusanus' party from the beginning to the end of December 1451; see *Acta Cusana: Quellen zur Lebensgeschichte des Nikolaus von Kues* [hereafter *Acta Cusana*], ed. Erich Meuthen (Hamburg, 1996), p. 669, no. 963.

[6] Koch, *Der deutsche Kardinal*, p. 3.

[7] Erich Meuthen, *Nikolaus von Kues: Profile einer geschichtlichen Persönlichkeit* (Trierer Cusanus Lecture, Heft 1; Trier, 1994), p. 15.

[8] Erich Meuthen, "Das Itinerar der deutschen Legationsreise des Nikolaus von Kues 1451/1452," in *Papstgeschichte und Landesgeschichte: Festschrift für Hermann Jacobs zum 65. Geburtstag*, ed. Joachim Dalhaus et al. (Köln, 1995), p. 476.

northward from Munich, they visited many historic towns, such as Freising, Regensburg, Nuremberg, Bamberg, Würzburg, Erfurt, and Halle, and then reached Magdeburg. Turning westward at Magdeburg, the party arrived at Minden on July 30, 1451, after traversing the area between the Elbe and the Weser rivers.

In the Low Countries the party went on to visit such places as Deventer, Windesheim, Zwolle, and Utrecht. Thereafter it came to Amsterdam, Leiden, Utrecht, and Roermond. Coming to the area between Belgium and Germany, it visited Maastricht, Aachen, Liège, Malmedy, Trier, Bernkastel-Kues, and Mainz. Like a football kicked around back and forth, the party turned around to go to Koblenz, Cologne, Aachen, Leuven, Brussels, Frankfurt am Main, and Aschaffenburg. It was on April 7, two days before Easter, in 1452 that the party reached Brixen.[9]

During this long reforming legation to the German territories, Cusanus held and presided over provincial synods at Salzburg, Magdeburg, Mainz and Cologne, which were the sees of the archbishops, and held a diocesan synod at Bamberg. The number of churches and monasteries which he visited and reformed between a few days and two weeks each amounted to about 80. In many places, he also delivered sermons either in Latin or in German, 51 of which have been preserved.[10] It is clear, as Meuthen has pointed out, that the whole itinerary was arranged for the purpose of the reform and reconstruction of the German church.[11] Forty years after the end of the journey Johannes Trithemius (1462-1516), the famous Benedictine abbot of Sponheim, wrote, "Nicholas of Cusa appeared in Germany as an angel of light and peace, amidst darkness and confusion, restored the unity of the Church, strengthened the authority of her Supreme Head, and sowed a precious seed of new life."[12]

Trithemius' remarks laid the foundation for very optimistic appraisals of the legation which prevailed for many years. But recent studies have revealed considerable difficulties and resistance which Cusanus experienced as he tried to

9 There are many studies of Cusanus' legation published since the nineteenth century. A recent, important one, in addition to the lectures cited in nn. 6 and 7 and a study in n. 8, is Erich Meuthen, "Die deutsche Legationsreise von Nikolaus von Kues 1451/52," in *Lebenslehren und Weltentwürfe* (Göttingen, 1989), pp. 421-499.

10 Donald Sullivan, "Cusanus and Pastoral Renewal: The Reform of Popular Religion in the Germanies," in *Nicholas of Cusa on Christ and the Church: Essays in Memory of Chandler McCuskey Brooks for the American Cusanus Society,* ed. Gerald Christianson and Thomas M. Izbicki (Leiden, 1996), pp. 167-175 at pp. 169-170. In his *Praefatio generalis* in *Nicolai de Cusa opera omnia*, 19 vols. (Hamburg, 1932-), 16:xlix-l: *Sermones 1 (1430-1441)*, Rudolf Haubst lists 46 extant Latin sermons which Cusanus delivered on the legation.

11 Erich Meuthen, "Die Synode im Kirchenverständnis des Nikolaus von Kues," in *Stadt, Kultur, Politik - Beiträge zur Geschichte Bayerns und des Katholizismus: Festschrift zum 65. Geburtstag von Dieter Albrecht* (Kallmünz, 1992), p. 17.

12 See Donald Sullivan, "Nicholas of Cusa as Reformer: The Papal Legation to the Germanies, 1451-1452," *Medieval Studies* 36 (1974): 383.

accomplish his reform mission.[13] During the Provincial Synod of Cologne, for example, a Franciscan friar attempted to kill him by poison.[14] One of the reasons for the existence and rise of anti-Cusanus attitude was the perception that, although Cusanus once tried to limit the powers of the pope by championing the supremacy of the council over the pope, he became a "traitor" by later joining the papal camp. Furthermore, at a time when a German cardinal was regarded as an extraordinarily rare phenomenon, like a white crow, it was deemed anti-German for Cusanus, a German-born cardinal, to attempt to reform German churches and monasteries and to distribute indulgences on orders from the pope. This kind of critical attitude towards Cusanus among the Germans was clearly manifested in Johannes Kymeus' *Des Bapsts Herald wider die Deutschen*, which was published in 1538.[15]

It was found out several years ago that at the Provincial Synod of Salzburg, which was convened as the first synod on Cusanus' legation, he presented a comprehensive plan for ecclesiastical reform. Although it is not signed by him, it is certain, judging from its contents, that the document was a declaration issued at the beginning of the legation by Cusanus who was very anxious to accomplish the reform of the German church. This very detailed plan, which was rejected by the Synod, seems to have remained unknown until recently in the library of Saint Peter's monastery in Salzburg.[16] As is well known, Cusanus wrote the *Reformatio generalis* in 1459, after moving to Rome under Pope Pius II.[17] It is clear that both during and after the legation, the reform of the Church was one of the most important concerns for Cusanus.

[13] See, for example, Koch, *Der deutsche Kardinal*, p. 14; Meuthen, *Nikolaus von Kues*, pp. 88-90; Sullivan, "Nicholas of Cusa as Reformer," pp. 404, 418 n. 116.

[14] Meuthen, *Nikolaus von Kues*, p. 89. The mendicant orders, both Franciscan and Dominican, which were directly subordinate to the pope, took Cusanus' attempts to reform them as interference with their internal affairs and often appealed to the pope during Cusanus' legation.

[15] Johannes Kymeus, *Des Babsts Hercules wider die Deutschen, Wittenberg 1538*, ed. Ottokar Menzel (Cusanus-Studien VI, Sitzungsberichte der Heidelberger Akademie der Wissenschaften, Philosophisch-historische Klasse, Jhrg. 1940/41, 6. Abh.; Heidelberg, 1941).

[16] Concerning the description and appraisal of this manuscript (HsA 203 f. 51r-59r) which was found in the monastery of Saint Peter in Salzburg, see Meuthen, *Die Synode*, pp. 17-22; idem, "Nikolaus von Kues und die deutsche Kirche am Vorabend der Reformation," in *Nikolai von Kues, Kirche und Respublica Christiana: Konkordanz, Repräsentanz und Konsens* (Mitteilungen und Forschungsbeiträge der Cusanus-Gesellschaft, 21; Trier, 1994), pp. 56-77.

[17] The text of the *Reformatio generalis* is found in Stephan Ehses, "Der Reformentwurf des Kardinals Nikolaus Cusanus," *Historisches Jahrbuch* 32 (1911): 281-299. An introduction and an English translation can be found in Morimichi Watanabe and Thomas M. Izbicki, "Nicholas of Cusa: A General Reform of the Church," in *Nicholas of Cusa on Christ and the Church*, pp. 175-202.

II. The Veneration of the Bleeding Hosts at Wilsnack

Because it is impossible, in a short article, to discuss the significance of many events that occurred during Cusanus' 456-day-long journey, we shall focus our attention especially on a controversial phenomenon, very well known at that time, but hardly remembered at present: the veneration of the bleeding hosts at a Saxon village called Wilsnack. What is its significance? How did it happen? On August 16, 1383, ten villages in the diocese of Havelberg within the archdiocese of Magdeburg, including Wilsnack, were burnt down by the noble Heinrich von Bülow and his followers. Heinrich had complaints against the bishop of Havelberg. A few days later, summoned by the repeated voice of an angel from nearby Gross Lüben, where he had spent the nights, the priest of the village church in Wilsnack, Johannes Kabuz (Cahlbuez, Calbuz) (d. 1412), began to assert that the three hosts on the altar not only remained undestroyed but had drops of blood in the center.[18] In the Prignitz region, where Wilsnack was located and where the natural religions of the Slavs were still strong, there had been pilgrim sites, such as Marienfliess near Stepenit (since 1231), St. Annenkirche in Alt-Krüssow, and Beelitz (1247).[19] But Wilsnack was something new; and it quickly began to draw pilgrims not only from northern Germany, but also from other European countries.

When informed about the news, Bishop Dietrich II (1370-1385) of Havelberg visited Wilsnack and confirmed the miracle. By 1384 Pope Urban VI (1378-1389) had granted the right to issue indulgences to those who visited Wilsnack.[20] Between 1384 and 1401 the construction of the mighty "Wunderblutkirche" (Wondrous-Blood Church) of Saint Nicholas was carried out by Bishops Dietrich II and Johannes II Wöpelitz (1385-1401) of Havelberg.[21]

[18] Since the sixteenth century, many studies on the veneration of the bleeding hosts at Wilsnack have been published. Some important recent studies to be mentioned are: Ludger Meier, "Wilsnack als Spiegel deutscher Vorreformation," *Zeitschrift für Religions- und Geistesgeschichte* 3 (1951): 53-69; Otto-Friedrich Gandert, "Das Heilige Blut von Wilsnack und seine Pilgerzeichen," in *Brandenburgische Jahrhunderte: Festgabe Johannes Schultze* (Berlin, 1971), pp. 72-90; Hartmut Boockmann, "Der Streit um das Wilsnacker Blut: Zur Situation des deutschen Klerus in der Mitte des 15. Jahrhunderts," *Zeitschrift für Historische Forschung* 9 (1982): 385-408; Charles Zika, "Hosts, Processions and Pilgrimages: Controlling the Sacred in Fifteenth-Century Germany," *Past and Present* 118 (1983): 24-64 at pp. 48-59. The oldest collection of important published sources is in Matteus Ludecus, *Historia von der Erfindung, Wunderwerken und Zerstörung des vermeinten heiligen Bluts zur Wilsnagk* (Wittenberg, 1586); and one of the most detailed, important old studies is Ernest Breest, "Das Wunderblut von Wilsnack, 1383-1552," *Märkische Forschungen* 16 (1881): 133-301.

[19] Ulrich Woronowicz, *Ev. Kirche St. Nikolai Bad Wilsnack* (Das Christliche Denkmal, Heft 92; Regensburg, 1994), p. 4.

[20] Meier, "Wilsnack als Spiegel," p. 54; Boockmann, "Der Streit um das Wilsnacker Blut," p. 389; Zika, "Hosts, Processions and Pilgrimages," p. 50.

[21] Rita Buchholz and Klaus-Dieter Gralow, *De hystorie unde erfindinghe des hilligen Sacraments tho der wilsnagk* [Die Geschichte von der Erfindung des heiligen Sakraments zu Wilsnack] (Bad Wilsnack, 1992), p. [4].

The enormous amount of money that was needed for the reconstruction of the church was raised through the sale of indulgences. By 1395 Bishop Wöpelitz, whose statute still stands in the Cathedral (Dom St. Marien) of Havelberg, made the property and possessions of the church of Wilsnack so much part of the diocese of Havelberg that all income from indulgences flowed into the treasury of the diocese.[22]

It is clear that by the end of the fourteenth century Wilsnack was certainly well established as a site of pilgrimage for the veneration of the bleeding hosts. The worship of the blood of Christ is believed to have increased considerably in late medieval Europe.[23] In Germany alone, there were over 100 pilgrimage sites, the most famous of which included those in Andechs, Waldrün, and Augsburg.[24] It is out of the scope of this paper to discuss the religious and psychological reasons why so many pious lay folks visited these sites as pilgrims. The religious and political confusion since the beginning of the Great Schism (1378-1417) and the spread of fear and anxiety as a result of the decline of the Holy Roman Empire certainly contributed to it. It is also probable that the approach of the end of the century fostered fear in the minds of pious but simple people.[25] It can be said, however, that, as Ludger Meier argued in his perceptive article, the phenomenon of pilgrimage does have certain aspects which can be understood not from the rational points of view but only by those who actually participated in it.[26]

In the fifteenth century, Wilsnack experienced further development as a pilgrimage site. When Archbishop Sbinko of Prague noticed in 1405 that an increasing number of pilgrims went to Wilsnack from his archdiocese, he decided to establish an investigative commission to find out about the validity of this pilgrimage.[27] One of the members of the commission was Jan Hus (c.1370-1415). The results of the commission's investigation are found in a synodal decree published in 1405. It mandated all priests to preach and advise against going to Wilsnack as pilgrims.[28] The same year Hus' book *On the Blood of*

22 Bruno Hennig, "Kurfürst Friedrich und das Wunderblut Wilsnack," *Forschungen zur Brandenburgischen und Preusischen Geschichte* 19 (1906): 78-79.

23 Meier, "Wilsnack als Spiegel," p. 53; Zika, "Hosts, Processions and Pilgrimages," p. 49.

24 Boockmann, "Der Streit um das Wilsnacker Blut," p. 380; Zika, "Hosts, Processions and Pilgrimages," p. 49 n. 76.

25 On the fear of the end of a century, see Norman Cohn, *The Pursuit of the Millennium* (London, 1957).

26 Meier, "Wilsnack als Spiegel," pp. 65-69.

27 Peter Browe, *Die eucharistischen Wunder des Mittelalters* (Breslau, 1938), p. 168; Meier, "Wilsnack als Spiegel," pp. 54-55; Boockmann, "Der Streit um das Wilsnacker Blut," p. 391.

28 Browe, *Die eucharistischen Wunder*, pp. 168-169; J. Fliege, "Nikolaus von Kues und der Kampf gegen das Wilsnacker Wunderblut," in *Das Buch als Quelle historischer Forschung: Fritz Juntke anlässlich seines 90. Geburtstages gewidmet*

Christ (De sanguine Christi), which clearly criticized the veneration of the bleeding hosts not only at Wilsnack but elsewhere, was published.[29] Despite criticisms from the archbishop, Hus, and others, the pilgrimage to Wilsnack further expanded and flourished. Not only did it draw pilgrims from Germany and Bohemia; but it also received them from Switzerland, Holland, Belgium, and the Scandinavian countries, thus making it one of the largest pilgrimage sites after Jerusalem, Rome, Santiago de Compostela and Aachen.[30]

Many inns sprang up in Wilsnack, such as Doppelter Adler, Goldener Adler, Löwe, Bär, Neuer Mann, Weisses Ross, Roter und Schwarzer Hahn, Weisse Gans, Ochsenkopf, Pflegel, Roter Ziegel, Windmühle und Hirsch.[31] Those who came from Berlin and its environment were on the "Heiliger Blutsweg" and reached Wilsnack via Tegel, Heiligensee, Flatow, Fehrbellin, Linum, Hakenberg, Garz, Wusterhausen, Kyritz, and Gross Leppin.[32] Those who came from Scandinavia left their ships at Lübeck whence, guided by a road sign that still stands today at Roekstrasse, they headed for Wilsnack. According to one study, the number of pilgrims is said to have reached 100,000 in a few warm months between spring and early autumn. On Saint Bartholomew's Day (August 24) the crowd was especially thick.[33]

But, between 1443 and 1453, Wilsnack became an object of heated debate mainly because of the activities of Heinrich Tocke (1390-1453). After studying theology at the University of Erfurt, Tocke became a professor of theology at the university in 1418 and a member of the cathedral chapter of Magdeburg by 1426. Because of his commoner origins and theological education, he belonged to a minority of the chapter that was critical of some church policies and practices. When he attended the Council of Basel between 1432 and 1437, he participated actively in the negotiations with the Hussites and may have met Cusanus. Although the exact year of authorship is not known, his book, *Rapularius*, written in the middle of the fifteenth century, reflects, like Cusanus' *De concordantia catholica*, the author's deep learning.[34]

(Leipzig, 1977), p. 63; Zika, "Hosts, Processions and Pilgrimages," p. 50.

29 Meier, "Wilsnack als Spiegel," p. 55; Boockmann, "Der Streit um das Wilsnacker Blut," p. 387.

30 Browe, *Die eucharistischen Wunder*, p. 168; Boockmann, "Der Streit um das Wilsnacker Blut," p. 385.

31 Rita Buchholz and Klaus-Dieter Gralow, *Zur Geschichte der Wilsnacker Wallfahrt unter besonderer Berücksichtigung der Pilgerzeichen* (Bad Wilsnack, 1992), p. 9.

32 Ibid., p. 16.

33 Ibid., p. 9.

34 Paul Lehmann, "Aus dem Rapularius des Hinricus Token," in idem, *Erforschung des Mittelalters*, 5 vols. (Stuttgart, 1959-1962), 4.187-205. For Tocke's other writings, see Hildegrund Hölzl, "Toke, Heinrich," in *Die deutsche Literature des Mittelalters: Verfasserlexikon*, 2nd ed., 9 vols. (Berlin, 1978-1995), 9.964-971.

To Tocke, the basic questions about Wilsnack were whether the hosts really had blood drops and, if they did, how they could be shown to be Christ's blood. In the famous speech which Tocke delivered at the Provincial Synod of Magdeburg in 1451, he declared, in the presence of Cusanus, that when he examined the three hosts carefully in Wilsnack on July 10, 1443, there were no red spots on the hosts, and that even if he had found them, he would not have been able to assert that they belonged to Jesus Christ.[35] Accordingly, he went on to say that the advice given to the laity to go to Wilsnack as pilgrims is based on the clergy's deception and superstition, as well as being a clever method of robbing the foreigners of money by distributing indulgences.[36] It should be remembered that the theological faculties of the Universities of Prague, Erfurt, and Leipzig took a similar position about this question.[37]

It is important to realize that behind the opinions of the theologian-reformer Tocke and the theological faculties, there was the position of the Dominican and Franciscan orders about the veneration of the bleeding hosts at Wilsnack. The Dominicans essentially took a negative attitude toward Wilsnack, basing their position on the *Summa Theologiae*, 3a, 54, 2-3 of Thomas Aquinas.[38] They concluded that, since Christ ascended to heaven with his sparkling body and full blood, it is theologically impossible to support the veneration of Christ's blood on earth. In contrast, on the strength of the theories of Bonaventure (1217/21-1274) and Johannes Duns Scotus (1265/66-1308), the Franciscans took the position that since part of Christ's blood remained on earth separate from the *unio hypostatica*, the veneration of the bleeding hosts can be affirmed.[39] Although there were few Dominicans who expressed their views on the Wilsnack affair, many Franciscans, such as Matthias Döring, Johannes Kannemann, Johannes Brewer, and Giovanni Capistrano, defended the pilgrimage to Wilsnack. Döring became famous as an opponent of Tocke; Kannemann was

35 Boockmann, "Der Streit um das Wilsnacker Blut," pp. 393-394; Zika, "Hosts, Processions and Pilgrimages," p. 55. For E. Breest's German translation of Tocke's synodal speech, see *Blättern für Handel, Gewerbe und soziales Leben* (Magdeburg, 1882), pp. 167f, 174-180.

36 Lehmann, "Aus dem Rapularius," p. 55.

37 Boockmann, "Der Streit um das Wilsnacker Blut," pp. 401-402. On the standpoints of the theological faculties, see Zika, "Hosts, Processions and Pilgrimages," p. 50; Rudolf Damerau, *Das Gutachten der Theologischen Fakultät Erfurt 1452 über 'Das heilige Blut von Wilsnak'* (Marburg, 1976).

38 On Thomas Aquinas's position, see *Thomae Aquinatis Opera Omnia* vol. 5 (Paris, 1872) pp. 278-280 [Art. 2: *Utrum Christi corpus resurrexit integrum,* pp. 278-279; Art. 3: *Utrum Christi corpus resurrexit gloriosum*, pp. 279-280]. See also Meier, "Wilsnack als Spiegel," pp. 61-62; Zika, "Hosts, Processions and Pilgrimages," pp. 52-53.

39 Boockmann, "Der Streit um das Wilsnacker Blut," p. 398; Zika, "Hosts, Processions and Pilgrimages," p. 50.

a theology professor at Erfurt;[40] and Capistrano was widely known as one of the greatest preachers of the fifteenth century.[41]

Another aspect of the Wilsnack controversy that must be taken into consideration is the political and ecclesiastical conditions existing in the province at that time. It is quite easy to understand that Bishop Konrad von Lintorff of Havelberg (1427-1450) was, as a financial beneficiary of the pilgrimage, a supporter and protector of Wilsnack. But Archbishop Friedrich von Beichlingen of Magdeburg, whose jurisdiction included the diocese of Havelberg, was reform-minded and critical of the pilgrimage to Wilsnack. Together with Tocke and other theology professors, he saw the demise of the pilgrimage as a first step towards church reform. On the other hand, the Elector of Brandenburg, Friedrich II (1440-1470), who ruled over the whole region as a secular head, was sympathetic to Wilsnack and on friendly terms with Bishop Konrad of Havelberg. In fact, Konrad was chaplain to the elector.[42] It seems also quite logical that Döring, a Franciscan, became advisor to the elector from 1443.[43] Archbishop Friedrich of Magdeburg, who was anxious to bring about church reform in his region, also was interested in controlling not only Bishop Konrad of Havelberg, who tried to be independent of him financially and politically on the strength of incomes from Wilsnack, but also the mendicant orders within his archdiocese, especially the Franciscan order. But to the Elector of Brandenburg, Archbishop Friedrich was the principal obstacle to the territorialization of the church under his domains.[44]

As stated above, in order to appreciate the significance of the Wilsnack affair, it is important to understand not only the movements of pilgrims, but also the development of theological debates and the struggle of political and ecclesiastical groups and forces. Furthermore, due attention must be paid to the reform movements within the monasteries that were spreading, as a result of the Council of Constance (1414-1418), in the Benedictine monasteries of Melk and Bursfeld and the Augustinian monastery of Windesheim.[45] The pilgrimage to

40 See Livario Oliger, "Johannes Kannemann, ein deutscher Franziskaner des 15. Jahrhunderts," *Franziskanische Studien* 5 (1918): 44-50; Ludger Meier, "Der Erfurter Franziskaner-theologe J. Bremer und der Streit um das Wilsnacker Wunderblut," in *Aus der Geisteswelt des Mittelalters: Festschrift M. Grabmann* (Münster, 1935), pp. 53-69.

41 Johannes Hofer, *Johannes von Capestrano* (Innsbruck, 1936).

42 Bruno Hennig, "Kurfürst Friedrich und das Wunderblut zu Wilsnack," *Forschungen zu Brandenburgischen und Preusischen Geschichte* 19 (1906): 83 n. 3.

43 On the elector, see Hennig, "Kurfürst Friedrich," pp. 73-104 (391-422). Also compare Boockmann, "Der Streit um das Wilsnacker Blut," p. 399; Zika, "Hosts, Processions and Pilgrimages," p. 51.

44 Zika, "Hosts, Processions and Pilgrimages," p. 52.

45 On Melk and Bursfeld, see Paulus Volk, *Urkunden zur Geschichte der Bursfelder Kongregation* (Bonn, 1951); Pius Engelbert, "Die Bursfelder Benediktinerkongregation und die spätmittelalterlichen Reformbewegungen," *Historisches Jahrbuch* 103 (1983): 35-55; Klaus Schreiner, "Benediktinische

Wilsnack is a good example showing clearly how religious practices could be affected by the double weight of church reform and territorial expansion.[46]

III. Cusanus and the Pilgrimage to Wilsnack

What kind of attitude then did Cusanus take toward Wilsnack? In 1446 Pope Eugenius IV approved in a bull the veneration of the bleeding hosts at Wilsnack; and the next pope, Nicholas V, declared in September 1447 that he supported his predecessor's decision. It is against this background that the problem of Cusanus' encounter with the Wilsnack affair must be considered. As has already been pointed out, Heinrich Tocke, in the famous speech at the Provincial Synod of Magdeburg, which had begun on June 18, 1451, argued clearly that the veneration of bleeding hosts at Wilsnack was a deception. How did Cusanus react to Tocke's assertion?

It was believed until recently that the same synod lasted till June 28, 1451, when Cusanus left for the next stop, Halberstadt, and that during his stay in Magdeburg Cusanus did not visit Wilsnack. But in a recent article, and then in *Acta Cusana,* Erich Meuthen, after noting the lack of any extant material or document about Cusanus between June 22 and June 24, pointed out that he found testimonies by two Dutch historians about Cusanus' visit to Wilsnack.[47] As Meuthen said, it is quite possible that Cusanus left Magdeburg on June 21 to go to Wilsnack, which was merely about 82 miles away down the Elbe river.[48] Cornelius von Zandvliet (d. ca. 1461), one of the two Dutch historians Meuthen cited, wrote in 1451 that Cusanus was in Wilsnack as papal legate.[49] Adriaan von Oudenbosch (d. ca. 1482), the other Dutch historian, also confirmed Cusanus' presence at Wilsnack.[50] But it is important to remember that the relationship between Archbishop Frederick of Magdeburg and Bishop Konrad of Havelberg was not really friendly. This is indicated by the fact that, in 1451, when the archbishop summoned all his suffragan bishops to the Provincial Synod of Magdeburg, Bishop Konrad sent only his ambassador and did not appear in person.[51] In fact, they would, as was stated earlier, excommunicate

Klosterreform als zeitgebundene Auslegung der Regel: Geistige, religiöse und soziale Erneuerung in spätmittelalterlichen Klöstern Süddeutschlands im Zeichen der Kastler, Melker und Bursfelder Reform," in *Beiträge zur westfälischen Kirchengeschichte* 86 (1986): 105-195. Windesheim is discussed in Wilhelm Kohl, "Die Windesheimer Kongregation," in *Reformbestrebungen und Observanzbestrebungen im spätmittelalterlichen Ordenswesen*, ed. Kaspar Elm (Berlin, 1989), pp. 83-106.

46 Zika, "Hosts, Processions and Pilgrimages," p. 52.

47 Meuthen, "Das Itinerar," pp. 484-485; *Acta Cusana*, 1/3.944-946, nos. 1401-1403.

48 Meuthen, "Das Itinerar," pp. 484-485.

49 *Acta Cusana*, 1/3.945, no. 1402.

50 Ibid., 1/3.945-946, no. 1403.

51 Gottfried Wentz, *Das Bistum Havelberg* (Der Germania Sacra, Erste Abt., Zweiter Band; Berlin, 1933), p. 54; *Acta Cusana*, 1/3.934, no. 1384.

each other in 1452. Did or could Cusanus visit Wilsnack in the diocese of Havelberg under these conditions without causing political and ecclesiastical repercussions? Although in all likelihood Cusanus was at Wilsnack in 1451, it would certainly be good to have more conclusive proof about his visit.

On June 25, 1451, probably after returning from Wilsnack, Cusanus issued seven decrees in Magdeburg,[52] and on June 26 and 28 one decree each;[53] but none of them had anything to do with the veneration of the bleeding hosts at Wilsnack. It was on July 5, shortly after arriving at the next stop, Halberstadt, that he issued a general decree prohibiting the veneration of bleeding hosts without, however, specifically mentioning Wilsnack. It is quite possible that as papal legate, he did not wish to contradict directly Pope Nicholas V's approval of Wilsnack in 1447. However, his decree was addressed to all archbishops, bishops, abbots, and other ecclesiastical officials in Germany, warning them that all those who exposed the bleeding hosts would be excommunicated, and that all territories where this practice continued would automatically incur interdict.[54] The reasons he mentioned were that, although the priests not only preached but also encouraged this practice because of the money it brought them, every occasion by which the unlettered are deceived must be removed.[55] It is quite clear that he was determined to carry out this decree, because he issued similar decrees in Hildesheim on July 12, in Minden on August 4, and in Mainz on November 20.[56]

Despite Cusanus' attempt to stop the pilgrimage to Wilsnack, it continued to expand and flourish. As a result, the archbishop of Magdeburg excommunicated the bishop of Havelberg on January 8, 1452 and placed Wilsnack under interdict. But, in turn, Bishop Konrad of Havelberg took the step of declaring the archbishop of Magdeburg excommunicated.[57] It is quite clear that the struggle that ensued between the two ecclesiastical heads was not

52 Ibid., 1/3.947-957, nos. 1409, 1410, 1412, 1414, 1415, 1417, 1418.

53 Ibid., 1/3.960-961, no. 1423; 962-963, No. 1428.

54 Hennig, "Kurfürst Friedrich," p. 101 (419); Meier, "Wilsnack als Spiegel," p. 51; Sullivan, "Nicholas of Cusa as Reformer," p. 403; idem, "Cusanus and Pastoral Renewal," p. 173; Meuthen, "Die deutsche Legationsreise," p. 486; *Acta Cusana*, 1/3.980-981, no. 1454. According to Koch, this decree was the thirteenth decree published by Cusanus on the legation; see *Nikolaus von Cues und seine Umwelt* (Cusanus-Texte IV, Briefe, Sitzungsberichte der Heidelberger Akademie der Wissenschaften, Philosophisch-historische Klasse, Jhrg. 1944/48, 2. Abh.; Heidelberg, 1942), pp. 112, 125.

55 Hennig, "Kurfürst Friedrich," p. 101; Sullivan, "Nicholas of Cusa as Reformer," pp. 403-404.

56 Fliege, "Nikolaus von Kues," p. 63; Meuthen, "Der deutsche Legationsreise," p. 486. Despite the fact that Cusanus was critical of the pilgrimage to Wilsnack and elsewhere, he made an exception for Andechs; see Zika, "Hosts, Processions and Pilgrimages," p. 61 n. 116.

57 Hennig, "Kurfürst Friedrich," p. 101; Meier, "Wilsnack als Spiegel," p. 58; Sullivan, "Nicholas of Cusa as Reformer," p. 404.

conducive to Cusanus' reform plans. In the meantime, the Elector Friedrich of Brandenburg went to Rome in 1453 to appeal to Pope Nicholas V; and Capistrano also sent a letter to the pope urging him to support Wilsnack. The pope issued on March 6, 1453 a decree in which he re-confirmed his decree of 1447, abrogated Cusanus' decree of July 5, 1451, lifted the excommunication of the archbishop of Magdeburg and the interdict placed on Magdeburg, and officially approved the continuation of the pilgrimage to Wilsnack.[58] Although Nicholas V and Cusanus were friends as humanists, the cardinal had no choice but to retreat in regard to the question of Wilsnack.

In the second half of the fifteenth century, Wilsnack reached its peak. According to some studies, it drew the largest number of pilgrims in Christendom.[59] But, after the Reformation, Martin Luther, in his "An Open Letter to the Christian Nobility of the German Nation," published in 1520, attacked Wilsnack, saying that the forest chapels and rustic churches to which the recent pilgrimages have been directed, such as Wilsnack, Sternberg, and Trier, must be utterly destroyed.[60] In 1552, Joachim Ellefeldt, the Protestant pastor, threw the hosts of Wilsnack into fire, thereby causing the pilgrimage to come to an end.[61] In 1906 a hot spring containing ferric-oxide was found by the town forester Zimmermann outside of Wilsnack. As a result, the name of the town was changed to Bad Wilsnack in 1929. But the church of Saint Nicholas, now a Protestant one, still stands in the middle of the town, which has a population of about 2,800.

Conclusion

During a legation that lasted one year and three months Nicolaus Cusanus observed directly the actual conditions in the German church shortly before the Reformation and tried to solve many problems. One of the most difficult was the veneration of the bleeding hosts in Wilsnack which had started about seventy years before. Despite critics like Heinrich Tocke and criticisms from the theological faculties of various universities, there was no sign that the cult would wane and decline. Its prosperity was based not only on the religious ignorance of especially medieval and uncultured people, but also on the manipulation and greed of some clergymen who took advantage of the psychological anxiety that existed among the simple, pious people. Furthermore, the problem was deeply related to a power struggle among the ecclesiastical and political leaders of the province who tried to expand their territorial and economic power and influence.

[58] Sullivan, "Nicholas of Cusa as Reformer," p. 404; Zika, "Hosts, Processions and Pilgrimages," p. 52.

[59] Hennig, "Kurfürst Friedrich," p. 102; Meier, "Wilsnack als Spiegel," p. 59.

[60] *D. Martin Luthers Werke* (Weimar, 1888), 6.447.

[61] Hennig, "Kurfürst Friedrich," p. 96; Meier, "Wilsnack als Spiegel," p. 61; Boockmann, "Der Streit um das Wilsnack Blut," p. 405; Zika, "Hosts, Processions and Pilgrimages," p. 50.

It is well known that ecclesiastical reform was widely recognized as necessary in the later Middle Ages and that, as a result, there were many reform movements within the churches and monasteries. It is clear that such developments and movements were strengthened by the conciliar movement that had started as a result of the Great Schism. For Cusanus, who participated in the Council of Basel as a supporter of the doctrine of conciliar supremacy but later switched to the pro-papal camp, the problem of ecclesiastical reform was one of the most important issues and tasks, as shown in his endeavors not only during his legation as papal legate, but also in the Tyrol after reaching Brixen[62] and in Orvieto and Rome towards the end of his life.[63]

But, like the reform proposals of other late medieval reformers, Cusanus' attempts to reform the church were essentially limited in nature and scope. Cusanus' legalism and inflexibility have often been mentioned as reasons for his failure as reformer. But reform did not mean anything really radical to him. It is quite clear that he tried to accomplish it within the existing framework of the medieval church. What he criticized and tried to correct within the church was degeneration or perversion, which was based on either lack of understanding the church's teachings or widespread superstition. As one commentator pointed out, on his legation Cusanus participated faithfully and diligently in the established practices and ceremonies of the church. The thirteen decrees he issued on the legation were almost all designed to effect a return to a rigorous but simple spirituality in harmony with the teachings of the church. "Cusanus remained firmly rooted in the conservative hierarchical tradition of medieval renewal."[64]

When this "restorative" reform attempt was not strongly supported or even was rejected by the pope, who was reluctant to carry on his own program strongly, Cusanus certainly was not able to become "a reformer before the Reformation."[65] The Reformation required a Martin Luther who, reluctant as he

62 On Cusanus' attempts to reform in the Tyrol, see Nikolaus Grass, *Cusanus und das Volkstum der Berge* (Innsbruck, 1972); Morimichi Watanabe, "Nicholas of Cusa and the Tyrolese Monasteries: Reform and Resistance," *History of Political Thought* 7 (Spring 1986): 53-72.

63 On Cusanus' reform at Orvieto, see Erich Meuthen, *Die letzten Jahre des Nikolaus von Kues: Biographische Untersuchungen nach neuern Quellen* (Köln, 1958), pp. 110-125, 249-300. Cusanus' attempt to reform the Roman curia is discussed in Morimichi Watanabe, "Nicholas of Cusa and the Reform of the Roman Curia," in *Humanity and Divinity in Renaissance and Reformation: Essays in Honor of Charles Trinkaus*, ed. John O'Malley, Thomas M. Izbicki and Gerald Christianson (Leiden, 1993), pp. 185-203; Watanabe and Izbicki, "Nicholas of Cusa: A General Reform," pp. 175-202.

64 Sullivan, "Cusanus and Pastoral Renewal," p. 174.

65 See Carl Ullmann, *Reformatoren vor der Reformation*, 2nd ed., 2 vols. (Gotha, 1866). The author has argued for the "restorative" nature of Cusanus' reform ideas in Watanabe, "Nicholas of Cusa and the Reform of the Roman Curia," pp. 201-203; idem, "Some Problems on the Study of Nicholas of Cusa as Church Reformer [in Japanese]," *Kuzanusu Kenkyu* [Cusanus Studies] 1 (1991): 32-50.

was at the beginning, began to go beyond the existing institutions of the church and criticized them strongly.

CONCILIARISM IN ENGLAND: ST. GERMAN, STARKEY AND THE MARSIGLIAN MYTH

Francis Oakley

Two centuries have yet to elapse since the English historian, Henry Hallam, writing in his *View of the State of Europe during the Middle Ages* about the scandalous spectacle of first two and then three rival claimants stubbornly competing for the papal office, interpreted the success of the Council of Constance in putting an end to the Schism by deposing the rival claimants as "a signal display of a new system . . . which I may venture to call the whig principle of the Catholic church." And the Constance superiority decree *Haec sancta synodus* (which provided the legal basis for such a deposing power by asserting the jurisdictional subordination under certain circumstances of pope to general council) and *Frequens* (which stipulated the assembly of such councils in the future at frequent and regular intervals) - those decrees he depicted as "the great pillars of that moderate theory with respect to papal authority which [not only] distinguished the Gallican church . . . [but] is embraced by almost all laymen and the major part of ecclesiastics on this side of the Alps."[1] Less than a century later, however, the conciliarist views, which Hallam had regarded as a live ecclesiological option to which most northern European Catholics in his own day subscribed, were not deemed worthy of having an individual entry devoted to them even in so comprehensive and learned a compilation as the *Catholic Encyclopedia* (1908). It is true that the subject was given some fleeting attention under the heading of "Gallicanism," but the author of that article was clearly confident that he was doing nothing other than expressing the prevailing sentiment of his day when he wrote:

> Stricken to death, as a free opinion, by the [First] Council of the Vatican, [theological] Gallicanism could survive only as a heresy; the Old Catholics have endeavoured to keep it alive under this form. Judged by the paucity of the adherents whom they have recruited - daily becoming fewer in Germany and Switzerland it seems very evident that the historical evolution of these ideas has reached its completion.[2]

What of course had happened, despite all the trials and tribulations endured by the papacy in the years supervening, was the dramatic rise to prominence of ultramontane sentiment in all the leading European nations. Evident already in the immediate aftermath of the French Revolution, given powerful voice in Josef De Maistre's contemptuous dismissal of conciliarist views (1819), it gathered strength and began to receive central direction during the crucial pontificate of Gregory XVI (1831-1846) and ended by triumphing over all opposition in 1870 with the First Vatican Council's solemn and historic definitions of the papal primacy and infallibility. In the wake of those definitions, the memory of the constitutionalist strand in Catholic ecclesiology was to fall victim for the better

1 Henry Hallam, *View of the State of Europe during the Middle Ages*, 3 vols. (London, 1901), 3.243, 245. The work was originally published in 1818.

2 A. Degart in *Catholic Encyclopedia*, 16 vols. (New York, 1914), 6.355, s.v. "Gallicanism."

part of a century to a (perhaps no more than half-conscious) ecclesiastical "politics of oblivion." Catholic theologians, that is to say, appear to have felt themselves left with no alternative but to bracket conciliar theory as a dead issue,[3] and Catholic historians with little choice but to align themselves with the doctrinally-conditioned historical viewpoint embedded long since in the controversialist works of such prominent papalists as Juan de Torquemada (d. 1468), writing in the era of the Council of Basel, Thomas de Vio, Cardinal Cajetan (d. 1534), writing on the eve of the Protestant Reformation, and Robert, Cardinal Bellarmine (d. 1621), writing in the aftermath of the Council of Trent.[4] Even in its inception, the historiographic tradition emerging from that rueful encounter was wracked by the internal tensions that the complex intersection of disparate interpretative criteria of historical, theological and canonistic provenance contrived to generate.[5] But such tensions notwithstanding, that historiographic tradition succeeded for long in framing the picture of the subject conveyed in our general histories, and not only those that were in some identifiable sense Catholic in their sympathies.[6]

Two features of that tradition stand out as particularly noteworthy. The first is the degree to which it contrived to identify the phase of conciliarist constitutionalism in the life of the Latin Church with the extraordinary circumstances characteristic of the ecclesiastical world during the first half of the

[3] Thus in the early 1960s Ladislas Örsy described conciliarism as "a false theory about the possessor of supreme authority in the Church" and as "a doctrine alien to the Catholic faith"; see the *New Catholic Encyclopedia*, 17 vols. (New York, 1967-1979), 4.111-113, s.v. "Conciliarism (Theology of)."

[4] See Thomas M. Izbicki, "Papalist Reactions to the Council of Constance: Juan de Torquemada to the Present," *Church History* 55 (1986): 7-20.

[5] The intrusion of theological and canonistic criteria (and the degree of contradiction, confusion, disingenuousness and disarray generated thereby) continues to be evident in the way in which the standard encyclopedias have treated the 15th century councils and the claims to legitimacy of the Avignonese and Pisan popes during the Schism, for which, see the discussion in Francis Oakley, *Council over Pope?: Towards a Provisional Ecclesiology* (New York, 1969), pp. 121-126. See esp. 125-126, as well as K.A. Fink, "Zur Beurteilung des Grossen Abendländischen Schismas," *Zeitschrift für Kirchengeschichte* 73 (1962): 335-337, for Angelo Mercati's 1947 revision of the official list of popes, which, for the first time, categorized the Pisan pontiffs as "antipopes." Although that shift (which ran counter to the direction of current historical scholarship) was presumably based on the unspecified "theological-canonical" criteria to which Mercati alluded, the revised list has now become the standard one - being reproduced, for instance, in the *Encyclopedia Britannica*.

[6] And in some residual measure continues to do so. Thus, for example, and less than a quarter of a century ago, Paul Ourliac could still depict the year 1440 as the great turning-point after which theologians turned energetically to the "constructive task" of vindicating the papal monarchy; see Paul Ourliac and Henri Gilles, "Les discordances d'une epoque," in *Histoire du droit et des institutions de l'Eglise en Occident*, ed. Gabriel le Bras, 18 vols. (Paris, 1956-1984), 12, pt. 1, p. 51; cf. Paul Ourliac, "La victoire de la papauté," in *Historie de l'Eglise*, ed. Augustin Fliche and Victor Martin, 26 vols. (Paris, 1934-1964), 14.285.

fifteenth century. The conciliar movement it portrayed as a temporary (if understandable) aberration spawned by the crisis and confusion of the Great Schism and brought to an end in the 1440s by Eugenius IV's final triumph over the conciliarist onslaught at the Council of Basel (1431-1449). Pius II's bull *Execrabilis,* which condemned appeals from the papal judgment to that of a future general council, was viewed as having proscribed as early as 1460 the ecclesiology on which the conciliarists had taken their essentially revolutionary stand. And the Fifth Lateran Council's 1516 decree *Pastor aeternus* was interpreted as having in definitive fashion consigned that ecclesiology to the outer darkness of heterodoxy, there to enjoy (it was implied) no more than an intermittent twilight existence under the guises of Gallicanism, Febronianism and Josephism. And the second noteworthy feature of this historiographic tradition was the degree to which it portrayed the conciliarist ecclesiology as an extreme position with little or no grounding in the orthodox doctrinal tradition and, according to some, with suspect origins in the speculations of those dangerous, pro-imperial radicals of the fourteenth-century William of Ockham (d. 1349) and Marsiglio of Padua (d. 1343).

Since the Second World War, however, the burgeoning of conciliar studies has called into question the validity of both of those features of the post-Vatican I historiographic tradition. A whole series of scholars - notable among them Hubert Jedin, Josef Klotzner, Olivier de la Brosse, Remigius Bäumer, Hans Schneider and Hermann Josef Sieben - have established the fact that the demise of conciliar theory in the century and more after the dissolution of Basel was neither as sudden nor as final as once we were led to assume, as well as the fact that it continued to enjoy, at least in northern Europe and on into the eighteenth century, a good deal more than an heretical half-life.[7] Similarly, so far as the matter of origins goes, it has been the great achievement of Brian Tierney to have made it unambiguously clear that conciliar theory was neither as recent nor as revolutionary in its origins as it formerly had become customary to suppose. Instead, it turns out to have had deep and unimpeachably orthodox roots amid the cozy canonistic respectabilities of the pre-Marsiglian era.[8]

It is upon this last point that I wish to dwell in this essay, with particular reference to the currency of conciliarist sentiment in early sixteenth-century England, and with a specific focus on the views of the distinguished Tudor lawyer, Christopher St. German (d. 1541), and of his contemporary, Thomas Starkey (d. 1538), a legally-trained writer of humanist sympathies whom Thomas Cromwell recruited into the royal service. As we have become better

[7] I draw here on the account given with full bibliographical references in Francis Oakley, "'Anxieties of Influence': Skinner, Figgis, Conciliarism and Early Modern Constitutionalism," *Past and Present* 151 (1996): 60-110 at pp. 77-84.

[8] Brian Tierney, *Foundations of the Conciliar Theory: The Contributions of the Medieval Canonists from Gratian to the Great Schism* (Cambridge, 1955), where, pursuing suggestions made over the years by Otto Gierke, Franz Bliemetzrieder, H.X. Arquillière, Walter Ullmann and others, he makes the case that conciliar theory, far from being a reaction *against* canonistic views, was in fact the logical outgrowth of canonistic thought itself, with some of its roots reaching back to the twelfth century.

acquainted with the conciliarism both of the classical (fourteenth-fifteenth centuries) and silver (sixteenth-century) ages, it has become increasingly clear that the views of Marsiglio of Padua stand out as so uncharacteristically radical that it would be a salutory clarification if, by general agreement, we could agree henceforth to withhold from him the conciliarist designation.[9] Certainly, though Dietrich of Niem (d. 1418) and Nicholas of Cusa (d. 1464) do appear to have garnered some material from the *Defensor pacis*,[10] Marsiglian ideas recommended themselves neither to the great conciliar theorists of the Council of Constance—Pierre d'Ailly (d. 1420), Jean Gerson (d. 1429), and Francesco Zabarella (d. 1418)[11]—nor to the leading sixteenth-century proponents of conciliarist ideas—John Mair (or Major, d. 1550) and Jacques Almain (d.1515). The last-named, indeed, was explicit in his rejection of such ideas.[12]

England, however, which had produced no conciliar theorists of note, and had played no more than a subsidiary role at Constance and Basel and none at all at the abortive *conciliabulum* of Pisa (1511), has seemed, because of the interest Tudor controversialists undoubtedly showed in the *Defensor pacis*, to constitute something of an exception. The first printed edition of that work saw the light of day only in 1522. And yet, within little more than a decade, William Marshall had published his (admittedly truncated) English translation.[13] Perhaps because of that striking fact, historians have been quick to detect the impress of Marsiglian ideas upon the views of a whole series of figures prominent in the era of the Henrician Reformation. They range from Thomas Cranmer, (d. 1556), archbishop of Canterbury himself, to Edward Foxe (d. 1538), bishop of Hereford, and Stephen Gardiner (d. 1555), bishop of Winchester, and include Starkey and

9 Though some scholars continue to classify Marsiglio as a proponent of an "extreme" variety of conciliarism, contrasting the latter with the "moderate," essentially Decretist, variety. Thus Remigius Bäumer, *Nachwirkungen des Konziliaren Gedankens in der Theologie und Kanonistik des frühen 16. Jahrhunderts* (Münster, 1971), pp. 12-16, 265. For the misleading nature of such classifications, see the remarks of Ulrich Bubenheimer in his review of Bäumer's book in *Zeitschrift der Savigny - Stiftung für Rechtsgeschichte*, Kan. Abt. 59 (1973): 455-465, and my own remarks in, "Conciliarism in the Sixteenth Century: Jacques Almain Again," *Archiv für Reformationsgeschichte* 68 (1977): 111-132 at pp. 129-32.

10 For these borrowings, see Johannes Haller, *Papsttum und Kirchenreform* (Berlin, 1903), p. 508; E. F. Jacob, *Essays in the Conciliar Epoch*, 2nd ed. (Manchester, 1953), pp. 41-42; Paul E. Sigmund, "The Influence of Marsilius of Padua on XVth-Century Conciliarism," *Journal of the History of Ideas*, 23 (1962): 392-402.

11 Though the claim is a rather sweeping one, A. E. Roberts is not far from the mark in claiming that "the work of extreme secularists like Marsiglio of Padua was of little use to the churchmen [assembled at Constance]" - see her "Pierre d'Ailly and the Council of Constance: a Study in 'Ockhamite' Theory and Practice," *Transactions of the Royal Historical Society*, 4th series, 18 (1935): 123-142 at p. 124.

12 Oakley, "Conciliarism in the Sixteenth Century," p. 120.

13 Franklin L. Baumer, *The Early Tudor Theory of Kingship* (New Haven and London, 1940), pp. 44 n. 27, 53.

St. German, two thinkers who were clearly conciliarist in their ecclesiological sympathies.

Thus in 1935, C. W. Previté-Orton having just argued for a Marsiglian imprint upon Cranmer's thinking, Pierre Janelle went on to postulate a veritable "chain" of ideological influence extending from the *Defensor pacis* to Foxe's *De vera differentia* (1535) and thence to Gardiner's *De vera oboedientia* (1535). In 1936, moreover, Franklin L. Baumer followed up with a full-scale attempt to establish Marsiglio as "the main source" of Starkey's political thought, and, a year later, broadened his general thesis by extending it to encompass also some aspects of St. German's ecclesiological and political thinking.[14] While, for the better part of a half-century, such claims proved remarkably robust, of recent years they have fallen into disfavor. And they have done so for three main reasons.

First, as Thomas Mayer has emphasized in relation specifically to Baumer's attempt to align Thomas Starkey's views with what he took to be Marsiglio's position, sixty years and more of Marsiglian scholarship have given historians a somewhat more secure purchase, not only on what that position actually was, but also on what was specific to it, rather than reflective of more widely-shared political and ecclesiological commitments in the later Middle Ages.[15]

Second, fashionable attacks in mid-century on the very viability of the "influence model" in the historical interpretation of intellectual phenomena, while not carrying the day, have left as their residue among students of art history, comparative literature and history of ideas alike a healthy astringency in the criteria deployed in order properly to assess the validity of influence claims.[16] These criteria have circumscribed within rather narrow limits the historian's license to advance such claims—and especially so with authors like Cranmer, Foxe, Gardiner and St. German who make no mention of the thinker by whom they have allegedly been influenced, and even with an author like Starkey who does mention Marsiglio, but only in a letter written in the last years of his life

14 Charles W. Previté-Orton, "Marsilius of Padua," *Proceedings of the British Academy* 21(1935): 137-183 at pp. 163-165; Pierre Janelle, *L'Angleterre catholique à la veille du schisme* (Paris, 1935), pp. 271-319, esp. p. 275. Both authors concede that direct citations from Marsiglio are lacking and base their claims, instead, on parallelisms of viewpoint and on common citations of scriptural and patristic texts. Franklin L. Baumer, "Thomas Starkey and Marsilius of Padua," *Politica* 2 (1936): 188-205; idem, "Christopher St. German: The Political Philosophy of a Tudor Lawyer," *American Historical Review* 42 (1937): 631-651.

15 Thomas F. Mayer, *Thomas Starkey and the Commonweal: Humanist Politics and Religion in the Reign of Henry VIII* (Cambridge, 1989), pp. 3, 139-147, 207, 215, 226-227.

16 See esp. Quentin Skinner, "The Limits of Historical Explanations," *Philosophy* 41 (1966): 199-215; and for an extended comment on the issue, Oakley, "'Anxieties of Influence'."

and in such a way as strongly to suggest that he had only just made the acquaintance of the *Defensor pacis*.[17]

Third, and calling for more extended comment (because it concerns the influence of Marsiglio on thinkers who can confidently be described as conciliarist in their sympathies), our knowledge of the circulation of conciliarist ideas in the England of the late-fifteenth and early-sixteenth centuries is somewhat less scanty and somewhat more nuanced than it was in the early years of the present century. Given the degree of royal control exercised over the English church in the fifteenth century, it is understandable that scholarly interest tended traditionally to focus rather tightly on royal policy and on the position adopted by the Crown in the complex politics and diplomacy of pope and council.[18] But it has become increasingly clear that one would be unwise to infer that royal policy necessarily reflected any sense of national unity on the conciliar issue. In relation to the Council of Basel and its era, Margaret Harvey has been at pains to warn that "we know very little about the debate, if any, behind the seeming unity and equally little about the views of individuals."[19] What we do know - largely because of her own researches and those of C. M. D. Crowder - suggests that while English churchmen certainly had access to the conciliarist literature (and among the Constance publicists inclined strongly to the writings of d'Ailly and Gerson),[20] and while "[English] conciliarists could be produced . . . when it suited the English government," there was "no standard orthodoxy" on the respective standing of pope and council.[21]

A few straws in the wind suggest that a similar climate of opinion continued to prevail on into the early years of the sixteenth century. However conciliarist in inspiration the *conciliabulum* of Pisa (1511) may have been, the

17 Mayer, *Thomas Starkey and the Commonweal*, p. 215.

18 See especially the contributions of C. M. D. Crowder and A. N. E. D. Schofield listed in Francis Oakley, "Constance, Basel and the Two Pisas: The Conciliarist Legacy in Sixteenth and Seventeenth-Century England," *Annuarium Historiae Conciliorum* 26 (1994): 87-118 at p. 90 n. 10, an article on whose findings I draw in this and the two succeeding paragraphs.

19 Margaret Harvey, "John Whithamstede, the Pope and the General Council," in *The Church in Pre-Reformation Society: Essays in Honour of F. R. H. Du Boulay*, ed. Caroline M. Barron and Christopher Harper-Brill (Woodbridge, 1985), pp. 118-122 at p. 108.

20 C. M. D. Crowder, "Constance *Acta* in English libraries," in *Das Konzil von Konstanz: Beiträge zu seiner Geschichte und Theologie*, ed. August Franzen and W. Müller (Freiburg, 1964), pp. 477-517, esp. notes at p. 479 that the English showed "a striking preference . . . for two works of Pierre d'Ailly, his *De potestate ecclesiastica* and *De reformatione ecclesiae*, with Gerson's treatise on the Church, published during the council, next in favour."

21 Margaret Harvey, *England, Rome and the Papacy, 1417-1464: The Study of a Relationship* (Manchester and New York, 1993), pp. 214-216, 222 and 242. She adds: "The most striking thing" about attitudes prevalent in England during the fifteenth century is the variety of available opinion "about the papacy and its relation to the universal church, especially the bishops."

lack of English participation in that predominantly French assembly no more provides grounds for speculation about the ecclesiological proclivities of English churchmen than does England's subsequent adhesion to the rival Fifth Lateran Council (1512-1517). Royal policy and the configuration of European diplomatic alignments dictated both moves.[22] In the subsequent years that led up to Henry VIII's breach with Rome, the evidence is lacking to suggest any clarity of commitment among the English bishops either to views that can properly be called conciliarist or to firmly papalist views. Indeed, given the behavior of most of the English higher clergy during the crisis years of the Reformation Parliament, there is little reason to believe that the clarity of papalist commitment that helped take John Fisher, bishop of Rochester, to his untimely death was anything but unusual among them. Instead, the ecclesiological position characteristic of the English bishops of the day seems likely to have had more in common with that of Sir Thomas More during the years *prior* to the composition in 1534 of his *Confutation of Tyndale's Answer*. In that year, out of office, out of royal favor and, finally, imprisoned, he came to focus more intently than heretofore on the teaching function of the general council and on its role as ultimate legislative authority in the government of the universal church. As a result, his conciliarist sympathies became fairly clear.[23] Before that, however, while affirming the authority of general councils, More had not really concerned himself with the central conciliarist issue of the authority of such councils acting in the absence of (or even in opposition to) their papal head.[24] And it seems likely that the English bishops were similarly positioned. Several years after Henry VIII had adopted a conciliar strategy in order to achieve his chosen ends in the divorce question, and even after he had gone so far as to appeal from the judgment of the pope to that of a future general council, the royal council was still so unsure about the position of the bishops on the question of whether "he, that is called the Pope of Rome, ys above the

22 See Augustin Renaudet, *Préreforme et Humanisme à Paris pendant les premières guerres d'Italie: 1494-1517*, 2nd ed. (Paris, 1953), pp. 524-590; cf. idem, *Le Concile Gallican de Pise-Milan: Documents Florentins, 1510-12* (Paris, 1922). Also Olivier de la Brosse, *Le Pope et le Concile: La comparaison de leurs pouvoirs à la veille de la Reformé* (Paris, 1965); Nelson Minnich, "The Healing of the Pisan Schism (1511-13)," *Annuarium Historiae Conciliorum* 16 (1984): 59-192.

23 *The Confutation of Tyndale's Answer* in *The Complete Works of St. Thomas More*, ed. John Guy et al., 20 vols. (New Haven, 1963-1987), 8.2, 937-938, 940-941; cf. pp. 520, 714-715, 872, 922-923.

24 Partly because of that, the issue of More's conciliarism has been much debated; see Brian Gogan, *The Common Corps of Christendom: Ecclesiological Themes in the Writings of Sir Thomas More* (Leiden, 1982). He concludes (p. 289) that "More was of a conciliarist bent" but that, nevertheless, "on the relationship between pope and council . . . [he] . . . did not have a great deal to contribute" (p. 292).

Generall Counsaile or the General Counsaile above him," that it felt the need to examine them on that precise point.[25]

It is clear, nonetheless, that the king's adoption in 1530-1531 of a conciliar strategy, along with the propaganda campaign that ensued, was designed not simply to wring tactical advantage from the legal maneuver itself but also to reinvigorate the conciliarist tradition, to acquaint English people with its central claims concerning the relationship of pope to council, and to generate a degree of sympathy with those claims.[26] Already in 1529-1530, during Reginald Pole's successful mission to secure from the theologians of Paris a satisfactorily supportive opinion on the question of the king's marriage, the members of the English delegation, especially Edward Foxe, Thomas Starkey and John Stokesly, had shown "a good deal of interest in individual conciliarists and conciliarist ideas." Stokesly later reported on a conversation he had had with John Mair, the most distinguished of the sixteenth-century Parisian advocates of conciliar theory, and a *liber conciliorum* was acquired for Foxe who may already at this time have begun to assemble the conciliarist arguments he was later to fold into his *Collecteana satis copiosa*.[27] And once Henry VIII, in the wake of the papal sentence of excommunication, had actually committed himself to appealing to a future general council, the pace of the campaign picked up, sermons being preached affirming that general councils were superior to all bishops, the pope included. One such sermon, attributed to Cranmer himself, invoked Gerson's *De auferabilitate papae* and noted (among other things) that "the Council of Constance and the divines of Paris had declared the Pope to be subject to a General Council."[28] Even after 1536, when Paul III convoked a general council to assemble in Mantua and the Henrician propagandists had now to face the uncomfortable possibility that a council under papal leadership might actually begin to address itself to the matter of church reform, they continued (while rejecting the papal claim to convoke councils and lodging that were prerogative in the hands of kings and princes) to reiterate the central conciliarist position on the superiority of council to pope, to support that claim with appeals to the

[25] *State Papers of the Reign of Henry VIII*, 11 vols. (London, 1830-1852), 1.411-412 ("Minutes for the Privy Council," December 2, 1533); Oakley, "Constance, Basel and the Two Pisas," pp. 91-92.

[26] For a recent account of these developments, see Hans-Jürg Becker, *Die Appellation vom Papst an ein Allgemeines Konzil: Historische Entwicklung und kanonistische Diskussion im späten Mittelalter und der frühen Neuzeit* (Cologne and Vienna, 1988), pp. 264-269.

[27] For which, see Mayer, *Thomas Starkey and the Commonweal*, pp. 78-79. In his *Opus eximium de vera differentia regiae potestatis et ecclesiasticae* (London, 1534), fol. 9r-v, 17r-v, Foxe had also bolstered his attacks on papal jurisdiction with an oblique nod in the direction of conciliar authority.

[28] *Letters and Papers Foreign and Domestic of the Reign of Henry VIII*, ed. J. Gardner (London, 1882), 6, nos. 1487 and 1488, 600-602. No. 1488 is the speech on general councils attributed to Cranmer; cf. P. A. Sawada, "Das Imperium Heinrichs VIII, und der erste Phase seiner Konzilspolitik," in *Reformata Reformanda: Festgabe für Hubert Jedin*, ed. Erwin Iserloh, 2 vols. (Münster, 1965), 2.476-507.

actions taken at Constance and Basel, to the teachings in general of "the divines of Paris," and to those in particular of d'Ailly and Gerson.[29]

In light, then, of these historiographic developments, it is not too surprising that a degree of skepticism has come to attend upon the claims once so confidently and sweepingly made for the particular influence of Marsiglio's *Defensor pacis* on the political and ecclesiological views of the Henrician publicists.[30] The less surprising, indeed, given the marked lack of specificity in their grounding. James McConica tells us that "the adoption of Marsilius as the semi-official theorist of the Henrician Supremacy . . . [has] . . . long been known." But beyond mentioning William Marshall's English translation of the *Defensor pacis* he offers no supportive documentation for that claim.[31] Christopher Morris, likewise, speaking of the Henrician propagandists, asserts that "almost all of their arguments are to be found in Marsiglio of Padua, whose work they knew and used," but he, too, fails to nail down that claim with specific textual evidence. And he blunts the sharp edges of the claim by noting that "some of their views [also] resemble Dante's" and, even, by speaking of their drawing "upon the anti-papal ammunition provided [not only] by Marsiglio of Padua" but also "by Ockham and Wyclif, or by the supporters of the fifteenth-century Conciliar movement"—an array of putative sources distinguished in some measure by their mutual incompatibility of viewpoint.[32]

Writing somewhat later, then, Harvey S. Stout was moved to concede that "although many students of the Henrician Reformation have recognized the figure of Marsilius looming in the background, none have delineated the precise relationship of his thought to the English Reformation." And, asserting that that Reformation was "a movement that clearly evidenced a positive dependence

[29] See P. A. Sawada, "Two Anonymous Tudor Treatises on the General Council," *Journal of Ecclesiastical History* 12 (1961): 197-214; Baumer, *The Early Tudor Theory of Kingship*, pp. 51-52.

[30] See, in relation to Thomas Starkey, W. Gordon Zeeveld, *Foundations of Tudor Policy* (Cambridge, Massachusetts, 1948), pp. 133-135; Gregoria Piaia, *Marsilio la Padova nella riforma e nella contrariforma: Fortuna ed interpretazione* (Padua, 1977), pp. 203-204; and, above all, Mayer, *Thomas Starkey and the Commonweal*, esp. pp. 139-146, 217, 226-227, 246. And, in relation to Christopher St. German, see *St. German's Doctor and Student*, ed. T. F. T. Plucknett and J. L. Barton (Publications of the Selden Society 91; London, 1974), p. xxi n. 2, where he comments that the definition of the church that Baumer viewed as distinctively Marsiglian "could have come just as easily from Gerson."

[31] James K. McConica, *English Humanists and Reformation Politics under Henry VIII and Edward VI* (Oxford, 1965), pp. 167, 136.

[32] Christopher Morris, *Political Thought in England: Tyndale to Hooker* (Oxford, 1953), pp. 54, 48. A. G. Dickens, *The English Reformation* (London, 1964), pp. 84-85, likewise canvasses the names of Dante, Ockham and Wycliffe as possible ideological influences on the Henrician reformers but singles out Marsiglio as the "greatest" and "most original of the medieval erastians," as well as "the one who provided the main fund of these ideas to the defenders of the Henrician Reformation in England." Without elaborating on the point, he goes on to identify among his debtors Christopher St. German and Stephen Gardiner; see pp. 97-98, 137.

on Marsilius's thought," that lack he himself set out to remedy.[33] But the "evidences" he adduces still move largely on the slippery and unsatisfactory plane of alleged similarities and parallels in positions taken—especially by Thomas Cromwell in the statutes he drafted or the policies, foreign and domestic, he pursued. Only when he adduces the fact that Marshall translated the *Defensor pacis* and goes on to cite Thomas Starkey's sympathy with conciliarist views and his mention of Marsiglio to Pole, does Stout become somewhat more specific.[34] In so doing, citing both Cranmer and Starkey, he concludes that "the conciliar principles of the *Defensor Pacis* were the most significant aspects of Marsilius's work for England."[35] That being so, and whatever one makes of the rather flimsy claims advanced from time to time in the past for the existence of links between Marsiglian ideas and those of Cranmer, Foxe and Gardiner, a particular pertinence attaches to the fact that the case made for the impact of the *Defensor pacis* on conciliarist sympathizers like Starkey and St. German have also fallen of late on rather hard times.

In relation to Starkey, and grounding himself both on the substance of that author's arguments and on the angle from which he approached political questions, Baumer had argued that the *Defensor pacis* was "the main source" of his political thinking. In its revolutionary nature and its absorption of Marsiglian "*democratic* principles," Starkey's political thinking reflected, he argued, "the lasting effect a study of Marsilius *must* have had on him" (italics mine).[36] While by the end of the 1970s doubts had begun to surface about one or other aspect of Baumer's case, it is only during the past decade that it has come under serious challenge, that challenge taking the form of a frontal assault launched in 1989 by Thomas Mayer.[37] Noting that so many of the similarities between Starkey and Marsiglio were either (as Baumer had conceded) "the common coinage of the time" or reflective of a common dependence on Aristotle, and cataloging a long and precise list of differences between the two

33 Harvey S. Stout, "Marsilius of Padua and the Henrician Reformation," *Church History* 43 (1974): 303-318 (at 308). Quentin Skinner, on the other hand, while citing Stout's article, refrains from making any unambiguous influence-claim. He does, however, suggest that "Marsiglio's . . . heresy—widely adopted in the course of the Reformation—was his insistence that all coercive power is secular by definition"; see *Foundations of Modern Political Thought*, 2 vols. (Cambridge, 1978), 2.37, 101.

34 Stout, "Marsilius of Padua and the Henrician Revolution," pp. 309, 311-313, 316.

35 Ibid., p. 316.

36 Baumer, "Thomas Starkey and Marsilius of Padua," pp. 205, 188-189, 199-200. Perhaps the most intriguing presence among the array of historians who have reacted positively (or, at least, not negatively) to Baumer's claims is that of Conal Condren, himself something of a skeptic about the usefulness of the influence-model in the history of ideas; see his *The Status and Appraisal of Classic Texts: An Essay on Political Theory, Its Inheritance, and the History of Ideas* (Princeton, 1985), pp. 265-268.

37 See above, n. 30.

thinkers, Mayer concluded that it remained to be demonstrated that Starkey "ever gave Marsilio much time" and that the linkage of the two men, "extraordinarily persistent" though it may have been, was "fundamentally wrongheaded."[38] Elsewhere, when he describes Starkey as having preserved "a record of almost unspotted conciliarism in the midst of all the smoke and fire of propaganda, even when conciliarism had gone out of fashion [in England],"[39] it is not Marsiglio but the great conciliar theorists of Constance (Gerson, d'Ailly, Zabarella) that he identifies as the source of such views. Starkey, he stresses, had had access to the ideas of those theorists via the teaching of Marco Mantova Benavides in Padua and Gianfranceso Sannazari della Ripa in Avignon, as well as during his visit with Pole to Paris.[40] "Apart from the immutable headship of the pope," he concludes, "Gerson's view of the ecclesiastical constitution was identical to Starkey's."[41] Towards the end of his life, certainly, when he undertook a critique of Albertus Pighius's *Hierarchicae ecclesiasticae assertio*, Starkey exerted no effort to defend Marsiglio against the sustained attack which Pighius launched against him in the fifth book of that work. On the other hand, he did make a point of rebutting Pighius's attack in the sixth book on the advocacy by Gerson and the councils of Constance and Basel of the superiority of council to pope. To Pighius's counter-insistence on the superiority of the pope he simply replied that "both councils and Gerson and the Parisian school stand to the contrary . . ., to which I [myself] thus far stand fast."[42]

While Christopher St. German's conciliarist sympathies were somewhat more fluctuating and less coherent than Starkey's, the familiarity with the conciliarism of d'Ailly and Gerson evident in England from the fifteenth century onwards is also reflected in his writings, too, and has long been emphasized in

38 Mayer, *Thomas Starkey and the Commonweal*, pp. 3, 77 and 139-146. The differences Mayer documents date even to the years after Starkey had made his solitary reference to Marsiglio.

39 Thomas P. Mayer, "Thomas Starkey, an Unknown Conciliarist at the Court of Henry VIII," *Journal of the History of Ideas* 49 (1988): 207-227 at p. 208.

40 Mayer, "Thomas Starkey, An Unknown Conciliarist," pp. 221-224; idem, *Thomas Starkey and the Commonweal*, pp. 81-83.

41 Mayer, *Thomas Starkey and the Commonweal*, p. 83.

42 Albertus Pighius, *Hierarchiae ecclesiasticae assertio* (Cologne, 1538), Lib. V (fol. clvi r-ccix r) is devoted to a critique of Marsiglio's views on ecclesiastical authority but has very little to say about matters conciliar. Lib. VI (fol. ccix r-cclxvii r) is concerned with the power of councils, but makes no mention of Marsiglio. It dwells lengthily, however, on Gerson and the superiority decrees of Constance and Basel. Starkey's critical notes on the *Assertio* remain unpublished. The manuscript is in the Public Records Office, London, State Papers, Henry VIII 1/141, fol. 188v ff. I cite the words in the text from Mayer, "Thomas Starkey, an Unknown Conciliarist," p. 29. Cf. the lengthier discussion in idem, *Thomas Starkey and the Commonweal*, pp. 82-83, 266-271.

the scholarly literature.[43] That familiarity with conciliarist thinking (in the case of Gerson, quite extensive) is manifest in his widely-read twin dialogues, *Doctor and Student* (1523-1531),[44] and, in two later works of controversy, though he attributes it incorrectly to Gerson, he also quotes at length from the *Concilium pacis* of another conciliarist, Heinrich von Langenstein (d. 1397).[45]

St. German was familiar enough, then, with the conciliarist authors of the era of the Great Schism and the Council of Constance, and we now know that he himself spoke to the authority of general councils not only in his *An Answere to a letter* (1535) but also in *A Dyalogue shewinge what we be bounde to byleve in thinges necessary to salvacion and what not* (1537). In the latter work, a newly-discovered and important treatise "hidden away for centuries in Cromwell's papers,"[46] St. German retreated, interestingly enough, from the position he had adopted two years earlier in his *Answere*. Though in 1535 he had not been unmindful of the importance traditionally ascribed to general councils, he had also noted that the popes had "in tyme paste . . . delayed such generall counseyls" and prevented their meeting "at certayne tymes appoynted by the lawe to redresse wronges done to the people." And that had led him to assert that in order to avoid long delay in the redress of wrongs done by the pope "the parlyement hath good auctority to remove such wronges in this realme." Speaking, moreover, of the even more fundamental need to resolve disagreements concerning the meaning of Scripture and noting that "all men agree that the

43 Thus Paul Vinogradoff, *Collected Papers*, 2 vols. (Oxford, 1928), 2, essay 9, pp. 190-204, noted that St. German borrowed heavily from him; similarly Baumer, "Christopher St. German," pp. 631-651 (St. German, he says, [p. 656] was "a profound student of Gerson"); Zofia Rueger, "Gerson's Concept of Equity and Christopher St. German," *History of Political Thought* 3 (1982): 1-30. Cf. *St. German's Doctor and Student*, pp. xxiii-xxv, li; J.B. Trapp, in the introduction to his [2nd ref—see n. 14] edition of *The Apology*, in *The Complete Works of St. Thomas More*, 9.xlvi-xlvii, says that "the author most frequently laid under contribution [by St. German] for general support is Jean Gerson." Similarly, J. A. Guy, *Christopher St. German on Chancery and Statute* (Selden Society Supplementary Series 6; London, 1985), pp. 35-36, 72-74.

44 The works cited are Gerson's *De unitate ecclesiae, De vita spirituali animae, Regulae morales, Tractatus de contractibus, De non esu carnium* and *Descriptiones terminorum ad theologiam utilium*.

45 St. German, *A treatise concernynge the division between the spiritualtie and temporaltie* (1532), printed with *The Apology*, in *The Complete Works of St. Thomas More*, 9.175-212 at pp. 182-185, and *A dyalogue betwixte two englyshemen, whereof one was called Salem and the other Byzance (1537)*, printed in *The Complete Works of St. Thomas More*, 10, Appendix B, pp. 323-391 at pp. 378-379, 382.

46 Thus *The Complete Works of St. Thomas More*, 10, Appendix C, "The Later Career of Christopher St. German," pp. 408-414 at p. 409; cf. *Christopher St. German on Chancery and Statute*, pp. 13-14, 49-53. The manuscript of the *Dyalogue* is to be found in the Public Record Office, London, State Papers, Henry VIII, 6/2, Theological Tracts, pp. 89-168. Guy analyzes its contents more fully in Alistair Fox and John Guy, *Reassessing the Henrician Age: Humanism, Politics and Reform, 1500-1550* (Oxford, 1986), pp. 210-222.

catholyque churche maye expounde scrypture," he had been willing to ascribe to the king-in-parliament that prerogative of interpretation. For as "the unyversall catholique people may not be gathered togyther to make suche exposycion," why should not the parliament assume that task in that it "representeth . . . the whole catholyke churche of Englande."[47]

Two years later in the *Dyalogue*, however, he backed off from that position and argued instead that the interpretative role, and the related role of deciding what books were to be regarded as scriptural, fell properly to "generall counsailes," though not to those "gathered by auctoritie of the bisshope of Rome." Instead, it was to be ascribed to those "gathered and orderyd according to Scripture" -- that is to say, those "gathered and kepte by auctoritie of kynges and princes and wherein notable men of the temporaltie (as they be called) shulde have voices."[48] And although he does not quite say it, perhaps it may be presumed that he saw it also as the (regrettably unfulfilled) responsibility of the general council to call to account those "bisshopes of Rome and other bishops" who had hidden "so ferre from the gospell of Criste . . . and his doctrynes."[49]

Given the degree of St. German's acquaintance with the views of the Constance conciliar theorists, notably Gerson's, and given his willingness openly to invoke their authority, it is not surprising that Baumer should have been somewhat more diffident in arguing for Marsiglian influence in his case than he had been, a year earlier, in relation to Starkey. Accordingly, he hedged around his claims with qualifications and conceded, even while insisting that Marsiglio was "a source of inspiration" for St. German, that the latter never in fact cited the *Defensor pacis*.[50] Nor is it surprising that other scholars who knew their St. German well should subsequently have called even that attenuated claim into question.[51] What *is* surprising, instead, is that J. A. Guy should have chosen of recent years to revive Baumer's claim. He has done so on the basis of what St. German had to say in the newly-discovered *Dyalogue*, arguing that it "encourages a return to Franklin L. Baumer's view that St. German had

[47] *An Answere to a letter* (London, 1535), sig. B vii v - viii r, and G v r - vi v.

[48] St. German, *A dyalogue shewinge what we be bounde to beleve*, pp. 103, 121-123; cf. p. 163.

[49] Ibid., 167-168. Note that in *An Answere*, sig. B vii v - B viii r, he had argued that general councils, having been required by law to meet at certain times, and the popes, having in the past maneuvered to delay their assembly, "there is no reason why they [i.e. the people] shulde susteyne wronge any one daye specyally by him [i.e. the pope] that differeth the meanes whereby they might have remedye."

[50] Baumer, "Christopher St. German," pp. 637-638, 650. Cf. idem., *The Early Tudor Theory of Kingship*, pp. 53-57.

[51] Thus *St. German's Doctor and Student*, pp. xxi n. 3 and xxiii-iv; also *The Apology*, in *The Complete Works of St. Thomas More*, 9.xlviii-xlix.

studied [Marsilius of Padua's] *Defensor Pacis*."[52] The question arises, then, as to what we are to make of that revived claim.

In making his own case for St. German's indebtedness to Marsiglio, Baumer had been moved by three strands in the former's thinking that he took to be powerfully reminiscent of the latter's views. First, the location of the (at least implied) line between things spiritual and temporal. That St. German had drawn, Marsiglian fashion, in such a way as to restrict the power of the clergy to (in the traditional medieval terminology) the *potestas ordinis* or priestly sacramental power. As a result, there was transferred to the temporal ruler the entire fullness of jurisdictional power in the public arena (*potestas jurisdictionis in foro exteriori*) traditionally wielded by the church.[53] Second, the prominence given to the role of kings and princes in relation to general councils.[54] Third, and most important because it is the premise on which the previous assertion depends, St. German's definition of the church not simply as the clergy but as "the hole congregation of Christen people," a definition "substantially different from the definitions set forth in the Middle Ages," and too similar to that proposed by Marsiglio in the *Defensor pacis* "to admit of much doubt as to where it came from.[55]

None of this, it must be confessed, amounts to very much. The line St. German drew between temporal and spiritual was something of a cliché among Henrician reformers—both those who can reasonably be classified as royal propagandists and such predecessors as Robert Barnes and William Tyndale who were men of genuinely Lutheran or Bucerian sympathies.[56] Here the invocation of Marsiglian influence constitutes something of a redundancy as it does also in connection with the dominant role ascribed to kings and princes vis-à-vis general

[52] *The Debellation of Salem and Byzance*, ed. J. A. Guy et al., in *The Complete Works of St. Thomas More*, 10.398 n.3. See also Guy, *Christopher St. German on Chancery and Statute*, pp. 40, 51-52.

[53] Baumer, "Christopher St. German," p. 638, where he concedes that St. German never precisely distinguished between "spiritual" and "temporal," but notes that "the cases at issue between clergy and laity which he cites are based on this fundamental distinction."

[54] Baumer, "Christopher St. German," p. 650. He cites St. German's *An Answere to a letter*, sig. G vi v, where, "in a passage which is peculiarly reminiscent of Marsilius," he says, "no man oughte to pretend that at a general counsell anye others shulde be juges but kynges and princes and suche as they wyll appoynte under them to have voyces therein, seynge that they have power and voyce of the whole people of christendom, which is the catholyque churche as is sayde before . . . ."

[55] Baumer, "Christopher St. German," pp. 637-638, where he cites the definition to be found in *The Power of the Clergy*, sig. D iii, and also in *An Answere*, sig. G iii v, and refers to Marsiglio's *Defensor pacis*, ed. Previté-Orton, p. 117.

[56] For a general overview, see Francis Oakley, "Christian Obedience and Authority, 1520-1550," in *The Cambridge History of Political Thought: 1450-1700* , ed. J. H. Burns and Mark Goldie (Cambridge, 1991), pp. 159-192 at pp. 176-181. Cf. W. A. Clebsch, *England's Earliest Protestants, 1520-1535* (New Haven and London, 1964), esp. pp. 54-65.

councils. Once it came to seem likely that the pope himself might convoke a council to pursue church reform, defenders of the royal supremacy had very good practical reasons for focusing on the relationship of royal authority to that of general councils.[57] As for the definition of the church as "the whole Christen people," Baumer's claim that it represents a marked departure from medieval norms is simply mistaken. And not surprisingly so because it is based on the odd assumption that a definition drawn from the writings of Robert, Cardinal Bellarmine in the sixteenth century could properly be taken to express "the medieval view of the church."[58] About St. German's definition, in fact, there was nothing at all noteworthy or new. It simply echoed a late medieval commonplace, and one popular especially among the conciliar theorists, with whom St. German was well-acquainted, and for whom the fullness of ecclesiastical jurisdictional power was seen to reside ultimately in the *congregatio fidelium* and the general council representing it.[59]

That being so, and the evidence supporting the claim for Marsiglian influence on St. German being so very weak, what, one has to ask, is there in the newly-discovered *Dyalogue* that would warrant Guy's attempt to refurbish that claim? And the appropriate answer, it must be confessed, is "little or nothing." What little there is all hinges on matters conciliar: that it was for kings and princes to summon general councils; that it was for such councils to decide what books were to be accepted as authentically scriptural, as well as to settle interpretative problems raised by scripture and thereby "to maynteyne oon catholyque feythe throughout all cristen realms"; that such councils represented the "hole congregation of Christen people," laity as well as clergy.[60] But while he suggests a Marsiglian origin for such views, Guy himself concedes that, so far as scriptural exegesis was concerned, St. German clearly agreed with "the Parisian conciliarist Jean Gerson" that the "authoritative interpretation came from the church." He further concedes that St. German's definition of the church

[57] As Pope Paul III did indeed do in 1536.

[58] Baumer, "Christopher St. German," p. 637, where he cites Bellarmine's definition from the *Catholic Encyclopedia.*

[59] See, e.g., for Pierre d'Ailly, Francis Oakley, *The Political Thought of Pierre d'Ailly: The Voluntarist Tradition* (New Haven and London, 1964), pp. 54-55; and for the conciliar thinkers in general, Tierney, *Foundations of Conciliar Theory*, esp. pp. 4, 23-24, 41-46. Similarly, among many others, Johannes Breviscoxe (d. 1423), *Tractatus de fide et ecclesia, romano pontifice et concilio generali*, in Jean Gerson, *Opera omnia*, ed. Louis Ellies du Pin, 5 vols. (Antwerp, 1706), 1.844-845: "Alio modo, capitur Ecclesia et proprie, pro congregatione omnium fidelium in hac mortali vita degentium."

[60] These last words are taken from St. German's definition of the church in *The Power of the Clergy*, sig. D 4, which Guy describes as "the definition of *ecclesia* set forth in the *Defensor pacis* of Marsilius of Padua"; see Guy, *The Debellation of Salem and Byzance,* in *The Complete Works of St. Thomas More*, 10. Appendix C ("The Later Career of Christopher St. German"), pp. 398 n. 3, 411. Cf. Guy, *Christopher St. German on Chancery and Statute*, pp. 40, 51-52. The passages in the *Dyalogue shewinge what we be bounde to beleve* occur at pp. 121-131.

"is so general that it could include sharply differing views about authority, hierarchy, and jurisdiction. More himself would have been quite willing to accept it."[61]

The *Dyalogue* notwithstanding, then, there is now, as there was a half-century ago, little or no reason even to link Marsiglio's name with St. German's, let alone to insist that he had some sort of shaping influence on the latter's thinking. And, given Mayer's parallel conclusion in relation to Thomas Starkey, there is, similarly, little or no reason to suggest that those of conciliarist sympathies in sixteenth-century England were any more notably indebted to Marsiglian ideas than were conciliarist thinkers in general. In the conciliarist thinking of Starkey and St. German, as in that of their fifteenth-century predecessors and seventeenth-century successors in England, it is the conciliar theorists of Constance, especially "the divines of Paris" and, most notably Gerson, who figure explicitly and appear to have been the shaping force.

That being so, and given also the vagueness of the "evidence" traditionally adduced for the impact of Marsiglian ideas on Cranmer, Foxe and Gardiner, one has to wonder a little about the marked preoccupation of commentators on the thinking of the theoreticians and propagandists of the Henrician Reformation with the question of Marsiglian roots. That is only part, of course, of a larger story and it leads one to ponder the strangely commanding position Marsiglio has come to assume in the eyes of historians of *modern* political thought. And, having so pondered, one is led to ask what exactly it was in Marsiglio's thinking that succeeded in transforming him into something of a Rorschach inkblot figure wherein interpreters of a multiplicity of later thinkers have been moved eagerly to detect the looming outlines of their chosen subjects' subsequent and disparate commitments.

[61] Guy, *The Debellation of Salem and Byzance,* in *The Complete Works of St. Thomas More*, 10, Appendix C, pp. 411-412, 398 n. 3. This concession is particularly damaging for Guy's whole claim for Marsiglian influence in that it pivots (like Baumer's) on the alleged novelty of St. German's definition of the church.

THE *CONSILIUM DE EMENDANDA ECCLESIA* AND THE 1555 REFORM BULL OF POPE JULIUS III: DEAD LETTERS OR BUILDING BLOCKS?

William V. Hudon

The history of reform in the Roman church is rich with examples of innovative change, renewal, and positive growth, but it is also studded with lofty ideals of limited significance. The very notion of religious reform is idealistic, deriving, in the Christian tradition, from the calls of Jesus of Nazareth for renewal in Judaism among his own contemporaries. Ideals, whether in pre-Christian Palestine, medieval Europe, or in twentieth century America, are established as new ways of thinking and living only with great effort. Ideals for ecclesiastical reform in the Roman church were sometimes of limited significance for that very reason: because they were either effectual for a very brief period or never implemented at all. From Jesus of Nazareth to the Council of Trent and beyond, calls for reform have consistently required both rejection of standard religious ideas and practice, and rejection of the attractions of this world, changes that are most difficult to achieve in practice. Early tenth century attempts at monastic reform initiated in reaction to the decline of adherence to the Benedictine rule, like the work of John of Gorze and Gerhardt of Brogne, had local importance. Abbots of Cluny like Berno, Odo, and Odilo, also established an affiliation of monasteries that spread the gospel of strict observance over the course of several centuries. In the end, however, this promising example of revival declined, as did that of the Cistercians who followed. While calls for respiritualization of the governing agencies of the church among both secular and ecclesiastical leaders in the eleventh century were vigorous, even vociferous, both lay and religious critics in the high Middle Ages, like Walther von der Vogelweide (c.1170-c.1230) and Catherine of Siena (1347-1380), could consider them of no long-term help in revitalizing Christian life.

In the sixteenth century, between the emergence of Martin Luther's call for change (1517) and the conclusion of the Council of Trent (1563), an incredible variety of reform ideals and initiatives developed among persons loyal to the Roman church. Some were more significant than others. Among the significant were the reformed Veronese diocesan administration of Gian Matteo Giberti, the re-establishment of the Roman Inquisition, and the confirmation of the final decrees of Trent. Against these, reform documents like the 1537 *Consilium de emendanda ecclesia* and the reform bull Pope Julius III commissioned in 1554 and completed in 1555 may pale in comparison. Giberti, after all, conducted diocesan visitations long before it was fashionable to do so, and had a practical impact on the work of, among others, the preachers of Verona. The Roman Inquisition, revived by Pope Paul III in 1542, is the one institution instantly recognizable to those with even a smattering of knowledge of the early modern world, even if their picture of the agency as a consistently vigorous pursuer of heretical behavior and ideology is a wildly stereotyped and simplistic one. The decrees of Trent, once finalized through the efforts of Giovanni Morone and other prelates gathered at the final sessions of the council, served as the foundation of Catholic doctrine and practice for some 400 years, right down to the era of the Second Vatican Council.

When viewing the two reform texts considered in this essay against such famous—and infamous—action, one might conclude that the *Consilium* was only a lofty reform ideal and that Julius' bull was simply a plan for action and nothing more. The *Consilium*, after all, may have been constructed by a blue-ribbon panel of curialists in a position to insist on action, but most of them fell out of papal favor or died before the real work of reform began.[1] A reform bull may have been drafted by the curial commission established by Julius III; but the document died with him, unnamed, unconfirmed, all but forgotten.[2] It is tempting to view both documents as dead letters of no real significance, and many have done just that.[3]

Careful textual analysis of the two documents, considered against the final decrees of the Council of Trent, reveals that both writings represent important steps toward the Tridentine plan for ecclesiastical reform. The idealism exhibited in the *Consilium* operated in the discussions of Julius' reform commission, and it continued to inform the work of prelates gathered at the final sessions of Trent nearly a generation later. In 1555, the authors of the reform bull of Julius originally conceived a plan for the implementation of reform decrees hammered out at the early sessions of the still incomplete Council of Trent. They engaged discussions and drafted recommendations, however, that went far beyond the initial Tridentine legislation. Based upon practical experience in diocesan administration, their plan for implementation included highly specific

1 The curialists who comprised the *Consilium* group were Gasparo Contarini, Gian Pietro Carafa, Jacopo Sadoleto, Reginald Pole, Federigo Fregoso, Girolamo Aleandro, Gian Matteo Giberti, Gregorio Cortese, and Tommaso Badia. The co-authors have often been identified as Carafa and Contarini, but this cannot be conclusively verified.

2 Membership in Julius' reform commission is unclear. He established one in February 1551 made up of Francisco de Turone, Alberto Pio de Carpi, Johannes Alvarez de Toledo, Marcello Cervini, Giovanni Morone, Girolamo Verallo, and Francisco Pisano. When meetings concerning the reform bull began in 1554, according to the extant diaries, the group included Cervini, Pietro Paceco, Iacopo Puteo, Sebastiano Pighino, Giovanni Battista Cicada, and Bernardino Maffeo. Cervini's fragmentary diary is in the seventy-volume collection of his papers in the Archivio di Stato, Florence: *Carte Cerviniane* (henceforth cited as *C.Cerv.*, with filza and sheet numbers following) 32/17r-v.

3 Recently, historians have presented the *Consilium* in an ambiguous fashion. John C. Olin included the text in two volumes of sources on the Catholic reformation, in the first calling it a document that indicated "reform possibilities" that were "not immediately realized," and in the second focusing on its preparatory nature in the history of early modern reform. See his *The Catholic Reformation: Savonarola to Ignatius Loyola* (Westminster, Maryland, 1978), pp. 182-183, and his *Catholic Reform: from Cardinal Ximenes to the Council of Trent 1495-1563* (New York, 1990), p. 21. Elisabeth G. Gleason, who also edited the *Consilium* text in a book of primary sources, cautioned that its immediate significance "should not be overstated." See her *Reform Thought in Sixteenth-Century Italy* (Chico, California, 1981). The author of the most recent attempt to summarize early modern Catholic revival never mentioned the *Consilium* at all, but devoted a paragraph to Julius' bull, where he described it as "repeatedly delayed . . . and filed away;" see Ronnie Po-chia Hsia, *The World of Catholic Renewal 1540-1770* (New York, 1998), p. 17.

suggestions in contrast to the sketchier overview embodied in the *Consilium*. The authors of the reform bull also formulated directives that anticipated later policies established in the final sessions of the council. In short, both these documents—one famous, the other forgotten—are a crucial part of the formation of the Catholic version of early modern ecclesiastical renewal embodied in the decrees of the Council of Trent. They illustrate the idealism and pragmatism, the posturing, and the compromising, that was required to secure even a plan for church reform—let alone its implementation—in the sixteenth century.[4]

The *Consilium de emendanda ecclesia* was a remarkably idealistic document, reflecting both the tradition of reform literature and the exigencies of its own time. The idealism evident in the rhetoric of the authors of the *Consilium* mirrored that of medieval reformers like Bernard of Clairvaux and Catherine of Siena. They all brought high-flung language to their calls for ecclesiastical renewal, praising the character of the very popes they were implicitly criticizing for inaction, while carefully laying blame for the condition of the church aside from the individuals they addressed. Bernard did so in his advice to Pope Eugenius III (1145-1153), urging him to "cut off the lying tongues" of "filthy," guilty curial attorneys and ambitious employees. For Bernard, it was Eugenius' job to root them out, just as Catherine later urged Urban VI (1378-1389) to prune the garden of the church and weed out clerics who were "so overflowing with miserable and wicked vices that they stink up the entire world."[5] While their language was not quite so colorful, the authors of the *Consilium* similarly indicated that the clergy was filled with the "unskilled," with adolescents, and with "men of the vilest stock and of evil morals." This rendered clerics, in their opinion, incapable of representing Christ to the faithful, generating not only scandal, but also contempt for the clergy. Like their medieval forebears, the *Consilium* authors looked to the pope himself to correct and redirect the process of clerical ordination and all matters of importance.[6]

[4] These texts are available, in the original Latin, in the series *Consilium Tridentinum*, 13 vols. (Freiburg, 1901-1938), 12.131-145; 13.261-312. This series is henceforth cited as *CT*. The original Latin text of the decrees of Trent is also readily available, in a single volume that provides an English translation as well; see *The Canons and Decrees of the Council of Trent*, ed. H. J. Schroeder (St. Louis, 1941).

[5] Bernard of Clairvaux, *De consideratione*. A portion of this text is available in a convenient English translation: *University of Chicago Readings in Western Civilization*, vol. 4: *Medieval Europe*, ed. Julius Kirshner and Karl F. Morrison (Chicago, 1986), pp. 237-246. For the quotation from Catherine's letter (c. 1378) to Urban VI, see *Le lettere de S. Caterina da Siena*, ed. Piero Misciattelli (Firenze, 1939), 3.221-228. The letter is similarly available in English; see Kirshner and Morrison, *Readings*, vol. 4, pp. 426-429. A complete English edition of Catherine's correspondence is in preparation; see *The Letters of Catherine of Siena*, trans. Suzanne Noffke, 2 vols. (Tempe, Arizona, 1999).

[6] "Primus abusus in hac parte est ordinatio clericorum et praesertim presbyterorum, in qua nulla adhibetur cura, nulla adhibetur diligentia, quod passim quicumque sint imperitissimi, sint vilissimo genere orti, sint malis moribus ornati, sint adolescentes, admittantur ad ordines sacros et maxime ad presbyteratum, ad characterem, inquam, Christum maxime exprimentem. Hinc innumera scandala, hinc

Like their predecessors, they were idealists who believed they clearly perceived the problems that required solution. Like most idealists, their clarity and certainty affected their plan of action.

The authors of the *Consilium* identified simple, one-dimensional answers to complex questions related to church reform. One of the fundamental problems at stake in the whole history of church reforms, the matter of dispensations, they passed over lightly and in an undefined fashion. Where clerical abuses were identified in the Middle Ages and in the early modern period concerning non-residence, accumulation of benefices, and other undesirable behaviors, canon law already existed which prohibited the behavior. The real problem lay in the reasons Roman administrators might employ to authorize exemptions from those laws. The *Consilium* authors treated both parts of this complicated problem in the same sentence. The first key point of ecclesiastical government, standing behind all others, they explained, was "that as far as possible," the "laws" must be "observed." They added that dispensations should not be considered licit, "save for a pressing and necessary reason." They left undefined what constituted gravity or necessity, but clearly they could conceive of some circumstances that might allow dispensation. Only definition of these terms and circumstances would have permitted their recommendation to address practical complications and move the curia beyond already established papal procedure.[7]

One-dimensional answers to complex reform matters can be found in other sections of the *Consilium,* as well. The authors of the text indicated that religious orders were suffering from deformity, a point that few, whether Romanists or Protestants, would have argued at the time. While few might have challenged the basic point, fewer still would have maintained that all of the orders suffered under the same degree of deformity. The authors of the *Consilium* treated them identically, however, recommending the simple abolition of them all. They also insisted that no cardinals should hold the office of bishop. They recommended this restriction with only passing, indirect reference to the expensive reality of residence in Rome, which had been among the reasons for granting cardinals episcopal benefices—and the incomes that came with them—in the first place. They even maintained that the pope ought to undertake all reform initiatives on his own, without acknowledging the more complicated realities of papal government. No matter how determined they were, few popes ever ruled by fiat.[8]

contemptus ordinis ecclesiastici, hinc divini cultus veneratio non tantum diminuta, sed etiam prope iam extincta," *Consilium* in CT 12.136.

[7] "Illud vero ante omnia, Beatissime Pater, putamus statuendum esse, ut dicit *Aristoteles in Polit.*, sicut in unaquaque republica, ita et in hac ecclesiastica gubernatione ecclesiae Christi hanc prae omnibus legem habendam, ut, quantum fieri potest leges seventur, nec putamus nobis licere dispensare in iis legibus, nisi urgenti de causa et necessaria," *Consilium* in *CT* 12.135.

[8] "Alius abusus corrigendus est in ordinibus religiosorum, quod adeo multi deformati sunt, ut magno sint scandalo saecularibus exemploque plurimum noceant. Conventuales ordines abolendos esse putamus omnes, non tamen ut alicui fiat iniuria, sed prohibendo, ne novitios possint admittere;" "Alius etiam abusus invaluit, ut Reverendissimis cardinalibus episcopatus conferantur seu commendentur non unus

The reform bull of Julius III began as an attempt to establish directives revolving around those matters already settled at the opening sessions of Trent, but its authors stepped far beyond. In fact, the final document indicates that the commission took seriously the work of the *Consilium* authors, as well as the work of the fathers gathered at the opening meetings at Trent. But their contribution to the debate on reform established curial positions that anticipated many of the dictates of reform decrees from the later sessions of the Council. The very opening chapter of the bull set the tone. Commission members indicated that human nature, which they defined as "more inclined toward evil than to good," helped to create the conditions they hoped to remedy. Cardinals in the curia, in the commission's vision, would lead the institutionalization of decrees laid down at Trent. The commissioners wrote an opening passage in which they also asserted the need for reapplication of laws that had fallen into disuse. They maintained further that the peculiar circumstances of the present time had created the need for vigorous, purgative reform. In their pessimistic assessment of an all-too-human set of ecclesiastical persons, they resembled the authors of the *Consilium.* But in their acknowledgment that contemporary circumstances complicated the picture, they hinted at what was to come in the bull, a more fully contextualized indication of ecclesiastical problems and how to solve them.[9]

tantum sed plures, quem, Pater Beatissime, putamus magni esse momenti in ecclesia Dei. Primo quidem, quia officium cardinalatus et officium episcopi incompatibilia sunt. Nam cardinalium est assistere Sanctitati Tuae in gubernanda universali ecclesia; officium autem episcopi est pascere gregem suum, quod praestare bene et ut debet haud potest, nisi habitet cum ovibus suis, ut pastor cum grege. . . . Nec ob id, quod cardinales sint, putamus eis magis licere transgredi legem; immo longe minus. Horum enim vita debet esse aliis lex;" "Haec sunt, Beatissime Pater, quae in praesentia pro tenuitate ingenii nostri colligenda esse duximus, et quae nobis corrigenda viderentur. Tu vero pro Tua bonitate et sapientia omnia moderabere; nos certe, si non rei magnitudini, quae nostras vires longe superat, conscientiae tamen nostrae satisfecimus, non sine maxima spe, ut sub Te principe videamus ecclesiam Dei purgatam, formosam ut columbam, sibi concordem, in unum corpus consentientem, cum aeterna Tui nominis memoria," *Consilium* in *CT* 12.138-139, 144.

9 "Varietas temporum et humanae naturae, quae magis ad malum, quam ad bonum prona est, imbecillitas exigit, ut si quae sanctissimae ac saluberrimae leges per desuetudinem obsoluerunt, per regentium providentiam restituantur, si quae vero malo usu depravatae sunt, purgentur. Quod sane remedium cum a nobis publica necessitas poscere videretur nostrique officii sollicitudo nos admoneret, non esse diutius differendum, nonullis primum S. R. E. cardinalibus fide, religione, integritate, doctrina et innocentia vitae praestantibus iniuximus, ut omni studio inquirerent et perscrutarentur, qui mores, quaeve consuetudines correctione indigerent, deinde ceterorum venerabilium fratrum nostrorum opera et diligentia usi sumus. Cum quibus omnibus matura discussione facta, quaedam, quae emendanda potissimum visa sunt, de eorum consilio et unanimi assensu collegimus et emendavimus et in canones regimus, ac canonibus in sacro Tridentino concilio super reformatione promulgatis adiungi et cum illis simul edi et vulgari praecepimus, quos a cunctis inviolabiliter observari, salva semper sedis apostolicae auctoritate statuimus et iubemus," *Bulla reformationis universalis* (*Varietas temporum*) in *CT* 13.261-262.

The authors of the bull provided one of clearest examples of their step beyond the confines of the early Tridentine decrees in the opening sections of the document. After the foreword, they composed a section on the pope, the cardinals, the bishops, and the provisions for cathedral churches. In the second major section they covered the ordination of clerics. In both they presented some material derived from the first reform decrees of Trent, but there they also drafted directives that anticipated much later work by the same council. They reiterated the conciliar prohibition in 1547 against the accumulation of cathedral churches. In so doing, they adopted a decree that required holders of multiple churches to divest of all but one. The decree also laid down deadlines for the divestment, after which time possession of the offices would be considered null and void.[10] The authors of the bull must have anticipated that the rule would lead to a rush of office holders seeking either reassignment or an opportunity to resign such benefices in favor of a relative. Both of these operations were consistent with the long-standing practice among cardinals of treating their incomes as property that could be bequeathed. The members of Julius' reform commission therefore reinforced the rule by insisting that any transferal from one major church to another, or any resignation in favor of another cleric, would have to be examined for propriety at the curial level.[11] Similarly, the commission adopted Trent's session 6 decree prescribing residence for bishops and other prelates holding the duty of the care of souls. That decree, while renewing old canonical legislation, also required forfeiture of twenty-five per cent of one year's revenue if violated. If the violation were to continue, even worse penalties were threatened.[12] In the

[10] The text of reform canon 2 from session 7 at Trent (3 March 1547) was adopted wholesale into the bull: "Nemo, quacumque etiam dignitate, gradu aut praeeminentia praefulgens, plures metropolitanas seu cathedrales ecclesias in titulum sive commendam aut alio quovis nomine contra sacrorum canonum instituta recipere et simul retinere praesumat, cum valde felix sit ille censendus, cui unam ecclesiam bene ac fructuose et cum animarum sibi commissarum salute regere contigerit. Qui autem plures ecclesias contra praesentis decreti tenorem nunc detinent, una, quam maluerint, retenta, reliquas infra sex menses, si ad liberam Sedis Apostolicae dispositionem pertineant, alias infra annum dimittere teneantur; alioquin ecclesiae ipsae, ultimo obtenta dumtaxat excepta, eo ipso vacare censeantur," Schroeder, *Canons*, p. 333.

[11] The added comment became paragraph 12 in the bull: "De resignationibus ecclesiarum cathedralium. Resignationes cathedralium aut maiorum ecclesiarum non admittantur, neque episcopi ab una ecclesia ad aliam transferantur, nisi ex causa in consistorio examinata et probata," *Varietas temporum*, in *CT* 13.264. There is a work illustrating the longstanding practice of such resignations and transferals in the early modern church: Barbara McClung Hallman, *Italian Cardinals, Reform, and the Church as Property* (Berkeley, 1985).

[12] "Si quis a patriarchali, primatiali, metropolitana seu cathedrali ecclesia, sibi quocumque titulo, causa, nomine seu jure commissa, quacumque ille dignitate, gradu et praeeminentia praefulgeat, legitimo impedimento seu justis et rationabilibus causis cessantibus, sex mensibus continuis extra suam dioecesim morando abfuerit, quartae partis fructuum unius anni, fabricae ecclesiae et pauperibus loci per superiorem ecclesiasticum applicandorum, poenam ipso jure incurrat. Quod si per alios sex menses in hujusmodi absentia perseraverit, aliam quartam partem fructuum similiter

following paragraph of their reform plan, the commission members then criticized many for employing false excuses in an attempt to avoid those penalties already written into the conciliar legislation.[13] They were clearly taking into account, and criticizing, the traditional, now ongoing, pursuit of dispensations from reform initiatives.

In the portion of their work covering the ordination of lower clerics, the commission members drafted rules that anticipated pronouncements at sessions of the Tridentine assembly many years later. This was especially true of the material they drafted on the reform of regular clergy. They created a fourteen-chapter outline of necessary changes that was detailed, specific, and written with cognizance of the dramatic problems existing in contemporary religious orders. Their dictates stood in between the broad stroke approach of the *Consilium* authors and the more moderate treatment of regular clergy by the Tridentine assembly in 1564. The *Consilium* group urged complete elimination of conventual orders. The reform commissioners took a rather different approach that blended specific, systematic reform policies and strong, but vague, criticism of contemporary practices. The fathers at Trent adopted virtually all of the suggestions of Julius' reform commission but not the strength of their language or the specificity of their recommendations. Commissioners began many of their chapters with a reference to the "scandalous" and "notorious" behavior in the past that had necessitated their legislation. The fathers at Trent even moderated some of the restrictions suggested by the commissioners. Commission members specified minimum age for, and manner of, profession of religious vows by dictating, for example a minimum age of 18 for men, and 16 for women, making profession. The Tridentine assembly compromised on the age of 16 for both men and women.[14] The commissioners also indicated in detail how

applicandam eo ipso amittat. Crescente vero contumacia, ut severiori sacro canonum censurae subjiciatur . . .," Schroeder, *Canons*, pp. 325-326.

[13] The added comment was chapter 16 in the reform bull: "Quia parvus admodum fructus ex praecedenti decreto, sive propter multorum praelatorum errorem, qui forsan seipsos decipientes, falso existimant se legitimum impedimentum iustasque et rationabiles non residendi causas habere, sive propter defectum executorum in fructuum amissorum apprehensione et applicatione, sive propter negligentiam metropolitanorum et aliorum episcoporum in ipsis contumacibus sedi apostolicae denunciandis, hactenus provenit, ne tam sanctum et salubre decretum suo fraudetur effectu, sciat quilibet episcopus, qui ut praefertur abfuerit, se praetextu cuiusvis impedimenti sive casae nisi impedimentum ipsum seu causam sedes apostolica approbaverit nequaquam excusatum iri, ita ut poenas supradicti praecedentis decreti per generales huius reformationis executores executioni demandandas omnino incurrat," *Varietas temporum* in *CT* 13.265.

[14] "Ut occasiones scandalorum huiusmodi tollantur, et ne, unde spiritualis profectus quaeritur, salutis dispendium subsequatur, nullus posthac, etiam quorumvis antiquorum iurium vel regularium institutorum seu consuetundinum praetextu, quibus in hac parte plene derogatum sit et esse censeatur, ante 18., neque ulla femina ante 16. suae aetatis annum, et nisi completo anno probationis, in quovis ordine regularem professionem facere tacite vel expresse valeat,"*Varietas temporum* in *CT* 13.279. The Tridentine legislation comes from session 25, chapter 15: "In quacumque religione tam virorum quam mulierum professio non fiat ante decimum sextum annum expletum, nec qui minore tempore quam per annum post susceptum habitum in

confessors for religious houses ought to be appointed, with their postings being confirmed by the local bishop. Commission members insisted on the importance of confession for all members of religious orders, detailing the biannual occasions (in the Advent/Christmas season and in the Lent/Easter season), on which they ought to be obligated to confess. The authors of the bull backed most of these chapters with either specific penalties for violation of the rules or with generic suggestions about the importance of "avoiding the vengeance of God and the indignation of the Holy See."[15] Where this latter comment was inserted, it was at the insistence of Pope Julius III himself.

The members of Julius III's mid-century reform commission created a document that reflects some of the same idealism of the earlier *Consilium de emendanda ecclesia,* but with far greater acknowledgment of the practical problems typical when attempting to actualize ideals. Their insistence that exceptions to the rule on resignations described above and dispensations on the minimum qualifications for appointment to positions in cathedral churches be examined by curial admininstrators certainly put teeth into the regulations that might make a cleric pause before requesting a favor. The same insistence also provided the curia with an avenue for moderation when necessary. Those avenues had been openings for abuse in the past, but the commissioners were apparently unwilling to block them completely. Many of the members, including the commission's president, Marcello Cervini, had utilized such loopholes over the course of their careers.[16] The authors of the *Consilium* wrote in a one-dimensional way about transfer from one benefice to another, defining any such arrangement as simoniacal. The authors of Julius' bull did not go so far but rather they referred questions on the legitimacy of transfers to the curia, once again providing a means for exceptions. The commissioners took a "no dispensations" approach on the retention of some multiple benefices, such as cathedral church benefices. Still, their determination to permit no exceptions was limited. They did not intend to force immediate resignation of incompatible and multiple cathedral benefices, but indicated that no *new* dispensations (emphasis mine) be granted to allow simultaneous holding of another benefice once appointment to a cathedral church had taken place. By implication, of course, clerics already in possession of dispensations could retain their multiple offices.[17]

probatione steterit, ad professionem admittatur. Professio autem antea facta sit nulla, nullamque inducat obligationem ad alicujus regulae vel religionis vel ordinis observationem, aut ad alios quoscumque effectus," Schroeder, *Canons*, p. 494.

15 "Caveant autem profitentium superiores, si Dei ultionem ac sedis apostolicae indignationem cupiunt evitare . . .," *Varietas temporum* in *CT* 13.279.

16 Cervini had been transferred from one bishopric to another, although he had never held two simultaneously. I treated his work as a bishop in my book *Marcello Cervini and Ecclesiastical Government in Tridentine Italy* (DeKalb, Illinois, 1992), pp. 92-160.

17 "Cum promoto etiam iuxta cap. *De multa* qualificato, si ex aliqua rationabili causa super retentione beneficiorum prius obtentorum dispensandum fuerit, nequaquam dispensetur, ut retinere possit, tam in titulum quam in commendam, ultra unum

The members of the commission permitted another sizable exception when considering, in general terms, all ecclesiastical benefices which had the care of souls attached. They reiterated the rule on such benefices that had been created by the Tridentine fathers in reform chapter 4 of session 7 (1547), but followed the rule with a substantial qualification. The Tridentine decree was itself a confirmation of the same canon law the commission members cited on the topic of cathedral benefices, the constitution *De multa* of Innocent III. The Tridentine decree established that persons accepting and holding incompatible benefices *in the future* (emphasis mine) would be deprived of their offices. In the paragraph following this one in the bull, the commission members allowed for dispensations from the rule. Exemption from the requirement should be permitted, in their view, if nobles who were graduated from either a public university or an approved college applied.[18] Such an exception may well have been drafted in order to quiet anticipated curial opposition to the regulation.

The authors of the reform bull identified the importance of local factors affecting ecclesiastical renewal and the need for improved diocesan organization to achieve it. The clearest example they provided of this view can be found in the bull's directives concerning preaching. The authors of the *Consilium* had only alluded briefly to the problem, suggesting that bishops examine preachers who had first been screened by their own religious superiors. Early in the Tridentine assembly—in fact, in its very first year—prelates meeting there went far beyond this point. The council fathers emphasized the duty of bishops, and of all those entrusted with the care of souls, to preach personally and regularly. Their first pronouncement urged care in modifying messages preached out of consideration for the intellectual capacity of the audiences, and stressed that bishops must be responsible for examination and licensing of all preachers in the diocese. All of this is covered in reform chapter 2 from session 5, drafted in 1545 and 1546.[19] When the members of Julius' reform commission took up the

beneficium curatum sive beneficium alias incompatibile cum ecclesias," *Varietas temporum* in *CT* 13.264.

18 The Tridentine legislation was as follows: "Quicumque de cetero plura curata aut alias incompatibilia beneficia ecclesiastica sive per viam unionis ad vitam, seu commendae perpetuae, aut alio quocumque nomine et titulo contra formam sacrorum canonum et praesertim constitutionis Innocentii III, quae incipit: *De multa,* recipere ac simul retinere praesumpserit, beneficiis ipsis juxta ipsius constitutionis dispositionem ipso jure, etiam praesentis canonis vigore, privatus exsistat," Schroeder, *Canons*, p. 334. The reform bull added this paragraph: "Dispensationes ad plura beneficia curata quibus concedendae sint. Dispensationes ad plura curata aut alias incompatibilia beneficia non dentur nisi nobilibus vel graduatis in publica universitate vel collegio approbato aut alias litteratis viris iuxta formam concilii Lateranensis ac Tridentini. Neque unquam tamen dispensetur ad duo conventualia vel claustralia," *Varietas temporum* in *CT* 13.270.

19 "Archipresbyteri quoque, plebani et quicunque parochiales vel alias, curam animarum habentes, ecclesias quocunque modo obtinent, per se vel alios idoneos, si legitime impediti fuerint, diebus saltam dominicis et festis solemnibus plebes sibi commissas pro sua et earum capacitate pascant salutaribus verbis, docendo ea, quae scire omnibus necessarium est ad salutem, annuntiandoque eis cum brevitate et facilitate sermonis vitia, quae eos declinare, et virtutes, quas sectari oporteat, ut

same point some ten years later, their instructions were far more detailed, and reflected their own administrative experience at the episcopal level.

The commisioners adopted, in its entirety, a long document on preaching that had been drafted by one of their key members, Marcello Cervini.[20] Cervini probably wrote the document in the fall of 1549, and it was based upon his activities in the diocese of Gubbio. He had worked to counteract preaching of questionable orthodoxy there during the previous Lent. The instructions for preachers that he wrote, which were later adopted by the reform commission, included both general remarks on the importance of stressing the foundation of the faith—that is, Jesus Christ—while eliminating "inane questions" and "windy disputations," plus instruction on specific topics to be addressed or avoided. The instructions stressed the need for clarity and comprehensibility, and listed the simple elements of the faith that ought to be emphasized to promote orthodoxy. The document recommended sermonized analysis of the unity of the church under Peter, plus preaching on the topics of original sin, justification, and free will that was in accord with the Tridentine doctrinal positions established in 1549. At that point only those topics had been treated at Trent. Beyond this reference to the Tridentine decrees, Cervini added his own concern that not just the dangers of Lutheranism, but also those of Manicheanism and Pelagianism be avoided. The instructions went on to treat the manner of explaining the sacraments, the Mass, purgatory, the invocation of saints, the use of images, and the concession of indulgences. None were treated in great detail, but Cervini recommended preaching on positions that were later formalized as official doctrines at Trent. Among the theological virtues, he emphasized the importance of charity. On the sacraments, he instructed preachers to teach the real presence of Christ in the Eucharist, and the sacrificial nature of the Mass. He told them to exhort their listeners to "contrition, confession, and satisfaction" for their sins. He insisted that they defend the existence of Purgatory and the legitimate dispensing of indulgences by the pope through the treasury of merits.[21]

poenam aeternam evadere et coelestem gloriam consequi valeant . . . Regulares vero cuiuscunque ordinis, nisi a suis superioribus de vita, moribus et scientia examinati et approbati fuerint, ac de eorum licentia, etiam in ecclesiis suorum ordinum, praedicare non possint; cum qua licentia personaliter se coram episcopis praesentare et ab eis benedictionem petere teneantur, antequam praedicare incipiant," *CT* 5.242-243; cf. also Schroeder, *Canons*, pp. 305-306.

20 Cervini not only served as the commission's president, but the meetings apparently took place in his Vatican apartments. One of the members of his cardinal "family," Bernardino Maffeo, maintained a diary covering the meetings; see Bernardino Maffeo, "Fragmenta reformationis (1552-1553)," *CT* 13.172-177.

21 "Caveant deinde, ne suam volentes ostentare doctrinam seipsos potius quam Christum Iesum praedicare videantur. Quamobrem ab inanibus quaestionibus et a ventosis disputationibus abstineant et, salutem dumtaxat animarum sibi proponentes, quae sunt populo christiano credenda, quae facienda et quae oranda, praedicent et explanent." "Et quoniam de peccato originali et libero arbitrio et de iustificatione contingit habere sermonem, sic eius peccati malignitas praedicanda est, ut non solum Manicheorum ac Lutheranorum, sed etiam Pelagianorum vitentur errores." "Hortandi ergo sunt auditores ad aemulandum illud nunquam satis laudatum charitatis donum, per quod fides vivit et operatur." "Quare et de sacrificio missae efficaciter praedicent, in

There is no doubt that Cervini's personal concern with the spread of heresy and his experience in Gubbio shaped the content of this portion of the bull, but the significance of the section is not limited to Cervini and his work. None of the paragraphs made it into the final decrees of Trent, once again illustrating the in-between character of the reform commission and its work. It was, apparently, clear to the commissioners that reform of preaching must operate on a local level. In this bull, the commissioners judged Cervini's experience to be sufficiently transferable to recommend his ideas to all. In the long run, the fathers at Trent accounted for the necessities of local reform not with paragraphs like these, but by empowering bishops to handle such matters personally, and by binding them to do so as a practical application of their care of souls.[22]

While these specific directives on preaching did not make their way into the final decrees of the Council of Trent, the members of that assembly did retain some other elements from both the earlier reform bull and from the *Consilium,* notably the lofty idealism embodied in the other two documents. They did so especially in the later decrees, in sessions 24 and 25. In 1563, the Tridentine fathers finalized instructions on the promotion of bishops, cardinals, and cathedral canons during session 24. They appealed to the necessity of "prudent and enlightened attention" in the election of bishops, insisting that "the entire household of the Lord will totter if what is required in the body be not found in the head." The authors of the Tridentine decrees recognized the realities, and variations, in contemporary episcopal election processes. They referred to the variety of persons, both clerics and members of the laity, who had a role to play in the elections. They also insisted on the development of local forms for the examination of candidates that would take into consideration what was "most useful and suitable" for each individual place. Still, they idealized both the action of the choosers and the character of the chosen in such elections. Those who participate in these promotions, the fathers wrote, must "above all bear in mind that they can do nothing more serviceable to the glory of God and the salvation of the people than to exert themselves" to the election of "good and competent shepherds." Electors, they added, were "partakers in the sins of others

Novo Testamento esse verum sacrificium veri corporis et sanguinis Christi incruentum, habens cruenti memoriam, quod et vivis et defunctis prodesse potest ad expianda peccata," "Exhortentur autem valido sermone peccarotes ad poenitentiam per contritionem, confessionem et satisfactionem. . . ." "Clare item et diserte declarent esse purgatorium post hanc vitam, quod et de scripturis sanctis elicitur et patrum traditione conciliorumque diffinitionibus comprobatur." "De indulgentiis denique tractantes doceant, esse vere inexhaustum thesaurum meritorum Christi et Sanctissimae eius Matris ac ceterorum sanctorum, et huius dispensandi thesauri per indulgentias summum pontificem tanquam Christi vicarium plenariam habere potestatem, reliquos iuxta sibi ab eo taxatum modum," *Varietas temporum* in *CT* 13.283-287. The commissioners worked with a manuscript copy of Cervini's instructions that still exists; see *C.Cerv.* 29/90r-94v.

[22] I have described and analyzed the document, and also identified the incorrect attribution of the text to Giovanni Morone, in two previous works; see *Marcello Cervini,* pp. 109-121, 149-150; and "Two Instructions to Preachers from the Tridentine Reformation," *Sixteenth Century Journal* 20 (1989): 457-470.

and sin mortally unless they strive diligently that those be promoted whom they judge more worthy and useful."[23] In reform chapter 12 of the same session, the council fathers spent a great deal of time legislating the specifics concerning age, prior clerical status, and required professions of faith for those gaining appointment to cathedral canonries, but again stated their aim idealistically. They hoped to create a body of assistants to the bishops who would "so excel in integrity of morals that they may with justice be called the senate of the church."[24]

The members of the Tridentine assembly reiterated other actions and attitudes idealized in the earlier reform documents. In 1563, again at session 24, they put together a brief coda to the earlier (session 5) Tridentine decree on preaching. The authors of the earlier decree had maintained that bishops must preach in their own churches personally. This order suggests that the members of the assembly had taken over the ideal of clerical residence—that drum so vigorously beaten by the authors of both the *Consilium* and of the reform bull—and were attempting to put it, and its logical implications, into practice. The fathers at session 24 reiterated the point, and created a parallel requirement for the faithful members of the laity. The bishops, Tridentine fathers asserted in 1563, "themselves shall personally, each in his own church, announce the Sacred Scriptures and the divine law." This must take place, they continued, "at least on all Sundays and solemn festival days, but during the season of fasts," (that is, during Lent and Advent), "daily, or at least on three days of the week." If such action were carried out, it clearly could obviate some of the problems that inspired the long preaching instruction Cervini had inserted into the reform bull of 1555. The fathers at Trent also directed bishops to "diligently admonish the people that each one is bound to be present at his own parish church . . . to hear the word of God." Apparently they hoped that the combination of these directives would not only insure excellent preaching, but that there would be audiences to

[23] "Nam totius familiae Domini status et ordo nutabit, si quod requiritur in corpore non inveniatur in capite. . . . Omnes vero et singulos, qui ad promotionem praeficiendorum quodcumque jus quacumque ratione a Sede Apostolica habent, aut alioquin operam suam praestant, nihil in iis pro praesenti temporum ratione innovando, hortatur et monet, ut in primis meminerint, nihil se ad Dei gloriam et populorum salutem utilius posse facere, quam si bonos pastores et ecclesiae gubernandae idoneos promoveri studeant, eosque alienis peccatis communicantes mortaliter peccare, nisi quos digniores et ecclesiae magis utiles ipsi judicaverint, non quidem precibus vel humano affecto aut ambientium suggestionibus, sed eorum exigentibus meritis, . . . Quoniam vero in sumendo de praedictis omnibus qualitatibus gravi idoneoque bonorum et doctorum virorum testimonio non uniformis ratio ubique ex nationum, populorum ac morum varietate potest adhiberi, mandat sancta synodus, ut in provinciali synodo per metropolitanum habenda praescribatur quibusque locis et provinciis propria examinis seu inquisitionis aut instructionis faciendae forma, sanctissimi Romani pontificis arbitrio approbanda, quae magis eisdem locis utilis atque opportuna esse videbitur. . . ," Schroeder, *Canons*, p. 461.

[24] "Vestitu insuper decenti tam in ecclesia quam extra assidue utantur; ab illicitisque venationibus, aucupiis, choreis, tabernis lusibusque abstineant, atque ea morum integritate polleant, ut merito ecclesiae senatus dici possint," Schroeder, *Canons*, p. 471.

hear the improved message.[25] Just one month later, in session 25, the council members expanded upon this idealized view of the preaching function to refer to the entire life of bishops as a "perpetual sermon," only to call them to yet another ideal. Like the authors of the *Consilium* and of the reform bull, the council fathers apparently loathed the fact that so many bishops used their offices to enrich members of their families, especially when they left a particular diocese or died. The Tridentine assembly, like the authors of the earlier documents, called all bishops to an opposite ideal. They ought to live with "moderation, modesty, [and] continency," and indicated that they were "forbidden to attempt to enrich their relations or domestics from the revenues of the church," for these "belong to God." This directive, so shockingly at variance with contemporary practice, was to be obeyed, they continued, "by all who hold ecclesiastical benefices, whether secular or regular," and "it applies also to the cardinals of the holy Roman church." They all must, the fathers concluded, "shine in the splendor of the virtues and in discipline of life." Thus council members reiterated some of the essential elements in the ideally reformed clerical orders presented in earlier sixteenth-century documents.[26]

Some historians assert that between 1537 and 1563 there was a progressively more restrictive approach to reform adopted in the Roman church, but comparison of the Tridentine decrees with the two reform documents illustrates that this assertion is untrue. The final reform decrees of the Council of Trent, for example, only inconsistently reflected some of the more

[25] "Praedicationis munus, quod episcoporum praecipuum est, cupiens sancta synodus quo frequentius possit ad fidelium salutem exerceri, . . . mandat, ut in ecclesia sua ipsi per se, aut, si legitime impediti fuerint, per eos, quos ad praedicationis munus assument, in aliis autem ecclesiis per parochos, sive iis impeditis, per alios ab episcopo impensis eorum, qui eas praestare vel tenentur vel solent, deputandos in civitate aut in quacumque parte dioecesis censebunt expedire, saltem omnibus dominicis et solemnibus diebus festis, tempore autem jejuniorum, Quadragesimae et Adventus Domini quotidie, vel saltem tribus in hebdomada diebus, si ita oportere duxerint, sacras scripturas divinamque legem annuncient, et alias quotiescumque id opportune fieri potest judicaverint. Moneatque episcopus populum diligenter, teneri unumquemque parochiae suae interesse, ubi commode id fieri potest, ad audiendum verbum Dei," Schroeder, *Canons*, p. 465.

[26] "Haec cum ad restituendam ecclesiasticam disciplinam praecipua esse sancta synodus animadvertat, admonet episcopos omnes, ut secum ea saepe meditantes, factis etiam ipsis ac vitae actionibus, quod est velum perpetuum quoddam praedicandi genus, se muneri suo conformes ostendant, in primis vero ita mores suos omnes componant, ut reliqui ab eis frugalitatis, modestiae, continentiae, ac, quae nos tantopere commendat Deo, sanctae humilitatis exempla petere possint. . . . Omnino vero eis interdicit, ne ex reditibus ecclesiae consanguineos familiaresve suos augere studeant, cum et apostolorum canones prohibeant, ne res ecclesiasticas, quae Dei sunt, consanguineis donent, . . . Quae vero de episcopis dicta sunt, eadem non solum in quibuscumque beneficia ecclesiastica tam saecularia quam regularia obtinentibus pro gradus sui conditione observari, sed et ad sanctae Romanae ecclesiae cardinales pertinere decernit, quorum consilio apud sanctissimum Romanum pontificem cum universalis ecclesiae administratio nitatur, nefas videri potest, non iis etiam virtutum insignibus ac vivendi disciplina eos fulgere, quae merito omnium in se oculos convertant," Schroeder, *Canons*, p. 500.

restrictively disciplining dictates of the 1555 reform bull, while stopping well short of the recommendations of the *Consilium* authors. Julius III's commissioners drafted a long section on the reform of the regular clergy. Their document did not repeat the blanket condemnation of all conventual orders implied in the suggestion to abolish them that was included in the *Consilium.* They did, however, insist on severe punishments when regular clerics serving as confessors "presumed" to grant absolution "in cases reserved to the Holy See or to the bishop."[27] These were to be suspended from office. The council fathers finalizing the reform plans of Trent did not even punish this confessional encroachment, let alone conclude that all conventual orders must be abolished due to their earlier deviations. In fact, as regards reform of regular clergy, one might argue for progressively more lenient, not more restrictive, treatment across the mid-sixteenth century. Further evidence can be located when comparing the 1555 bull against the final Tridentine decrees. Council fathers adopted the reform commission's view that confession and communion ought to be mandated for nuns—and even more frequently than the commissioners did—as they considered these sacraments a kind of fortification against the assaults of the devil. They did not, however, order the same for regular male clerics. While there is no mention of the frequency of confession and communion for regular clerics, nuns were required to do so once per month according to the dictates at Trent in session 25.[28] This was the case despite the 1555 commission's assertions on the importance of confession for all regulars.[29]

27 "Caveat quicunque ad audiendas confessiones deputatus, ne etiam praetextu alicuius generalis privilegii in casibus sedi apostolicae vel episcopis reservatis, nisi in mortis articulo vel licentia et potestate prius habita, se intromittat, neque in ipsa confessione directe vel indirecte, etiam loco elemosinae, a confitentibus aliquid petat, neque pro satisfactione poenitentiali poenam aliquam pecuniariam sibi ipsi persolvendam imponat. Qui contra hoc facere praesumpserit, ab audiendis confessionibus atque etiam ab officio et beneficio arbitrio superioris suspendatur," *Varietas temporum* in *CT* 13.281.

28 "Attendant diligenter episcopi et ceteri superiores monasteriorum sanctimonialium, ut in constitutionibus earum admoneantur sanctimoniales, ut saltem semel singulis mensibus confessionem peccatorum faciant et sacrosanctam Eucharistam suscipiant, ut eo se salutari praesidio muniant ad omnes oppugnationes daemonis fortiter superandas," Schroeder, *Canons,* p. 491.

29 "Ut sanctissimum poenitentiae sacramentum pure, integre et cum animi ac conscientiae tranquillitate tam a regularibus quam a secularibus recipi queat, et ne regulares ipsi ob metum et reverentiam superiorum suorum aliqua peccata confiteri praetermittant, quod interdum evenisse dicitur, habeant monachi, fratres et moniales omnes cuiuscunque ordinis, ter in anno, videlicet a prima die adventus usque ad ultimum diem octavae Nativitatis Domini nostri Iesu Christi, et a primo die Quadragesimae usque ad ultimum diem octavae Pascatis, et a kalendis Augusti usque ad ultimum diem octavae gloriosissimae assumptionis Immaculatae Virginis eligendi una vice in quolibet praedictorum temporum presbyterum saecularem seu regularem, quem maluerint, cui peccata sua confiteantur, et a quo beneficium absolutionis, etiam in casibus eorum superioribus reservatis, obtinere valeant, quovis instituto seu consuetudine, quacunque ordinatione, etiam sedis apostolicae auctoritate roborata, non obstante, amplam et liberam facultatem et potestatem," *Varietas temporum* in *CT* 13.281-282.

The reform commissioners, even outside of the section of their bull related to the regular clergy, sometimes sought to impose rules that were actually tougher than those that emerged later from Trent. They laid down heavier penalties for violation of jurisdictional norms. If a bishop, for example, should ordain priests outside of the territories and persons subject to him without the permission of the local ordinary, both the bishop and the new priest should be suspended from office. The commissioners did not indicate any specified length for the suspension.[30] The council members at Trent did not mention suspension for violation of this rule at all, until considering bishops who might issue dimissory letters permitting such ordinations. Then the Tridentine prelates insisted only on a limited, one-year suspension, a penalty to be applied only against the bishop.[31] The reform commission also suggested adaptation of a general rule against the appointment of titular bishops. They stated that such appointments ought to be exceedingly rare, if they occurred at all. They included the point in the section of the bull that treated incompatible benefices, suggesting that the concept of a titular bishop was something of a contradiction in terms.[32] Despite their general focus on bishops, the problems they faced, and the powers they needed in order to handle those problems, the council fathers at Trent surprisingly took no general stand against such appointments.

The reform commissioners, by and large, were also tougher than the council fathers in recommending restrictions to be placed upon the very highest levels of the ecclesiastical hierarchy. When they were describing the quality of persons who ought to be cardinals, they did not restrict themselves to vague language and platitudes. After referring to the cardinals as "brothers" and "assistants" of the pope, they appended a list of requirements. New ones ought to be "serious, learned, and modest." The commissioners hoped, moreover, that they would be persons publically known for their commitment to ecclesiastical discipline. They also indicated that the number of cardinals should not be increased without good reason.[33] When the members of the Tridentine assembly

[30] "Nulli episcopo liceat cuiusvis privilegii praetextu pontificalia in alterius diocesi exercere, nisi de ordinarii loci expressa licentia et in personas eidem ordinario subiectas tantum. Si secus factum fuerit, episcopus ab exercitio pontificalium et sic ordinati ab executione ordinum sint ipso iure suspensi," *Varietas temporum* in *CT* 13.266.

[31] "Abbatibus ac aliis quibuscumque quantumvis exemptis non liceat in posterum intra fines alicujus dioecesis consistentibus, etiamsi nullius dioecesis vel exempti esse dicantur, cuiquam, qui regularis subditus sibi non sit, tonsuram vel minores ordines conferre; nec ipsi abbates et alii exempti, aut collegia vel capitula quaecumque, etiam ecclesiarum cathedralium, litteras dimissorias aliquibus clericis saecularibus ut ab aliis ordinentur, concedant. . . . Concedentes autem dimissorias contra formam decreti ab officio et beneficio per annum sint ipso jure suspensi," Schroeder, *Canons,* p. 442.

[32] "Episcopi titulares non fiant nisi perraro et cum causae cognitione," *Varietas temporum* in *CT* 13.264.

[33] "In sacrosanctae Romanae ecclesiae cardinalium (qui pontificis maximi fratres sunt et eidem in executione sacerdotalis officii coadiutores assistunt, et quorum

got around to identifying desirable characteristics for cardinals during session 24 in 1563, they did so in a reform canon that dealt with bishops as well. They had a great deal more to say about bishops than cardinals, and instead made a vague recommendation to future popes. They were to appoint, and thus to associate themselves with, only the "most select" persons.[34] The reform commissioners even recommended legislation against potential papal abuses. After alluding to the great duties that were the responsibility of the pope, they indicated that these could not be met without the temporal possessions that make spiritual work possible. They warned that the pope ought not be permitted to alienate that property. This section becomes more comprehensible when considering that the persons behind this bull (Julius III who commissioned it, and Marcello Cervini who was instrumental in drafting it) were cardinals—and papal legates—under Paul III. His alienation of sizable portions of the Papal State, most notably the cities of Parma and Piacenza, in the form of gifts to his son, were difficult for legates to defend. Thus, the authors of the bull indicated that the alienation of all church property—not just cities and territories, but any non-moveable goods—was bad.[35] The legislation that the fathers at Trent established concerned alienation only by cardinals and bishops.[36]

Still, it would be an equally unwarranted oversimplification to suggest that no disciplinary intentions beyond those already expressed by previous reformers stood behind the work of the prelates gathered at Trent. The same evidence that illustrates slightly greater conciliar leniency toward regular clerics, for example, also demonstrates their intention to lay heavier burdens upon female religious. On some other regulations, the council fathers stepped beyond the recommendations of the 1555 reform commissioners. Both groups wanted to legislate against the private ownership of property by male and female members of religious orders. The council fathers legislated more vigorously on this than

consilio universalis regitur ecclesia clarum ac spectatum collegium nonnisi viros graves, doctos, modestos, quique in disciplina ecclesiastica cum laude versati fuerint, cooptari, neque eorundem numerum nisi ex rationabili causa, quae rectum possit pontificis maximi movere iudicium, augeri decet, ne tam excellens et praecipuus honor sui numerositate vilescat. Si quando eos vero cooptari contigerit, id praecipue praecavendum erit, ut canones quoad aetatem uniuscuiusque ordinis observentur," *Varietas temporum* in *CT* 13.263.

34 "Postremo eadem sancta synodus, tot gravissimis ecclesiae incommodis commota, non potest non commemorare, nihil magis ecclesiae Dei esse necessarium, quam ut beatissimus Romanus pontifex, quam sollicitudinem universae ecclesiae ex muneris sui officio debet, eam hic potissimum impendat, ut lectissimos tantum sibi cardinales adsciscat, et bonos maxime atque idoneos pastores singulis ecclesiis praeficiat. . . ," Schroeder, *Canons,* p. 462.

35 "Pontifici maximo canonice electo curae potissimum esse debet, ut bona temporalia (sine quorum auxiliis vix spiritualia subsistere possunt) conservet. Proptereaque ab alienatione non solum civitatum, terrarum et locorum status temporalis, sed aliorum quorumcumque bonorum immobilium, praesertim pretiosorum, ad apostolicam ecclesiam pertinentium abstineat," *Varietas temporum* in *CT* 13.263.

36 See the passage cited above, in n. 26, from Session 25, reform chapter 1. Schroeder, *Canons,* p. 500.

the reform commission, adding teeth to their directive. Those in violation of this revised version of the old rule of strict poverty would lose their voting rights in the community. "Should anyone be discovered or convicted of possessing something in any manner," the members of the assembly asserted, other than use consistent with the profession of poverty, they "shall be deprived for two years of [their] active and passive voice and shall also be punished in accordance with the prescriptions of [their] rule and order."[37]

Perhaps the single most surprising difference among the reform suggestions embodied in the *Consilium,* in the reform bull produced by the commission of Julius III, and finally in the reform decrees of the Council of Trent, lies in the varying mechanisms each established for carrying out reform. It is common to assume that repressive, disciplining action by a Roman church attempting to force its version of orthodoxy down the throats of an unwilling population became gradually more acceptable, more intense as the "counter" reformation went on, and certainly across the years between 1537 and 1563. It is clear that the authors of the *Consilium* wanted vigorous, repressive action taken—in the abolition, through attrition, of all conventual religious orders, for example—but they wanted reform initiatives implemented through the pope himself, with limited curial involvement. They clearly, and rightly, feared curial opposition to their reform initiatives. The reform commissioners of Julius III envisioned a very different implementing institution. In the final paragraph of their bull, they directed that the power to execute all of the directives they had enumerated to that point be given, not to the pope, but to the cardinals already established to extirpate heresy through the Holy Office of the Inquisition.[38] They may well have hoped by this means to underline their determination to effect real reform, if not to inspire fear outright. It is exceptionally important to realize that the Council of Trent, in its final sessions, did no such thing. The council fathers incorporated a considerable portion of the specific reform plans that the commission and the authors of the *Consilium* had advocated. They did not, however, adopt either version of a centralized, reform-implementing authority, whether papal or inquisitorial. Instead, the members of the Tridentine assembly indicated that the bishops must do this work. In so doing, they were privileging the local situation and the importance of making decisions that took local conditions into account. This decision reflected not only the experience between 1555 and 1563 of the operation of the Roman Holy Office, but also the

[37] "Nemini igitur regularium, tam virorum quam mulierum, liceat bona immobilia vel mobilia, cujuscumque qualitatis fuerint, etiam quovis modo ab eis acquisita, tamquam propria aut etiam nomine conventus possidere vel tenere . . . Mobilium ver usum ita superiores permittant, ut eorum suppellex statui paupertatis, quam professi sunt, conveniat, nihilque superflui in ea sit, nihil etiam, quod sit necessarium, eis denegetur. Quod si quis aliter quidquam tenere deprehensus aut convictus fuerit, is biennio activa et passiva voce privatus sit, atque etiam juxta suae regulae et ordinis constitutione puniatur," Schroeder, *Canons,* p. 486.

[38] ""Parum est leges condere, nisi sint, qui eas observari curent. Nullis autem commodius consultiusve onus eiusmodi demandari posse censetur quam illis cardinalibus, qui pro tempore extirpandis haeresibus et sanctae inquisitionis negotio praefecti erunt," *Varietas temporum* in *CT* 13.290.

experience of the bishops gathered at Trent. Who better than those increasingly resident bishops to decide that the implementation of reform must vary according to local conditions? Who better than those prelates in 1563—after the notoriously personal and vindictive operations of the Inquisition under Paul IV—to recognize that Julius' reform commission was wrong to hand over such important work to an institution with a track record of manipulation? It was manipulation of the "rules" related to clerical life and behavior, after all, that these reform initiatives—and many others—aimed to control.

In the end, these texts, once considered in a careful, comparative fashion, hold even broader significance. They clearly illustrate that the work of ecclesiastical reform in sixteenth-century Italy was a process more reliant upon creative experimentation and compromise than upon stultifying dictation and repression. All the recent literature on implementation of the decrees of Trent—implementation both inside and outside of Italy, in fact—is pointing to this model. This recent literature relies upon analysis of the administrative records of individual dioceses and bishops, records that have proven especially interesting and useful.[39] In many ways, it could be argued that the history of reform can only be understood through such study. One could go further to insist that what passed for the "history of reform" in older historiography was really only the history of reform *ideas* and of reform *ideology*. If this is the case, then historians have only begun to write the real history of reform. The newer approach to considering the process of ecclesiastical reform, whether one considers it the "true" history of reform or not, is absolutely essential. The method properly traces reform by relying more heavily upon the practical, day-to-day process of implementation, than upon investigation of the ideologies developed by reformers over the years. The results of the new method must be fully incorporated into the picture of post-Tridentine Roman Catholicism if historians are ever to gain a truly contextualized view of the period. These works show that the disciplining intentions of post-Tridentine bishops had only limited success. They show furthermore that where such bishops were successful in effecting change, they did so through a process of negotiation and cooperation with local persons and institutions, from confraternities and convents, to cathedral canons and lay catechists. But even study of reform by an older method—careful analysis of texts elaborating reform ideas and reform ideology—can help point scholars in the same, correct direction, to this proper conclusion. The *Consilium* and the unpublished reform bull of Julius III were not dead letters at all. They were connected to earlier calls for ecclesiastical reform. They fed

[39] See, among others, *Le visite pastorali: Analisi di una fonte*, ed. Umberto Mazzone and Angelo Turchini (Bologna, 1985; 2d ed. 1990); *Visite pastorali ed elaborazione dei dati: Esperienze e metodi*, ed. Cecilia Nubola and Angelo Turchini (Bologna, 1993); *Riforma pretridentina della diocesi di Verona: Visite pastorali del vescovo G. M. Giberti 1525-1542*, ed. Antonio Fasani, 3 vols. (Vicenza, 1989); Cecilia Nubola, *Conoscere per governare: La diocesi di Trento nella vista pastorali di Ludovico Madruzzo (1579-1581)* (Bologna, 1993); Craig Harline and Eddy Put, "A Bishop in the Cloisters: the Visitation of Mathias Hovius (Malines, 1596-1620)," *Sixteenth Century Journal* 22 (1991): 611-639; and Craig Harline, *The Burdens of Sister Margaret: Private Lives in a Seventeenth-Century Convent* (New York, 1994).

ideas into the final decrees of the Council of Trent. They did not, however, feed ideas into the later decrees in a simple, linear fashion, merely adding positions and legislation gradually, one piece on top of the other. Hence, even the "building block" analogy is not fully applicable. Stiff, sometimes belligerent, postures adopted by the authors of the *Consilium* and by the authors of the reform bull of Julius III at times gave way to rethinking at Trent that stood behind the later synthesis on clerical reform. The texts reflect the difficulty of changing ingrained procedures and behavior. They illustrate that commitment to inquisitorial control over the reform process was a short-lived phenomenon. They illustrate the *longue durée* of reform history, from the development of theory to thc process of implementation and practice. They show that a long process of negotiation, not dictation, was characteristic of reform in the early modern period. These texts show that negotiation took place at the theoretical, church-wide level, before the negotiations over the implementation of the theories began at the diocesan, local level. Study of these texts, and of the local implementation process, provides an essential portion of a consistent, logical, and human explanation of reform in the sixteenth-century Roman church.

INDEX

Persons

Places

Subjects

Studies in the History of Christian Thought

EDITED BY HEIKO A. OBERMAN

1. McNEILL, J. J. *The Blondelian Synthesis.* 1966. Out of print
2. GOERTZ, H.-J. *Innere und äussere Ordnung in der Theologie Thomas Müntzers.* 1967
3. BAUMAN, Cl. *Gewaltlosigkeit im Täufertum.* 1968
4. ROLDANUS, J. *Le Christ et l'Homme dans la Théologie d'Athanase d'Alexandrie.* 2nd ed. 1977
5. MILNER, Jr., B. Ch. *Calvin's Doctrine of the Church.* 1970. Out of print
6. TIERNEY, B. *Origins of Papal Infallibility, 1150-1350.* 2nd ed. 1988
7. OLDFIELD, J. J. *Tolerance in the Writings of Félicité Lamennais 1809-1831.* 1973
8. OBERMAN, H. A. (ed.). *Luther and the Dawn of the Modern Era.* 1974. Out of print
9. HOLECZEK, H. *Humanistische Bibelphilologie bei Erasmus, Thomas More und William Tyndale.* 1975
10. FARR, W. *John Wyclif as Legal Reformer.* 1974
11. PURCELL, M. *Papal Crusading Policy 1244-1291.* 1975
12. BALL, B. W. *A Great Expectation.* Eschatological Thought in English Protestantism. 1975
13. STIEBER, J. W. *Pope Eugenius IV, the Council of Basel, and the Empire.* 1978. Out of print
14. PARTEE, Ch. *Calvin and Classical Philosophy.* 1977
15. MISNER, P. *Papacy and Development.* Newman and the Primacy of the Pope. 1976
16. TAVARD, G. H. *The Seventeenth-Century Tradition.* A Study in Recusant Thought. 1978
17. QUINN, A. *The Confidence of British Philosophers.* An Essay in Historical Narrative. 1977
18. BECK, J. *Le Concil de Basle (1434).* 1979
19. CHURCH, F. F. and GEORGE, T. (ed.). *Continuity and Discontinuity in Church History.* 1979
20. GRAY, P. T. R. *The Defense of Chalcedon in the East (451-553).* 1979
21. NIJENHUIS, W. *Adrianus Saravia (c. 1532-1613).* Dutch Calvinist. 1980
22. PARKER, T. H. L. (ed.). *Iohannis Calvini Commentarius in Epistolam Pauli ad Romanos.* 1981
23. ELLIS, I. *Seven Against Christ.* A Study of 'Essays and Reviews'. 1980
24. BRANN, N. L. *The Abbot Trithemius (1462-1516).* 1981
25. LOCHER, G. W. *Zwingli's Thought.* New Perspectives. 1981
26. GOGAN, B. *The Common Corps of Christendom.* Ecclesiological Themes in Thomas More. 1982
27. STOCK, U. *Die Bedeutung der Sakramente in Luthers Sermonen von 1519.* 1982
28. YARDENI, M. (ed.). *Modernité et nonconformisme en France à travers les âges.* 1983
29. PLATT, J. *Reformed Thought and Scholasticism.* 1982
30. WATTS, P. M. *Nicolaus Cusanus.* A Fifteenth-Century Vision of Man. 1982
31. SPRUNGER, K. L. *Dutch Puritanism.* 1982
32. MEIJERING, E. P. *Melanchthon and Patristic Thought.* 1983
33. STROUP, J. *The Struggle for Identity in the Clerical Estate.* 1984
34. 35. COLISH, M. L. *The Stoic Tradition from Antiquity to the Early Middle Ages.* 1.2. 2nd ed. 1990
36. GUY, B. *Domestic Correspondence of Dominique-Marie Varlet, Bishop of Babylon, 1678-1742.* 1986
37. 38. CLARK, F. *The Pseudo-Gregorian Dialogues.* I. II. 1987
39. PARENTE, Jr. J. A. *Religious Drama and the Humanist Tradition.* 1987
40. POSTHUMUS MEYJES, G. H. M. *Hugo Grotius, Meletius.* 1988
41. FELD, H. *Der Ikonoklasmus des Westens.* 1990
42. REEVE, A. and SCREECH, M. A. (eds.). *Erasmus' Annotations on the New Testament.* Acts — Romans — I and II Corinthians. 1990
43. KIRBY, W. J. T. *Richard Hooker's Doctrine of the Royal Supremacy.* 1990
44. GERSTNER, J. N. *The Thousand Generation Covenant.* Reformed Covenant Theology. 1990
45. CHRISTIANSON, G. and IZBICKI, T. M. (eds.). *Nicholas of Cusa.* 1991

46. GARSTEIN, O. *Rome and the Counter-Reformation in Scandinavia.* 1553-1622. 1992
47. GARSTEIN, O. *Rome and the Counter-Reformation in Scandinavia.* 1622-1656. 1992
48. PERRONE COMPAGNI, V. (ed.). *Cornelius Agrippa, De occulta philosophia Libri tres.* 1992
49. MARTIN, D. D. *Fifteenth-Century Carthusian Reform.* The World of Nicholas Kempf. 1992
50. HOENEN, M. J. F. M. *Marsilius of Inghen.* Divine Knowledge in Late Medieval Thought. 1993
51. O'MALLEY, J. W., IZBICKI, T. M. and CHRISTIANSON, G. (eds.). *Humanity and Divinity in Renaissance and Reformation.* Essays in Honor of Charles Trinkaus. 1993
52. REEVE, A. (ed.) and SCREECH, M. A. (introd.). *Erasmus' Annotations on the New Testament.* Galatians to the Apocalypse. 1993
53. STUMP, Ph. H. *The Reforms of the Council of Constance (1414-1418).* 1994
54. GIAKALIS, A. *Images of the Divine.* The Theology of Icons at the Seventh Ecumenical Council. With a Foreword by Henry Chadwick. 1994
55. NELLEN, H. J. M. and RABBIE, E. (eds.). *Hugo Grotius – Theologian.* Essays in Honour of G. H. M. Posthumus Meyjes. 1994
56. TRIGG, J. D. *Baptism in the Theology of Martin Luther.* 1994
57. JANSE, W. *Albert Hardenberg als Theologe.* Profil eines Bucer-Schülers. 1994
59. SCHOOR, R.J.M. VAN DE. *The Irenical Theology of Théophile Brachet de La Milletière (1588-1665).* 1995
60. STREHLE, S. *The Catholic Roots of the Protestant Gospel.* Encounter between the Middle Ages and the Reformation. 1995
61. BROWN, M.L. *Donne and the Politics of Conscience in Early Modern England.* 1995
62. SCREECH, M.A. (ed.). *Richard Mocket, Warden of All Souls College, Oxford, Doctrina et Politia Ecclesiae Anglicanae.* An Anglican Summa. Facsimile with Variants of the Text of 1617. Edited with an Introduction. 1995
63. SNOEK, G.J.C. *Medieval Piety from Relics to the Eucharist.* A Process of Mutual Inter-action. 1995
64. PIXTON, P.B. *The German Episcopacy and the Implementation of the Decrees of the Fourth Lateran Council, 1216-1245.* Watchmen on the Tower. 1995
65. DOLNIKOWSKI, E.W. *Thomas Bradwardine: A View of Time and a Vision of Eternity in Fourteenth-Century Thought.* 1995
66. RABBIE, E. (ed.). *Hugo Grotius, Ordinum Hollandiae ac Westfrisiae Pietas (1613).* Critical Edition with Translation and Commentary. 1995
67. HIRSH, J.C. *The Boundaries of Faith.* The Development and Transmission of Medieval Spirituality. 1996
68. BURNETT, S.G. *From Christian Hebraism to Jewish Studies.* Johannes Buxtorf (1564-1629) and Hebrew Learning in the Seventeenth Century. 1996
69. BOLAND O.P., V. *Ideas in God according to Saint Thomas Aquinas.* Sources and Synthesis. 1996
70. LANGE, M.E. *Telling Tears in the English Renaissance.* 1996
71. CHRISTIANSON, G. and T.M. IZBICKI (eds.). *Nicholas of Cusa on Christ and the Church.* Essays in Memory of Chandler McCuskey Brooks for the American Cusanus Society. 1996
72. MALI, A. *Mystic in the New World.* Marie de l'Incarnation (1599-1672). 1996
73. VISSER, D. *Apocalypse as Utopian Expectation (800-1500).* The Apocalypse Commentary of Berengaudus of Ferrières and the Relationship between Exegesis, Liturgy and Iconography. 1996
74. O'ROURKE BOYLE, M. *Divine Domesticity.* Augustine of Thagaste to Teresa of Avila. 1997
75. PFIZENMAIER, T.C. *The Trinitarian Theology of Dr. Samuel Clarke (1675-1729).* Context, Sources, and Controversy. 1997
76. BERKVENS-STEVELINCK, C., J. ISRAEL and G.H.M. POSTHUMUS MEYJES (eds.). *The Emergence of Tolerance in the Dutch Republic.* 1997
77. HAYKIN, M.A.G. (ed.). *The Life and Thought of John Gill (1697-1771).* A Tercentennial Appreciation. 1997
78. KAISER, C.B. *Creational Theology and the History of Physical Science.* The Creationist Tradition from Basil to Bohr. 1997
79. LEES, J.T. *Anselm of Havelberg.* Deeds into Words in the Twelfth Century. 1997
80. WINTER, J.M. VAN. *Sources Concerning the Hospitallers of St John in the Netherlands, 14th-18th Centuries.* 1998

81. TIERNEY, B. *Foundations of the Conciliar Theory.* The Contribution of the Medieval Canonists from Gratian to the Great Schism. Enlarged New Edition. 1998
82. MIERNOWSKI, J. *Le Dieu Néant.* Théologies négatives à l'aube des temps modernes. 1998
83. HALVERSON, J.L. *Peter Aureol on Predestination.* A Challenge to Late Medieval Thought. 1998.
84. HOULISTON, V. (ed.). *Robert Persons, S.J.: The Christian Directory (1582).* The First Booke of the Christian Exercise, appertayning to Resolution. 1998
85. GRELL, O.P. (ed.). *Paracelsus.* The Man and His Reputation, His Ideas and Their Reputation. 1998
86. MAZZOLA, E. *The Pathology of the English Renaissance.* Sacred Remains and Holy Ghosts. 1998.
87. 88. MARSILIUS VON INGHEN. *Quaestiones super quattuor libros sententiarum.* Super Primum. Bearbeitet von M. Santos Noya. 2 Bände. I. Quaestiones 1-7. II. Quaestiones 8-21. 2000
89. FAUPEL DREVS, K. *Vom rechten Gebrauch der Bilder im liturgischen Raum.* Mittelalterliche Funktionsbestimmungen bildender Kunst im *Rationale divinorum officiorum* des Durandus von Mende (1230/1-1296). 1999
90. KREY, P.D.W. and SMITH, L. (eds.). *Nicholas of Lyra.* the Senses of Scripture. 2000
92. OAKLEY, F. *Politics and Eternity.* Studies in the History of Medieval and Early-Modern Political Thought. 1999
93. PRYDS, D. *The Politics of Preaching.* Robert of Naples (1309-1343) and his Sermons. 2000
94. POSTHUMUS MEYJES, G.H.M. *Jean Gerson – Apostle of Unity.* His Church Politics and Ecclesiology. Translated by J.C. Grayson. 1999
95. BERG, J. VAN DEN. *Religious Currents and Cross-Currents.* Essays on Early Modern Protestantism and the Protestant Enlightenment. Edited by J. de Bruijn, P. Holtrop, and E. van der Wall. 1999
96. IZBICKI, T.M. and BELLITTO, C.M. (eds.). *Reform and Renewal in the Middle Ages and the Renaissance.* Studies in Honor of Louis Pascoe, S.J. 2000
97. KELLY, D. *The Conspiracy of Allusion.* Description, Rewriting, and Authorship from Macrobius to Medieval Romance. 1999